# PHOTOGRAPHY AND AMERICAN COLONIALITY

## AFRICAN HUMANITIES AND THE ARTS

*Series Editor*
Kenneth Harrow

The African Humanities and the Arts series mirrors the agenda of the African Studies Center at Michigan State University and its commitment to the study of Africa. The series examines all aspects of cultural research—including art, literature, film, and religion.

# PHOTOGRAPHY AND AMERICAN COLONIALITY

## Eliot Elisofon in Africa, 1942–1972

RAOUL J. GRANQVIST

MICHIGAN STATE UNIVERSITY PRESS | EAST LANSING

♾ The paper used in this publication meets the minimum requirements of
ANSI/NISO Z39.48-1992 (R 1997) (Permanence of Paper).

Michigan State University Press
East Lansing, Michigan 48823-5245

Printed and bound in the United States of America.

26 25 24 23 22 21 20 19 18 17    1 2 3 4 5 6 7 8 9 10

LIBRARY OF CONGRESS CATALOGING-IN-PUBLICATION DATA
Names: Granqvist, Raoul, 1940– author.
Title: Photography and American coloniality : Eliot Elisofon in Africa 1942–1972 / Raoul J. Granqvist.
Description: East Lansing : Michigan State University Press, [2017] | Series: African humanities and the arts | Includes bibliographical references and index.
Identifiers: LCCN 2016027759| ISBN 9781611862362 (cloth : alk. paper) | ISBN 9781609175184 (pdf) | ISBN 9781628952889 (ePub) | ISBN 9781628962888 (Kindle)
Subjects: LCSH: Elisofon, Eliot—Travel—Africa. | Photojournalists—United States. | Africa—Description and travel. | United States—Foreign relations—Africa—20th century.
Classification: LCC TR140.E4 G73 2017 | DDC 770.96—dc23 LC record available at https://lccn.loc.gov/2016027759

Book design by Charlie Sharp, Sharp Des!gns, East Lansing, Michigan
Cover design by Shaun Allshouse, www.shaunallshouse.com
Cover image: Eliot Elisofon filming Twins Seven Seven, the Youruba artist, and his jazz band, Golden Gabretas, at the Oshogbo Artists Center, January 1971 (photo Maya Bracher).

Michigan State University Press is a member of the Green Press Initiative and is committed to developing and encouraging ecologically responsible publishing practices. For more information about the Green Press Initiative and the use of recycled paper in book publishing, please visit www.greenpressinitiative.org.

---

Visit Michigan State University Press at *www.msupress.org*

*For his wisdom,*
*I dedicate this book to the memory of*
*Chinua Achebe.*

# Contents

# Preface

The paramount empirical base of *Photography and American Coloniality: Eliot Elisofon in Africa, 1942–1972* is the memory bank of two archives containing replications of the photographs that Eliot Elisofon collected over the course of three decades (1942–1972) of travel in Africa: Eliot Elisofon Photographic Archives, Smithsonian, National Museum of African Art (EEPA),[1] and the Harry Ransom Center, the University of Texas at Austin (HRC).[2] The book is a close reading of a single American photojournalist's visual contact with Africa formatted within the interface of colonialism and the Cold War. By pairing the inner and outer cores of the book's rhetorical address—the biographical (Elisofon) mindset of liberal conciliation, on the one hand, and the ideological efforts of imperial structure building, on the other—my aim is to construe a postcolonial minihistoriography that, using Ali Behdad's words, "can provide a critical genealogy to explicate the political shift from European colonialism to US imperialism."[3]

"Everything in the European dream of possession rests on witnessing, on witnessing understood as a form of significant and representative seeing," claims Stephen Greenblatt, who ends his argument with a worried question: "Why should my eye-witnessing be trusted?"[4] In looking for the guidance I needed to meet the challenge of the project at hand, writing an intellectual chronicle of Eliot Elisofon's pictorial and graphic narration of Africa,[5] Greenblatt's question has inspired me to respond to the aspirations of Robert Young's call: "A major task of postcolonialism must be the production of a 'critical ethnography of the West,' analyzing the story of a West haunted by the excess of its own story."[6] So placing myself as a critical witness of what has been witnessed (Elisofon's Africa), I hope to contribute to the probing or the dismantling of this "excess," not simply seeing it. As a large part of Elisofon's field collection of eighty thousand black-and-white prints and thirty thousand color slides are reproducible, his ongoing Western/American story takes on contemporary global/imperial dimensions. It is a storied excess that begs for scholarly attention in its own right, but also since it has not been told before in book form.

The theoretical and discursive structure of my work is set in the interface of Walter Mignolo's *Local Histories/Global Designs: Coloniality, Subaltern Knowledges and Border Thinking* and Sabelo J. Ndlovu-Gatsheni's *Coloniality of Power in Postcolonial Africa: Myths of Decolonization.* It is from within the perspective of decolonization as illusion, and a devastating one, that the history of Eliot Elisofon's paramount and iconic role as a photographer of Africa will be contested and its entanglement with the continent unveiled. Coloniality, as Mignola understands it, takes place *in* and *from* the borders and from local histories of modernity/coloniality. Elisofon's local histories are the hundreds of photographs that he constructed and that I have examined and contextualized. They embody the space that, in Mignola's world, harbors subaltern border thinking and that I have translated as representing images of Africans looking back. Coloniality also incorporates the place where home, in this case the United States, adopts and integrates the images in the metaphorical names of mission, salvation, and modernity. It is a physical and imaginary location in which the possessive coloniality of power confronts the Other. I have been inspired by Allan Sekula's theoretical discussions confronting economic systems with photography and art, especially his *Photography against the Grain.*[7]

More explicit, and as aspiring and provocative as Young's admonition and Greenblatt's question, is a comment in Ruth Mayer's introduction to her *Artificial Africas* (on the issue of the undercurrents of the "political unconscious"): "A new historicist combination of contextualization and close readings might help to come to terms with the paranoiac tendency slumbering in the project of tracing a set of stereotypical patterns through time."[8] Ambivalence, contradiction, paranoia, and their connections with the discourse of political shift, to pick up Mayer's central appellations, are considered in depth in both *Postcolonial Studies and Beyond* and *Relocating Postcolonialism*, two recent and highly authoritative collections of postcolonial critique that have been of great help to me. The editors of *Postcolonial Studies and Beyond* postulate that the book "need[s] to keep alive particular metanarratives for critical purposes, while minimizing and accounting for their Eurocentric traces."[9] The editors of *Relocating Postcolonialism,* in turn, ascertain, as respectfully, that postcoloniality has adopted an ethical enterprise through its pervasive focus on destabilizing antifoundationalist binarisms, whether they concern politics or literature.[10] The efforts of critiquing power structures aligned to essentialist subjectivity and nationalism, as this book attempts to do, never cease to be inhuman and problematic. They must be confronted, I claim, although it may well be that, in certain circumstances, it is "at the crossroads of contradictions that strategies for change may be best found."[11] My ambition is different. The political shift discourse, the second appellation, is duskily relativist. So to examine the subjective agency of Elisofon in the collusion with the shifting power elites of colonial Africa, Mobutu's Zaire/DRC and the United States, I have sought additional insight from the theoretical domains of reception studies, historicist studies, and visual studies. How does Elisofon, the American male person(a), adjust to or engage with the flux of his encumbered spatial time, "the binary axis of time" (McClintock 1995, 11), I ask.

Elisofon inhabited a complex mythological cosmos, "a sovereign self of Europe,"[12] that contained, first, his own construct of it; second, that of a complementary and conciliatory environment surrounding him (ongoing); and third, the design of the social and political structures of his time. He was both agent and victim of his history (Sekula). The history of colonialism (also his adaptation of it) "has left in its wake a legacy of worshiping freedom-as-individual autonomy, and of defining freedom according to its distance from custom and tradition (rather than tracing freedom as a form of agency *through* custom and tradition)."[13] Elisofon, the mythic ego of the self-made man of action, fits, I find, Immanuel Levinas's definition of radical freedom: "self-possession that extends itself to anything that threatens its identity."[14]

It was not coincidental that Elisofon traversed Africa driving a Land Rover from the Cape to Cairo in 1947 for *LIFE*, climbing 14,500 feet of one of the Mountain of the Moon craters in 1951, spending ten weeks faring along the Nile from Lake Victoria to the Mediterranean, and hovering over the Kilimanjaro in 1966 in a two-engine plane with a pilot's oxygen line clogged for some baleful seconds. He was the last war correspondent to leave Cape Cod on 15 May 1943, but was to be publicly more noteworthy for snapping a picture of an army transport plane colliding with his own while he was scrambling out of it. This spectacular World War II moment was another of his acclaimed fire-eating deeds. Such feats of masculine physical prowess, endurance, and risk-taking, endlessly cited and reproduced in American media and by Elisofon himself, symbolically demonstrate, as solo ascents of mountains and penetrations of jungles always have, national upper-hand perspectives and, obliquely, African lack and inadequacy. "As powerful masculinist discourses, adventure and exploration writing proved to be instrumental in the construction of rationales for imperialism."[15] His off-the-cuff photography and its allusions to patriotism and dauntlessness shaped a topic that he nourished throughout his life. The longevity of these circumnavigating legends was part of a collective mythic conspiracy. The self-promoting myths were upheld by the media industry's fascination for them. They were rehashed even after his *LIFE* magazine commission terminated in the early 1960s. The problem is that the Elisofon myths are still uncritically repeated and, with them, understandably, his equally snappy one-liners, from those about Tarzan to women's coiffures and Swedish meatballs. The fortieth-anniversary celebration called "Africa ReViewed: The Photographic Legacy of Eliot Elisofon" (2013–2015), as well as some of its press and image releases and reviews, recapitulated and embellished a number of these myths and their visual offshoots, anchoring his legacy even deeper in a false dream world of misrepresentation.[16]

Elisofon's mythmaking habitat is the smallest doll in a matryoshka world of similarities, the largest being the Western fabrications of the myths of Africa, all too familiar to require any extended exposures here. It camouflages and hides the Other (Africa) and naturalizes the receiver of the "gift." Elisofon gazes at Africa; Africa looks back at him.[17] Since Africa's looking has gone unregarded, critical research about Elisofon in Africa has been delayed. Suffice it to say that the West beats the drum for the most prominent domains that Elisofon's photojournalism is encased by. They were the border landscape with the river, the mountains, and the cities as demarcations; the peoples ("tribes") as predestined distinctive groupings; disregarded individuals, anonymous group members, and "families" (either replicas of the Western nexus family or its perversion); men's work and leadership, women's chores; the woman's body (disabled, scarified, sexualized) as a fetish; the savage, the monster; the masquerade as spectacle; tradition as museum; modernity as import; the African city as a monument for transnational capitalism; animals; and paradise. Each of these imperial domains, down to its smallest specific, was construed as a binary, a unilineal movement of domination, from Frantz Fanon's white "well-fed town" to the "hungry town . . . a town of niggers and dirty arabs."[18]

It was not necessarily a historical concept but a persistent viewpoint postulating the imaginary of the (post)colony.

If Joseph Conrad, as Mayer suggests, approached the myth of the Congo jungle with the "image of white power-weakness [that] seems to allegorize the conditions for imperial rule, with the white man in utter dependence acting unabashedly superior" (172), Elisofon, half a century later, did it with the myths not only intact but bolstered, entering (post-)colonial Africa with a "power-weakness" that was by nature logistical and by economy controllable. His entrance was an American manifesto of sheer power. He was a white man of liberal independence and as "unabashedly superior" to the Africans as his predecessor had been. His mission was not the territorial advancement of Europe and the saving of two men left behind after the expedition, Kurtz and David Livingstone; it was to "verify the many rumors of distant places and people,"[19] update and revamp the master narrative of Africa, and with his camera produce symbolic images of excellence (which he did, in a way) and displace hooked up trophies for the grandiose home of the postcolonial globe.[20] Africa was his treasure trove and fertile ground for a heritage venture supported by the elites of Washington.

Any of the mythic domains that Elisofon frequented could be split up into the vocabulary of its colonial specifics, which he stood by, irrespective of the postcolonial adjustments and the guerrilla activity that confronted it throughout his African sojourns. Carolyn Martin Shaw's description of the colonial landscape in its Kenyan mold could stand as a prototype of Elisofon's photo vistas.

> The political geography of this gaze [Karen Blixen's] from the heights figures importantly in colonialists' appropriation of Africa: the feeling of being in the air, on the top of the world, a small part of a great landscape, but the pinnacle of the human pyramid. Colonialists could own all that they could see, people and land, or could claim the wilds of Africa as their happy hunting ground, slaughtering many of the species Western environmentalists now try to protect.[21]

It is a gendered and binary landscape. Elisofon pursued it in its guise of the unacculturated, unknown, and irresistible, hoping to capture "the godlike Big Picture" at each click.[22] His compatriot Ernest Hemingway hungered for it with as much masculine spleen: "I loved the country so I was happy as you are after you have been with a woman that you really love" (Hemingway 1935, 72). The gendered landscape spilled over to the imageries of the peoples that populated it. Elisofon's considerations and photographing of the Kikuyu, Maasai, and Mbuti ("Pygmy") populations, to mention three registered "tribes" only, were anchored in racial stereotypes of long-standing: the Maasai, the cartoon's "paradisiacal tribe," loyal colonized with the savanna as their turf; the Kikuyu, brutal freedom fighters, disloyal colonized in the mountain forest or British households; the "Pygmies," the primeval, animal-men, sluggish colonized in the jungle. Such time-space clichés, impregnated by the pre-Victorian myths, revised by the colonial rhetoric, and adjusted by the modernist and Cold War impact of the postwar generation of travelers to Africa, "were formalized, racialized, creolized, and imbricated sets of relationships [that] have developed essentialized 'European' and 'Non-European' designations, where the former exerts hegemony over the latter."[23] Elisofon's visual voice made him the postwar United States' most influential and knowledgeable media populist with Africa as his target.

> As a technology of surveillance, photography was central to the rationalizing of working class leisure and work time. As such, it was associated with those other panoptic Victorian phenomena—the exhibition, the museum, the zoo, the gallery, the circus—all of which involve the fetishistic principle of collection and display and the figure of panoramic time as commodity spectacle. (McClintock 1995, 123)

What is remarkable about Anne McClintock's overview of the social realms that Victorian surveillance penetrated is not its totalizing impact for its time but its relevance for qualifying the much later width of Elisofon's photography. Only the zoo and the circus were foreign to his interventions; the other multigenre references were not. "Photography's wild hallucinations about phantom Africa"[24] have fostered all kinds of anomalies, and even if Elisofon's were less wild, modest rather, researching and writing the story of his photography have required scholarly openings from several compendious sides—simultaneously. His approach to photography was a combination of the intuitive snap of the moment; a catalyst of the already-seen but improvable; the attempt at aesthetic completion; the quest for a narration that claimed to be scientific, essayist, or documentary. Even if the result was a conventional flattening of Africa in pictorial homogeneity and a reduction of its history, to decode it, I have needed to know the width of his intentionality, to what degree it succumbed to the visual grammar that he was child of, his personality as an aesthete, and the outside requirements (serving as a member of the *LIFE* staff was one of them). Visual studies were long a sidetrack of colonial travel inquiries and literary analyses, but not so any longer. The "male gaze," the "panoptical eye," and concepts related to exoticism and power, the sublime landscape, stereotyping, and imaginings, all of them central for my study, have diverged into visual preoccupations within a number of disciplines. The normalizing "ethnographic gaze,"[25] the "media gaze," and "colonial nakedness"[26] are such signature newcomers with great relevance for the project.

The indexes of a photographer's surveillance act involve the framing of the object for reasons that in one way or another register, classify, organize, or institutionalize it. It is a "scientific" approach that may be misleading. To take an example, the Niger "Delta's myriad rivers and creeks not only define a geographic region; they also form a cultural confluence whose 'water ethos,'" explain Martha G. Anderson and Philip M. Peek, "surfaces in shrines, masquerades, and rituals associated with water spirits, as well as in aquatic exhibitions and performances on land that incorporate canoes and paddling displays."[27] A simple visual metaphor for the opposition of variability and ethnic fusion is the conventional still-photograph, the formulaic and homogeneous composition of kindred items. In fact, Elisofon's photography and his watercolor paintings (of flowers and women's bodies) were commensurate. In his African cosmos, these still lifes could represent a panoptical view taken across Albert Park (now Virunga National Park) with Rwenzori Mountains as background, a group portrait of "docile bodies" (Foucault), representing the Mangbetu chief Teingu and his thirty-six wives, or the analytical mug shot gaze, front and side, of a scarified Congolese woman. His thousands of administrative or power portraits (all men) of chiefs, kings, and political leaders were choreographed along similar ideological patterns, some of them interpersonal, others empowered, and not a few exoticized. He applied what could be called a discursive tactic of surveillance contrast when documenting appositional time and space zones. "Old," then, could represent an Igbo mask dancer during the Onwa Asaa festival outside Enugu, a cultural site he followed with enthusiasm and which mask he desired to own, or the same "Old" could epitomize African managerial systems to be replaced—allegedly for their own good—by superior Western structures. Elisofon's photographic surveillance accommodated primary avenues to documentary, cultural, and ethnographic "knowledge." This knowledge was absolutely and ultimately that of the Same. The Virunga scene, the two portraits, and the many others require their particular theoretical reading for them to open up. I decode these "knowledges" independently in the course of my photo analyses.

The body of the Other is located in the surface, in the coat of paint, as much as "racism is always located on the surface of other things." Paul Gilroy's double backtalk that I cite here is meaningful for understanding Elisofon's ambivalent fetishism for the territory of African surface reality. "We increasingly face a racism which avoids," Gilroy continues with reference to Britain, "being recognized as such because it is able to link 'race' with nationhood, patriotism and nationalism, a racism which has taken a necessary distance from crude ideas of biological inferiority and superiority and now seeks to present an imaginary definition of the nation as a unified *cultural* community."[28] Mapping Elisofon's fetishlike practices is indexing one of colonialism's major fields of Othering. It covers class and ethnic cross-dressing, sexual difference, and fixations with women's body parts such as head, breast, and torso. The cross-dressing playmate is not the Victorian soap and the white clothes empire (McClintock 1995, 207–31); it is far subtler. It involves the dramaturgy of the absent Same-scene and the presence of its aberrant Other. By controlled posing and choreographing of the African masquerade, Elisofon created falsified "tribal purity" with a persistence that was unconditional, in this way evoking Same-scene ideals of Western cultural and political stability. The sexual difference token of dancing young women with dangling breasts, another frequent "scene" of African deviation, intimated normalcy of similar Same-scene gender conformity. It was a photography that lured "imperial modernity deeper and deeper into consumerism" (McClintock 1995, 125, on colonial photography) and into the morals of "nationhood" and "(anti-) racism" (Gilroy).[29]

The framing of the image and the containing of the same image in a museum is a double mode of encapsulation and abridgement. This rather trivial statement metamorphoses into an observation of bearing when adjusted to Elisofon's double-sized photographic practice of appropriation: bringing home, if possible, both the object and the subject of his shooting. He worked as explorers always have done: "through an archive of pre-exist[ing] images and tropes."[30] The world was there waiting for him to report about it; that was his thesis and gospel. This could materialize only, he realized, through images that were identifiable and known to the American viewer or the reader. For the already-seen and the already-said to be recuperated and verified, they needed the newcomer's (his) registering touch as well as the codification of their reception. Like Henry Morton Stanley, he was extremely concerned about the verification of his "discoveries." Elisofon's "Africa" would not be real without American proofs of authentication and applause. His loyalty to his "American family" (Kozol 1994) involved bouncing back his photo rolls and the cultural artifacts that he was collecting. The rolls also contained in situ pictures that he had taken of the artifacts, thus doubly marking them as possessions. His photography derives from within a long tradition of Western explorer practices, as hosted by travel and empire studies.[31]

Quasi-scientific definitions go on reproducing tropes of registering and cataloging as well as the technology of racialized mapping, of which Elisofon was both an architect and a mediator, and of which the Smithsonian indexing monitors seem to be current archival amplifiers. This is how the decolonial site has shifted geographically but not the core of its language. The two questions by Okwui Enwezor and Octavio Zaya in *In/sight: African Photographers, 1940 to the Present*: "Can decontextualized images be facts contained within an embellished history?" and "Can they represent an empirical record of experience or serve as objective stand-ins for history?"[32] carry the same weight for me as Greenblatt's "Why should my eye-witnessing be trusted?" My answer to the questions by Enwezor and Zaya is a critical "yes." Observatory dominance is at the center of the study, for which Richard Vokes's edited anthology *Photography in Africa: Ethnographic Perspectives* has been instrumental in providing approaches to the role of the backdrop in colonial photography and works such as Wendy Kozol's *LIFE's America: Family and Nation in Postwar Photojournalism*, Erika Doss's *Looking at LIFE Magazine*, and John Loengard's *LIFE Photographers: What They Saw* for the increasing scholarly interest on the other side, the locality and the mechanics of coloniality's think tank.

Ever since 1935, when Elisofon saw the groundbreaking "African Negro Art" exhibition organized by the Museum of Modern Art, one of the first exhibitions in the United States to display African sculptures as works of art rather than as ethnographic objects, he was fascinated by them. Throughout his eleven trips to Africa he collected objects that were sent to his home in New York, in most cases with the assistance of American embassies or American organizations. He bargained, he conned, he made purchases with pearls—using the established methods of the colonialists or the missionaries of returning the cultural "trophies" home for the moral and national enlightenment. Eventually his collection of approximately seven hundred objects ended up at the National Museum of African Art (NMAfA).

> Elisofon was a collector of art and brought back more than 700 objects from Africa during the course of his life. These objects are part of the museum's exhibition, as well as some of Elisofon's photographs of them. [Amy Staples cited:] "The large details and multiple views of the objects highlight their beauty. . . . Where previously they might have been thought of like anthropological artifacts, he helped people see the work as artistic and abstract forms."[33]

The objects have navigated between the labels of ethnographic generic types and aesthetic dislocated passive products. In both cases they have been alienated and, metonymically, so have their former keepers. In the archives (EEPA/Washington and HRC/Austin), I have been able to track the less pleasant routes of many of these objects (including photos), from the moments of their acquisition in villages in the Congo and elsewhere to their deification on lofty national pedestals in Washington, D.C. A Western institution has emerged, proudly as it seems, as a distancing device, marginalizing the Other in the name of foreign "beauty."[34] The question, rhetorical or not, asked in one of several recent studies of Western museum collections holding colonial material is: "How do objects become repositories of meaning and value as they are de-contextualized and re-contextualized in new places, times, and situations?"[35] Sandra H. Dudley's comment about the "museum as container" discourse takes the question further: "Museums' long-held aura as authoritative temples of enlightenment and culture rests upon the socially widespread belief that they hold in perpetuity, for the benefit of society, historically established data-sets comprised of objects and their documentation."[36] Anne Maxwell's *Colonial Photography and Exhibitions*, Annie E. Coombes's *Reinventing Africa: Museums, Material Culture and Popular Imagination*, and Sidney Littlefield Kasfir's *African Art and the Colonial Encounter* have been important for me in formatting theoretical structures for the discussion of Elisofon's frantic search for "authenticity" and the "spectacle" and his choreographing or construing the events as if they did not show up by themselves. Of extreme importance proved to be the anthology *The Scramble for Art in Central Africa*, edited by Enid Schildkrout and Curtis A. Keim, for two of its bearing themes: "the relationship between the intentions and agendas of the collectors and the narratives and texts that were constructed to display the objects to the non-traveling Western public" and the notion that "exhibitions . . . become historical artifacts of history and grist for the mill of cultural criticism."[37] Paul S. Landau's statement in his introduction to *Images and Empires: Visuality in Colonial and Postcolonial Africa* is opportune: "In its curatorial organization, the African art museum, like ethnographic collection before it, corresponds less to any African category than to the history of colonial expropriation" (7). So is also the following passage in *The Scramble for Art in Central Africa*:

> One theme running through this book is the relationship between the intentions and agendas of the collectors and the narratives and texts that were constructed to display the objects to the non-traveling Western public. We are interested in the

> changing intersecting space between collection and representation. In the decades since these collections were made, the explanatory labels attached to many of the objects, in museums, galleries and books have changed. Fetishes have become power objects; curios and specimens have become art. . . . Today we can see . . . displays as expressions of European arrogance and greed, blatant reflections of the colonial expansion. . . . Exhibitions become historical artifacts of history and grist for the mill of cultural criticism. (Schildkrout and Keim 1998, 28)

The bothersome feeling it created in me came from the insight that I could have formulated the theme of Elisofon's role as collector in very similar terms, except that mine would contain a sharp distinction. I could focus on a theme that was far less dynamic than Schildkrout and Klein's. This is saying that a progressive or precocious intersection between collection and representation never occurred in Elisofon's time in Africa. He appropriated the object. Its multiple or obscure representation was flattened out during its migration into canonical art. Even today, as I have noted, the official Smithsonian Elisofon world remains doggedly intact, along which orthodox parameter Elisofon, the deified photographer-collector, upholds with curatorial help the appropriable imaginary of Africa. The only chance for a museum such as NMAfA, this book suggests, is to allow the objects—whether they are iconic photographs or cherished pieces of African "art"—to tell their own stories about the "then" and "there," where and how they were once collected, and encourage us to invite their present-day possessors to face the responsibilities of ownership and reconsider their consequences.[38] As Wyatt MacGaffey argues in one of the most thrilling chapters in *The Scramble for Art in Central Africa*, canonized "power objects" and relocated "African art" (the latter concept fabricated by Western travelers, connoisseurs, and collectors) need to be reconsidered or better reorganized into new medial formats, as they falsify, abridge, and misrepresent, or simply, inviting them to retaliate, return or die. Nothing is permanent.

*Photography and American Coloniality* grew out of a complexity of historical settlements, all of them aligned, but differently, with my biographical time as a scholar with cultural studies as a major professional avenue. Cultural studies with Africa as a focus pulled me from the start into nonconventional affiliations of topics of studies and fields of theory making, combining the literary with the visual, the low with the high (whatever they mean), the footnote with the image, and so on, endlessly. This is the intellectual terrain of the book. Another alignment that it shares generally with the discipline of my research, as it has evolved through the years, is my political captivation with the West versus Africa dichotomy, with Africa, dependably and contrastively, representing the injured and consumed party. The book conjoins these parameters with their intricacies and loopholes, and in particular those that concern the abuse of the continent.

For a book about a photographer, it may seem bizarre, perhaps even unacceptable, that it does not contain a single photography by the master himself. The issue has been a most troublesome crux that I have been struggling with from the beginning. For a long time, the pros of including the photographs seemed to be the winning game plan, for reasons that are self-evident and may seem incontrovertible: visual analyses require the pictorial representations for them to make sense, for the reader to comprehend the arguments, or even better challenge them. Pictures provide a sense of physical presence, a "now" laden with feelings, and can provide detailed documentary knowledge through lens and color manipulations (and Elisofon was an expert in this area). The pro list could be endlessly long, so also that of the cons. My cons were as muscular from the beginning, invigorated by the exclusive character of the book as not a visual study of Elisofon's photography but an intellectual chronicle of his Cold War mission with Africa as his target and the United States as his beneficiary. Of the thousand pictures I have browsed, the 160 that I discuss cannot be represented by single photos spread decorously and equally across the nine chapters. They would distract and confuse, I told myself.

The Smithsonian Institution Research Information (SIRIS) is a subjective but consistent system of indexing, as all systems should be. Its prejudices are lodged in its ambivalent world of promoting a scientific perspective through a classification system in tune with the sexist and colonial ideologies embedded in Elisofon's photographs. It is a realization that became obvious to me the further I advanced my burrowing into the material. I employ here the consequentiality and the transcendence of SIRIS to advance the present discussion.[39] Those photos that I have selected for examination, which can be viewed on the SIRIS website, are paradigmatic of Elisofon's style, thematic, and technique.[40]

There are many inconsistencies of orthography, mainly related to names of persons and places throughout the book. These are due to particular circumstances, including the political and historical passage from colonial to postcolonial, Mobutu's authenticity program of changing names, the divergences of spelling as norms rather than exceptions, and multilanguage mixes.

# Acknowledgments

In spring 2010, I was fortunate enough to "settle" at Harry Ransom Center (HRC) in Austin, Texas, for a three-month fellowship to work on a project called "Colonial Photojournalism and the Western War: Ernest William Smith and Eliot Elisofon in Africa" (David Douglas Duncan Endowment for Photojournalism/The Andrew W. Mellon Foundation Research Fellowship Endowment). The project was initially intended to be a study of the colonial writing and visualizing of two war battlefields on African ground: the Boer War (1899–1902) and World War II fighting in North Africa (1942–1943). The questions that I wanted to examine were: How is "Africa" conceptualized in such encounters? How can the very absence of "Africa" be defiant and subversive? What functions of alterity (subversion) can be discovered in military photography and war journalism? How does an image or a snapshot authenticate its Western actor (invisible/not-heard) rather than the African (visible/heard)? How can the posing or the choreographing of/by the Other intensify meaning-making documentation or resist or parody it? How can the colonial nationalistic self-image in its turn be distracted?

It did not take me long to discover that I would need to abandon Ernest William Smith, the British *Morning Leader* and the *Star* writer and photographer, and capitulate without reservations to the *LIFE* magazine camera magician, Elisofon, despite the fact that Smith was one of the first war correspondents to use a portable roll film camera with instantaneous shutter speed and had written articles and children's stories (as had Elisofon). It was not, however, Elisofon's visual magnetism—which this book will deconstruct—that changed the direction of my archival digging; it was other things. First of all, having acquainted myself with the format and depth of the Elisofon collection at HRC, which encapsulates in such immense detail his time in Africa, I fully realized—if not during the first month but the second—that the questions that I had formulated for the original project also proved to be wide and provocative enough to address the physical objects of archival reality with another reality, that of the interpretive schemes and postcolonial theories contained in my questions and all the others that would follow. In other words, I had to write a book about the American photojournalist. This book is a chronicle of an American journalist's photographic positioning by a scholar of African literature.

Writing Elisofon's story about Africa has incorporated studies of his photography, books, essays, and letters; lengthy research stints at the two archival resources (HRC and Eliot Elisofon Photographic Archives, EEPA, Washington, D.C.); examinations of external material from within an eclectic scholarly source bank; and interviews, talks, and discussions with scholarly friends, special persons, and the few alive who had met or worked with him. As a witness of another witness, I have stayed close to the primary records. Christraud Geary, Teel Senior Curator Emerita of African and Oceanic Art at the Museum of Fine Arts, Boston, was one of the first to welcome the direction of my project plan. Her views came in at an early stage of my writing and were reassuring and energizing. This is what she said in a letter to me (11 January 2012):

> I think that it is high time for a reassessment of Elisofon's work in Africa. At the Museum of African Art, where I was the head of the Eliot Elisofon Photographic Archives for 13 years, his photography never got the attention it deserved, mainly because the then directors had little interest in it and only considered the images as contextual documentation, i.e. illustrations. There is so much more to his photography than the images everybody knows.

I too claim—for other reasons than Geary, naturally—that "there is so much more to [Elisofon's] photography than the images everybody knows." My critical views of them, my "much more," are founded on a scholar's exploratory postulations and have taken me into the messy and complex infrastructures of Elisofon's photography.

EEPA opened their historical archive for me in 2013 with consideration, and lead curator and chief archivist Amy Staples has shared her multiform knowledge about the photographer with readiness and engagement. HRC has been welcoming from the start. In my very first talk with Roy Flukinger, senior research curator, carrying a familiarity of the photographer's papers, drew a sketchy bio-outline of Elisofon as a "one-man band" with youthful exuberance, a persona that would turn out to be a warning as well as a stimulating prompt in my navigating in and between the more than 2,000 HRC documents that I examined at the archives. Linda Briscoe Myers, associate curator of photography at HRC, has been a congenial star for me, always there to assist, also when I was waving nervously from the other side of the ocean. I also want to thank Mary Alice Harper, head of photography and art cataloging, and Bridget Gayle Ground, academic affairs coordinator—Mary for her help in my strenuous one-year-long quest for the enigmatic ABC *Africa* film, and Bridget for her friendly counseling and assisting me as a newcomer to Austin in 2010. All in all, the Center—for me, and, I am sure, for all visiting scholars—is a unique scholarly environment for the combination of ambiance and authority it embraces.

I am grateful to Hila and Gerald Feil, who, as a courtesy, opened their Montreal home for me for a week in October 2013, providing me with a long-cherished chance to view several screenings of the ABC *Africa* that I had thirsted to do for so long. And not only that: I was invited to discuss with them their thirteen-month filming adventure on location in Africa in 1966–1967. It was a remarkable bonus for a scholar—and definitely for the book. So was also my exciting meeting with Maya Bracher (Sernhac, Gard, southern France), who, with her husband, Georges, worked for Eliot for five months (1970–1971). She was Elisofon's script girl at the filming of the *Black African Heritage* (1972). Generously, she entrusted me not only with her memories of the collaboration with the American but also with copies of letters that she wrote to her parents in Switzerland. I am indebted to her. Merci-Danke!

Among others who have backed up my research and the book project in various ways, I wish to acknowledge in particular Philippa Levine (University of Texas at Austin), James Gibbs (Bristol), and John Mraz (Universidad Autónoma de Puebla, Mexico). Thanks to Catharine Walker Bergström, senior lecturer of English at University West in Trollhättan, who early read and commented on the book manuscript. Bernth Lindfors, professor emeritus at University of Texas at Austin, also examined the early stages of *Photography and American Coloniality*. But more than this, he introduced and encouraged me to apply for a research fellowship at the Ransom Center; second, he bonded with me, in various fashions, in the research on Western commodification and visualization of Africa for years; and, third, he and his wife Judith, offered me accommodation for lengthy periods in their Austin home. I thank you two heartily! With equal warmth I want to acknowledge Hertha D. Sweet Wong, associate professor at the Department of English, Berkeley, who has followed my writing the book from the beginning as a judicious counselor and loyal companion. To the same category I wish to allocate Kenneth W. Harrow, distinguished professor of English at Michigan State University (MSU), for his teammate trust in me and his activist's yell: "Go for it; don't give up!" So I didn't give up! Also thanks to Alex Schwartz, MSU Press senior acquisitions editor, who with equal consistence pushed me forward, and a last-minute salute to MSU's Anastasia Wraight and Robert Burchfield, whose forthright editorial skills brought an up-to-date facet to the book (in my view) by inducing me to reconsider conventional patterns of academic writing.

CHAPTER 1

# En Route from Scandinavia to Africa, 1942–1944

## On Becoming a Trickster with a Hungry Camera and a Loud Mouth

Eliot Elisofon's photographic map of World War II scenes is as far-reaching as his efforts to be a global photographer. As it happened, his first stop in October 1939 was my native country, Finland, where he was sent (accompanied by the legendary photojournalist Thérèse Bonney) by *LIFE* to cover the upcoming Olympic Games, but he found himself in the midst of frantic Finnish war preparations; his second stop was a seven-month assignment as a pool photographer (from October 1942 to May 1943) for the North West Africa Sea Frontier Command in Tunisia; the third was a commission to photograph the installation of pipelines to Alaska (for the Northwest Service Command) and covers his residence at arctic Aklavik on the west side of the Mackenzie Delta; and the fourth was his service as war correspondent and combat propagandist under Dwight Eisenhower's and the Allies' London-based Supreme Headquarters Expeditionary Forces (SHAEF).[1] His stay in neutral Sweden and Stockholm would last from February to November 1944 and also involve a dramatic excursion to northern Finland (September–October) to document the expulsion of the Nazis from Finnish territory.

I have chosen to dwell upon Elisofon's Scandinavian sojourns as they were two substantial stopovers on his route to the Africa of my study. The time in Sweden was different from the other war scenes he experienced. His time there offered a normalcy of sorts: he witnessed people—seemingly free—walking in the streets, flirting in restaurants, skiing, and debating. But Stockholm, Eliot's home base, was anything but an orderly Swedish city; it was the world's largest treasure trove for gossipmongers, diplomats with plans, and others just as dedicated to undermine the same—Nordic Casablanca. The palavers were not only about the ongoing war and what means were required to stop it, or Sweden's kissing in the dark with Nazi Germany, but also produced the formulations of conditions for peace to emerge and addressed the shaky future Sweden embraced. Alliances, large and small—transnational, idealistic, and political—were construed and dissolved. Hierarchies of power builders were created. By the time Elisofon entered this arena, the staff at the American legation had increased from four in 1940 to four hundred four years later.[2] It is in this milieu that he developed his skills in calibrating his hand and eye, in sweet-talking with persuasive conviction, in taking individual risks also outside the trenches, in refining his American profile as "the world's best *Life* magazine journalist," and, as such, on occasions, bolstering arrogant national superiority, side by side with spates of aphoristic wit. In Scandinavia, he became the trickster with a hungry camera and a loud mouth.

Stockholm, the only free-talk marketplace in Europe, was a perfect site for imperial show-offs, as postcolonial Africa would also be. Yet the Swedes needed to dismantle their stereotype of the United States, in their turn, as a country of nylon socks and chewing-gum only, Eliot would have riposted. Not all winners, whether war-faring Americans or nonviolent Swedes, have won it all. The mediation by a trickster is full of loopholes.

## Finland: Orientalism

Eliot Elisofon's very first foreign assignment for *LIFE* sent him to Finland, where he was going reluctantly, as he said, "to do tourist pix." Finland would host the Summer Olympics the following year, and the Americans needed to be informed. But the Finns would have to wait until 1952 before this could take place. "Was there a week when the war broke out, realized Finland would figure. Changed story to emphasize military aspects," Eliot wrote to his bosses in New York (HRC 2.20).[3] Eliot was accompanied across the Atlantic on the *Queen Mary* by the already famous photojournalist Thérèse Bonney, who was forty-four years old (Eliot was twenty-eight). They were the first of the 266 accredited journalists from twenty-three countries to arrive in Finland. Bonney was an influential agent in the American intelligence service[4] and was also writing articles about Finland for *Collier's*, for which Carl Gustaf Emil Mannerheim, commander in chief of the Finnish troops during the three wars, rewarded her with a medallion of honor. She traced the Finnish contacts that were needed to produce the 1939 *LIFE* story, but the photography and the storyline that it contained were all Eliot's.

The photo essay title "Finland: Soviet Russia Crowds a Nation of Democrats" (*LIFE*, 30 October 1939, 69–76) recognized the two military combatants, Communist Russia and Democratic Finland, but hid the third, the righteous one, the United States, or expected magazine readers to take its presence as a given. Also at this stage, as the verb "crowd" implied, the Russian aggression and threats had not yet catapulted into brutal invasion, but it was close (which would bereave me of my father for five years). I have not yet found a *LIFE* story without the casting of "America" as the prime protagonist, so this one was not unique. It played out an Orientalist morality where Finland was a threshold, borderline figure, an aspiring fledgling in the Western democratic club, headed by the United States, whose duty it was, the essay intimated, to assist. The rhetorical appropriation of heroic Finland definitely had goodwill effects at the time (*LIFE* would have one section each week about Finland as long as the one hundred–day Winter War lasted), but its patronizing impact was to be more penetrating. It was along the thematic parameters of East and West, servitude and freedom, bad and good, Byzantine extravaganza and Christian liberalism that the visual material of a Western-biased morality was organized. Finland's paying off its war debts was lauded with benign pats on the head. With the country's problematic and murky alliance with the Germans, Elisofon's admiration for the dogged Finnish determination turned sour, and would not be rehabilitated by the Finns expulsion of the Nazis from Finnish territory in October 1944. The Finns were to remain an irresolute, threshold "race." But at this early stage (1939), he was all in favor of them/us.

The forty photographs dominate the eight-page essay, followed (in this order) by the captions, the titles, the subtitles, and the contextual narrative. The text (excluding the title texts) contains only one thousand words (in ten columns/132 rows); it is supplementary, a figurative guide only pointing to the visual material for clarification. The photos can be arranged into aerials, portraits, archetypal family pictures, and group pictures. Each of these categories or groups is meaning-bound; the individual photo within the group is a variance of the norm. The collage of the nine aerials sketched a topocentric narration of a young, independent (southern) Finland threatened by an imperial monster of aberrant culture and religion. The panoptical air-flight loop captured the president's summer residence Gullranda on the western coast (Naantali), the icon for Western democracy, contrasting it with its imaginative counterparts, the Orthodox Valamo (Valaam) monastery in the east and the Fort Slava ruins on the island of Kukouri (just outside the city of Kotka) in the southeast.[5] Together with the vignette for the essay, the conventional aerial of the "land of thousands of islands," these images drew the geographical and ideological boundaries of the package called Finland (only half of the country). The remaining aerials closed in on the capital of Helsinki and its major historical attractions and administrative buildings completing the snapshot overview: the town hall, the Swedish legislature, Russian czar Alexander II's statue, the Great Church, and the Olympic Stadium. The next move was to fill the package with men of power—and one woman (Fanni Luukkonen, chief of the Lotta Svärd band)—all of them, the essay assured, were ready for the war and its sacrifices. The photo of Jean Sibelius with the caption ("who gave Finns an anthem in his tone poem *Finlandia*"), not taken by Elisofon, accorded smoothly with the elegiac, mournful sentiment of the photo essay.

The portraits of single military leaders in uniforms, the group pictures of veterans in strict military poses, World War I volunteer soldiers marching, young men swearing the oath of loyalty in the Lutheran church, men heating up in the sauna, and others doing gymnastics, keeping healthy, construe the concept of a pious, united, and decisive nation. The additional four collages of pictures reinforce this ethics; their metonymic rubrics only confirm: "Finns love flags," "Finns are religious," "Finns are clean," "Finns are honest." These are typical exotic clichés, visual or nonvisual, that Eliot could have found in any tourist brochure, in any travelogue about Finland, then, and even now. What is of interest for me (and for the thesis of the book) is the skill, and this essay is a prime example, with which Elisofon domesticated and imputed the-already-said/seen with the viewer's prejudices, desires, and expectations—of his specific time. Its blend of an accommodative narrative structure, its chauvinistic rhetoric, and its journalese foreshadow Eliot's conditional writing of Africa.[6] Told as an orientalized simile of redemption and patriotism, the implications of which hardly any middle-class American *LIFE* reader would have missed, Eliot and the New York staff (and Bonney) had produced one of the magazine's most influential photo essays of the

1940s (he thought that it was his best prewar production) (*LIFE*, 13 April 1940, 13), as well as a problematic one.

Eliot's second trip to Finland (25 September–14 October 1944), during the last phase of the Finnish wars, bore little resemblance with the one five years earlier.[7] The small group of international journalists (British, American, Swedish) he accompanied were sent out to report on how Finland handled the armistice agreement with Russia, and, in particular, the lease of the Porkkala region, only 19 km west of Helsinki (returned to Finland in 1956), where they were shipped for a day's visual observations. On their return to Helsinki, Eliot and his colleague John Scott persuaded the Finnish intelligence officer Heikki Kekoni to permit the group to travel to a newly formed front in the northern Baltic Gulf area where the Finns were landing matériel and soldiers in what was to be their very first confrontation to intern the German forces in the north in compliance with the Allied Control Commission's decision (Eliot rightly called it the "Russian" Commission: it consisted of two hundred Soviet and fifteen British members). Kekoni hardly had any problems with letting the journalists travel, since Finland sought eagerly to be recognized for its endeavor to clean up the North.[8] The skirmishes that Eliot and his colleagues were to witness on 3 October in the Kemi-Tornio area were among the very first battles in what was to be called the Lapland War (ended in April 1945).

From what was planned to be a somber report about a particular instance (the evacuation of Porkkala) in wartime Finland, given this chance to travel, Eliot would broaden his photojournalistic focus to the theme of "a country at all odds arising from war"—in other words, to writing the sequential chapter of his 1939 article about the country preparing for it with such determination and energy. It is in this vein that he, on the one hand, took pictures of devastation and decay, of bombed bridges, of torn houses with sandbagged windows, of women wearing wooden-soled shoes with paper composition uppers, and men in full uniforms with rows of ribbons. On the other hand, he made ample but uninspired efforts to document a country returning to a normalcy, a country lacking the material prerequisites for it to develop. He visited a chemical factory whose staff were instructed to cultivate their own potatoes on rented land, and took an astounding picture of women queuing for potatoes handed out from a freight train wagon, both in Helsinki. He visited hospitals for evacuees and invalids in both Oulu and in Helsinki; he scanned a school for rehabilitating and teaching disabled ex-soldiers to accustom to new life activities—all these activities at a speed that left no room for either meditation or concentration. On his way back from the north he met Niilo Kanto, director of a paper mill in Kajaani (northeastern Finland) who told the story of the Finnish cellulose products emerging from the forest outside the mill into the world market. It is another moral tale of intrepidity and stamina about the small versus the big, the leitmotif of the former photo essay. So is also the aura that surrounds his second industrial project, a very brief call at (now) Ovako Imatra Steelworks, not far from the Russian border (which Eliot approached without permission and from which he was brusquely dispatched). The Allied Control Commission required the Finnish forces to demobilize while advocating, conflictingly, that the country throw out the Germans. Eliot encountered the two sides of this paradox during his two-week travel. He took snapshots of happy Finnish soldiers waving their demobilization documents on the way home; he ran into the less happy Russian prisoners and noted them with detachment. He did not interview Finnish soldiers, but he saw them in action, and cursed their commanders, high and low, for incompetence. Nor did he talk at any length with the many Karelian evacuees he met frequently and photographed.[9] It was not prewar Finland, war-faring Finland, postwar Finland he was engaged in; it was he himself as a combatant American photographer that he focused on as his job.

On 3 October, the press corps were transported—again the initiative was Eliot's—at nighttime in a small open boat from Oulu to the port of Röyttä, a few kilometers south of the city of Tornio, from where they were taken to the Finnish-German front, a short distance farther south, midway between the two cities of Tornio and Kemi. It is as if the journalists and their host egged each other on. By this flanking maneuver by both sea and land, the press reached the military bull's-eye they were anxious to watch. Apart from Elisofon's increasing irritation with what he thought was negligent and inept Finnish command, his focus was on taking photos of Stuka bombs, advancing Finnish soldiers "dispersed over a large open area," and fallen or injured troops.[10]

Three of the photographs and the comments he made about them were meant only for Wilson Hicks, photographic editor at *LIFE*. The first describes a pretty conventional use of a camera angle to achieve the effect he desires. "I walked around shooting the very bare looking chimneys and found several places where some contrasts helped out. One I framed against some very much alive birches, in others I used a white ruined church for contrast" (HRC 6.10, 4). Producing the second, he admitted that the same viewing (if not necessarily the same technique) had created ethical problems for him:

> There was one dead German in a fat pasture fringed with spruce trees and cut by a split rail meandering its middle. Above the trees a beautiful cloud sat with fine shading and edges. I broke one of my rules and put a filter on my Rolleiflex to overemphasize the clouds and the landscape so as to make a greater contrast to the still figure stretched full length in the grass. (HRC 6.10, 6)

The third photo portrayed a wounded Finnish soldier carried into the theater on a litter made of birch logs and being nursed by a military doctor.

> The medical captain of the battalion had a look and there was one moment when the captain laid his hand on the wounded leg and near his easy hand the soldier's tense hand made great contrast. It was a fine picture and was lucky enough to get it just that way. (HRC 6.10, 6)

In all the three montages, contrast was a decisive factor, both as an aesthetic factor and an ideological medium. The picture with the bare-looking chimneys may signify both sadness and hope. The smoke from the home or the factory reversed the freshness of birches and the whiteness of a church wall. That is contrast that any war is embedded in. In the next, Eliot's manipulation of the camera lens intensified the play of colors surrounding the corpse of the invader in his grassy *lit de parade*. It is as if the verdure of the Finnish spruce forest and a split rail had taken revenge. The visual sympathy rested outside the body. The professional malaise the photographer felt creating this picture was replaced by his feel-good for the next. The latter's narrative is impromptu, self-produced. These two pictures were about life and death. The one with the German was anchored to the lowest ladder in the hierarchy of political order and denied the right to Elisofon's caring hands and neutral eyes.

In the next few hours during the same afternoon things would change. The press was about to board their boat to take them back to Oulu, when they heard the aircraft. Six Stukas (Junkers JU 88) dropped their bombs at 5:03 p.m.; two of them exploded so close that Eliot was tossed up in the air, his mouth filling with dirt. He repeated the incantation that "saved his life" when the same Luftwaffe attacked in Tunisia, "maybe this is it," adjusting it to, "I guess this is it" (HRC 6.10, 7). About a week later he was back in Stockholm, having interviewed Jean Sibelius at his home in Ainola and taken a series of photographs of the aging man, sitting on a bench and walking in the park (HRC 6.10, 11–12),[11] but having failed—to his bitterness—to revisit President Gustaf Mannerheim, "very old and terribly vain," for another session.[12] Elisofon would rest in Sweden, hospitalized, for a month, and a week in an American military hospital in London, suffering from a brain concussion and a blood clot as a result of the bombs. "What a hell of a show" (HRC 6.10, 14), he concluded his Finnish report. Finland remained an aberrant showcase in *LIFE* storytelling.

## Social Hierarchies in Formation, Swedish Welfare, Swedish Glass

We will step back in time to 17 February 1944, when Elisofon arrived in Stockholm and settled in the hexagon-shaped Room 325 in the Grand Hotel with windows facing the Parliament Building and the Royal Palace—a perfect vista for spies. As he explained cryptically in an interview in a Swedish weekly, I was "here to see if something would happen."[13] And "something" was no less than a Nazi invasion of Norway and/or Sweden. Eliot had traveled from New York to Liverpool in a merchant ship convoy provocatively called *Liberty*. The ship *Samuel Backe* "41," with the Norwegian captain Jacob Olsen and a cargo of aerial bombs, carried Elisofon and his colleague Bill White of the *Associated Press* (later the *New York Times*) to Liverpool. The Atlantic crossing was horrid, with frequent warnings for submarines and the constant fear they experienced of being hit or even touched (and so also the lethal cargo) by the two other ships, the port "31" and the starboard "51."[14] Having sworn his loyalty to the Allied Expeditionary Force (SHAEF) in London and received the credentials as a combatant *LIFE* photographer/journalist and informant, Elisofon faced another war-time-innuendo-ordeal: the six-hour flight to Stockholm from Leuchars in Scotland in a freezing cold and blacked-out Douglas DC3 Transport plane—with an oxygen mask on.[15] The luxurious hotel room waiting for him must have been a haven.

For more than seven months in Sweden, Elisofon would be navigating in and out of individual liaisons of colleagues, diplomats, ambassadors, and ordinary people of differing affiliations and nationalities, including both presumptive friends and presumptive enemies, facing an ordeal of another kind than the physical and mental one that took him to Scandinavia. His Scandinavian sojourn would have a lasting impact on his view of the inequalities of the world and his part at its top. The practice of categorizing and classifying people, both in an essentialist (unchanging/

inherent) and a taxonomic (hierarchical) mode, had a heyday during the years of the Second World War, imbricating, variously, not only the round-table negotiations between diplomats and peacemakers but just as much an embedded American journalist's fieldwork and its complex infrastructure.

His roommate, Scott, who would accompany him to Finland later in the year, organized a welcome party for him in his hotel room with fifty persons, among whom were the British minister, Victor Mallet, and the American minister, Herschel Johnson. Two days after his arrival he photographed J. K. Paasikivi, the Finnish ambassador to Sweden, on his balcony. Paasikivi was discussing the conditions for peace in Finland with A. M. Kollontaj, the Soviet ambassador. Two Scandinavian journalists, photographer K. V. Gullers and his Danish associate, Kurt Schneider, introduced him—the same week—to the Swedish "smörgåsbord" at the "Gyllene Freden" (the Golden Peace). This triad of people, here metonymically representing Allied diplomats, correspondents, and, as Elisofon himself would categorize them, "pro-Allied Swedes," codified his ideological panopticon with its harsh claim of Swedish validation, acceptance, and standing ovation. It resounded power. From Scott's side, it could sound like this:

> In Stockholm, Sweden, in the barbershop of the Grand Hotel, there was a deadly silence as three men sat side by side. One was the British Ossian Goulding; on the other, a German Legation attaché. In the middle was Dr. Juho Paasikivi, Finland's possible negotiator.[16]

This somewhat theatrical sketch of a meeting in the hotel lounge not only tries to capture a tense moment with unspoken consequences, it narrates something about the political role in media coverage in the terminating phase of the Second World War, when inclusive words had become more significant than conclusive bombs. Ossian Goulding, like Scott, was not in the hotel to be informed about the current situation on the Nordic scene, Finland's arduous and mandatory exit out of war. They were agents in a political movement of insight dictated by their employers' and the British and American intelligence services' ambitious efforts to stop German hegemony, whether it was war-faring as in Finland or linked to trade agreements with Sweden.

In other words, a Goulding, a Scott, and an Elisofon had informal mandates; they were far more than journalists.[17] Elisofon would entertain Malet and Johnson at different events in May–June, not only photograph them. He would do the same with the movie executive of Paramount Studios Stanton Griffis and the Red Cross vice-chairman Douglas Poteat. The two were dramatically flown into Stockholm in a darkened Mosquito to meet the two brothers Jacob and Marcus Wallenberg for a palaver about the Swedish ball-bearing trade with Nazi Germany.[18] Their return on 12 June was even more dangerous; their plane had to return, as its wings were covered with ice, adding to their postwar heroism. At his second Stockholm home, Norr Mälarstrand 34, on 5 June, Eliot treated the American couple to an extravagant dinner, topping it off with four "beautiful Swedish girls."[19] Griffis's often-quoted bombastic threats, à la Humphrey Bogart, about the risk that Gothenburg could be mistaken for Hamburg by American army bombers unless Sweden bent, was affective newspeak that appealed to Eliot and his colleagues at the time but hardly to those who knew about the complex background of the Allies' deals with the enemy.[20]

Using his position as one of *LIFE* magazine's "star photographers," a reaffirming self-nomination that he never had any problem with, and arguing for the tourist value of his narrative photography for Sweden abroad, he managed to be authorized to travel and work in protected military zones, in Skåne (along the southeast coastline), in southern Lapland near the Norwegian border, and on the island of Gotland.[21] He recruited the best assistant he could think of in the art historian Gustaf Munthe, who, miraculously, in his person combined Elisofon's primary competences and needs: Munthe was a captain in the Swedish Security Service; head of the Swedish Traffic Association (meaning tourism); head of Röhsska Konstslöjdmuseet (today Arts and Crafts Museum) in Gothenburg. Was this Swedish passive or pacifist naïveté? Hardly, Sweden had its own lurking agenda in encouraging foreign correspondents to report from and about Sweden. Letting the boyish, loud-speaking, famous war correspondent Elisofon and *LIFE* magazine roam the country under soft vigilance would benefit the country.[22] About his day on Gotland (17 August 1944), he wrote with self-confidence and pride: "I am the first foreigner since 1939 to be permitted entry there." Munthe was his guide among Visby's historical remains and also observed Elisofon riding, as he said, "in one small light tank, Royal Gotland Infantry to make pictures of three others churning dust into my face from ahead." Far more exciting was his account of another image whose aesthetic and thematic making reminds us of the three he would take at the Finnish front: "A significant shot was a soldier on guard near a bunker and below him a small boy, naked, playing unconcernedly in the sand at the water's edge" (HRC

5.30, 2). Elisofon transferred a collection of select photographs from the three trips to the British and the American intelligence.

A major occupation of Elisofon's SHAEF commission was, as he himself explained, buying pictures from Germany.

> Part of my job was to go through the picture releases from Berlin and buy any suitable for *Life*. I also tried to pick up pictures brought out of Central Europe by refugees or neutrals. The spring of 1944 saw an all-out bombing attack against Germany and all of us were very anxious to get pictures of ruined Berlin. The U.S. Army Air Corps was extremely interested in seeing close-up pictures of the damage, made from the ground level.[23] (Elisofon 1948, 52)

The trafficking with close-ups, such as Elisofon's own photo of the German dead at the Finnish front line, exacerbated in his encounter with the legendary Jane Horney-Granberg, the "red-haired spy, Mata Hari," who wanted to sell him "pictures from a boyfriend she had in the German K., 'Propaganda Companies.'" A friend of his brought her to his home at Norr Mälarstrand for lunch. I can only guess who it could have been.[24] "When it was over, we began our talk," and he continued excitedly, as if a hero in a Hollywood Nazi espionage thriller:

> Meanwhile, just for fun, I had been flirting furiously with the girl whose first name I discovered was Jane. On the pretext of personal talk, Jane and I went into my studio. . . . I was curious to see how far Jane would go considering her professional interest in me but I was also worried about the possibility of a frame job being pulled on me with a fake attack. So I went slow and she took out a few pictures. They were terrific. (HRC 52.18)[25]

He browsed through hundreds of them, most of dead Germans from an attack near a railway terminal in Berlin, many of them, Elisofon observed, still clutching the handles of their burst bags. He selected around forty and agreed with Horney-Granberg on the price. She left, only to return in the afternoon, claiming that the photos had to be returned to her; if not, the Germans would kill her (she was killed by Danish resistance in January 1945). Before she arrived, within fifteen minutes, he copied frantically ten of the best (no doubt, the ones he commented upon), which he refused to hand back to her. British intelligence was willing to transmit these photos to the *LIFE* London office, where they were to be censored and confiscated for "dealing with the enemy." He managed, however, to smuggle copies of them to New York via, he explained, "a confidential channel," Mavis Lyons, his wife (Elisofon 1948, 56).

Within his cocoon of Americans, war correspondents, diplomats, and pro-Allied friends, Elisofon's reputation as a photographer of high rank was indisputable and so was, from his point of view, the privileged and anointed axiom about his mission of "setting things right." This was his duty-bound commission as an American "soldier" abroad. In Africa, the mission was similar, even its gladiatorial tendencies, only that its home market was different, more demanding, more sophisticated. What went on in his encounters with just "ordinary" Swedes in this "no-ordinary" time and place?

The following confrontation was not typical or representative of him, not at all, but it demonstrates his self-defending irritability in his role at the time as an emissary of another biosphere. He is in Uppsala to document Swedish student "Spring Rites" celebrated at the university on the Valpurgis Night (30 April). After a long day of photographing white-capped drunken students climbing walls and listening to tedious student union speeches at a dinner, he begins a conversation with Anders Klein, favorably introduced in his report home as one of "Sweden's most favored desk newspaper generals . . . who has a pro-allied reputation," whereas his wife, Else Klein-Möller, turned out to be a "a nasty little woman." What motivated these diverging judgments about the couple? The overture was innocuous. She said, and I quote, that the flowers on the table were the spring's first.

> I put my feet into it at once . . . and said wasn't it a pity that Germany was getting about two million dollars a year out of Sweden for flower bulbs so she drew herself up and said we have to live, that was that. The old man's contribution was that after all America was fighting to preserve international law[26] and Sweden was living up to it and he meant ball bearings no doubt. (HRC 6.13, 3)

Why was Else Klein-Möller a "nasty woman" in his eyes? She countered him. Her pragmatism provoked Elisofon, I believe.

The week before his Uppsala visit, he and a small group of friends, most of them refugees in Stockholm, traveled by train to the Bydalen ski resort in Jämtland to enjoy skiing. Elisofon's intention was to do another picture story about national rites—this time about the Swedish art of skiing, and, in his case, also to learn the art. It took some time before he received his hotel room. No big deal but he was affronted, not as a person but as an American journalist: "Don't they know now what a story in *LIFE* is worth in post war tourist trade. . . . In the U.S. . . . in most cases the owner would move out himself before saying there is no room" (HRC 5.21, 3).[27] His story, "Skiing in Sweden," a self-stigmatizing wailing about his incapacity to get down the hill in style, can be compared to his stooping experience—as a naked man—of being washed by a woman ("let me tell you she was about fifty") after the bath and "*löyly*" (hot steam) in a public sauna in Helsinki, 1939 (Elisofon 1948, 26–29).[28] No text and pictures were published in *LIFE* about his skiing experiment, and he explained why it lacked his familiar spirit: "As far as the story was concerned there weren't enough pretty girls." Cultural normalcy was transformed into a cultural anomaly: Swedish "skiing" and the Finnish "sauna" confirmed their exoticism and Otherness, reverberating Elisofon's or *LIFE*'s overall clichéd frameworks of the two countries.

## Racism in Saamiland (Sapmi)

On 21 June he departed to Lapland, on train to Östersund, changed into another "genuine back water small town local job" for Vilhelmina, and from there in a wood-burning bus to Saxnäs, stopping at the two rapids of Harrforsen and Bieliteforsen (where he would take pictures on the way back) before arriving at Saxnäs, where he spent the night and a day. Here, while he had time, he decided to learn about the Saami and their seasonal meeting, "so I would know a little about it before I started shooting" (HRC 6.14, 2), which meant interviewing the owners of the inn. Exactly as extempore as a journalist on the jump does it, and Elisofon had made that posture his own. The next day a boat took him and twenty others to the destination, the Saami Church Village at Fatmomakke in southern Lapland, with its cone-shaped wooden huts, rough log houses, and the white church. Here he would spend a night in a "*kåta*" (a cone-shaped small house). "And I saw my first Laps," he reports.

He saw if anything the racist caricatures of Saami people or his own modified versions of such phantoms. He first wondered about their "costumes," disappointed at witnessing so few wearing traditional Saami dress. "It seems that they think the civilized costume is more classy" was his snappy resolution. Eventually Elisofon approached a "finelooking Lap to pose for a color shot," the eldest brother of four and a sister that made up the Baer family, but he was not interested. Elisofon promised to send them copies of his photos, but the Saami man did not believe him. His experience was: journalists do not keep their word. "How do you like that—and in Lapland," was Elisofon's response, similar to the one at the ski resort.[29] Elisofon prevailed, however, as his habit was, bought them Pilsner, and got the picture of the Baers in the end. The spokesman for the family, the fifth absent member, was represented by the friend (to the extreme left in the photo), who acted as an indifferent or hostile bystander, a visual commentary of a situation that Elisofon hardly understood. In the evening at the dance session, Elisofon observed that the Swedish boys liked to dance with the Saami girls,

> who were not bad looking. They have a sort of slanty eyes, broad faces and high cheek bones. I would not call them pretty but oddly attractive. I danced with the Baer girl once but she was a very bad dancer. I guess that New York and Lapland have their own ideas of dancing.[30] (HRC 6.14, 4)

They would not *yoik* (for) him. Why would they? The *yoik* is a personal or spiritual kind of Saami singing, which he was informed about in situ (Elisofon 1948, 55–57). Engaging in unequal power dynamics (how dare you question my rights to "possess" you?) and having his camera construe a material (the dress) and sexual (woman's body) specimen, Elisofon had typified the Baer family into nonexistence. This colonial encounter, as I read it, would have been perceived to be normal, trivial even, exotic and hilarious perhaps, by those Swedes at Fatmomakke who happened to be around, watching a foreign cameraman running to and fro like a hungry arctic fox. The Saami have been the objects of discrimination and racism for centuries, a discrimination that dies slowly. At least Elisofon acknowledged the resistance he was exposed to, but he was unable to understand its language and rationale.

We have by now reached the bottom level of the hierarchy that constitutes Elisofon's Scandinavian worldview (Finland-Sweden), with himself, the single combatant persona at the top and, then, in descending order: the Americans; the Western journalists; the political refugees; the pro-Allied Swedes; the neutral, the skeptical, the critical Swedes; the Finns; and the Saami. His low-profile categories, the Finns and the Saami, were besotted by racial or racist assumptions.

But there is another side to Elisofon's Scandinavian time, which liberated him from the combat zone and which merits him to be called the "trickster with a hungry camera." On the Stockholm cultural scene, among peace-loving artists of all kinds—sculptors, painters, actors, and actresses—meeting them, photographing them at work, and eating with them, he metamorphosed into the artist that he most of all wanted to be. Two interviews he gave during his time in Sweden demonstrate these two conflicting aspects that only postwar peace could assuage. In Hans Meyer's interview in the *Folket i bild*, Elisofon's twelve photographs from Tunisia with their narratives did not dominate (as they would have done in a *LIFE* essay). The interview was detached and unsentimental, devoid of the high-pitched national pathos that overpowered Elisofon in similar interviews with American newspaper journalists.[31] In the second portrayal of him, in the *Vecko-tidningen Såningsmannen*, a follow-up of the previous story, as it seems, the themes of his self-presentation were shaped by his civilian career, the role of his working-class background as the son of a poor Russian emigrant family from the slums of New York's Lower East Side, and his desires to devote his professional life to the creative intersection of social documentary photography and art. He met actresses[32] and singers for photographic sessions at the Royal Dramatic Theatre, the Royal Swedish Opera, and the Royal College of Music; photographed students at work at the Royal Institute of Art; and was fortunate to be in Stockholm while the exhibition "Nyttokonst" (Applied Art) at Stockholm National Museum was on deck. He took shots of crystal decanters, cut crystal vases, claret decanters (eleven of them were published by *LIFE*), and explained enthusiastically:

> Swedish glass combines . . . utility with beauty. In warring Europe Sweden leisurely pursues the arts and crafts of peacetime. One of these is the making of beautiful glass. . . . The glassware in this exhibit was made with a practical sturdiness by artists who have held to the same functionalism in design that has recommended Swedish architecture to the world for over decade. ("Swedish Glass," *LIFE*, 7 August 1944, 65–68)

His African photo work, its problematization of conventional boundaries between artisan craft and fine art, has its artistic origin in the social aesthetics that governed this exhibition and also Alva Myrdal and Sven Markelius's "Little Utopia," the cooperative apartment building on John Erikssonsgatan 6 in Stockholm (it is still there) that Elisofon wrote about with as much fervor (HRC 6.24).[33] Thanks to the salaried babysitters in the house, the combined nursery-kindergarten, dumbwaiters that led from the central kitchen to all the six floors, and the ground floor cafeteria, he speculated, the divorce rate in the communal house was as low as two cases in ten years. And the building was beautiful.

Throughout his stay in Scandinavia, whenever he had time, Elisofon made simple pen drawings of boats, buildings, statues, trees, flowers, nets, reindeer antlers (but he never saw a reindeer, to his regret), panoramas, posing nudes, or what caught his curious eyes or the camera lens. At convenient free moments, he worked these sketches into aquarelles or croquises. His artwork and photography were inseparable. "The nearer the act of photographing comes to the act of seeing the better the report will be," he wrote (Elisofon 1944, 8). His pen sketches were part of this visual dynamics. This "rapport/report" was also the topic for his essay "The Relationship of Photography and Painting" printed in the pamphlet *En amerikan ser på Norden*[34] for the exhibition of the photographs and artwork that he produced during the seven months' stay in Scandinavia. The exhibition took place at Tekniska muséet, Stockholm, Röhsska Konstslöjdmuséet (Museum of Arts and Crafts), Gothenburg, and Malmö Museum, Malmö, opening on 24 November 1944 with a launch party in Stockholm with sixty invited guests, the cultural elite of the capital, his colleagues and friends.[35] This date was also that of Elisofon's farewell to the North. The Swedish reviews of the exhibition were positive, many of them wondering at the American's hazardous versatility and vitality. I see him in a photo leaving the Tekniska muséet, bent forward and looking tired, on his way to an American army hospital in Britain for observation.

## Food, War, and Spying

Writing, photographing, painting, cooking: all these capacities were intermixed; Elisofon was multifaceted. He was a rambler, talkative, and intelligent with a charming ego; he was a good liar, a ladies' man, and a skilled photographer. Painting in the morning, writing in mid-day, photographing during the rest of the day, to finish it off by cooking for friends: "I do photography for a while, I get hungry for the softness of watercolor"; "I am a visual man." No wonder he produced several cookbooks with his own pictures, among the first in the genre. Writing came as early as the other activities. Cooking was a formative structure of his social life as it evolved during his time in Scandinavia.

Food for Elisofon was not only an array of condiments organized along certain rule systems called recipes; it was not, as he wanted us to believe, only "a four letter word" that materialized in meals and eventually in his book *Food Is a Four Letter Word* (1948). Gypsy Rose Lee, ex-girlfriend, an ecdysiast (a more modest word for a striptease artist), and author of the preface, knew, if any, that there was always a foreplay to it, that even if it occupied its own center, the meal had consequences, sour, sweet, neutral, for its performers or agents. When Eliot eats, she explained, either unsatisfied or relieved, "there's no time for witty sayings, and as for décolletage, you could sit at the table half naked and if the food was good, Eliot wouldn't look up from his plate" (vi). This was, in any case, a half-truth. The meal was a metonym for a story of many entrances and exits, the "*bon mots*" or the woman's "décolletage," in Eliot's case, suggesting both intellectual and sexual exercises. What happened to this "story" when we move, with Eliot, from the New York restaurants or apartments to another time and other sites, the war scenes of 1943–1945, and how does it interact with my other observations?

Two wartime African gourmet sessions will be our starting points for his Scandinavian crusade between the tables. The first portrays the sensual dating between an American lieutenant, a patrol plane commander, and a blond French nurse. Elisofon escorted the characters to a picnic on the Sidi Abd er-Rahman sand dunes, consisting of canned sardines, boiled eggs, toasted bread, oranges, and wine, to a lunch at the famous Papa Gouim's, Casablanca's "best chef," renowned from Paris, he added. The annexed picture and its caption, "Jim lights a U.S. Cigarette, America's Greatest Gift to North Africa, as Nikki holds his Naval Officer's cap," completed the sweet fable about the alliance of the righteous.[36] The caption's innuendo about the "American gift to Africa" took on a far more sinister and multilayered meaning in the next eating performance where the roles of the haves and haves-not, the powerful and the powerless, were inverted. It is the Caid Al Ayydi of Rehemna, a French colonial handyman, who offered the Americans a gift (for "keeping the Nazis out") by inviting General Mark Clark, commander of the U.S. Fifth Army and his twenty-person staff, to indulge in a "Morocco Feast," off-bounds, far away from the Mediterranean coastline.[37] Of Elisofon's five pictures of the officers enjoying the honey drunk chicken meal—the fourth of nine dishes—three targeted Clark eating with the right hand and licking his fingers, with the Caid on his left watching him, worriedly. Is this American (Clark/Elisofon/*LIFE*) ignorance of Muslim etiquette or defamation of Muslim hospitality? The two introductory paragraphs of eighteen lines, through their abounding detail, construed a menu of excess that was enhanced perversely by the human misery outside the striped banquet tent—pitched on a seized continent. "The food was superb," exclaimed Elisofon (20). But what did he really mean?

Let's move to a site with other more prosaic attributes, but where a Second World War buffet could be as significant, Elisofon's apartment in Stockholm, Norr Mälarstrand 34. It is here with the assistance of his Swedish cook and housekeeper,

Ingrid Magnusson, he prepared meals that, according to him, became "the talk of the town" (Elisofon 1948, 36–37), but it was a talk of a special kind. It was always exclusive, for the select. We have to remember that Eliot was a spy. He had the U.S. minister for Sweden, Herschel Johnson, over for dinner. Johnson's engagement during spring 1944 concerned Raoul Wallenberg's mandate to help Hungarian Jews to leave the country for Sweden. The meal for Johnson consisting of cold borsht, cold salmon, and breasts of guinea hen with potatoes and trifles harmonized well, Elisofon must have thought, with the positive aura that possessed the concurring Swedish-American dialogue about the refugee question. The second high-profile dinner that Elisofon mentioned with pride from his time in Stockholm was the buffet he and his partner served the tough and rough American diplomats Griffis and Poteat (37–40), who, we remember, were invited in the company of four women (one of whom was Maude Siri Maria Anna Blomberg, alias Betty Maud[38]). Elisofon's roommate, Malvin Fagen, American/British political adviser for SHAEF, a real spy, was also present. Only that the palavers on this June evening, if any, must have been conducted in whispering asides. Opportunely, the informal serving and dining of a buffet gave the men the chance to chat about what were the best tactics to force the Swedes to give up their silly loyalty to the Germans (which they partly did on 12 June).

Elisofon was host, cook, entertainer, the loyal Allied combatant, all in one person. He would manipulate this fictional "persona" when he considered the situation appropriate, as in my third example of his Stockholm dining politics. It relates to Jane Horney-Granberg, whom he had invited, we remember, to a simple lunch, foreplay for the hoax about the commercial exchange of German pictures. His multileveled "talent" would be tested.

> The problem arose of what to feed this Mata Hari. We kept it simple. Some Smörgåsbord, mostly little tidbits from previous meals, things like cold guinea hen, sliced chicken, smoked salmon, smoked eel, and so on. The main dish was to be Parisian Sandwiches. (52–53)

He also tagged the recipe for the "Parisian Sandwiches" dish in the book. To my mind, it was not a bad lunch, and far from "simple." However, I am not sure that it took place at all. He may have fabricated the story about its apex, the photo commerce, in order to make the rendezvous with Horney-Granberg fall into the titillating and variegated thematic of the *Food* book, which "is about practically everything, with a small plot, some humor, some love, some travel stories, and—some food."[39] The far less melodramatic, the somber, and the most likely variance is the one he told in the interview "Recapitulation of Elisofon's War Record" for *Time* Inc. Archives on 21 October 1945, only a bit more than a year after what he called "The Affair with the Redhead" in Sweden. In this account he explained how the "Redhead" came up to his house to tell him that she was traveling to Germany, and offered to take pictures for *LIFE*, provided that Elisofon lent her a camera and picked out what to shoot. "He stalled her off, not daring even accept the feminine favors she had mutely offered him along." Next day, he is quoted as telling her on the phone: "Don't you know that under Swedish law it would be illegal for me to have any such dealings with you" (HRC 72.9). No mention in this talk with the interviewer of his "heavy entertaining" and the ensuing lunch with Horney-Granberg, and the setting up of the commercial negotiations about the photographs. In the latter version, he verified his loyalty with the SHAEF assignment by taming his "natural" instincts, resisting her sexual solicitation; in the parallel narrative, the same masculine drive was an idle weapon with a sting. One suited the book of food, travel, and frivolity; the other, the military report. Which of them was true, if any, is insignificant. The three Stockholm meals discussed have dealt with food as a masculine discourse propagating political negotiations, a political power game, and political seduction.[40] We have confronted a *LIFE* magazine photographer engaged in wartime espionage with his five-room apartment as the base. For Swedish meatballs to excel, Elisofon advised, "be careful not to overcook." He "overcooked" the "Redhead" affair.

What did food signify for Elisofon under the pressure remitted by the Finnish-German war front in the north? He filled his "Tunisian" haversack and musette bag in Stockholm before departure not only with his photo equipment (several cameras) but also with Swedish crispbread (*knäckebröd*), salami, sardines, smoked mackerel in oil, and some Pommard ("the real stuff 1929 vintage") (HRC 6.10, 3). In Helsinki, happy to learn that the visit would be extended to include travel to the Kemi-Tornio war front, and the "feeding" of five American war correspondents (including Scott and Elisofon) and three British citizens, Elisofon's food storage was supplemented with several roast chickens, cans of Argentine corned beef, and bottles of Chablis and Rhine red wine. Throughout the round trip, Elisofon, "Mess Officer for the Allied Press," doled out the food to his colleagues at mealtimes and "when the Finns were not ready for us" (61–62). Eating would be a bonding, compacting, solacing, and exonerating act, a liturgy of a kind, as we will see.

At an Oulu Rotary club lunch of salmon and wild duck, Eliot and Ossian Golding (the *Daily Telegraph* journalist mentioned earlier) were sitting close to Hjalmar Siilasvuo, a Winter War hero and commander of the Army Group Lapland, now fighting to throw out the Germans. Time was running out, the Allied ("Russian") Control Commission's deadline (1 October 1944) had passed. The Finns had to demonstrate their determination. Siilasvuo saw his chance. He also knew the risks of taking a group of foreign journalists to a place that offered no shelter. At the table, the most spectacular event of the Lapland war was at hand, the shipping of twelve thousand Finnish soldiers in five flanking maneuvers by ships to Röyttä (1–5 October), the beachhead outside the city of Tornio. Siilasvuo asked: "Would you like to go there?" The war correspondents said yes; they in their turn had no idea of what Siilasvuo could foresee. The Rotary Club lunch in Oulu on 2 October 1944 was momentous.

In the cabin back at Oulu, escaping from the deadly Stuka bombardment, Elisofon was resting, faint after the concussion, but not for long.

> I felt OK again and I laid out a big dinner of some of the smoked fish, two chickens I had held out, a tin of beef, and two of sardines. I had plenty of real tea I had brought from Sweden, and we had a hot quart each. We also had a bottle of Bulgarian Schnapps which had on the label . . . Herzlichen Gross Euch Nicht . . . Wir Vergessen Euch Nicht . . . Heil der Führer . . . Dr. Göbbels. It was awful stuff. (HRC 6.10, 8)

It is a meal of both thanksgiving and desecration, of the right and the wrong, of friends and enemies—and of Elisofon's good heart. It is advocating one justice only—that of the winning team. About the next meal, Elisofon said: "It was fantastic!" The host was Niilo Kanto, manager of Kajaani OY, a private paper mill at the city of Kajaani (UPM) that would operate until 2008. Indexing Elisofon's Scandinavian meals, this one was celebratory of a future that was as unimaginable as that of Finland. Elisofon's rhetoric was drunk on illusionary, culinary joie de vivre. That is power and it was his, too. It also provides me with a smooth possibility to end this chapter and to start probing the meanings of "what not" as they emblematized on another continent.

> It had everything. Plates of roast beef really rare, tongue, veal, ham, lobster salad, caviar, lax, anchovies, chicken salad . . . all this was the smörgåsbord. Then cream of asparagus soup . . . after that breast of partridge. The extraordinary thing about

the dinner was that it came after hours and hours of drive through wood after wood from Oulu. It was as if we were in czarist Russia and had driven for days through forests to come finally to some great castle and find strawberries and what not waiting. (HRC 6.10, 9)

CHAPTER 2

# Colonial Travel and Colonial Habits

## Early Years, Elisofon in Africa, 1947 and 1951

Elisofon's half-a-year-long (January through June) trip through Africa in 1947 was his first of eleven (not including his World War II commission as pool photographer in Morocco/Tunisia 1942–1943). The second, in 1951 (March–mid-July), with his wife, Joan Elisofon Spear, was also for *LIFE*. They were events of enormous significance, for him personally as a flourishing photographer with Africa as an appropriated field of specialized knowledge, and for the *LIFE*'s Cold War project of making the continent look recognizable.

It is important to realize that any photograph that Elisofon took for *LIFE* was the result of an array of interlaced pulls. The photo narratives he produced were informed by the contextual material he culled from various sources and what the *LIFE* editors supplied him with. But there was more to this photography. "*Life*'s special gift," explains Wendy Kozol, "was to make change seem traditional by locating the tensions of an unfamiliar world within the seemingly familiar and nonthreatening orbit of the "happy" nuclear family."[1] Kozol's political imaginary of the curative 'happy American family' is useful in discussing Elisofon's rhetorical application of colonialist conventions as they formulated the narratives of Africa, the "unfamiliar" Other. Normative colonial practices related to the eye, the camera, the "African" body, and the "African" landscape, embedded in the West's visual archive of long-standing, governed what Elisofon chose or was compelled to see and reproduce. The unfamiliar world was masqueraded. His photographs were confirmations and refinements of fantasies-already-seen that he wished to display anew for an audience that he believed needed guidance and clarifications. His narrative in images about the continent was subordinate to a domesticated rehearsal. Their modulation and mediation for the American readership was more important; Africa was a palimpsest. To retell the "old" African story was his "gift." Colonial travel or missionary travel was double-faced. It connoted the arrival-passage-return from the outer (Africa) to the inner (the United States). Photographing the Kuba king, for instance, was such a roundabout exercise. Elisofon returned repeatedly to the canonized imaginary of him after 1947. The reinvented photographs that he took were republished and robbed of their context. They still are, continuously distancing African cultural and historical conditions, revisiting their colonial and racist mythologies.

The second theme—as is also inferred in the previous paragraph—is how the parallel and interlocutory myth of Elisofon being a popular *LIFE* photographer, animated collector, and specialist in African "art" was shaped over the course of these travels. We will see him taking photographs of objects in the museums in Kinshasa and in Lubumbashi that he thought were extraordinary (in the latter museum of a chair "whose feet end in four stylized human feet with toes pointing forward"; another of a sculpture of "man and woman with their organs in union"). We will also witness him taking pictures of objects in people's houses (called "huts") and in outdoor public spaces, and buying and haggling for artifacts as any colonial tourist with "Africa" as his marketplace would do (HRC 9.22, report 3, 31 January 1947). These activities provided material for one of his most cited and informed visual essays for *LIFE*, "Mystic Art of Tribal Africa: Images of Early Negro Culture Influence Native Life of Today" (8 September 1952, 116–25) as well as his renowned book *The Sculpture of Africa* (1958). They were domestic prolongations of the 1947/1951 travels.

## Elisofon's Retour of Africa: From Cape Town to Cairo

Masculine traveling is first of all a project of solidification and completion, of the individual making a decision, mapping and measuring the ground under his feet, and reaching his goal personally fulfilled and socially sanctified. It is exploratory, possessive, and, by its historical nature, imperial. The African continent in this imaginary is crisscrossed with canonized tracks, from historical pilgrimages in the footsteps of Stanley or John Hanning Speke to the more mundane but as questionable "safari" races in the Kilimanjaro region, which variously have contributed to the map-making industry of the continent.

Elisofon's 1947 trip, "from Cape Town to Cairo," was—grandly and metaphorically speaking—the beginning of his colonialist mission of Amer-European postwar aggrandizement. Ironically, this spatial trope coincided with the logistical expansion of the British Empire by its connecting South Africa, Botswana, Zimbabwe, Zambia, Tanzania, Kenya, Ethiopia, Sudan, and Egypt via the highway (today called Trans-Africa Highway 4).[2] And even more representative irony can be won from the fact that the formal reason for Elisofon's travel to South Africa was an assignment to photograph part of the British king George VI's two-month African visit. In *LIFE*'s sardonic taunt, the king's role was to perform the "solemn obligations of Empire . . . enacting against the darkening backdrop of imperial calamity" and open the parliament of the Union in Cape Town that a king never had done before ("England's King Visits South Africa," *LIFE*, 10 March 1947, 23-27). Elisofon dropped out of following the royal family because of the "bad treatment that he and other journalists had got" (report, HRC 10.2, 21 February 1947), except for taking a series of photos of dancing "heir-apparent Elizabeth." This may have been one reason, but there were others.

Cape Town had for centuries been an iconic meeting place for seafarers and adventurers, and later, eighteenth-century and nineteenth-century botanists and explorers. It had been a borderline site for expanding frontiers for as long, and right now, in front of Elisofon's eyes, it was a white laboratory experimenting with racial orders. In Cape Town during these weeks in February 1947, he was caught in a hotbed of racist politics. He registered it, commented on it, and shared his thoughts with his peers in New York. He pronounced what *LIFE* magazine would not do, that the king had come "to reinforce Smuts [Jan Smuts, the Union's governor-general] to cut down the growing desire for a republic [1961]" and that the Indians were boycotting the visit. He reported that he had witnessed non-European traffic cops correct European women jaywalkers and had read about a trial against an instigator of a strike, which he believed rather was a trial "against communism per se." He discussed apartheid with other journalists and with people he met. The following quote from the Cape Town report, rare in a sense as he seldom and only unwillingly discussed politics in public forums, sums up his apprehensive viewpoints at the time. They would have indistinct consequences for the orientation of his African photography.

> It is becoming more and more obvious to me . . . that various governments in Africa are sitting on black dynamite. . . . Here [in contrast to Alexander Bustamante's anticolonial activism in Jamaica] there are practically no native leaders but the natives are getting more and more restless. . . . After seeing some of their land (the Bantu who are allowed to hold only ten per cent of all South African land and this within special reservations in the Natal Province), I am convinced they have been treated well compared with the American Indians who were in the same position as the Bantu here. (HRC 10.2, 4)

Before he managed to procure a ticket to New York in 1905, Elisofon's father almost died from impoverishment in South Africa struggling in the diamond mines, and for his son Cape Town would also constitute a point of departure, a no-place as ephemeral as an insignificant spot on his map. South Africa remained a complex Terra Horrifica for him, representing, on the one hand, Boer energy and intrepidity that he admired, and, on the other, racism that he disliked ("but the natives"). Except for a couple of mandatory weeks during his Literary Africa tour in 1959, he would not travel to South Africa. His library of photographs from South Africa is significantly meager.

On 25 February, he left Cape Town—a young knight at the beginning of his apprenticeship, of the visits to the African and British royals, and of his "African art" chase, and ready for the first courtly stop at the Victoria Falls. Each stop would mediate an exclusive story that was self-sustained and embellished with details of its particularity. Elisofon's tour can be divided into ten sequential stations, where each break generated a sequence of connective photos and an explanatory graphic narrative destined for the *LIFE* office. Elisofon knew personally his peers in New York, their idiosyncrasies, what food they ate, what women they gazed at (as heterosexual men), and their take on the day-to-day media politics at *LIFE*. His visual and written address, the package of rolls and the telegrams he sent them, were skillful adjustments to the protocols of caption formulation, *LIFE*'s Africa politics, and the determinants of his gender-centered heroic passage along the predestined route to Cairo, and its extension—"home." Elisofon knew that only a winning string of communication, between him and them, would guarantee success: a published photo essay. A question such as Caren Kaplan's, "if we gain possession of something by taking a photograph, what do we gain writing about it?" (or vice versa), troubled any *LIFE* photojournalist, and in particular Elisofon, skilled in each art.[3]

Elisofon's remaining stops were the visits to Zanzibar, the Maasai safari, "guide to Kenya," the Nile, the Shilluk, and Egyptian art. We remember his usage of panoptical aerials to box in his fantasy of what was to constitute oriental Finland. The holistic creation of his stop at the Victoria Falls (6 March) was molded in a similar panoptic traffic from top to bottom. The dichotomy would connote formations in the landscape but also shifting narrative perspectives from the Falls' iconic history to a subjective camera observation of a woman tourist's hat challenging the Zambesi River. Such metonymic shifts are legion in his visual narratology. His stop at the Victoria Falls was not only a pilgrim paying respect at one of the Tour's mandatory highlights. It was Elisofon's first nostalgic contact with David Livingstone, one of the three Victorian explorers (the two others were Stanley and Speke) whom he admired and emulated. He spent three days at the Falls, photographing ethnographica (African masks, chairs) at the Livingstone museum, quoting Livingstone extensively in his journal/report, and observing gleefully: "Livingstone had no camera."[4]

Elisofon's (also) three-day trip to Zanzibar (after his three weeks in Nairobi, which he left on 17 April) was narrated in the fashion of an eighteenth-century rational travel writer with the world as information (history, geography, nature), a universal rationalism that was fouled by his colonial gaze, as when photographing and choreographing the seating of Sultana and Sultan Seyyid Sir Khaliga Bin Harub (he called it a "scoop"). The actual photo, as often is the case, fools you at first glance, but reading Elisofon's unofficial caption for it, your perception is cleared and the real is no longer real but paranoia. The Sultana, he wrote to Wilson Hicks,

> looked as if she had dipped her face into a box of hard white powder and carried on like a rhino in a mud bath. The most difficult job being to have the Sultan sit in the chair and hide the lower portions of the Sultana behind him. It took considerable maneuvering. (HRC 10.6, 3)

Apart from his anxiety about border sanitation and his camera's efforts to police a woman's body, the photograph is one of hundreds similar in his African album of the family as a social hierarchy sanctioning subordination of woman to man. The bestial trope, "the rhino in a mud bath," takes the Sultana's degeneration even a step farther down the Darwinian ladder.

At the beginning of May, he was ready for what was to be the most memorable stretch of his Tour, the stern-wheeler cutting down the White Nile through the papyrus swamp area of the Sudd to the confluence of the Blue Nile at Khartoum. His narrative of the passage described visual scenes that he either ran into or organized at places and cities—among them Malakal, Fashoda, El Jebelein, Omdurman/Khartoum, Shendi, Meroë, Batn el Hagar, Abu Simbel, Aswan, Luxor, and El Faiyâm—before, one month later, he hit the Delta and Cairo. The plaque commemorating Speke's first sight of the Nile leaving the Victoria Nyanza (28 July 1862) was not merely an object to visit for a formal camera shot. To start his visual covering of the Nile at the Ripon Falls was a way of ritualizing the affinity he acclaimed with other Nile scholars and explorers. And he would definitely make a visual global impact. More than half of the 280 photos that were published in his *The Nile* (Elisofon 1964) were taken during his 1947 Tour (the others date from four other travels: 1951, 1959, 1961, and 1962); 125 were exhibited at New York's Museum of Natural History on 8 December 1950 through January 1951.[5]

Despite its extempore narration, Elisofon's ten-week and seventy-five-page-long Nile field report matches any contemporary travelogue in formation through its restless but intense focus on the volatile and unveiling detail. His visual observation and linguistic formulation do not necessarily jibe; they may represent different aesthetic experiences. A mother carries her child using a "fascinating contraption" that

> consists of shoulder straps made from animal skin, usually goat, a small wooden round bar on which the baby sits with his or her feet hung near the mother's sides, some cross straps to keep the baby from falling out, and over the baby's head and shoulders a small woven basket shaped like a bowl, which covers the baby to the waist or lower. (HRC 10.9)

Its visual version fails to embody this complex construction, but it adds to the riverbank atmosphere it was momentarily part of. Another mother carries her baby in a woven basket strapped to her back, and the caption, in contrast, is meaningless (Elisofon 1950, 60). With intense ethnographic voyeurism he inspects the scarification patterns on women's and men's bodies, their different geometrical crossings, and ancillary body ornamentations. He takes photographs that have become iconic—for reasons that are not always defensible.

There are a Madi girl "with large triangular welts on the torso and thick, vertical scars along the forehead and arms" (Elisofon 1964, 57); the Shilluk girl with a necklace of aluminum "from a plane wrecked in the area" (78);[6] a "girl of the Hamar tribe" who wears "a leather amulet containing sacred writings from the Koran transcribed by a holy man" (86, 87); a Nuer youth with "six horizontal scarification bands on his forehead" (82); and another young male covered with "ash from burned cow dung" (67). The addenda or the attributes, however exotic, charming, and informative, hide the unexpressed main clause: "I See and Understand It All." Paddling into the Muslim regions and leaving the "savage tribes" (119), Elisofon's focus shifts from photographing individuals to photographing groups of people (women winnowing grain or bathing in the river; men carrying sand to reinforce the dikes along the Nile). The anonymous individuals are profiled by skin and other ornamentations, the women and men in groups by Muslim dress codes. There are three portraits of individuals in his Sudan-Egypt gallery, all men of authority, all honored by their full names, all in dress; there is one fully dressed woman, an anonymous "Berber girl" from near the Egyptian border who wears "the black cotton costume customary among the women of Upper Nubia and is adorned with a silver necklace and leather amulets around her neck; the silver ring in her nose is called a *nibla*" (102, 115). A dressed woman in the colonial Nile context is a phenomenon that exacts an ethnological commentary; dressed men from the same regions are self-explicative. Nudity is banned in the Republic of Sudan, explains Elisofon, as a retort to my innuendos, but "in the Sudd the law is more honored in the breach than in the observance, for its inhabitants are among the most independent people on earth" (61). His mistake was triple: one, the "naked" African woman or man who was exhorted (alternative verbs are abundant) to step up in front of Elisofon's camera (or was not even exhorted to pose) did not act out of any conscious sensibility of freedom/independence, whatever that word meant; two, as colonized under the British and the Belgians, the idea of "freedom" could only be asserted by rebellious body language, sneers, and so forth, that, three, Elisofon was blind to, caught, as he was, in the commercial and popular imaginary about the "racially pure" Shilluk (or it could be the Maasai). We will have many reasons to return to Elisofon's blind or false spots about the "primitive" in the course of the discussions to come.

Elisofon's intuition for the African "spectacle" as both "trophy" and "curiosity" was filtered through a liberal conscience of many layers—critical, ethical, and acquisitive—that seemed to interact without causing him either scruples or hesitation. He accompanied a colonial judge (D. D. Donald) to a trial in a village outside Kwon Fashoda with elders listening to a woman who refuses to return her daughter to a man she married (66, 75); he witnessed the lengthy purification ceremony,[7] with a goat sacrificed, after lightning had struck a house and burned it to ashes (66, 76); he organized a war dance of celebration with two hundred men north of Malakal by paying them with beer (HRC 10.9, 15). The photo of the wild-looking "Shilluk brandishing his spear" (72–73; also in the Nile *LIFE* essay) is one of many in his genre of the choreographed "African savage."[8] Having reached the rock temples in Abu Simbel (they were disassembled and reconstructed with the construction of the Aswan High Dam in the 1960s) in southern Egypt, Elisofon changed focus, in line with his last program, to document pyramids, temples, reliefs, and wall paintings. The remaining fifty photographs of his Nile book are accordingly an Egyptian art catalog, except for the last five, which view women planting rice shoots and children picking worms from cotton plants in the Delta area. *LIFE*'s metaphor of the Nile as "mistress and handmaiden of all who live along its banks" (Elisofon 1950, 119) falls into the subaltern ethos of these five pictures.

Elisofon was a traveling master of mobility, with the camera sweeping leisurely over river scenes, buildings, thorny acacias, market places, and expanding its hegemonic claims with aerials of the confluences of the White and Blue Niles, the old Aswan dam, and the First Cataract, and, eventually, at the heroic exit out of his Tour, the Damietta branch with its flow into the Mediterranean Sea and the New World. "Elisofon saw," *LIFE* summarized,

> the panorama of racial groups and civilizations through which it flows. He visited savage tribes in Uganda, pastoral people and desert nomads in the Sudan, Arab villagers, Egyptian *fellahin* farther north and the cosmopolites of Cairo at the river's end. (Elisofon 1950, 119)

To make all this possible, he needed all kinds of assistance, numerous letters of reference, which he got with ease. Via the British embassy in Nairobi, he received names of colonial administrators whom he would contact from the first day of his Nile itinerary. Throughout his travels, he was aided by local British functionaries, police, judges, and intermediaries; he had a power-based crosscut to events, places, and people he wished to document. Accompanying or being escorted by key individuals, British or Sudanese (even by the *reth* or the king of Shilluk, Anei Kyr), he was more of a colonial coadjutant with a camera than a *LIFE* journalist. The Juba Round Table Conference, where the North and the South (the latter reluctantly) agreed to pursue a united Sudan to be represented by a legislative assembly, took place on 13–15 June, within Elisofon's hearing range and sight. A couple of years later the British had started the process of Sudanese "self-rule." The avid photojournalist he was, he navigated adroitly into the midst of these historic and fateful controversies, as he had done in Stockholm three years earlier. He was present in April at the installment of Sir Robert Howe as governor-general (1947–1954) for the Sudan who was to pave the way for decolonization. Nor did he miss a dinner party in Omdurman, in May, with twenty nationalists of the Sudanese elite, only that "they all looked alike to me and to my camera as well" (HRC 10.9, 30). With no little confidence, he could write to the *LIFE* office in New York:

> There is no question in my mind that the British have done more for the Sudan than Egypt ever would. The loud screams for "Unity of the Nile Valley" by the Egyptians is a shrill sour note in an already discordant orchestra. . . . The Sudan at this time is being administered with a definite attempt by the British to give the country self-rule. (HRC 10.9, 24)

These viewpoints—and not only his twenty-one photos in it—decisively influenced the Nile essay. The *Sudan Herald* quoted him (on 7 May 1947) as saying: "I am glad to have arrived in one part of Africa where the people have reached a level of education which is beneficial to the community at large . . . in great contrast to the Union of South Africa where the native is regarded as pure labor" (HRC 10.10). This was Elisofon sweet-talking.

## Eliot Elisofon and the Colony (Belgium and the United Kingdom)

In his role as an American photojournalist, Elisofon very seldom encountered any problems with catchall traveling in Africa, whether before or after 1960. His intrepid take-it-for-granted attitude that the red mat would be rolled out for him was in itself a winning strategy. And seen from the other side, the thought was, what were there but advantages to gain welcoming Elisofon with official kudos? The premise was that he was more of a big gun as a formal representation of accumulated empirical power than was the elusive impression of the small hyperactive man turning up with cameras dangling around his neck. Furthermore, the argument ran, we can use him for our own purposes.

The Belgian curator, Adrien Vandem Bossche, at Le musée de la vie indigène (The Museum of Native Art) in Kinshasa (11 January 1947), where Elisofon started his first peacetime African visit, welcomed him for the best reasons in the world. Both were patriots, each World War II combatants with Africa as the arena, and each fascinated by "African art." Only three years earlier (1944), Bossche had produced an exposition dragging 4,600 artifacts from the Leopoldville museum across (or around) the continent. This gigantic nationalistic showcase, "L'art indigène à l'honneur. Les expositions d'art colonial belge au Moyen-Orient," traveled from Cairo to Alexandria, Jerusalem, Damascus, and Bayreuth. It was a Western self-manifesto of possessiveness.[9] The Belgian Information Center in New York published simultaneously a sixty-six-page pamphlet called *The Belgian Congo at War*. Its purpose was "to tell the American public how this African territory, as large as one third of the United States, is bracing itself to an ever increased effort for the Allied victory" (2).[10] By successfully filling Belgian museums with treasure troves of looted goods, both at home and abroad, as well as fighting a morally inferior European nation (Germany), the Belgian colonialists claimed to be enlightened warriors brazening out their history. That they had appropriated African land and African people for their warfare was of no importance.[11] "The tremendous sacrifices Belgium has imposed upon Itself to help the Congo native out of Arabian slavery and to deliver him from disease, have been rewarded by the loyalty and the devotion of the 15,000,000 Negroes in the Congo" (2), the propaganda leaflet declared. Stealing from Africans as well as using them in their war paradoxically freed and cured them. This is Belgian colonial history-writing:

> The first pioneers came back to Europe laden with the treasures of the Africa Tenebrosa. Ivory, leopard and lion skins, arrows, spears, and musical instruments were heaped in decorative piles, resembling the cartouch of Baroque architecture. Naturalists and ethnologists were eager to share the major spoils, leaving the less important pieces to collectors of exotic curiosities. Masks and figures, arms, and carved tools, basket-work and clothes were studied, compared, classified according to their tribal origin. The religious, military or domestic meaning of every single object was explained by learned men who soon were able to write exhaustive books on the subject. . . . Since that time, the Ethnographic Museum of the Belgian Congo, created in 1897 in Tervueren (Brussels), by the foresighted genius of Leopold II, became the most important European center for the study of African art. The collections, arranged and classified by the first director of the Museum, Baron Alphonse de Hardleville, finally contained the finest examples

> of Negro craftsmanship as well as the most touching and significant statues ever carved in wood by the black race.[12]

Elisofon spent two days at Bossche's museum,[13] photographing diverse objects, two of which were published in his book *The Sculpture of Africa*, which contains in all 405 objects photographed by him. Only 17 of them were located and shot in Africa.[14] Is his *Sculpture of Africa* an exhaustive book by a learned man? Is its title defunct? Could its asymmetrical displacement of Africa and the Rest of the World be juxtaposed, theoretically, with the storyline of the British district commissioner's coming thesis called "The Pacification of the Primitive Tribes of the Lower Niger" (the last words in Chinua Achebe's political allegory *Things Fall Apart*) and his ruminations at witnessing dead rebel Okonkwo dangling from a tree having committed suicide? I am insinuating that both the British colonial and the American photographer saw what they were conditioned to see. These are sad presumptions based, however, on facts that Elisofon himself, at this very moment entering the Kuba kingdom, recognized, but never addressed, saying, "Most of the best African art is not in Africa but in museums and private collections, the British museum having the greatest . . . [so] my intention is to photograph what examples one can find in Africa still in the hands of the natives and being used by them as a part of everyday life" (Report for *Time* via air mail on 24 January 1947; HRC 10.1). "Authentic native sculpture" meant for Elisofon indigenous sculpture made and used for traditional purposes—with him as its tactile temporal observer and often pillaging collector. Notice the temporal amplifier "still," the nostalgic suggestion of which Elisofon undermined at every second step he took during his African fieldwork.

The environs of the city of Mbandaka (then Coquilhatville), near the confluence of the Congo and Ruki Rivers, was a site relatively "untouched," implementing the second proviso for a sculpture's desirability, and Eliot was ready to board a riverboat, a canoe, to travel to Mbandaka (in an earlier report from the same Bakuba trip, on 12 January in Kinshasa, HRC 9.22). But the trip did not materialize. Being an expert on Kuba cups and embroidered raffia textiles himself,[15] Bossche had a more conservative, safer, and enriching plan that, he also knew, the colonial administration not only preferred but demanded.

Kubaland, bordered by the Sankuru, Lulua, and Kasai Rivers in the southeast, had an exceptional place in the Belgian colony. The kingdom cooperated smoothly with the colonial administration throughout the period, even during the war, when the villagers were freed from cultivating cotton as a compulsory contribution to the Belgian war costs. The indirect rule worked as long as the king's men would do the job that normally (in other parts of the colony) was done by the Belgians, such as counting the subjects and preventing unrest. They in their turn would enjoy privileges, salaries, and tributes, and again were expected to return services, such as entertaining important foreign guests by grading gift giving, demonstrating their artistic skills, and dancing for them.[16] By the time of Elisofon's two days at Mbop Mabinc Kyeen's (ruled 1939–1969) court, the Kuba kings' reputation for the richness of textile art, wood-carving skill, sumptuous narrative ballets, and (conditional) hospitality extended half a century back to include many famous overseas visitors such as the anthropologist Emil Torday (1900–1907),[17] the photographer Casimir Zagourski (who took a picture of Mbop's elder brother and predecessor, Nyim [king] Kvet Mabinc Kyeen [ruled 1919–1939]), and a royal tourist with a camera such as the Belgian Queen Elisabeth in 1928. The Kubaland was the very opposite of the "untouched" landscape; its reputation as a treasure store and cultural mine was kept alive by the colonial administration, in the colony's own interest as its humanitarian guardians.[18] Elisofon was only one in a long line of Western visitors under colonial surveillance—for a purpose.[19]

Elisofon flew to Luluaburg (now Kananga) and took the train from there to Mweka, where he met Gabriel Hunin, the territorial or the "cultural" administrator who, by the governor-general, had readied for him the passage to Mushenge, the capital of the Kuba. On the next day, before he confronted the royal court in its full activity and splendor in a photographic onslaught, he had some extra time of reconnaissance with the king, letting him know what his plans were, stealing into his rooms uninvited, photographing carved columns, a collection of knives (two with European shears), and a reclining chair.[20] He also saw "the crown prince," probably Kwet aMbwek III, who, according to Eliot, spoke French fluently and called himself Joseph (HRC 10.1, report 2). From conversing with this Bushong intellectual, he picked up the addictive tall tale that "the Kuba were cannibals fifty years ago," which helped to set the adventurous mood for his shooting and the annexed "African Big Shot" *LIFE* essay (based on Elisofon's New York letters).[21] The two hierarchical systems, those of the colonial and the Kuba, complemented each other in forging the mix of real and imaginary. In her brief essay "Two Days in Mushenge: Eliot Elisofon's Images of the Kuba (1947)," Christraud Geary writes:

> The photographer constructed his view of an African king and the arts and artists surrounding him, no doubt with the thought of publishing the pictures. The king presented himself and his subjects as he wanted them to be seen by the foreigner and by outsiders in general. Judging by the continuing popularity of these photographs, both photographer and king succeeded in creating a lasting image of the Kuba.[22]

Yes, it is one of Elisofon's most published photos, and one that he promoted himself whenever he saw a chance. But what kind of "lasting image" of the Kuba does it promote?[23] We need to recognize that Elisofon profited from the colonial situation, of which the king was the victim despite his relative elbowroom within it, and that Elisofon's two-day photo work was embedded in structural lopsidedness.[24] It was Eliot who was the king and the master, Bope/Mbop a stage director of a cultural carnival adjusted to the white man's camera, with another white man's permission. Even if he profited from the attention and the advantages he gained as being the chief mediary of "Kuba Kingdom [as] a showcase of benign Belgian colonial rule in the Western rule," he was still its servant.

Eliot was not interested in Mbop, the individual, the skillful politician, and the sculptor, but in what he stood for, his royal pompousness, the regalia, his appearance, and in particular his female entourage, his "harem of wives." This is how Elisofon saw him: "[He] turned out to be quite ugly with coarse features and a pot belly so heavy that it bore him down. . . . He was dressed in a simple skirt of wrap-around material and a large collection of tight copper leg bracelets and a smaller collection on his wrists" (HRC 10.1, report 2). Posing for him, after three hours' grooming, then wearing the luxuriant robes ("Bwaantshy") covered with beads, bells, cowrie shells, and King Leopold II medals, the headdress ("Ntshuum Aniym"), the necklace made of leopard teeth ("Lashyaash"), the sword ("Mbombaam"), and the lance ("Mbwoom Ambady"), the ugly but the real and private man was translated into the public "African Big Shot," a black clown. With its myriad of connotations, the following extract from the *LIFE* essay encompasses the devious "image of the Kuba." It is still active, I am afraid.

> In his court is a minion called the Yumi whose function it is to rub red pepper into the eyes of the monarch's 350 wives if they become disobedient. He even gets tribute from the outside world receiving a yearly grant of 86,000 francs from the Belgian colonial authority, which recognizes his power in keeping the

> once-cannibal subjects under control. Bope has one ambition: to visit America. He thinks American blondes are fascinating. (Elisofon 1947, 129)[25]

In her study of William B. Fagg's photographic archive of Africa, Deborah Stokes makes a few observations that are relevant here. Like Elisofon, his partner in the production of the book *Sculpture of Africa* (1958), Fagg was drawn to the thematic of kings and chiefs, to their power-based allure rather than their personalities. In Fagg's case, it was the "ritual symbols of office [of Yoruba kings]: beaded crowns, shoes, staffs, fly-whisks, and other accoutrements of royalty" that were central. His portraits were straightforward, dignified, and unemotional. They look like, Stokes writes, "clinical studies" by a colonial outsider who is documenting a particular "type," frozen in time and space.[26] Elisofon's portrait of the Kuba orthodox dignitary was also a refashioned conventional product by an outsider but by one with far more subjective attitudes than those of the British governmental scholar. Eliot's image-text is a perversion on two parodied levels: first, through its individual bodily and ritual excess, second, by its cultural affiliation with savage backwardness, erotization, and polygamy. During his Mushenge days, he took about one hundred photographs that documented the royal court activity with the "wives of Kuba" (fewer men) either "tribal dancing," singing praise songs to the monarchy, carrying water gourds, or embroidering, among them the earliest "specimen" in Eliot's enormous gallery of scarified half-naked women (Elisofon 1947, 130–32).

Juxtaposing the two synchronous Elisofon royal *LIFE* stories, "The Fat Black Monarch" and "England's King Visits South Africa," or rather its appendage "The Trip Down to Capetown Was Fun and Visit Got Off to a Good Start" (separated in real time by a month but in moon time by one hundred years), is forcing one party of the dichotomy, liberal Western monogamy, to confront or cure the other, degenerate African polygamy. The narrative figuration is of the Kuba king turned into a deformed synonym for idiosyncratic perversity. On photographing the British king and his family on 17 February in Cape Town, back from the Congo, Eliot, in his typical brusque fashion, walked up to George VI "standing practically alone" and told him that he had visited the Kuba king and his 350 wives; the "king laughed and said: 'It would keep a man busy, wouldn't [it]?'" (HRC 10.2, "Report of Union of South Africa," February 1947, report 4, 11). The curt byword is one of hundreds in Elisofon's private store of one-liners that he tossed around (and the media with him) at appropriate moments to enhance a twist in his conversation, but, more importantly (and sadly), it represents here a repartee of conventional, trivial male shoptalk that he occasionally extended into male sexism or chauvinism of the worst kind. The following is such an example. Elisofon was sharing with the New York photo editor Hicks his experiences of photographing the women of the Kuba royal court dancing in front of his him and his camera:

> The leader had a special gourd which had a necklace of tinkling objects around its neck. She set the rhythm for the others. The others . . . all kinds . . . fat and skinny, tall and short, young and old, smooth and wrinkled, some with breasts so pendulant that they were revolting to see, backs and stomachs tattooed in intricate beautiful patterns, a touch of tattoo near the forehead, some with clean shaven hands, other with tight black curls, and all wearing the attire of the harem, an orange wrap around skirt with a billowy edging. . . . I got tired of photographing old hags with horrible figures and picked out a nice young one with a fine figure, only she said she couldn't dance. (HRC 10.1)

It is as if the women's bodies, depending on their degree of mutability, decay, and constitution, were caught in a losing battle against the invincible permanence of the "attire," the raffia, the hairpins, and the necklaces that they wore. The bodies that carried them were replaceable (or almost), Elisofon meditated, but not so the collectible and photogenic objets d'art. The stereotypical narration of an African dance scene, like the Victorian interline of the normalcy ("family") and the abnormality ("harem") of the two kings, can be analogously compared (and for the same reason) with a series of three photos that Elisofon took of the "heir-apparent Elizabeth" (now Queen Elizabeth II) swinging around on the deck of H.M.S. *Vanguard* with midshipmen in Cape Town harbor. The caption of the dance scene read:

> The playful princess . . . dodges about in a spirited game of tags. . . . Leaping to elude the pursuer (top), she gets trapped between two more (centers), finally falls into a historic hug with a brash but happy officer (bottom). (*LIFE*, 10 March 1947, 28)

In the Kuba scenes, the women were reduced to their bodies, body parts, body decorations, age, and beauty. Elisofon's visual navigation between attraction and revolt prevented him from seeing their dance performance. In the Cape Town scenario, on the other hand, he was intrigued by what was its center, the step-by-step impromptu movements of the individual dancers. Here he saw the out-of-the-ordinary moment, the British princess dancing with sailors, did not distract him as did the de-individualized Kuba women with pendant breasts. The thematic of "us and them" required separate lenses and mindsets. Elisofon's objectification of women was an enduring passion for him throughout his professional career, whether it was the portrait of Swedish Ingrid Bergman or the Kuba king's wife, but still fundamentally different.[27]

He made observations of another sort, grosser or just naive. Passing through Zappo Zap (near Kananga) in Kasaï-Occidental, heading for Lubumbashi (and its museum) during the last stretch of his Congo trip, he wrote (letter 31 January 1947; HRC 9.22, report 3):

> I met the Basonga [Songye] in the village of Zappo Zap I was immediately struck by the beauty of the women and I was afterwards told that these women are most popular with white men who are unmarried. They are not only pretty but clean and are good housekeepers. I made portraits of typical women and the most attractive was the wife of the local chief.[28]

He speaks, without self-awareness, as if women were commodities and he an agent in human trafficking. There is a triple racial categorization in Elisofon's pondering, through his attribution of not only physical and aesthetic attributes to these women but moral as well. It may well be that the hearsay about their qualities that Elisofon had picked up was a twisted reflection of Zappo Zap history as a center for the slave and ivory-rubber trade and the site from where King Leopold recruited his middleman to chop down forests to get at the rubber.

Elisofon would return to the Congo six times in all before his last stop in 1972. By that time the dictator, and Elisofon's patron, Mobutu, had been in office for seven years.[29] The apartheid-inspired Belgian colonial system kept Africans out of top jobs in the government, the army, and the companies; forbade them from attending universities; and suppressed all attempts at political protest using military force, to mention a few circumstances known to Elisofon. All this did not seemingly concern him at the time, nor would he hesitate to work alongside of and seek assistance from the Mobutu regime later. And why would he as long as neither the Belgian colonials nor Mobutu dictatorship undercut his U.S.-sanctioned and privileged work with the camera? The question must be asked, however: what Congo did his camera see? Was it in any way different from Stanley's colonial discourse of a "consciousness of absence with the structures of imagination and desire?"[30] What do the presences say about the absences in Eliot's post-1947 "Congo"? I will return to these concerns in much detail in later chapters.

British Nairobi welcomed Elisofon with kudos rather than with the polite indifference of Belgian Kinshasa. On arriving in Nairobi on 10 March (during his Cape Town–Cairo travel) and checking in at the New Stanley Hotel, the (also) new owners, the Block family, I am sure, gave him a crash course in the latest news mongering about the British plantocracy and their hedonistic lifestyle ("Are you married or do you live in Kenya?"), their sophisticated hunting manners, and their relationship to their African servants.[31] In the hotel, he drew the outlines of what he planned to achieve during the three weeks available. He called the plan "a simple coverage of the English way of life in an African setting," which in fact was far from simple. The "African setting," the auxiliary theme, he explained, would incorporate a documentation of the "original inhabitants of Kenya both human and animal," natural history, mountains, plains, lakes, the Great Rift Valley, and local color collected from the downs in the Mombasa harbor, the Nairobi streets, and the Karatina open air market in Nyeri. The animals he wished to shoot were giraffes, rhinos, and buffaloes; the other species, the "original inhabitants," were the Maasai and the Kikuyu.[32] Like Karen Blixen in *Out of Africa*, comparing the gazelle and the Maasai, he conjoined the African animal and the African human.

There are plenty of "LORDS" around, Elisofon wrote mockingly to Hicks, among them Alexander Cambridge, the uncle of the Queen of England,[33] and the "Lady" who has been "cited in the notorious Erroll murder." Elisofon was talking here about the murder of Josslyn Victor Hay, the Twenty-Second Earl of Erroll (in January 1941) by—most likely—the American heiress and absinthe-drinking party-girl Alice de Janze, who committed suicide eight months later.[34]

> I do not know how *LIFE* will be able to play the social decadence of the Kenya smart set and get away from libel suits. Most of the infamous characters are dead or have gone away. Those that are left are completely camera-shy.

As the case was open and on everybody's lips, it was no wonder that Eliot was pulled into the aroma of "the social decadence of the Kenya smart set," the intrusive and sneaking *paparazzo* he could be, which epitaph he would have endorsed with relish. The anonymous "Lady" proved not to be shy, and he took four pictures of her, which I have not been able to trace, nor have I come across any evidence that *LIFE* took the risks of publishing either pictures or bits from his writing about the Erroll case.

He visited three wealthy conservative British landholding settlers: Lady Genesta and Lord Claud Hamilton, the Pitt-Moore family, and Donald Ker, "one of Africa's great white hunters" (Elisofon 1964, 6), all leading figures in the settler community. They all knew Bror and Karen Blixen and Lord Erroll. The first couple took him to their designed and built Nderit House (today Lake Nakuru Lodge) on the shores of Lake Nakuru, where Elisofon took pictures of their fine cattle and "wild Maasai herders." He spent a weekend at the Pitt-Moore coffee plantation in the Kiambu district counting 160 acres of land, a workforce of 70 farmers, 150 tile-workers, and 500 pickers who got four cents for four gallons. The land of these families had been confiscated from the Maasai (as the Blixens' was) and the Kikuyu alternatively; the Kenyans who worked for the British were poorly waged, landless, and racially abused. By 1945, 10,000 European settlers owned 43,000 square kilometers of the most fertile land, only 6 percent of which they cultivated.

As part of his English lifestyle project, Elisofon went on a luxurious "Maasai safari." Three cars carried the company with the "boys," a bathtub, folding tables, chairs, china, and silver, to the famous Treetops Hotel in Aberdare National Park on the southern side of Mount Kenya. Here Elisofon tried to take pictures of the mountain, which was invisible due to fog and inaccessible for his camera. The tourists were entertained by a "white hunter" who stunned Elisofon with his skill in weaponry. On their way back they passed the township of Nyeri, making brief stops at a Maasai *manyatta* and the Karantina market on the Nyeri-Nairobi highway. They were at a height of 1,966 m (6,450 ft) above sea level on the Aberdare Range, in the midst of the Mau-Mau territory from where the operations against "loyalists" and white farmers would start in two years. In June, Jomo Kenyatta would be elected president of the first colony-wide African political organization, the Kenya African Union (KAU), which had been formed two years earlier.

Elisofon met the reputed Kikuyu colonial chief Koinange Wa Mbiyu and his son Peter Mbiyu Koinange, educated in the United States and a minister for sixteen years (1963–1979) in the country's first cabinet under Kenyatta. Under the supervision of a colonial information officer, the chief was dressed up in "attires of monkey skin" to subserve ceremoniously to the foreigner's camera, in the best Kuba king fashion. After the photo rehearsal, the chief turned up metamorphosed, Elisofon complained, into the paragon of a "well-dressed executive similar to a Washington clerk of the Negro race." "He was wearing a blue serge suit with a shirt and a tie, black oxfords, had a gold chain dangling from his lapel to his breast pocket" (HRC 10.5). We recognize the identical irritation that Elisofon expressed observing a number of Saami costumed as "civilized" at the Midsummer Night celebrations in Lapland/Sweden in 1944. The Kikuyu chief, in contrast to the Kuba king, had transgressed the rule of subservience and the stereotype of himself only (in Elisofon's eyes) to move into another. The problem was that irrespective of how the chief or the king (the Buddha, the Fat Man, and the Big Shot) did anything, it was wrong; the two remained black clowns, by being black. Photographing Kikuyu women squatting near their woven baskets at the Karatina market, Elisofon made the following remarkable comment (to which I will return): "Their postures and natural positions made picture after picture as easy as copying old masters in the museum" (HRC 10.5, report 6, mission March–April 1947). In other words, as long as the "original inhabitants" stayed put within their God-shaped or stereotypical formats, they answered to his visual and preconceived perceptions of them. Their "natural positions" were there to be copied by a sly camera, to be ossified and published for the world. He continued his marketplace chat with Hicks:

> I used the Rollei over my head down so that I could see the subject over my head [or the camera could]. They hadn't the faintest idea that I was shooting them and were very unconscious of the camera. I found great similarity in the native markets of Africa with those of the West Indies, especially the one of Port-au-Prince, Haiti.

The efforts made toward independence from Great Britain (or Belgium) were not on Elisofon's agenda in 1947 (and would never be), first of all out of courtesy, as he was an honorable guest among the settlers. It was not that he did not care. It was that any outspoken vacillation about the colonial status quo within which he could operate so smoothly would have been canceled out by his commission as a *LIFE* Cold War photojournalist and also be disordered by his own ideological and aesthetic conservatism. He was all for social reforms, but from *within* the given systems only—and slowly. The Kikuyu chief should stay an "authentic Kikuyu chief," at least as long as he was a subject for Elisofon's camera. Commenting on an article in *East African Standard* (1 April 1947) about strikes in Mombasa for higher salaries among the stevedores, he explained:

> On a question of pure economics, which, I am afraid, had been the one and only factor in persecution, the native is way down. For the preservation of fat incomes and a fine way of life the native's real advancement will be fought tooth and nail

in Africa as he has been and still is being fought in the Southern United States. (HRC 10.5, 14)

Elisofon's analysis of the interdependence of colonial economy and discrimination was a carbon copy of the litanies that he overheard at the New Stanley Hotel dinner palavers. "The native's real advancement" in Kenya, Belgium, and South Africa, as well as that of the blacks in the southern United States, could not take place without the undermining of their common suppressive systems. This was another statement for debate traveling to and fro between Cape Town and Nairobi, London and New York. The sarcasm of the "fat-incomes-and-a-fine-way-of-life" about the aspirations of Kenya's "squatters" and landless originated in coloniality's racist think-tank. At this time southern (U.S.) legislatures were actively busy keeping lynching legal and blacks disenfranchised. Elisofon knew what went on in the South, of course, as he must have realized that Kenya was turning into a full-fledged apartheid state, only one step away from the institutionalized separation of races that would be implemented by the Boer regime in 1948. "There is no question that East Africa needs plenty in the way of medical attention and education," he entreated, modifying it by suggesting that "the Kenyan native is much better treated than his southern brothers" (meaning South Africans). He was a blindfolded liberal.

Elisofon's photo essay about Kenya was never published by *LIFE*.

## The Beginning of a Collector's Shopping Tour in Africa

Collecting and photographing were, for Elisofon, inherently similar acts of appropriation to the point that in theory neither would claim first concern. Quite often the two activities, however different logistically they were from each other, merged or concurred. Many of his photographs of objects in situ were acquiesced and removed straight out of their organic milieu to be photographed (by him) anew transposed into another site-specific situation—an exhibition, a museum, an art book—into another cultural frame of reference, for which he has been endlessly celebrated. Elisofon was a multidimensional agent of desecrating cultural objects while deifying them through a process of reconstitution, translation, and replacement. Collecting, for him, was as prima facie as was taking pictures; it was doing a job that could be problematic but never reprehensible as such. Its character of dispossessing the Other was not an issue. It was submerged by the higher ideals of national self-centeredness that have characterized the Western presence in Africa for centuries.

Collecting was a priority long before Elisofon arrived in Kinshasa in January and resolutely made the local art museum his very first stop. He himself repeatedly pointed to the famous exhibition of "African Negro Art" at the Museum of Modern Art in 1935 as the kickoff moment not only for his love of this art but for collecting it, identifying it, and registering it.[35] Collecting and photographing went hand in hand. The didactic information with labels, stickers, as with captions, in Elisofon's case in his photojournalistic practice, was a way of communicating with the museum viewers, legitimizing the object.[36] Ethnographic objects were moved out of the continent and fashioned into African sculptures. The century-long colonialist trophy-curio racket was in the 1960s and 1970s turning into a professional and semiprofessional art-dealing industry. It is easy to understand the fascination that this metamorphosis had for an aesthete such as Elisofon, of realizing that he could be part of it and become an aspirant connoisseur. It is logical to think it all started at the New York exhibition in 1935, he as one of its forty-five thousand visitors. His lifelong argumentation for the impact of African art on painters such as Picasso and Matisse, also as a supportive prompt for his own combative enthusiasm, it is safe to claim, had its origin in the display techniques of the exhibition.

The building of Elisofon's African art collection, then, was never a subsidiary project. It was an ongoing activity that infiltrated each photographic bout along his itinerary from Kinshasa in January to Cairo in June, as it would all his other ten African journeys for the coming three decades. By then he had amassed about seven hundred artifacts, most of them crowding his New York apartment until the time of their final translation (1972) from private into public space took place, and eventually into a safer life in the catacombs of the National Museum of African Art in Washington, D.C. In his letters to Hicks, he regularly noted en route what his acquisitions were, small or big; how he went about procuring what he wanted; whether he paid or not, bargained, or simply snatched the object. To please Hicks, he did not only send him his well-formulated, often amplified travel anecdotes but also memorabilia that could be anything from Nazi sleeve insignia and shoulder boards that Elisofon cut from uniforms of dead German soldiers in Finland in 1944 to African vases and cups. He practiced two modes of collecting, one more aggressive and diverse, the other improvised and straightforward.

The one in Zappo Zap had all the qualities of the first. He choreographed men, women, and children to engage with the objects that he cherished, here musical instruments, swords, and masks, and then took the pictures. Naming the interaction between the object and its holder variously "authentic," "natural," or "real," Elisofon's deified and legitimated the transaction, fabricating his own illusions. Requiring or buying the objects was a given outcome of an unsigned deal. Elisofon got his musical instruments and swords. Yet he could also meet with resistance. At Zappo Zap, a couple of villagers refused to let their personal icons go. He was as baffled as he was at Fatmomakke in Lapland, and for the same reasons (HRC 9.22, letter 31 January 1947). The Saami and the Zappo Zap situations are prototypical.

The purchasing event in Tanzania, south of the Kilimanjaro along the Moshi-Arusha road, involved Maasai men and women whom he encountered on his travel north for the first time in his life. But what he saw was not real; it was rather the classic popular distortion of it. His camera depicted the cartoon's "paradisiacal tribe." Purchasing copper earrings, a bow, and arrows from them was both illustrative and consequential. Elisofon enlisted individuals from a group of Sudanese Shilluks on the Nile north of Malakal, prototypical photogenic "savages," juxtaposing them with the "tributes," as he called the material that he acquired, paying five shillings "for a pipe with two bowls in the shape of a hyena or a dog" and trading beer for aluminum plaques by Adieng Lion, a local artist (HRC 10.9, 15).Generally, the Smithsonian curators have loyally interpolated with Elisofon's field-note protocols (as we will see other instances of later) extending merely the representative ethnographic material they carried.[37]

Meeting Bope, Elisofon had been informed about the Kuba custom of the grading gift giving, but he may not have understood or may have simply ignored the fact that it was a respectful gesture to entertain a guest and not similar to an auction sparked by the step by step raising of the value of the object with one winner emerging at the end. The Kuba king gave his photographer an intricately carved wooden cup in the shape of a man's head and several carved boxes of intricate design and animals in relief. The following is one of Eliot's many tall tales about his tactics at this gift-giving spectacle:

> I wanted a superb mask [EEPA EENG 01867] in the household . . . and I knew that if I offered him something he'd be forced to respond according to the native custom. I gave him 50 dollars [in fact 500 francs]. The Nyimi's [the king's] chamberlain, in turn, gave me three eggs. So I raised the price. The chamberlain produced a hen. By this time I was worried. I recorded reading about explorers who had swapped mirrors, gimcracks that sort of thing, and as an afterthought, I had purchased some

> gold chains at the Five and Ten ["Woolworths" in the report for *Time*, HRC 10.1]. . . . I took out the chains and placed them around Nyimi's neck. . . . When he beamed I heaved a sigh of relief, and a rhinestone fountain pen was the final thing that closed the deal. I felt as I was back in the era of the explorer, Stanley. I could have got myself killed for that mask [Bope gave him another mask; who fooled whom?].[38]

Bope wanted a camera, and Eliot sent him a Brownie reflex when back in New York, suggesting infamously that he could take pictures of his own people to be shared with Eliot. That this did not happen was what he and Joan were to realize at their next visit to Mushenge, in May 1951 to their disappointment. The "vanishing savage" did not perform as he should.

Elisofon's "colonial habits," from their dependence on feudal map knowledge to "imperialist nostalgia" (Rosaldo 1989a), were infiltrated with a peculiar rebellious frame of mind that both boosted and interjected his advance. We saw that he rejected, in fact refused, to fulfill what he had been assigned by *LIFE* to do, write a full-length story about King George VI in Africa while still adjusting to the colonial social and political rituals. We have followed him conforming rigorously to "the hierarchicalization of space" (Harley) while transgressing from the canonical itinerary at times when running into a visual allure that he could not resist.[39] These instances, and similar, did not alter his basically lifelong colonial frame of mind. He was a loyal rebel; his "rebellion" was a tactic to see better, not more. The "mourning" of a loss, for which "we" are ourselves responsible, and the wearing of what Taylor called the "Many Masks of Eliot Elisofon" (1958b) to hide "our" facial grimaces (as Elisofon's double-crossing with the Conradian harlequin) are circumstances that I will have Rosaldo's laboratory diagnose:

> Imperialist nostalgia revolves around a paradox: A person kills somebody, and then mourns the victim. In more attenuated forms, someone deliberately alters a form of life and then regrets that things have not remained as they were prior to the intervention. At one more remove, people destroy their environment and then worship nature. In any of its versions, imperialist nostalgia uses a pose of "innocent yearning" both to capture people's imagination and to conceal its complicity with often brutal domination.[40]

The paradox in the *LIFE* journalist "hunter hero" (Richard Slotkin) narrative does not resolve necessarily (but almost) around "killing" and "crying" but around stealing, disappearing, and reconfiguring, formulating rhetorically another version in Rosaldo's album of nostalgic tropes. On reaching Kinshasa in 1947, the creating of his elegiac montage of Africa and the mythologizing of himself as One and the Rest as Others was in full operation. "Stealing" is an umbrella term that I use for the white man's jubilant conquistador travel along the life-line, the Cape Horn–Cairo route; for the passing of the canonical Speke, Livingstone, and Stanley spots; for reaching, deified, the Mediterranean West. Before being heroically Reconfigured into another Stanley, the passage had to be mesmerized by further Stealing, the collecting of images and artifacts, a picture there and a mask here that were paid for with "innocent yearning" pearls. Also "I could have got myself killed for that mask," we remember Elisofon telling an interviewer (Taylor 1958b) about the Kuba visit transaction. Reconfiguration started when the missionary circle was completed, when the object and the story had been domesticated. It contained Elisofon's unlucky fantasy about producing the photo book in the footsteps of Stanley; his aesthetic purifying of the photos of troubling contextual details; the depiction of "traditional" Africa as an obligatory narrative preamble for a documentation of modernist postcolonial Africa. Colonial Reconfiguration stopped when America had seen it, read it, heard it, responded to it, and endorsed "its complicity with often brutal domination." This is the theme that instills in some way or another all the remaining chapters.

CHAPTER 3

# African Women Walk, African Men Sit, African Children Are

## Gender as Difference, Exclusion, Segregation, and Passage

Stanley's visual configuration of the African geography as a sensory patchwork and a hierarchical system of the overlying and the dismal was a sinuous segment in Elisofon's visual platforms from where he construed his artistic photo art surveillance. Lakes, confluences of rivers, mountains, waterfalls, and cataracts were for him, as they were for Stanley and his followers, topological breaking points, binary dramas, separating low from high, small from big, water from soil, mapping a mental and physical image of a recognizable normative Africa, that still haunts us mainly for what it leaves out. To plant his "Kilroy was here" signature at these canonical sites and modulate his visual narration of the continent along the established Victorian parameters of the colonial space was, for Elisofon, passion, desire, and lust. He constructed an explorer-persona of himself from within the canon of the Victorian explorers. His was the call of a masculine pilgrim, in Simon Ryan's defining words about the explorative gaze, "a voyeur 'unveiling' a feminized landscape; a reader construing the land as text; an elevated eye, with a viewpoint regarded as privileged."[1] Rewatching and renarrating the Victoria Falls and the Murchison Falls, for instance; researching, photographing, and writing about the river systems and cultures of the Nile and the Congo; transforming his traveling into the pursuit of not only the best photo of the artifact but the possession of it,

Elisofon's mission was to bring back his neocolonial trophy to the United States, if possible, for admiration, recognition, and consumption.

Animal life, wildlife, and panoptical landscape portraitures as safari leisure activities for the rich were accessories of a colonial lifestyle and infrastructure that Elisofon enjoyed replicating throughout his time in Africa, barely, as he would have claimed, for the bettering of Africa camera work. Elisofon's photographs of peaceful river scenes, rhinos kissing, and the "sublimity" of Rwenzori and the Victoria Falls are masterpieces in their own right, but do they represent more than themselves? Was it the "real" Africa? Almost a century had passed since Stanley's time, and the politics for understanding the continent had changed and, one would expect, so also the photographs that "followed the steps" of the originator would have, however loyal the visual scribe was. But no, Stanley's phantom blocked the entrance of Africans into Elisofon's album, and the thousands that were permitted to enter his visionary contact zone were redressed to sanction it. Stanley had neither the patience nor the equipment to characterize Africans in photographic terms. Elisofon had not the time either, but he had the skill and the equipment. No reader/viewer can take away from them their compelling power of charm. But what is charm? Elisofon's schemata and thematic were to portray Africans in groups, and as individual women, men, and children. From within such broad gender domains, the notions of landscape, place, and body became interceding constituents of the photographs. Stanley will be watching.

Out of Elisofon's travels in 1959, which are the empirical core of my investigation, came 8,271 black-and-white pictures, negatives, and color slides, a great number of which have been digitized and are freely accessible on the Internet.[2] I will only comment on a small selection of them. The *LIFE* assignments of this 1959 trip constituted what Elisofon mostly called Literary Africa and the documentation of the political campaign (rigged, some think, by the British[3]) in Nigeria for the 12 December election. The five-month trip was the most all-embracing of Elisofon's African travels. He visited Sudan, Uganda, Kenya, Tanzania, South Africa, the Democratic Republic of the Congo, Nigeria, Ghana, Mali, and Liberia, a trajectory that offers a broad, and timely, ideological canvas for my study of his gender constructions. Colonialism as a political setup was capitulating; coloniality was not.

## Women Walking

Elisofon's photographing of African women walking and at work was uninvited, what one could call an intervention into the muscular rhythms and timetables of their daily chores. Colonial Africa of that time lacked words to escape his eye, but it could look back. It did. The "time-geography" that Elisofon took for granted was that of an opulent master from another planet confronting the "time-geography" of the less beautiful, less advanced, and explorative planet.[4] The *LIFE* photographer mapped the terrain in front of him as if he were a god out of fear, lust, and curiosity, to seek control at least for some minutes of what he saw or rather what he had been culturally conditioned to see. The women, whom his camera would sneak onto for it to possess, reacted with rampant indifference and tacit loyalty, intimating that the cameraman was equally or perhaps even more inhibited than they were, that the colony enclosed both the colonists and the colonized. The American with the ogling camera was a troublesome intruder. Michel Foucault was right in generalizing that "we are neither in the amphitheater, nor on the stage, but in the panoptic machine," that surveillance's self-regulating power concerns us all.[5] True, self-regulation may minimize or intensify intersecting gazes; the Other was in trouble.

Elisofon took forty color sequential slides of "Gwari women carrying firewood in baskets [on their way to the market], near Kaduna, Nigeria" and over forty of "Nupe women carrying enameled tinware with flexible woven cover, Wuya, west of Bida, Nigeria" ("Nupe woman walking in narrow street surrounded by mud wall fences, Bida, Nigeria").[6] None of the other collected samples of women as walking objects reach this volume (many of those with men at the center supersede them by the double). Reading each of these two collections of photographs as a filmic narrative along the parameters of time and space/place provides the individual photo with a contextual meaning that it may avert in isolation. The story that emerges is revelatory of the photographer's intentions or intuitions. It provides an insight into his clash with the essentialist stereotype of African women as carriers of heavy burdens—with more than half of their body weight on their heads or backs. The clash meant the paradox: upholding a conventionality, the exclusive African image, by strengthening or weakening it. The Gwari group of about eight adults and one child about nine to ten years old walked single file along the edge of a road, crossing a river on a bridge (with a railroad bridge in the background), without stopping or talking, while ignoring the photographer strutting at their side, behind, in front, except once when the woman with a red shawl reciprocated by dropping him an evil eye, as if to say, "You trespass, leave us, we want to walk in peace, we are busy for the market." This was the women's life-serving time-geography. The time it took to do so (about twenty minutes) and the distance they covered (about 500 m) were the only experiences they had in common.

By shifting angles (half back, side, half front) and alternating distances to include six, four, or two women walking, Elisofon placed the focus on the body carrying the strenuous yoking of the wood load. To achieve this technique, he had to run up the road a bit, wait until his favorite quartet (with the red shawl woman and the child) would pass, and then shoot with his camera parallel to their bodies, as if tracking shooting with himself on a camera dolly. The sensation of power, energy, and speed of the image was deepened by the horizontal contours in the landscape, the rails along the bridge, the railway, the never-ending road (EEPA EECL 8337). The heightening or the punctuation of the stereotype might have occurred in instances when a man on a bicycle and an insouciant young man with a stick in his hand passed in between the women and the photographer (EEPA EECL 8334). A small road kiosk with drinks in the back would be a third provocation of the norm or its very opposite. Elisofon's dominant visual regime of the women carriers, his aesthetics, and egocentric impatience (he did not celebrate the women's arrival at the market) formulated his time-geography.

The "Nupe" collection takes us to Wuya near the city of Bida at the east bank of the Kaduna River village. Here Elisofon witnessed women walking ashore to continue to the local market at Wayazuwaku village. That was real, but the rest was not. Elisofon's sets of pictures of women as porters navigated from producing a panorama of a still river landscape to a group of twenty women disembarking languidly from a long dug-out male-maneuvered canoe and close-ups of a few of the prettiest individuals. This decorative picture painting could have been taken out of any nineteenth-century colonial travelogue, only surpassing it technically, celebrating the timeless gendered landscape waiting to be explored. Stanley's voyeuristic observations of the virgin landscape have had many copyists. The scenery relates to the photographic studio of the 1860s where the backdrop of relics and other memorabilia around the sitters, McClintock has argued, "signify an anachronistic relation to the technological time of modernity" (125). The "relic" here is the river landscape sensualized by the anonymous female figures, the life-bearers in the male canoe; the "modern" was the viewer seeing it all, controlling time, theme, and the aesthetics (EEPA EECL 8617). The "woman" is Nature; "he" is Culture. The two time-geographies cannot be more separated than here. In a set of eight photographs, Elisofon returned to his stalking technique, photographing from the back and the front a Nupe woman with a child, a baby, and her load of nutriments on/at her body walking on a narrow path into a compound fenced in by mud walls. As in the other Nupe pictures, the woman, minimized and distanced, was denied a presence of her own. She merged with the mud walls, with the landscape, the Mother of abundance she was. With her deleted, what dominates this bunch of pictures is the abandoned path leading to Nowhere (EEPA EECL 7937).

## Women Working

What do these women do? Or rather what situations with women at work did Elisofon opt to document? The following are the nearest I could get to him examining female activities related to work. I have found him photographing women selling calabashes on the east bank of the Niger River at Onitsha (EEPA EECL 8555); women removing beans from cocoa pods at a family farm in a Yoruba village; women collecting water at a spigot from a piped water system in Katsina; women pouring out threshed millet at Barhin village, near Katsina (all these places are in Nigeria); women pounding millet at Bin and Ireli Dogon villages in Mali; women transporting water in the Nile Delta region, Egypt; and women carrying/displaying cloths for sale at a market in Kumasi, Ghana. Highly traditional women's work and workplaces—then and now—and, I could add, exhausted century-old visual themes in Western photography and African travel writing. That Elisofon honored par preference what he defined as the tradition-borne, ancestral, customary, we know by now, whether it constituted the preservation of old dance forms or Bakuna masks. Adding photographing women at work to his conservatory practices could be a comment on the threats caused by modernist and postcolonial prompts for change. But this was not the case.

The fact is that these photos did not portray African women at work. Their work and their supportive bodies were assistants or cover-ups for engendering other ideas. The color slides of the terraced riverbank commerce with the panorama across the wide water Onitsha landscape would come to life only on the pages of a commercial travel brochure or on a postcard for the West African port city. The caption about the four mannequins in the foreground selling calabashes was a fake. They had been bereft of their livelihood. The same had happened to the women selling and carrying the colorful clothes market in Kumasi literally, now drowning, disappearing in the colors. The caption here too was a misrepresentation. The Katsina millet scene was aestheticized into an excess. In repetitive shots the color slide sequence captured the solitary figure of a woman at a tree during the last minutes of the sunset (EEPA EECL 7839). She was pouring the millet with one arm raised, which extended her body, licensing the voyeur to incorporate the full curvature of her body landscape.[7] The image was overloaded with safari eroticism: the sunset, the body, the yellow terrain. The lore of nakedness and barrenness impregnated all these pictures.[8]

The picture of the two Bin village women also pounding millet was organized in a similar manner, with less studied craftsmanship but with the same sexism (EEPA EENG 03493). Another photo from the same village portrayed a single woman who had been decoyed, without her allowance, for no other reason than to stir the sexual fantasies of the heterosexual photographer and the (implicit) male spectator (EEPA EENG 03491). In the second Mali photo (Ireli), the pounding women were devoured by a gigantic baobab tree. Shot from a distance, the women were hardly recognizable, compressed into tiny gesticulating miniatures as if shrieking for help (EEPA EENG 10049). In the spigot drama with two women collecting water, helping each other to move the water baskets onto each other's head, the pictorial centerpiece has been replaced by a thirsty helpless donkey.

The final exemplary serial image when extended into its maximum translates into a visual story about the cocoa farmer Michael Ige and his three wives and twelve children. Elisofon took thirty-eight pictures (of forty-one in all) of the farm, starting his shooting of the compound from a distance of 50–60 m, moving step by step, picture by picture, in the same straight line close enough to take snapshots of the youngest wife removing beans from the pods (EEPA EECL 10655). In the process of approaching her, he documented the farmhouse, what it produced (a shot of a heap of beans), the sixteen family members (a portrait), and the third wife looking disinterested and aloof at the man with the camera (EEPA EECL 10661; EEPA EECL 10659). The picture of Ige's prettiest wife (although less abstracted than the others) is emblematic of Elisofon's view of woman at work. She is a shadowy, secondary figure, an allegorical object befitting his visual aesthetics and imperial desire, the phantoms of which he was looking for nervously in both material and human culture in Africa. He recapitulated his angst for her in the photography we have examined. Rose quotes, conveniently here, C. M. Armstrong on comparing the female nude in Western art to the landscape.

> The female nude, when free of narrative situations, is most often constituted frontally and horizontally—as a kind of landscape, its significant part the torso, its limbs merely elongations of the line created by the supine, stretched-out torso. (1996, 96)

"The same sense of visual power as well as pleasure is at work as the eye traverses both field and flesh: the masculine gaze is of knowledge and desire" (Rose 1996, 97–99).[9] I wonder if Stanley would have enjoyed accompanying light-footed knowable Elisofon during his photographic peregrinations from one colonial safe haven to another with colonial administrators as his assistants. Yet many of the reviewed photographs, examined from other perspectives, would by many be considered executed with great skill. And they are. It is only that the sophisticated photo such as the one of the Habe woman with the stretched-out torso against the sunset emanates male sexual possession rather than producing knowledge about women's food work that its caption anticipated it to do. The gap between the *LIFE* photographer's intention and Elisofon's practice was a quandary.

## Portraits of Women

Even if we are half a century away from the hey-day of anthropological genres of photography as instruments to chart physiognomic characteristics of different "tribes" and body decorations as evidence of ethnic boundaries, they actively impact in various ways on Elisofon's work. The explorer's privileged eye, his multiple armchair identity told him, served to formulate a thematic overview for the details it embraced to become visible and registerable. The mapping of this confluence, the transfer from the panoptic to the myopic (or vice versa), was Elisofon's insignia. The scarification pattern on the woman's (less compelling on the man's) body, the detail, was identified with its parity with other body significants, which as an entity would support (extremely seldom negate or deflect from) the individual body's group (ethnic) affiliation. The pseudoscholarly rhetoric would not by definition favor ambiguity. The following cases are, here too, exemplary. At Zarenda village, east of Jos, the capital of Plateau State, Elisofon was attracted by the multicultural diversity around him and took photos of what he (?) registered as women from three distinct ethnic groups: Hausa (6),[10] Fulbe (5), and Zulawa (57). The two "girls" dressed in traditional bubas, wrappers, and head ties, and with painted faces, were singled out (by EEPA staff based on "photographer's notes") as Hausa (EEPA EECL 2630), and the woman wearing an "elaborate headband and colorful beaded necklaces," respectively, a "brightly tasseled hat," as Fulbe (EEPA EECL 2669). But do we know for sure?[11] But it was, as we understand, the half-naked body-modified "Zul(awa) women" (EEPA EECL 2685) on the same marketplace at Zaranda (where he picked out the Hausa girls) that provoked Elisofon to shoot fifty-odd photos of mainly their heads—from all imaginable angles.[12] The likes of Zaranda village "Hausa" and "Fulbe" girls/women Elisofon could see walking the streets of New York; they have therefore left little trace in the EEPA Zaranda album. Not so the Zul women "with disk inserted into their upper lip and facial scarifications" and "the characteristics of degeneracy and deviance writ large on the physiognomy of the subject." The latter quote is from Coombes's discussion (1994, 38) of early twentieth-century photography of ethnographic selections but applies with little modification (deletion of "degeneracy") to the material we are concerned with here. What is the difference between bringing a group of "Pygmies" to London from the Ituri forest for display and photographing in 1905 (Coombes 1994, 139, 144–45; Murray 2011) and Elisofon's photographing them side by side with Joan in April 1951 or his mug-shooting of the Zula in 1959? In each case the idea was to display deviant or deformed "types" from the Lost World for the Civilized World of "normalcy."[13]

None of the women I have discussed in this chapter have names, or better, they have names but they do not feature in the Elisofon archive as individuals in their own right. They are women, emblems, attributes, specimens, bodies, breasts representing twenty "cultures" where each cultural affiliation is a theoretical assumption: correct, half-correct, wrong, half-wrong. Among the 870 documents in the EEPA (1959) register under "woma/e/n" I can find only two women (Joan Elisofon not included) who are named: Aissa Alimiri, a single-stringed lute musician from Timbuktu (23) and Conde Tiemoko, also from Mali (8), "wearing large gold bicone bead" (which EEPA [EEPA EECL 2538]), mysteriously, advises us to devalue, and cite as: "Conde Tiemoko, a nurse, wearing a straw necklace").

## Men Working

"Many [*LIFE*] photographers did not want suggestions and felt that their best pictures depended on spontaneity that no one could predict," writes John Loengard in his introduction to LIFE *Photographers: What They Saw*, a generalization that Elisofon would have accepted also as his.[14] But only to a point. The "spontaneity" he confessed to was not uncontrolled abandon. In general, his visual stories moved along avenues that were partly predestined and planned, partly improvised and intuitive, but reservedly conditioned by his sensibility to their chance to connect with the audience. He listened to "suggestions" from others and nurtured his loyalties, but such prompts or scripts would always be modified when subjected to his own scrutiny. In practice, his route was a shuffling, unruly movement. Studying the photographic material involving his photographing "men's work" and "men working," we recognize that it was his controlling apparatus that was pushing. Africa was facing a new epoch, and the United States needed to be told what was going on. This was also the rhetorical call coming from New York. His 1960 *LIFE* story, "The Hopeful Launching of a Proud and Free Nigeria: New Nation Is a Model of Preparation in a Turbulent Continent" (26 September 1960), was executed with accuracy, bravura, and all-inclusiveness. It was the result of postcolonial aspirations. The second *LIFE* story "Africa's Savage Beauty" (13 October 1961), also photographed in 1959, was its regressive die-hard counterpoint. These photographic essays represent two of Elisofon's many confusing masks.

The men in my examples from the EEPA 1959 feature as bodies united by a common cause or forced commitment, whether it is through workplace contracts, military service regulations, or cultural obligations. They are men interacting in groups, small and large, often with their backs to the camera; men at such a distance that they merge into each other or are obfuscated (as we saw women's bodies deleted) by enlarged "details"; men (which we also saw discussing the women figures) that are transmuted by the work itself, theorized into becoming instruments (a classic Marxist image). It is not self-evident that Elisofon's shooting was consciously political, that he was searching for scenes that could be interpreted by his peers as critical; it is only that many of the men we confront on the pictures worked in such slavelike conditions that no peering camera watching them for whatever purpose would miss registering that. Elisofon's was no exception. I would argue that he adopted the normative perspective of documentation, focusing on what he considered interesting, without attempting to thematize it beyond the expectations of his readership. He was not a David Douglas Duncan.

For instance, he must have known about "The Iva Valley Shooting" when, on 18 November 1949, twenty-one miners at Ekulu coal mine were killed and fifty-one wounded by the British government after strikes and unrest among the miners due to the colliery management holding back their pay. And he also must have known about its role in the ongoing election and for Nnamdi Azikiwe, the nationalist leader of the National Council of Nigeria and the Cameroons (NCNC) whom he photographed in Onitsha and Urualla during the electoral campaign. At the time Elisofon took his pictures of the "surface laborers" pushing coal tubs on a rail toward the terminus of an aerial ropeway, where the photographer was situated, the Ekulu mine employed the astounding number of eight thousand men—now the Iva Valley mines are unused. From his height he could shoot the approaching workers to whom he would eventually reach out for seven close-up pictures out of only nineteen, which was all. His access to the mining site for a wider documentation had not been allowed. Not so a month earlier, when in South Africa working on his "Savage Africa" story he was, noticeably, permitted to take pictures of the Swaziland "hammer boy" and the "spanner boy" at Daggafontein gold mines (outside the city of Springs) drilling a hole in the rock to fill it with dynamite for the blast, as the caption informs us. We also learn how the water emerging from the end of the hammer washes out the drill cuttings and reduces the dust. In conjunction with his judicious camera shots of the two migrant workers, the caption intimates much more than it exposes (perhaps more than Elisofon knew of). Together they ushered in a slice of apartheid history about the humiliation of migrant workers and their horrible working conditions.

Another project with bearings on British postcolonial interests was the building of the Bornu extension of Nigerian Railways from Kuru (outside Jos) to Maiduguri in Bornu state, a distance of 885 km. Elisofon took almost fifty pictures of the work,[15] of the workers dropping side panels on wagons, shoveling ballast of wagons onto the ground and pounding it into place, slinging rails on sleepers, bolting tracks down, and a heap of variations of these operations. Bare-footed Hausa ("northerners") men chanting, struggling, working for three pence a day, Elisofon's field-note informs us. And he added the explanation: "The project is of great importance because it will permit tapping the vast agricultural potential of the north-east part of the country, and will stimulate demand for consumer goods in that area." For such a self-serving scenario to materialize, we saw, the British manipulated the election, placing their thrust on the Northern Nigerian political elite. The extended northern railway would be finished by 1964. This is to say that Elisofon was more than welcome to spend qualitative time shooting every single maneuver of the Bornu extension work teams, but would not be invited to let his camera explore the coal mining community in

Enugu. Only ten years had passed since the massacre by British colonial policemen took place at Iva Valley; maybe it was too close.

As we have observed, Elisofon's documentary field photo sequences of "bodies" alternate between distances where they collapse into their own shadows and proximity, where s/h/e is metamorphosed into an intervening organ or a tool in a system. Neither strategy provides the objects individual space. The image documentations of social context, manufacture, performances employing masks or techniques used in producing pottery, iron, leather, and woven goods venerate the surveying camera and its holder as magic apparatuses of what Western audiences would see as authentic knowledge.

The next photo documentaries, each firmly anchored in the colonial history of British trade and landowning, were ambitious coverage of two enterprises, one focusing on the workforce, the other on the industrial milieu. The forty shots Elisofon took of the backs of men "carrying bags of groundnuts, on the premises of P. S. Mandrides & Co.,[16] Ltd., oil mill, Kano, Nigeria," as the SIRIS title read, were formatted as if they were stylized, undulating rows in a dance (EEPA EECL 10409). The images dissimulate the workers' drudgery, depriving them of space and seriousness. The photos are self-absorbing. Elisofon's added field-note that the Hausa men earned from seven to ten shillings contravenes opportunely the assonance of the photos.[17] The second, a much more ambitious industrial photo project, concerned African Timber & Plywood Limited plant at Sapele.[18] The SIRIS album registers at least ten visual motifs comprising 161 documents in all that span pictures, taken from a distance, of the sawmill with its cranes with the Ethiope River (a tributary of the Benin River) as their soft frame, freighters being loaded and unloaded, mahogany logs floated, and portraits of the lumber and rubber businessman Joseph Asaboro and a worker pouring latex into a bucket at a rubber plantation (EEPA EECL 13179). The boss has a name, not the worker.

The remaining three sequences of pictures that I will comment on have at least one thing in common—in addition to Elisofon's own penchant for it—the well-ordered spectacle of men. He visited the Hawan Sallah that has been performed by the people in Katsina now for over a century and took eighty-three pictures of the equestrian pageantry (EEPA EECL 6299) and as many of soldiers of "the Nigerian Army third battalion" training on Victoria Beach, outside Lagos.[19] The first day of the Igbo new yam jamboree "Onwasato" at Ugwuoba (on the Enugu-Onitsha route) with Elisofon fervidly present was rainy (EEPA EECL 3794). This did not stop him from taking over eighty shots, both portraits of the most gruesome masqueraders and of their agile masculine jolting up and down the village.

In all three photo sessions (as in so many others) Elisofon's massive shooting had little to do with pursuing single-photo excellence. The stories they mediated have no beginning, no end, only an extended passage. It was his desire to communicate the embodiment of power, action, and resoluteness as it was manifested in men moving, on horseback, in military attack or defense operations, and the Igbo fanfare for the yam, king of the crops. The men depicted here were not "walking like women," they were "strutting like men" (cf. Okonkwo in Achebe's *Things Fall Apart*). Elisofon, in his turn, pranced and cackled (body language plus English), directing his protagonists to assume the postures to his liking. The Igbo masqueraders as well as the elite bodyguards of the Emir of Katsina were organized to form a half-circle in front of his camera; the soldiers were adjusted unmistakably, they too, by the cameraman's orders, the ex-combatant he was. All wore masks.

## Portraits of Men

Most of Elisofon's portraits of women, as we saw, were designated by profile views, full-face views, and three-quarter views, profiling "ethnic" orientation or aesthetic preference. In most cases these women were young, beautiful, and anonymous. With male portraiture at least the first and the last attributes were the opposite. The anthropological three-dimensionality, if not totally bailed out, was displaced by a focus on variations of what could be called the constructionist (an idea), the environmental (environment), and the candid (no posing) approaches. A photographer's constructionist method was, for instance, Elisofon asking Field Marshal Baron Carl Gustaf Emil Mannerheim (*LIFE*, 23 October 1939) to step down one level on the stairs for the pose (which he did not); the environmental was to coax the Kuba king to exhibit his representative setting of artistic excellence, decorative luxury, and political sovereignty; the candid was when amplifying the symbolic or political formality of the portrait by supplementing it with pictures captured in motion, as when Elisofon accompanied Nnamdi Azikiwe to take pictures of him during the political rally in 1959. Here, as elsewhere in this chapter, I am investigating how epistemological gender asymmetry and commensurability impregnated Elisofon's 1959 photography. I have organized these male power portraits in three groups: those of politicians, rulers, and judges. All the subjects were Nigerians.[20]

It is also Nigeria in transit he was to explore, its rejection of the foreign masters and molding of the new. So Elisofon, like any Western commentator on Africa these days, was absorbed by the dichotomies of the old and the new—in Elisofon's case by a dogged veneration of the ceremonious, the traditionalistic, the die-hard pompous, and modernity (that he represented) as their guardian angel and tower of strength. It is something of this ambivalent depository impact he wished to achieve with his work for the *LIFE* Nigerian essay that not only would document how the largest country in Africa was campaigning in the federal elections, going democratic as it was believed, but what its achievements were in preparing for a postcolonial life, and as a promiscuous undercurrent in Elisofon's thinking, what its losses were. It can be no surprise that the *LIFE* team focused on the top candidates in the election and on prestigious northern leaders whom the British escorted into victory.[21]

They were premier of Eastern Region Nnamdi Azikiwe and Minister Michael Iheonukara Okpara (who succeeded Zik as premier after the election, 1959–1966); premier of Western Region Obafemi Awolowo, founder of the Action Group (AC), and the lawyer Samuel Ladoke Akintola (who was premier 1960–1966); premier of Northern Nigeria Alhaji Sir Ahmadu Bello (the Sardauna of Sokoto) and Sir Abubakar Tafawa Balewa who (with Bello) had founded the Northern People's Congress (NPC). He was independent Nigeria's first prime minister (1960–1966); Zik would be sworn in as the first Nigerian president in 1963.

These men were the major executors of the First Republic, three of them were to be killed—Akintola, Balewa, and Bello—in the military coup in January 1966 that punctuated the regime. Elisofon was around these political leaders for days (with British administrators at his feet). He allocated his attention in relation to each protagonist's position, comportment, and entourage with their eye-catching attraction for an American audience as his yardstick.[22] He accompanied Zik in his traditional purple robe from his home in Onitsha to a rally at Urualla, picturing him introducing candidates, one of them being Felicia Obua, an executive member of the NCNC, a rare specimen in Elisofon's lopsided (not only his fault) 1959 photo album (EEPA EECL 1679). Zik's political enemy Awolowo and his party (AC) received even more media attention. Elisofon captured him—he wore a green robe—in a number of sequential close-ups, took panorama pictures of a crowd of over two thousand rallying in Sokoto with Awolowo giving a speech in English (translated into Hausa). In Zaria (346 air km from Sokoto) he photographed AC campaign leaflets promising "the good things of life" being dropped from a helicopter at the Institute of Administration. In Sokoto, too, he took over fifty individual pictures, studiously depicted, of the Sardauna of Sokoto, Ahmadu Bello wearing his embroidered robe and winding turban, markers of his caliphate status and prestige, and of Bello's companion, Abubakar Tafawa Balewa, at his office in Lagos, who radiated the power and self-reliance to be expected from a prime minister.

While in Lagos and in Kaduna, Elisofon took photos of the leadership within the federal judiciary. One was Sir Adetokunbo Adegboyega Ademola, chief justice of the Federation of Nigeria, and the other Diekola Ogundere, crown counsel at the Federal Legal Department (picked out from the local staff by Elisofon, I believe, because of his "Yoruba facial scars"). Both were "been-to" as were all the Nigerian elite I am introducing. In Kaduna, then the capital of the northern region, Elisofon documented the new Law Courts building dedication, taking pictures of (again) the Sardauna of Sokoto and of the emir of Katsina, Sir Alhaji Usman Nagogo, with a couple of British members of the High Court of Justice. Now it remains for us to visit the nonsecular rulers whom Elisofon would go on visiting until the end of his travels in Africa, if not necessarily the sites that I examine. They are Sokoto, the Seat of the Caliphate, in the extreme northwest; Abeokuta in Egbaland in the southwest; Ede and Ife, both in Osun State; Akure in Ondo State; Owo, halfway between Ife and Benin City in Edo State; and Big Qua Town in Calabar. It is not Elisofon's itinerary; it is mine.

The character and style of the portraits he produced depended on the approachability of the rulers, their religious and cultural protocols, and, of course, their personalities. If the meeting between the photographer and his object proved to be fittingly bilateral for whatever reason, if it said "click," Elisofon's portraits developed into either cascades of individual shots from various angles, postures, and settings or fascinating ministories for any SIRIS student interested in his photographic energy and inventiveness to browse. The thirty-odd photos he took of Oba Ademuwagun Adesida II, the Deji (ruler) of Akure, the man with the beaded veiled crown, do not come near to telling any story about an African kingdom in decline. What they do is illustrate Elisofon's skill in formulating a categorical image of the dignity of the Deji by not circulating vertically or horizontally around his object, but taking it from an indisputable front, only alternating the distance. He used the same approach factoring his portraits of the Abeokuta Aleke, Sir Ladapo Samuel Ademola II, and his son, the chief justice of the Federation of Nigeria, as well as of the two kings, Sir Adesoji Tadeniawo Aderemi, Oni of Ife, and Olateru Olagbegi II, the Olowo of Owo. Both the Oni and the Olowo smile, maybe because they sensed the vibrations of freedom closing in on them.[23]

The remaining three portraits, the one of the Sultan, of Timi of Ede, and of the Calibar ruler of the Qua clan, apart from being disparate demonstrate above all Elisofon's knack for filmic photojournalism. His presentation of the Sultan is distanced in two fundamental ways. The Sultan hid the lower part of his face inside his white veil-cum-turban as Elisofon's camera approached, looking away or astray in concordance with the Islamic principle of modesty. The photographer, in his turn, positioned himself (or was advised to) behind the backs of the retinue who accompanied the Sultan on horseback to attend the juma'at (Friday) prayers at Masallacin Bello mosque, a disassociating courtesy that was respected also on their return from the mosque.

The story of Timi of Ede, the Yoruba king with the leopard crown, was impinged by sentiments—in contrast to the previous—of reciprocity of another kind. The king, the centerpiece and the focus of his attendants, the drummers in front and the photographer around him, communicated with these protagonists separately and, astonishingly, with seeming ease, fostering a communal presence that impregnated the photos. Elisofon's camera responded, with or without his assistance, to the atmosphere that prevailed on the site. A sequence of photos of the king's Sango shrine collection of carvings finished his series.

The final power portrait concerns a jubilant series of sixty-six shots generated by Ntoe Ika Oqua II and members of his people performing an Obon dance procession for the *LIFE* photographer. The portrait of the elderly paramount ruler of the Qua Clan in front of his palace in Calabar (attested to by the shield on the wall behind him) with a cannon at his feet pointing at you, talked—whipped up comedy (EEPA EECL 1576). The feathered Western vaudeville hat he wore and the U.S. flag used in the procession announced—knocked together carnival. Or in each case, could it be anticolonial politics, a tribute (ironic or not) to the *LIFE* icon or a memento mori of the Atlantic slave trade?

## Children Are

Children are addenda, or? They surface, it may seem, in Elisofon's photographs as if by mistake, cropping up when he is the least prepared for them, staring at him, moving in and out of his camera focus like rabbits. As a matter of fact, they respond to his ideal of the situational prerequisite for candid photography—being just they. (An ideal, by the way, that he abandoned as many times as he preached its values.)

Scrutinizing Elisofon's photographs on the lookout for children, I learned, however, that their subsidiary presence did not signify negation or dismissal; their showing up in the photos had a function, in fact several functions. It did not occur accidentally. Elisofon saw the children and allocated them distinct roles in his visual play. They were neither addenda nor rabbits.

He was purposefully interested in photographing children, in telling their lives through images. He started taking such photos as a very young man in the 1930s, when he realized that he could sell them to support his poor Russian family. An exhibition of such photos, perhaps his first, originated literally in his backyard, with children playing in the poverty-struck Lower East Side, Manhattan, amid broken glass, car parts, and debris. Then much later and now in the gravy, he would lecture about how to photograph children (1962), and in the early 1970s he started to make photo books for children. His third children's book in Crowell-Collier's Face to Face series was his first about Africa—and which also proved to be his only one: *Zaire: A Week in Joseph's World* (1973).[24]

These are the first four lines in *Joseph's World*, prototypical for a Western children's book for a nine-year-old. All is there: place, family, and the father's profession: "Joseph Mobobi lives in Zaïre [at Lake Albert], a large country in central Africa. He has two sisters and a baby brother. His father is a medical assistant, and takes care of sick people."[25] The week in Joseph's life as Elisofon narrated it could be any middle-class American's, a stark contrast to the family extravaganza he arranged to represent the African family on so many occasions. Two examples: the 1970 portraits of Mangbetu chief Teingu and his thirty-six wives, twenty-five children, and Sabina Abirangoma, his young wife and the Basonge children whom he photographed with fetishes in their hands during his 1947 Congo collecting escapades (HRC 9.22, report 3). Joseph's monogamous and Christian family was qualified for having left the same "natural setting" (Teingu). The Basonge children were authenticated camera objects for being "in their natural setting." Paradoxically, as it may seem, the dialectical amalgam of these "two" worlds was the elixir in Elisofon's photography in Africa. Made in April 1970, during a most frenzied year of his traveling in the Congo and West Africa, Elisofon had the plan to annex *A Week in Joseph's World* with another Macmillan series for children to be called "The Five Faces of Africa." The booklets and the filmstrips would document the three rivers of the Nile, the Congo, and the Niger, an outgoing "tribe" (the Yoruba), and an incoming nation (Ghana). All the material was there; in fact, there was such abundance that it was overwhelming. He broke the contract, and the series was never completed.

Scanning the scene through the viewfinder, creating his visual representations, Elisofon would routinely try to see or rather construe what he called "contrasts." This meant adjusting visual order or disorder into a predetermined narrative of dichotomies. It is as if the contrast only needed the secondary eye, the camera, for it to produce the desired narrative meaning. Without the camera: pandemonium! Children would not easily feature in such plot constructs or dramas. If they sneaked in without having been asked, the risk was that they harmonized or neutralized the image-making, suspending its tension, making the picture lie, which could be another way of telling a truth. Children at the beach in Accra (Ghana), in a market in Monrovia (Liberia), at a canal in Mit Rahina (Egypt), at the ruins of Sophiatown (South Africa) did this. The residents of Sophiatown were removed by force in 1955, thirteen miles from the city to Meadowlands (now part of Soweto) as a consequence of the Group Areas Act (EEPA EECL 1251). The children Elisofon photographed playing in the ruins, if they do not counterbalance segregation, exhibit it by the mere fact of being there: a life-must-go-on perseverance, a gesture of normalcy as resistance. The photograph is about their activist presence.

Being annexed to position (not pose) in social partnerships with other members of their families, age, and gender groups, or communities, they are also ascribed with a particular power, however innocent it may be. Typical captions read: "Domestic scenes outside a Dogon settlement"; "Child and old man, Bin village"; "Children fishing"; "Man and child sawing logs, El Batanon" (Egypt); "Mother washing her child at outdoor public laundry, Lagos"; and "Family members of Yoruba farmer sorting kola nuts, Adamo village." Elisofon did not particularize children in portraits to demonstrate ethnic affiliations, other than undedicated commentaries such as "Tuareg children with turban" and "Nupe children wearing traditional clothes." The last picture is the only one I have for which he had asked the boys to pose for him.

In many photos by Elisofon from the Second World War fronts in Morocco and Tunisia (November–May 1942–1943), the children occupy a central function, even if they were framed peripherally. In his detailed reports to the New York staff to go with the contact prints, narration, and visuality, children, narratively, alternate in taking the action forward on complex levels. Photos of an air raid in Casablanca depict a woman pressing her child against her breast, a dog on the alert, and children seeking protection from the air raids as much as they do from the camera (December 1942, HRC 4.23). The photos (with the captions and the report) formulate the same vulnerability shared by the child and the cameraman as the war's ultimate borderline subjects.

> Searchlights and anti-air-craft fire, shooting down a plane, shattered ware house, street crated; 1–2 R58 native soldiers clearing ruins from bombed Arab house; 4–6 native soldiers functioning as work companies only. . . . Arabs looking through ruins for dead or belongings. . . . Arab women, dead man in the ruins; man with seven year old son both have hands up as if to keep debris from covering them, hand significant in Mohamed religion; women crying, lost children, dog looking for his master; mother removed with her six year old boy with hardly a scratch. (HRC 4.24)[26]

In his documentation of the "new" Africa, schools, education and research were of particular importance. He photographed teaching activities in a number of places: students at Shell-BP at Port Harcourt doing exercises on lathes, shaper and automotive and diesel; a nurse lecturing mothers on infant feeding in an Infant Welfare and School clinic in the Oko-Awo area of Lagos Island. He documented teacher training classes in Ibadan; art classes at the Nigerian College of Arts; and town planning in Zaria. The "newness" was an announcement and a statement: technology and modernity were available to a first generation of Africans. The two primary and secondary schools he visited were solidly entrenched in the routines of the colony, with both American and British instructors. Here "newness" was conditional. The pictures he took of the hustle at Seventh Day Adventists Secondary Modern School in Ife, of boy and girl students entertaining themselves in separate groups at the schoolyard, and of Hazel Ryckman, an American Baptist missionary teacher, reading to children under a huge tree at Zagun Village, west of Jos, hardly pointed forward. In fact, any of them could have been published in a Western missionary tract right at the beginning of the same century, so enthusiastically conventional they were (EEPA EECL 12008). What engaged his eye creating the first photo was its visual geometry, the circular and the vertical movements of the students playing ball (boys) and singing-dancing (girls). In the second his focus was likewise on the composition of the picture: the tree dominating the center, the minuscule kids at its root, and the gray-haired missionary on a wooden chair looking down on them. What was taught and how it represented modern Nigeria were not issues. Elisofon was simply not interested nor had time to stay longer, anxious as he was to go to the next city (Bauchi). The third school scene deviated from these two by the presence of its protagonists, its intimacy, and its expressiveness. The setting was a street in the old town of Kano accommodating two students studying the Quar'an with their mallam-teacher at their side. They sit publicly on a small stage, as it were, a stone bench protruding out of the wall, with men, and a woman covering her face, passing—also a donkey that Elisofon would not miss shooting. The series of thirteen shots (SIRIS) was taken within a time span of ten to fifteen minutes, which means that a diminutive street story can be reconstructed based on the shifts from one frozen moment to another. This is the SIRIS summary of the picture context:

> The children of the main walled (old) town are largely non-literate, heavily reliant on the old caliphate system of patronage to survive. The family's Islamic education is organized around makarantum Allo (school-of-tablet, Qur'anic school), headed by a mallam who can trace the chain of his tutorship to the first disciples of the Islamic reformer, Shehu Danfodiyo. Emphasis in these schools is placed on rote learning; and sabka "completion of study" takes place when a pupil's recitation meets a particular standard. (EEPA EECL 11982)

The apocalyptic story that concludes this chapter took place in Kenya in 1973. It also involves serendipitous children. A colleague of Elisofon's, Robert Halmi, photographer-writer at *LIFE*, had produced a photo essay saga about the friendship across the borders between an American boy, Kevin, and the Maasai chief's son, Dionni. The narrative is simple: how the two ventured forth, following rhino tracks, Kevin learning to throw spears and Dionni to play baseball. Young Kevin wrote the story based on his diary, and stepfather Robert took the pictures.[27] A decade later, Halmi into documentary television, decided to attempt a big screen show based on his photographing "I Go Visit a Chief's Son." He needed a writer to produce a synopsis. He got his hands on Elisofon, who was more than willing. Apart from the writing of the script, to which he had agreed, Elisofon suggested that he would film a second unit sequence on "Kevin lost up on Kilimanjaro and a hunt for him, if you decide it can help dramatize this story."[28] The timing for the filming would concur with a most spectacular event, the total solar eclipse that was to occur in Kenya on 30 June 1973. The American Astronomical Society would organize a major "solar eclipse site" at Lake Rudolph (now Lake Turkana, northeastern Kenya, near the Ethiopian border) for scientists to do observations and for the press to document. Elisofon saw his chance to exploit what nature so timely threw a spotlight on and also NASA's generosity to share its data, egged on as the agency was by the moon-landing craze in full operation. Denver-located Key Travel Service whipped into shape a monthlong "Special Itinerary for the American Astronomical Society" (21 June–21 July 1973) that, apart from incorporating the visit at the eclipse camp with astronomer guides, included a long trip through the Serengeti for game viewing, a visit at Olduvai Gorge Dr. Leakey's Camp, the "home of Neolithic Man," and the Masai Amboseli Game Reserve passing Kilimanjaro. Elisofon and his camera were to participate (HRC 59.4).

Halmi's feature film would begin with the four-minute eclipse, which was rearticulated by Elisofon's clever naming of the synopsis, "Passage" (two pages, EEPA D-9). In other words, the planetary eclipse and the shrouding out of boyhood were to be considered congenital phenomena. The scene he wanted to film himself, Kevin's disappearance, he imagined happening in this way:

> With Kilimanjaro close at hand, a great scene could be added by having Kevin leave the camp to try climb the mountain on his own. There are areas on this mountain with great twisted trees all hung with dripping moss which could be an extraordinary setting for a search for Kevin by his father and his people.

Besides the simile of the young boy's ritual act of initiation with father as custodian, the Kilimanjaro Mountain in Elisofon's narrative is more than a place he had visited and photographed several times, down to its dropping moss and twisted trees. It is, as with Rwenzori, a contestant figure for Africa as image of Western mastery and possession. I return to the thematic of mountain bravery later, but here it is enough to recognize how the trope "Eliot in Kevin," the ever-posing, insecure, fetish-collector, the adult-as-child syndrome perpetuates Elisofon's photography. Africa has never been only a storehouse for Western acquisitiveness and greed but as much a laboratory for butterflies' maturity and strenuous coercive masculinity.[29] There are further Western strings attached to the plot. The cast listed a "black white hunter, a new element in East Africa which has been receiving recent attention" (originally he was an Oxford-educated Maasai), a "female young student of the Anthropologist [*sic*] in Africa working on her doctorate," and the father an anthropologist "who needs to record the Maasai in film before their culture is completely adulterated." It is the alleged loss of a culture that motivates, the argument expounds, the presence of the Americans in the film. However, it can be argued, it is the same anthropologists and photographers (including Elisofon) who, through their salvaging mission, would no more than belittle it. In a mix of exoticism and racism.

> Passage is a lyrical and meaningful story which will make a superb feature film of the type that Walt Disney made famous. The setting is one of the most dramatic and

> beautiful in the world. The Great African plains are literally covered with almost a million animals, and a great mountain almost twenty thousand feet high capped with eternal snow serves as a backdrop. The Africans who are integral part of this film are the Masai. They are almost from another world slim and tall, and even elegant in their utter simplicity. Unlike their black Bantu neighbor, the Masai are copper brown with thin aquiline features. Their everyday costume is a length of ochre colored fabric draped over one shoulder like an ancient Roman's toga. Their women are almost covered from chin to shoulder in huge circles of colorful beads, their earlobes distended and pulled down by enormous copper earrings.

Halmi's semidocumentary film to be called *Visit to a Chief's Son*, with John Philip Hogdon as Kevin and with Halmi and Lew Amack as writers, was broadcast in 1974. It was no longer Elisofon's. His Maasai "Passage" argument had dematerialized to end up in the archives. He never traveled to Kenya to film the eclipse and search for his Kevin, nor to Africa anymore. He passed away in New York City on 7 April 1973.

CHAPTER 4

# From Colony to Colonized

## Elisofon Fashioning Nigeria

Eliot Elisofon's African photographing, we have noted, was embedded in a Western colonial visualscape tradition of long and widening standing, with ethnographic intrusiveness and anthropological depersonalization as its backbone. It was a power dynamic that he made his own, sharpening it with the aesthetics and the methodology of a painter. *LIFE*'s pursuits, particularly in their African context, of clinching the popular, the educational, and the political, ideally designing the single photo to stand for the whole, evolved into a public doctrine that Elisofon appropriated squeamishly. "Photography is more than art. . . . In photojournalism it is knowledge" was a slogan that had a particular significance for African photography, not only for Elisofon.[1] For him it was double-edged, as few things for him weighed more than art, were it not a beautiful woman or a good dinner. The second *LIFE* policy convention, also voiced in the memory book LIFE *Photographers: What They Saw*, was more in tune with Elisofon's thinking: "*Life* magazine for me [Alfred Eisensteadt] was like the American flag. . . . We felt a great responsibility photographing for *Life*. We educated the world" (Loengard 1998, 20). Knowledge about the "new" Africa had to be filtered through American ideology for it to take shape. Elisofon's fluctuations between his photographic sensibility and the regularizing photographic regimes forged complex Western/

American imaginations of Africans. Elisofon's tropes of "transient Africa" and the "independence of Nigeria" as they modulated his portraiture of Nigeria had their lineages in prior Cold War *LIFE* narrations of Africa.[2]

## Alexander Campbell's Project 1953

In *LIFE*'s African historical archive, the special issue Alexander Campbell's "Africa: A Continent in Ferment" stands out in many ways.[3] The issue was divided into twenty-four files, each of which resembles a chapter in a travelogue ushering the reader/viewer into a ten thousand–mile African tour that "begins at northwest corner in Tangier, winds through Morocco, Sahara, Egypt, skips to west coast, traverses central Africa and the Congo, finally ends up in Union of South Africa" (9). *Time-LIFE* correspondent Alexander Campbell, with a journalistic past in South Africa, organized the four-month journalistic project that engaged the six legendary photographers—Jack Birns, N. R. Farbman, David Douglas Duncan, Eliot Elisofon, Alfred Eisenstaedt, and Dmitri Kessel—to produce their particular stories, assisted by the South African writers Stuart Cloete and Alan Paton.

The advertisement for the issue claimed that the photographers that were sent out by the magazine "had encountered enough material for an H. Rider Haggard novel." That *LIFE* used Haggard, the extraordinarily popular African storyteller at the time and the smart liberal (British) imperialist, as a springboard for its formidable 178-page publishing venture was editorial tactics of the double-talk. By all means, it advocated, marvel at what you see and read about an expansive continent but moderate your expectations and, above all, beware of what might happen. The bulletin board of the *New York Daily News* (30 April 1953), in flaunting the forthcoming issue, formulated an ominous scenario of the "explosive continent of Africa," housing the lapse of the Ivory Coast into "a laboratory for native self-rule," the "murders by the Mau," the "vague hints of Communist filtration in a land that supplies half the free world's uranium," and the "crushing victory of the 'white supremacy' government of Daniel Malan" (his anti-British Unity Party winning the election on 17 April).

Campbell's introductory account centered on the daring assumption of the "white man's burden" originating in self-implanted greed that his colonial lust for land was to destroy him. "This year, in South Africa, the Rhodesias and most dramatically in Kenya, it begins to seem as if the whites are behind their own bars, while the blacks peer menacingly in" (Campbell 1953, 9).[4] Colonization was disintegrating piecemeal, violently or with style, things were falling apart. The metaphor of the liberated oppressed should be interpreted not only as a dictum of threat but the right and the consent to protest. And with the same inverted logic, the 1952–1953 Mau violence exonerated the Rift Valley colonials from guilt, making them unfree or at least free to leave the country. Jomo Kenyatta, the Mau manager, was sentenced to seven years of hard labor for "peering in": for violating his most precious Western gift, the Christian faith (150). "The Mau Mau took over most of the mumbo-jumbo of the dissolved *Dini ya Msamba*" [a cult, one of many, combining Kikuyuism and Old Testament bloodthirstiness], wrote Campbell (10).

It is from within these parameters of have-nots and haves, savagery and civilization, African "awakening" and American marketplace hopes that the visual narratives of the *LIFE* issue sought their educational directions and inspiration. The photographers' applications of these guidelines varied, as we will see, depending also on their individual political temperament and what regions they visited. Both Birn's contribution "Tangier, a lure for Europeans" and Farbman's "The splendor and problem of Morocco" started with the Western fantasy of the Orient, in the fascination for the excessive, the exuberant, the promiscuous. Birn's photo of Countess Phyllis della Faille de Leverghem stretched out on her divan weighed down among the green cushions by five dogs and two parrots and Farbman's six pictures, each of which portrays a man of extreme wealth but where the waning power relation of the two (colonials and non-European Sultans and Pashas) resembles that of degenerate Countess Phyllis and her miming parrots. The two photo collages are sardonic, not less so by being grimly juxtaposed by photos of two American air bases (French Morocco) with the bold Cold War caption "almost unreachable [by land] from Soviet Russia" (35).

"Sardonic" is not the word to use when categorizing Duncan's three-pack photographs for Campbell's massive Africa story. They are critical of colonialism and apartheid, both in a direct and indirect manner: (meaning that) saying what can be said is a defamation of what cannot be said. Unsteady double-talk never captivated Duncan's images, whether they were produced in South Africa or in Vietnam. In southern Algeria, in the "rocky Sahara," with Ahaggar Mountains as a tradition-bound background, he photographed a shaky Swiss tourist couple on a camel tour in the sand with "veiled" Tuaregs as their company (36–38); in northwestern French Guinea his topic was the French administrator Georges Ducrest of Youkounkoun and his "rough life in the service of France" (47–48);[5]

for Campbell's South Africa segment, he was assigned to tell the raw truth about the regional election on 15 April 1952. His contribution was a two-page brusque, open and shut handout (175–76) that contained his single photo of Daniel Malan, winner of the election, figured as a close-fisted ringleader (the other five images were taken by Magnum Photos); the alarming signature rubric reading "Malan in his great triumph;" and the captions (all by Duncan; not only his own) pointing at the discomforting consequences of the Union rushing deeper and deeper into the Apartheid republic.[6] The *LIFE* readers, I am sure, were cognizant about its message and its tie-in with his individual photo essay from the year before, "One Fifth of a Nation Celebrates" (21 April 1952),[7] as much as they would have understood his seemingly trivial metaphoric field-note account of the Election Day—had they had a chance to read it: "Whites, blacks and coloureds all seemed rather depressed. The weather that had been beautiful and clear during the Election Day, turned cold and rainy and bleak" (HRC 24.8). Duncan's clever 1953 South Africa snippet was a reenaction of the "Nation Celebrates" essay that, surprisingly, had admitted two antisegregationist pictures that he took during the Cape Town's Van Riebeeck festival (5 April 1952). One of them, "Sneaking a peak" (30), depicted black youths creeping under stands that in fact had been reserved for them, but which they were not allowed to use because of the nonwhite electoral boycott. A few whites had moved in (on their seats). The second, captioned "Only babies ignore politics" (31), was a photo of the "blond three-year-old Nüta Aschengorn, daughter of an Afrikaner artist . . . who makes friends with Kau, an 18-month-old Bushman [black child]."[8] *LIFE* or Hicks in New York condoned pictures that sketched segregation politics, but not images that related to organized black resistance, such as those he took in secret of the protest meeting at "Freedom Square" in Johannesburg on the next day. Duncan's narrative of the "Day of Protest by Johannesburg's Non-Europeans" and his account of the Boer histrionics were both dismissed. In the memorandum that went with the Johannesburg photo essay and the rolls to New York (14 April), Duncan argued—in vain: "these pics serve to complement the festival ones, to demonstrate some *black* activity, at least" (his emphasis; HRC 22.9). Provocatively, the famous rally was organized a day after the Van Riebeeck racist Boer festival in Cape Town.[9] These two photo documentaries are unique and, what is unhappy, ignored.

Liberia, "Africa's only republic," emerges in *LIFE*'s listing as an African model state "humming with economic activity" (51), idealized for its historical and economic allegiances with the United States. American investments, such as those by the Firestone Rubber Company and Liberia Mining Company, and the building of Monrovia port and a huge airfield, underpin the priggish epithet of the country as a "little bit of America," an ironic contravention of the postcolonial process. Eisenstaedt, the American flag bearer, was not responsible for the portraiture of Liberia but for those of the three British colonies of the Gold Coast (Ghana 1957), Nigeria, and Kenya, the first two to his mind thriving like Liberia, the third under colonial siege. Prospering local business and subtle small-scale entrepreneurship of the Gold Coast and Nigeria are contrasted with the ordeals of the British farmers barricading themselves behind bars (embodying Campbell's metaphor), losing property, hiding, running away.

Eisenstaedt's fairy-tale portrait of the "million-dollar operator" Mary Nzimiro, owner of a fleet of trucks doing business in wholesale trade in cloth, sipping champagne at the breakfast table with her husband, Richard, arbitrates with the photographer's shot of another idyll, that of the mixed family, J. E. S. de Graft-Hayford, secretary at Cocoa Marketing Board (army trained at Sandhurst) and his "white" wife (no name), at the luncheon in Accra. The Harcourt "Manny Trader" couple's planned to visit England to "see the coronation" during the summer, the caption added, emphasizing the colonial veneration. The thematic of the West Africans learning, adapting to, accommodating Western habits, conventions, and thinking were embedded in the visual tropes of Eisenstaedt's photographs from champagne glasses, the whig and the mace of the Gold Coast Legislative Assembly, the hawkers' capitalist advertising style, and premed student Florence Martins's "European-style dress" in the dormitory room wardrobe at the University College of Ibadan. The cautionary tale of the "good" as the wise provider and the "poor" as the humble beneficiary transmit to the viewer the concept of change and transition as acts of unilateral faith. Eisenstaedt figured colonialism as a disbeliever's avocation. His stay in Nairobi turned the West African fairy tale upside down, fracturing the delusive romance and exposing the face of the Other: a "poor" reciprocating—unappreciatively, acquisitively, and brutally. Eisenstaedt arrived in Kenya amid settler hysteria with the State of Emergency in full operation, with sensational murders of Europeans at the hands of the Mau Mau, and with Kenyatta serving the prison term in desolate Lokitaung. He documented two settler families, one on the Mau Mau death list (Michael Blundell, a leading settler politician), the other frozen into a private combat zone, both armed to the full, and a community paralyzed by inertia and fear, with elderly white men in Nairobi cocktail lounges shouting "extermination." Out of the fourteen photographs of Eisenstaedt's that were printed, only two were allocated to the Kikuyu: one a portrait of Kenyatta, the second illustrating a "loading" of Kikuyu into trucks taking them from their homes to the reserves. He commented: "On the already overburdened, starved land of the reserves the impoverished Kikuyu face starvation and their resentment against the whites is only increased by such forced measures" (146). Eisenstaedt did not draw the same parallels as Duncan did for South Africa, but he perceived and pointed to the problem. *LIFE* would publish five photo essays (including Eisenstaedt's) about the Mau Mau during this year (1953). The most ostentatiously racist among them was fashioned by the American big-game hunter Robert Ruark, entitled "Your Guns Go with You." His follow-up warning to visitors was as snappy: "If you keep Kikuyu on your premises, you are inviting murder" (120).[10] Elkins writes:

> The press releases were not mere spin doctoring. They also reflected a colonial world that was organized according to a strongly hierarchical scale of humanity. White racial supremacy in Kenya had long manifested itself in various kinds of primitive settler justice, including public floggings, beating deaths, and summary executions. . . . The nature and demands of Mau Mau led to an even greater pathological fear by the whites of the Kikuyu. It was the distinctive quality of Mau Mau oathing rituals, and methods of killing, that transformed the virulent racism that had been the cornerstone of settler racial attitudes for over half a century into something even more lethal.[11]

The title of Dmitri Kessel's contribution to the *LIFE* issue, "Modern Congo Is Born from a Jungle-Edged River and a Sorcerous Past," enfolds the master dichotomy of the Western writing on Africa of almost any category and of a long time to go: the jungle, the river, savagery/ sorcery/civilization/ progress, site and time, and their interactive shifting meanings. Also, and this makes Kessel's photography important for the further discussion about Elisofon's Nigeria essay and, indeed, as a general comment on Elisofon's African aesthetics, that its visualization of the ideological time shifts does not attempt at representing the provisional and the progressive but the stationary. In graphic terms, this simile in Kessel's presentation of modernity gripping colonial Belgian Congo reads like a propaganda text for homeopathy:

> But out of the savage land and the savage people the Belgian businessmen have created a prosperous colony where the Congolese lead a fuller, healthier life at the same time that European capital makes a handsome profit. Almost buried in heat but rich in vital resources, the Belgian Congo is an outstanding argument for

"enlightened colonialism," which here has found a highly profitable compromise between the primitive and modern worlds. (131)

"Enlightened colonialism" or Western profit-making required a loser and a winner—and no compromises. Kessel's twenty-four photos were all designed along such axes of asymmetrical and aberrant differentials. Here are six, all embedded with colonial assumptions—and captions: (1) the photographer, the caption explains, had to submit to being flogged to be allowed to take the photo of the "Secret society of Lilwa" with the chief exhibiting two masks; (2) grave combines a "Westernized tombstone" with "native customs of burying important dead along the roadways [a truck driver]"; (3) miner wears goggles and tattoos; (4) plane passengers and families arriving in Elizabethville to take mining jobs; (5) "modern gadgets," produced in Belgium, are sold in an "electric appliance store in Elizabethville"; (6) mining center of Kipushi "has a broad street and neat rows of two family houses of brick supplied to workers by Union Minière." The pictures do little more than elicit from the viewer/reader exclamations of "Ugh" or "Bravo," or both, signing passively the contract with *LIFE* magazine as projector of normalcy and civilization and rejection of what Kessel called "sorcery." But what about the compromises you claim were made, the same viewer might have asked? Did you communicate on matters of nonnegotiable deviance, on what took place in the "jungle twilight" (91)?

The fact of the matter is that none of the six *LIFE* photographers did, except for Kessel's lame gestures, nor were they allocated visual space to examine, for instance, a Maasai *manyatta* or plumage-marked chiefs. Elisofon, the given candidate for this kind of project, was commissioned to do other things.[12] The *LIFE* editors solicited visual material from the veteran safari traveler Attilio Gatti's and his twelfth African expedition (October 1951) to fill the lacunae of the primitive. The twelve pictures were all in color with one exception, a portrait of a woman named "Tribal beauty," Tutsi princess Emma Bakaishongo, with "finely chiseled nose, delicate lips that reflect possible Caucasian strain in ancestry" (100). The Gatti album of stereotypical conceptions of ethnic "types" (Maasai, Sonjo, Hutu, Luo, and Zulu, with the support of Elisofon's photo of Tutsi dancers) counteracts the fatalistic rubric of the set: "Black Africa primitive society holds out south of the Sahara." For how long? is the implied question. "Long" was Elisofon's quick reply. He had already installed a rescue plan.

The second hedging of Duncan's photos of a public event of incompatible importance for South Africa would leave the Africa issue bereft of both words and images of the South—except for the photo of victorious Malan and the brief electoral résumé. This was not satisfactory at all. Two stalked South African writers were invited to provide their views of the current situation, to speak as freely as they thought possible, Stuart Cloete (111–26) and Alan Paton (163–70). They tried. The three self-reflective ruminations about the "black man" and "himself" (Cloete) fail to intervene with the rest of the *LIFE* issue. This is to say that the few Africans in it who are invited to speak do it by proxy. These are the quotes.

> The native sees the white man divided. He sees white men who refuse to acknowledge his humanity. He sees others who . . . would give him full equality. . . . He is beginning to see that we have sold him a secondhand religion with our secondhand clothes—that we pass on to him only the things we no longer want. But all this he would tolerate as long as he had hopes for the future, as long as even a few could escape from the penalty of being born black. (111)
>
> His aim is to copy, not surpass. He cannot believe that we fear his knowledge as much as we do, or that we are jealous of his expensive clothes. (113)
>
> But if a man can read the instructions for servicing a tractor he can also read the Communist Manifesto. If he can read he can communicate with his fellows and organize. (113)

Cloete was engaged in an interrogative, temporal, and spatial dialogue.[13] His moment and body interact with 1950s' racist South Africa. It is interesting to compare the three photographs by Kessel that were to "illustrate" Cloete's story. They misrepresented it. The captions read:

> *Man in transition*—and unaccustomed white man's clothes—a native casts a bewildered glance in the camera in furnace room of a Congo smelting plant. (111)
>
> *The color bar* is Africa's ever present reminder of domination by whites. This railing in a Belgian Congo drugstore separates two races buying same goods. (114)
>
> *Savagery and civilization* combine when Lusambo, chief of Yalikanda, in the Belgian Congo, leaves a ritual meeting in the trappings of his secret society. But he also wears a Western waistcoat and mounts a modern bicycle that, as befits a distinguished chief, is one of the best, complete with two bells. (120)

The colonial camera ogled. It did not recognize reciprocity. Kessel did not see the worker in the plant watching him, calling him into question. He turned his focus inward, modeling a chimera of self-defense. Similarly, in the second photograph, he reached no longer than chaffing the bizarre order in the store with the customers doing business separated in two groups. He did not question the nucleus of "white domination." Lusombo, the ridiculous combo man in the third photo, a figure all too well known in colonial novels, alias the village chief, returned, he too, the photographer's sneering glance—with dauntlessness. Kessel confounded him, as he did Cloete's article. Even worse: he hardly realized this.

Paton was angry. Malan, his enemy, had won, and nonwhites, he prognosticated, will "face government by irreconcilables committed to enforce white supremacy at any price" (163). He was right. Paton's essay, "'Impending Tragedy': South African Elections Widen the Areas of Discord," written in an anger that made him prioritize politics till the end of the 1960s, cofounding the same year the nonracial and anti-Communist Liberal Party of South Africa (1953–1968). Our only hope, he said at the end of his article, was "that sufficient numbers of Afrikaner Nationalists should come to their senses and see the ideal of white supremacy for the madness that it is." But "at the moment it does not look as if there is or can be" (170). It is noticeable, as I have mentioned, that none of Duncan's encompassing field photos (except the formal Malan portrait and that of Johannes Strydom [Strijdom]) of electoral activities were published to go with Paton's free-speech text whose genesis was the same event.

What remains then to be discussed is Elisofon's famous "Mountain of the Moon" pictures and those of wildlife in adjacent Virunga National Park, which were taken, we remember, in October 1951 (at the same time as the Gatti expedition roamed in the vicinity). With these twenty-one pictures only, Elisofon certified his lifelong commitment to photography as art, of "seeing better" (Elisofon 1944, 5). In the issue they stood out even more so by being placed right at the center preceding Gatti's stock images. Each of the close-ups and the panoramas of vegetation and the volcanoes, hippos, and buffaloes was studiously elaborated to achieve monochromatic uniqueness, what he called photographic harmony. "The photograph must be an image organic to the nature of the material," he explained, where the "material" can be interpreted as a combination of his technical use of lenses and his timing of the sunset. His fantastic panorama photo of the bluish Rwenzori glacier at 12,400 feet, with two members of the climbing expedition crawling in snow toward the darkening cliffs sucking them in (84, 86), corroborates what Elisofon meant about aesthetics and technique converging, not scattering, creative impressions of mood. Standing on a rock pinnacle and producing a photo of this kind is "the determining factor between distinguished and run-of-the-mill results," between good and bad photography, he claimed (Elisofon 1961b, 10). The result (good) of his photographic essay differed from all the others in the *LIFE* issue (bad) not because the latter were less distinguished, and more prosaic and mediocre. The difference is that his African collage has turned off, as it seemed, the special issue's programmatic limelight about Africa in transit. If the dictum that "photography is more than art . . . photojournalism . . . is knowledge," was to stay intact, Elisofon's essay, it would seem, had abdicated it. To prevent such a rift, the *LIFE* editors may have thought it central to clarify the essay and format captions such as "Albert Park . . . Africa's Wild Paradise," "The Lava Devils . . . Still Alive," "Twisted Shapes, Quiet Lakes," which replicated the subjective discourse of the sensory, the phantasmagoric, and the wondrous, but also, with as much transience, insinuated Elisofon's masculine pursuit of reaching out, as number six in a row, for the top of the mountain, metaphorically and physically. By involving Stanley, the God-Father Pursuer, in the Elisofon story, *LIFE* established the canonical link between his forging of the Rwenzori photographs and the American history of African exploration. In the preamble of the essay, this partnership was undersigned:

> *LIFE* sent Photographer Eliot Elisofon there [Albert Park and the Rwenzori] to take these pictures, which show Africa as it was when the American explorer Henry Stanley looked wide-eyed at the big game moving across the savannah and discovered the square-browed summit of the Ruwenzori, the long-lost Mountains of the Moon, rising out of the leaden mists. (75)

Elisofon not only observed, but more so, he saw what he looked at through the mists. But this was not enough. As the only photographer in the Africa issue, Elisofon was endowed with a half-column-long afterface (86) called the "Photographer's Nine Worst Days." The nineteen members' climbing through muggy, tropical heat and icy cold was retold as a hazardous undertaking with only three of them making it to the highest level. Here Elisofon took the ultimate photo of the two men on the blue glacier (EEPA EECL 26393). It is a great photo in its own right; it is an African photo; it is a patriotic American photo.

If the exploits that Elisofon performed did not have "as Stanley had a direct bearing on the development of imperial mercantile projects," the sites of his itinerary that unite the Cape, "Mountain of the Moon," the Nile River, and the Mediterranean represent transcontinental meaning-making tropes for Western conjunction and civilization.[14] As Hermann Wittenberg explains in his thesis on "The Sublime, Imperialism and the African Landscape," the Rwenzori, is not simply an obscure mountain range in Africa but a significant ideological location for its virginal snow-capped peaks, its permanence of whiteness (connoting the universal), surrounded by a hostile "black" jungle (this would be Stanley's and Elisofon's "Pygmy" landscapes) and positioned midway between the Cape and the Mediterranean. Elisofon visited the mountain region as a believer of a holy place, each time making benighted observations about the snow. Stanley addressed the mountains in a racialized discourse of difference: a "lofty mountain king, clad in its pure white raiment of snow, surrounded by myriads of dark mountains, low as bending worshipers."[15] "By designating the mountains [by Claudius Ptolemy, an Alexandrian second century A.D. cartographer whom Stanley copied] as the fabled source of the Nile, the mountains assume a mythical prehistory which detaches them from their African locale and purports to link them organically, through the Nile, to the Mediterranean roots of Western civilization" (Wittenberg 2004, 89, 90–95). Congo was the jungle; Zaire was Kinshasa, with a back-reference to the colonialist dichotomy. Elisofon's narration of Africa as a project, whether in books, captions, photographs, or films, and his scrambling for African art were saturated by the same detachment: the bring-it-home dialectics à la discourse of the "Mountain of the Moon" or *The African Queen* (1951).

## Robert Coughlan's Project, 1959

Six years later, *LIFE* sent another reporter, Robert Coughlan, to take the pulse of Africa. After stumbling across eighteen countries or territories, interviewing new leaders, missionaries, and administrators, he returned with more or less the same message as Alexander Campbell, formulated along the rattletrap parameters of Darwinian change. Introducing his exemplars of modernity-building in Africa, he filtered them through a conservative archive of preexisting images and tropes that were sabotaging his own observations. Renato Rosaldo has called this phenomenon the "white man's burden, where civilized nations stand duty-bound to uplift so-called savage ones" (Rosaldo 1989a, 107-22). Vulnerable elephants were juxtaposed with landing airplanes, the "juju" magic market of leopard claws and dried mice with the close-by Ibadan University buildings, the Stone Age with a follow-up in the Atomic Age. For more than a decade, these binaries (not only in this context) were endlessly recollected and rehashed in the Western configuration of Africa, in visual forms, in the media, in social and political discourse, in literature. They were like the opening stock phrases in a conversation, meaningless but necessary, as was believed, for their levels of argumentative posture. They were literary hotbeds for smug bombast, as was Coughlan's input: "Awakening from the sleep of ages, still sluggish and half-bewildered, this vast section of humanity comes lurching onto the world scene trailing anachronisms."[16] Cynically, one could ask: which section of humanity did he mean? It is an arrogant, dramaturgical act of provocation, a guilt-born symptom of the "white man's burden" (to be assisted by Rosaldo again). The passage linking the rhetorical poles of de-colonization, in Coughlan's vocabulary, a "sudden, uncontrollable and violent eruption," was a threat not only against the Africans. Also simplistically, Campbell's "fervent," energetic, and vibrant concept, stood for a process, something less abrupt, that of the good-natured revolution. The two *LIFE* representations of Africa (1953–1959), it needs to be said, represented differences in outlook that mirrored the time periods they were covering (the shift from "fervent" to "eruption") rather than a momentous change in internal media policies.

Worried about the white man's postcolonial hangover, Coughlan asked rhetorically "Does the white man have a future in Black Africa?" In arguing for a stiff "yes," he evaluated the administrations of the African countries on the shaky bases of their status as independent, near-independent, or not-independent, listing Guinea, Ghana, Ethiopia, Sudan, and South Africa in the first group, Nigeria and Somalia in the second (and the Francophone nations in formation), and the rest in the third, flaunting particular fretfulness about Tom Mboya in Kenya and anti-white rioting in the Congo. Not a word passed over his tight(ended) lips about apartheid's South Africa.[17] Nor was the heritage of the white man in Africa a problem for him. In fact, the opposite ruled. He indulged in literary escapades into safari romances and witchcraft and "juju" medicine lore[18]—and celebrated outgoing colonialism. Concluding his Sigma Delta Chi awarded series of Africa, he paid homage to the European Christians' roles for their civilizing efforts, thanked *négritude* for neutralizing and harmonizing antagonisms, and, with a wink to the home markets, posted a solicitation to American capitalists to make a determined entrance in Africa: "The best way to prevent African socialism from developing into Communism is to season it with enlightened capitalism" (96).[19] This was the "control" that he ordained for managing "Black Africa." Campbell, on the other hand, was less resolved about the direction of white presence, pointing to the vagaries of British colonialists in coming to an honorable end. "From their 'creative abdication' in the Gold Coast to their human zoos in possessions like Basutoland, the British have tried virtually everything, without being any surer which policy will eventually leave them with the least sense of guilt." In the postscript to the 1953 editorial, the situation was summarized in these moderating terms:

> No white definition of African civilization will come true without a universal idea that commands black assent. That certainly implies racial equality and, on the long path to it, mutual respect. One does not show respect for the African by pretending to believe in his rainmakers; nor by denying him what he has earned, whether a Gramophone or the vote; nor by withholding what he needs and desires, notably education. (178)

It is from within this linguistic framework from the "fervent" to the "rupture" that I examine Elisofon's twenty-four photographs of Nigeria, taken in November 1959, their affiliations with themes and genres discussed, their spots of divergences and accommodations, and, perhaps more interesting, the level and content of Elisofon's individual and conjoined attributions in their making. How do they manipulate ethnographic and anthropological stereotypes vis-à-vis gender, "primitivism," modernity; how do they reflect on the postcolonial process, on the British versus Nigerian (the federal election in December), on the United States and Africa/Nigeria?

## Nigeria, October–November 1959: Eliot Elisofon on the Rush of Wings

Elisofon's shooting in Nigeria during the month of November right up to the House of Representatives election on 12 December 1959, when he returned to New York after almost a year in Africa, was backed up with an organizational resoluteness that placed travel logistics and photo thematic on equal footing. The time and the place for the shooting had to coalesce with the topic. In other words, the photo to be was "foreseen," a theoretical image that merged several time and authorizing zones for it to qualify as one of the twenty-odd to be sanctioned for publishing almost one year after its shooting. In this complex process Elisofon was the major actor, but one of many inter-actors. The buildup of the *LIFE* Nigeria project demonstrated not only Elisofon's share in it but also the multiplex basis that characterized it.

It started with the two-week-long reconnoitering trip he and the much younger journalist (1926–2009) Judson Gooding made around Nigeria in October, covering 2,500 miles by car, seeing the places they were to visit and talking with the people they would shoot, and making agreements concerning the portraits they would make of the political leaders, of the industrial sites they would visit, and of arrangements for the dancing and horse shows.[20] But above all it was during this trip that they acquiesced to the theme for the story, to go for the contrast wherever it popped up and whatever it held, whether it involved regional varieties, differences between old and new, man and woman, or skirmishes in politics, religion, and education. And we will do it all in color, Elisofon assured the New York staff. The contrast-mongering would also include gutsy Americans "helping" Nigerians, "Nigerianization" (Nigerians replacing the "whites"), Lagos slums locking horns with new office buildings, and exoticizing scenes such as "a woman in native dress with a baby strapped on her back reaching into a frozen food display case at one of the modern stores, or a man in turban and Moslem robes doing the same."[21] The itinerary included detailed suggestions for extensive shooting, some of it already arranged, as well as alternatives in case the prime ones failed. The trip was recklessly compact, by modern standards, one- or two-day stops at twenty-odd cities with their environs, spread around the country, starting in Kaduna (14) on 4 November (by air from Lagos and by car) through Jos (18), Bauchi (3), Zaria (6), Kano (13), Katsina (11), Sokoto (10), Bida (2), Jebba (1), Ibadan (14), Oye-Iseyin and Ede (3), Ife (3), Akare (2), Benin (6), Sapele (9), Umuede (6), Onitsha (9), Enugu (6), Aba (2), Port Harcourt (7), Calabar (7), and from Calabar by air back to Lagos (37) on 28 November, with the election just in front (12 December).[22] It was an encyclopedic shooting venture, heroic and breakneck. But how did it go apart from its logistics? Did he succeed in adjusting his lens in tracking or discriminating the assumptions of unlikeness in the politics and the particularities of time and space?

There are two major areas that tie up the visual material, confronting each other, one representing the instrumental potentialities for change, two-thirds of the photos; the rest, and the much smaller group, African Otherness. Inequality permeates their subdivisions as well. This means that the pictures related to politics, buildings, education/religion, and industry, in the first group, are structured antithetically; the second of "local color," scenery, art, and portraitures of "ordinary people" principally in the same contrastive vein. So it takes little dissecting effort, knowing the epic storyline of Elisofon's and *LIFE*'s Nigerian project and their colonial background, to position the individual photograph along these conflicting parameters.

Of the forty-three albums that composed the largest of the four groups in the first section, the one on politics was a given outlet. This was the electoral year when Nigeria was preparing to say goodbye to Frederick Lugard's 1914 institutionalized and flawed indirect rule, because the new era spelled independence. *LIFE*'s Nigeria essay (1960) and Elisofon's pictures (1959) were focused on the count down, the drama of the transit, the British replacement tactics, and American intervention. He photographed (as I have mentioned) the most prominent political leaders and judges of the country: Abubakar Tafawa Balewa, Ahmadu Bello, Obafemi Awolowo, Samuel Ladoke Akintola, Nnamdi Azikiwe, Michael Iheonukara Okpara, and the judges Adetokunbo Adegboyega Ademola and Diekola Ogundere—a formidable group and formidable pictures. Twice he ran into the AG's electoral campaign while en route, naturally using the encounter for his own purposes, shooting from a helicopter in Zaria (8 November), the AG flamboyantly dropping campaign leaflets at the Institute of Administration. The leaflets promised "the good things of life" and "free education for all," and the building, as optimistically, was prepared to serve as a site for training northerners to fill clerical and administrative posts in local government units.[23] The AC propaganda and the building shared the same vision of change and progress. In Sokoto four days later, Elisofon heard Awo of the AG give a speech, in English translated into Hausa, for a crowd of 2,500, and in Kaduna a week earlier, in an extensive rush of arranged shooting, he not only took the individual picture of Bello that would qualify to be published in the essay a year later but also several album photos of the ceremonial attendance of the new Law Courts building dedication with British dignitaries at the premier's side. The picture composition was significant, insinuating aberrant and fragile interdependencies that Elisofon invites us to juxtapose with the promising aerial view in Zaria of the five-hostel-block-large Nigerian College of Arts, Science and Technology. The straightforward pictures of Zik, the third domineering politician, were taken outside his simple apartment house in Onitsha (21 November), and a few of them at a rally in Urualla (forty miles from the city); the photographs of all the other dignitaries on my list were taken in Lagos in early December.

Elisofon's portraits of the emirs and the kings were far more contextual, focusing on their exotic Otherness rather than their authority, which of course was far from petty in these times of regional electioneering. In Katsina during the festival of Sallah, at another special prearrangement for the American, Elisofon photographed the emir of Katsina, Sir Alhaji Usman Nagogo; he was equally privileged to shoot Sarkin Musulmi alhaji Sir Abubakar, the sultan of Sokoto, both going to and returning from Friday worship at Masallacin Bello mosque. These two albums are documentary in two directions, demonstrating Elisofon's cautious physical maneuvering with a candid camera in the emir's environ and the slow shyness of his objects. With the southern kings he needed to show fewer circumferences; most of them were actively interacting with the colonial elite. The Alake of Abeokuta, Ladapo Samuel Ademola II, one of the British favorites, distinguished by them as the Sole Native Authority for Abeokuta, would occupy a whole page in the *LIFE* essay together with his son Adetokunbo, chief justice of the Federation of Nigeria, also a British son of the empire. The same pictorial adulation gratified two political animals, Oni of Ife, Adesoji Aderemi, on the picture throning under an umbrella, and Oba Olateru Olagbegi II, then Olowo (king) of Owo, sitting as symbolically between two ivory tusks.

As to the remaining four extended portraits of southern rulers, Elisofon again took on the broader spectrum. His interest in John Adetoyese Laoye I, Timi of Ede, one in a line of spectacular power-dressing African kings, was the reverse of the political and religious leaders through his passion for talking drums and poetry.[24] Oba Ademuwagun Adesida II, the Deji (ruler) of Akure, agreed to sit for Elisofon in his palace courtyard with two boy attendants at his side and the beaded veiled crown on his head, translating the situation of meeting the *LIFE* photographer into a ceremonial pseudopolitical occasion that justified the royal presence. That presence was missing when Elisofon visited the house of the Oba in Benin City, its owner, Oba Akenzua II, was not at home, the man best known for starting to return to Nigeria the stolen Benin bronzes in the punitive Benin Expedition in 1897. The last stop in Calabar (26 November) was bound to succeed as it was one of the many of Elisofon's prearranged meetings. This was his fabulous meeting with Ntoe Ika Oqua II in Big Qua Town and his photographing of the Obon (King) dance procession.

## Education and Industry as Photographs

We have seen how the modus operandi or the dialectics of what Elisofon designated as "contrast" saturated the political domain. His extended portraits of politicians, religious leaders, and tradition-borne kings were invited to declare, on the one hand, we will build the new nation with our own hands and brains, and, on the other, stop, we need help. Or rather, such reservations emanated from the cameraman's and his employers' political-economic pipe dream and were not necessarily a reflection of the fragmented world he was viewing. The contrast was fictive, constructed. If we look at the pictorial material representing the interlinked domains of education and industry, the dreams and hopes it invoked was not only a given for any postcolonial, developing country but, as important, it betokened, was the bonus for the industrial world. The deceptive internal contrast that characterized the former group of pictures I analyzed will be replaced in the following by the external asymmetry (also as a given) of capitalism. The new Nigeria is there to serve in another dress.

Elisofon's documentation of the advances of the federal-colonial government within the two branches of education and industry is a lusty and straightforward story. He visited a number of educational institutions, in Lagos, Ibadan, Zaria, and Kano, took pictures of the buildings (often from a helicopter) of both in-complex class-room scenes and advanced theaters of instruction, such as of a lecture for mothers at a clinic for undernourished children in the Oko-Awo area of Lagos Island and a gynecological operation in progress at Lagos General Hospital by the first woman doctor from Nigeria, Abimbola Awoliyi, educated in Dublin, surrounded by student nurses. Many of the albums featuring instruction involve American teachers, for contradicting purposes, as we will see. Here are four examples. Elisofon set prime visual focus on Dr. W. McDonald, an American entomologist engaged in a medical experiment at the West African Institute for Trypanosomiasis Research at Kaduna; on Mary McDonough at the University College, Ibadan, as one of seven teacher training instructors from Ohio University, teaching a class of students in English; and William H. E. Herbert monitoring a class of young men in motor mechanics at Kano's Government Trade Center. The fourth is the most stereotypical of them all: Hazel Ryckman, we saw, a Baptist missionary teacher in Africa since 1922, reading from the Bible to children under a tree at Zagun Village, west of Jos (published in the essay). All the four could have been taken out of a photographic documentary of a Western mission in Africa, so orthodox are they in composition and ethics. This was Elisofon's overt idea for silhouetting Americans:

> I think it would interest readers to see Americans at work in Nigeria, and it would enable us to show some things, like trypanosomiasis and missionary work, which might otherwise have to be omitted. In short, I think it might make a good spread in the story, and furnish a pleasant change of pace. (itinerary for the Nigerian trip, EEPA, S.1.1, 5)

In its conventionality this is true and credible, but it misses of course the myopic slant that I am adhering to it, the *LIFE* confirmation of the dichotomy of the rich and the poor, center and the periphery, what is often called in relation to Nigeria "nurture capitalism."[25]

The impression one gets covering Elisofon's overattentive and somewhat nervous occupation with the industrial sector is that the level of its prioritization was not his choice. Industry was not only a must as were politics and education, it was their motor, and the narration of this interacting drama the very apogee of the essay and the photographer's work. The *LIFE* organizers of the Nigerian double roundabout did not need to bother (at least Elisofon did not) about the American role in the colonialists' search for cheap raw materials and the expansion of markets for their products. The team focused on the novelties in the colonial administration's 1950s' program: on how the Nigerian resources could be domesticated, on improvements in the general health, and on how education was expanded at various levels. The colonial economy enterprises, both long-standing ones and newcomers were favored. Among the novelties were the many research institutes that were started at this time. One was the West African Institute for Trypanosomiasis Research in Kaduna that we saw Elisofon visit; another was the West African Institute for Palm Oil Research, where he took pictures of workers spraying cocoa trees on experimental plantations in the Benin City area. But the most towering one was to be the commercial exploitation of oil in the Niger delta, today a terrorized zone. Oil was first discovered in quantities large enough for commercial exploitation in 1956; the first shipment left Nigeria in 1958. Elisofon was witnessing the first year of an economy of dependence under oil, a Nigerian nightmare economy brand. He spent two days in Port Harcourt harbor photographing (from a helicopter) Shell-BP oil drilling rig and barge, the widening of the harbor, and freighters entering and departing, and followed classes with British instructors at the Shell-BP Trade School teaching welding, diesel theory, and duel injection, the first generation of the management of oil exportation.

The more established colonial enterprises he viewed during his nationwide round were agricultural produce sites (fruits, timber, palm oil, groundnuts, sow farms, brewery, skin manufacturing) and a tin and a coal mine. Most of these would remain foreign-owned or diversify into global conglomerates. The Lafia canning factory (Ibadan), a venture by Awolowo (1954) to provide farmers with an alternative income to failing cocoa, was to be a successful British exporter of pineapples, oranges, and grapefruits from Africa to Europe. The caption of the published photograph in the *LIFE* essay carries, however, the following haunting and prototypical note: "Managed by a European, it has serious trouble with careless workers breaking delicate machinery" (Elisofon 1960, 65). The feeding of "English Large White Sows," the title of photographs Elisofon took at a farm in Kano, was established, he added in his notes, in 1943 by Kalil Maroun to provide pork for U.S. troops stationed in the city. British-American connotations filter also his commentaries of the photos of workers carrying bags of peanuts, on the premises of the P. S. Mandrides & Co., Ltd., oil mill, also in Kano. The African carrying the white man's burden on his back, here consisting of bunches of palm fruit, is a visual trope in a rich album of a single worker at the Calabar Oil Palm Estate (COPE) in Calibar.[26] A brewery plant and a soap factory (both in Aba), the Oji River Power Station, and "The African Timber & Plywood Limited at Sapele finish this inventory of the agricultural sites he documented that are narrated along the axis of local production and foreign consumption.

The pictures of draglines and sluices at Amalgamated Tin Mines on the Jos plateau, south of Jos, and of workers at the Ekulu coal mine, near Enugu, are interesting for the reason that *LIFE*, by incorporating the activity from the two mining sites, completed its encyclopedic mapping of the Nigerian economy as an exporter of agricultural and mineral produce. In combining the Ekulu coal mine with the oil-producing Niger delta and the harbors, the image of Nigeria as the peripheral nation, there primarily for us, was perfected. But, also interestingly, there seem to have been problems. The Ekulu event is not listed in the itinerary as a site that Elisofon had planned to visit, and once some kind of permission was granted him en route, he and his camera had to stay on the ground, which he must have experienced as a mishap. The workers pushing coal tubs towards his camera, click by click, were surface laborers, not the compeers of machine boys, hammer boys, or spanner boys he had photographed two thousand feet down in the Daggafontein Mines, Ltd. gold mine, east of Johannesburg, in the spring of the same year. His observations were curtailed. It could well have been that letting a *LIFE* photographer take close-up pictures from the work on coal seams might have added sympathy to Zik's NCNC, the valley incident being a Zikist tool, undermining the colonial administration's siding with the northern political elite. The *LIFE* editors had no such intentions; the "surface" pictures from Ekulu did the job of being emblematic only.

So what remained to wind up the *LIFE* story of Nigeria as an economic mainspring for Britain and the United States were complementary pictures of the maintenance of the northern profile and the widened infrastructure for the outlandish export. They were fetched from Elisofon's shots of a rail-laying crew building the Bornu extension of the Nigerian Railway from Kuru to Maiduguri outside Jos and the enlargement of facilities at the Port Harcourt, Sepele, and Lagos docks. The photos of the railway workers slinging rails on sleepers, dropping side panels on wagons, and ballast shoveling of others (published in the Nigeria essay) were meticulously done, demonstrating Elisofon's skill in capturing the intensity of bodywork movements; the ones overlooking piers, docks, berths, and cranes loading or unloading ships display another talent of his, that of using aerials for narrative syntheses. If the Northerners were successful in pressurizing the colonists into building the railway, the English were as smart in securing *LIFE*'s voice.

## Local Color and Nigeria

We have reached the second and much smaller group of the Nigerian albums (65 versus 117), and the one whose thumbprint is Otherness. In other words, what Elisofon defines as a "local color" topic is the contrast's underdog that reflects, registers, and confirms normalcy and "us" in their manifold configurations. Local color is not, then, a sideshow or an appendage to the master narrative; it is its sustainer. In the north–east–west travelogue, it contains an array of stereotypical shots of street and market scene exotica (snake charmers, street vendors, and "mammy wagons"), aerials of river scenes (Sapele, Niger), slums (Lagos), huts, and so forth. Elisofon's wandering camera never rests; it fills in the interludes between the designed stops, providing the cotraveler (the reader/viewer) a shared sense of the sentiment. It helps me distinguish the photographer's angle of view (the contrast) and his control of the lens aperture.

Elisofon incorporated the women he photographed (seventeen albums), most of them from the north, into the local color discourse of the stereotypical, racialized, and sexualized. He abdicated to a visual automation of Western racist dependence. The captions he added may repeat dog-eared clichés of long standing in the colonial visualization of African women, but they also demonstrate the thematic and the structure of the photographs. Here are (again) the most prominent: "Gwari women carry firewood in basket" (Kaduna; in all forty documents in the SIRIS collection); "Izere woman with facial scars carrying basket on a wooden headboard" (near Jos); "Nupe women carrying enameled tin ware with flexible woven cover" (west of Bida); "Fulbe woman wearing elaborate headband and colorful beaded necklaces" (east of Jos); "Zul woman with disk inserted into upper lip" (east of Jos); "Habe women pouring out millet, Barhin village" (near Katsina).[27] One of the albums, in contrast with all the others, was "laid on," indicating its high local color status. This was "the Irigwe women dancers of Miango village, Jos Plateau," a dance he arranged in October when passing and which was performed on 7 November. In the photo caption Elisofon wrote: "Bunches of leaves suspended from a waistcloth to hang over the buttocks of the women may be seen in family compounds, but women today wear blouses and wrappers at the market and in public spaces" (EEPA EECL 4564). The Miango girls dancing in a public space surrounded by men dancers did not break any dress codes, as their seminaked dance was duplicating a marriage celebration dance where the only customary body adornments were kerchiefs, leafy boughs, and the waistcloth. Elisofon had engaged the dancers to perform the fake marriage dance in front of his camera. As hypocritical as is the earlier caption is the pseudocultural explanation accompanying the two-page color picture:

> Nudity in Nigeria occurs only in occasional remote areas, sometimes the result of poverty. But in most cases it is ingrained custom—or even a form of high fashion—and clothes are considered the trappings of the sick. The government is quietly campaigning against nudity. Very sensitive to any implications the Africans are still close to savagery. Nigeria wants to foster the image in the world of a modern progressive country. The hope is that the normal course of education will solve the problem. (Elisofon 1960, 63)

The women dancing for him had been transported into a local color imaginary of place and time to justify the Otherness of the dance.[28]

The women, the relatively few of them who appeared in Elisofon's Nigerian albums, we have already observed, walked, worked, and danced. They had no names. The men and they were in an overwhelming majority, posed, standing or sitting. They had names. Among them were sweet Hausa barber and father Ibrahim Maidonaba with daughter, at Maikujeri (near Kaduna);[29] young and brisk Achebe (Enugu), the novelist; Ben Enwonwu, artist at work (Lagos); and the political elite we have faced up to. Anonymous men were—among others—Fulbe herders (Sokoto), prisoners carrying grass (Kano), railway workers (Jos), and Igbo mask dancers during the Onwa Asaa festival at Ugwuoba village (between Awka and Enugu). They all had a job to do for Elisofon, too; they were guiltless members of his contrast dramaturgy. The seven-photo album of Achebe ("a young Nigerian whose book has been praised"[30]) produced in his home in Enugu on 22 November 1959 could be any respectful portrait of an ascending writer, Western or African. And it was, no doubt. Yet studied from within the dialectics of subservience that is the topic of this book, another interpretation will be at hand out of which emerges the Igbo writer with the two books in front of him, the English and American editions of *Things Fall Apart*, as a masquerader, an impersonator, the colonial trope of the colonized in the white man's borrowed clothes. The contrast here entangled the false "authenticity" of the Onwa Asaa mask dancer with the First World War hypo helmet (EEPA EECL 3764) and the double-dealing of Achebe.

## The Twenty-One Magazine Photographs, 1960

Out of the library of 3,391 color photographs[31] that Elisofon took during his travels in November, twenty-one photos were selected to be published (on 26 September 1960) almost a year after their execution. Each *LIFE* essay photo, it could be argued (for lack of other arguments), stood for 161 documents. The two shooting trips around Nigeria and the pictures' one-year of fermenting (to use the term from the 1953 *LIFE* Africa issue) form a problematic that impinges on what differences and similarities there were between Elisofon's *LIFE* essay and its 1950s' predecessors.

As the two dozen photos were the payoff of an itinerary of double-checking and planning, the *LIFE* editorial commando group must have considered that Elisofon's massive shooting venture was worth the money, that the twenty-one pictures would do the trick—the trick being a strong support of the British politics of keeping Nigeria colonized in a "nonsavage" (modern) way, which also would further American interests. To this could be added logistics of another kind. Elisofon was at the end of almost a year in Africa, having finished his research and shooting for his second *LIFE* essay born out of the same 1959 visit ("Africa's Savage Beauty" to be delayed even longer, published on 13 October 1961). Extending his time to cover the Nigerian electoral year was a practical decision, all the more so as the "savage beauty" essay, his number one, needed to be confronted by an accessory of soberness and intelligence. Elisofon's October–November prolonged stay in Nigeria was a patriotic duty.

The categorization of the twenty-one follows at large the groupings I took on in my overview cataloging of the albums, the larger one containing exemplars with references to politics, religion, industry, and education, and the smaller one what

I, with Elisofon, called local color representations. The essay in its turn exhibited five political portraits, four with religious connections, three with education, and four with industry. The remaining local color five pictures were definitely out of place with their also relatively speaking much larger resource bank, as they were with the essay statement in their own right. But they had no other right than reminding us of Otherness as the lower level in the world of the contrast. That was their contribution to the essay. They were the photos of the Igbo masquerade, the Habe tribe millet threshers, the Irigwe dancers, and a Hausa family compound. A combination of curt caption phrases ("juju gods," "thresh millet in the primitive African way," "Africans are still close to savagery") and candid visual gestures epitomize nostalgic obscurity, titillating perversion, orthodoxy. That is the opposite direction of where "we" are going, and what direction of onward modernity Africans should conform to. The fifth of this group is provocatively antagonistic. It points forward. It is the warm portrait of father Ibrahim Maidonaba with his one-year-old daughter in his lap.

The composition of the pictures on and between the pages and their sizes conform to the essay principle of lauding the sanguinity of the British, and its complementary agenda of notifying the Americans of their future chances on the continent. The vignette photo, in black-and-white for contrast (all the others were in color) and seriousness, of Governor-General Sir James Robertson awarding a medal to Edward Ogedegbe for oil palm research was doubly emblematic. First of all, Sir James was the architect of the federal elections and their manipulation leading to the northern overtake; second, oil research was typically celebrated, not advances within health and nursing. The opposite page characteristically holds the Igbo "juju gods . . . with the bizarre addition of an antique gas mask" (44–45). In fact, it is an extremely interesting and unique photo in Elisofon's gallery of images, as having survived a cleansing operation, postulating Otherness and cultural deviation.[32] The theme of contrast is then highlighted from the start. The theme of the next spread is power politics. The pages are crowded with the five portraits of the Oni of Ife, the Olowo of Owo, Ahmadu Bello, and a two-page picture of father and son, the Alake of Abeokuta and Sir Adetokunbo. The three regions were represented except the Eastern (Zik), a choice hardly Elisofon's. The spread (next) with the three threshing Habe women and a man struggling with a load of fruit on his back at Calabar Oil Palm Estate illustrate, among other things, outmoded work methods; the following four-picture spread narrates the competing religions of Islam and Christianity. Christian missionary work is lifted to the sky.

> The first in the country, the [Christian] missionary schools are still in the first rung in the ladder of civilization for thousands of young Nigerians. Sometimes nearly naked (see next page) they come to the church boarding schools from thatched, mud-hut villages. They learn to wear clothes, wash, eat with utensils, manage pocket money and to be literate in English. Without missionaries in Nigeria, there would not have been an educated class to take over from the British. (61)

Does this mean that the "nearly naked" on that next spread have not been to a missionary school, and not learned the good manners, for which Elisofon should be but happy, for had they, according to himself, he would not have had a chance to take the, by now, iconic picture? His Irigwe young woman of 1959, with her centralized buttocks, is a Smithsonian market-place top-high (EEPA EECL 4564). The mud-hut village on the next page, side by side with one of the four industry pictures that follow, takes us, as the rubric of this section indicates, contrastively from mud huts to a modern world, with the added conditional comment: "Wisely, Nigerian leaders hope to keep their British coaches indefinitely." One of them might be the "white inspector" who controls the Bornu railway workers in one of these pictures. The editorial rider words "wisely" and "indefinitely" are significant for the skepticism that haunts the article, as it does Elisofon's Nigeria work as a whole. Education, the last photo group, with the grand panoramas of the new University College of Ibadan and a graduation ceremony, hardly modifies this attitude and position. The illiterate barber's daughter adorned with the "brilliant beads" around her neck, on the last page of the article, epitomizes the delusive "light at the end of the tunnel" scenario. This is the last sentence of the article: "She will be raised to think with pride of her African heritage, but her national ambition will be to match in years the white world's centuries of progress" (68).

At large, the twenty-one photos, their captions and the rubrics, that are the designed visual and the graphic material of "The Hopeful Launching of Proud and Free Nigeria," concur very well, proportionally, thematically, and politically, with their core as I have structured it. The references to the American presence in Nigeria, as missionaries, educators, and businessmen, reverberate in the article as a self-serving conjoint political crusade. The ambiguous and contradictory title is imbricated in the dialectics of the contrast discourse. There are a few small shifts between my analytic examination of the fieldwork and the finished product; thus education within the religious frames is held up and the local color complexity cut down, although Elisofon does make a point of the cultural "mistake" of the juju man wearing a gas mask at the Igbo yam festival. In other words, the one-year time span as a changing parameter does not show. The rhetoric of the *LIFE* title described the outsiders' lineup, not the Nigerians'. The "launching" ballgame was a British enterprise, the attributes "proud" and "free" to designate Nigeria-to-come depended on who was speaking, and out of which position. As to pride, Achebe said this many years later: "Most of us were ready to take destiny in our hands, and for a while at least, it worked quite well" (2012, 49). The problematics and the double-dealing of the concept "free" hide in the reservation in Achebe's statement, as they form the backbone of the *LIFE* article.

Compared with the other Africa texts examined in this chapter, Campbell's photographic project (1953) and that of Robert Coughlan (1959), Elisofon's is similar in its upholding of what I have called the contrast. Only that Elisofon widens and, at the same time, problematizes it. The contrast for him is not simply the mechanism generating the conventional Western stereotype about the African or Africa, but a discourse, an ellipsis for asymmetrical differences and affinities between me/he and Africa. He was not anybody or nobody; he embodied the middle-class, the well-educated, and the traveled American—the typical reader of *LIFE* magazine. Neither Campbell nor Coughlan shared these affinities, and in particular they did not share his aesthetics and his love of the flag. So the differences between them and their presentations are obvious. Elisofon's article is the best ever produced about any region in Africa or about Africa in general by *LIFE*, at least thus far, in its conjoining the pedagogical researched overview with the personal comment and advanced photo shots that nobody other than Elisofon was able to make. The encyclopedic documentation of Nigeria—its politics, religion, education, and social life all set within a single year, and more than that, the year of the country's stumbling into independence—was an achievement that would be undermined by nobody else but himself one year later. That the article also was a propaganda tool in Western postcoloniality is my postulation.

CHAPTER 5

# Elisofon's and *LIFE*'s Literary Africa

## White Mythologies, Racism, and Cold War Politics

Only quickly browsing through my home library of African books in English, German, and Swedish—travelogues, documentaries, and missionary reports—was sufficient to convince me that the relationship between the image and the text, down to the visual layout of the double-page spread, was frighteningly compatible and foreseeable, despite the disparity of the books. The text-image discourse followed similar patterns of recording and evaluating landscapes and cities, flora and fauna, animals and people, conjoining simplistically two representations of the world: one descriptive, the other figurative or imagined. A taxonomic mishmash or a myth about Africa was the result.[1] The pictorial part of the discourse—sketching, drawing, painting, or photographing—was supplementary, offering its advisory touch and a thrilling look to its viewer. In almost any of the one hundred books spanning an equal number of years (1870–1970), the visual codes remained the same, whether the volume was the American Stanley's *The Congo* (1885), the German Leo Frobenius's *Kulturgeschischete Afrikas* (1933), or the Swedish Albert Henrik Mohn's *Kongo kallar* (The Congo Calls) (1961). These visual codes were enabled by wood-engravings, dry-plate photography, or Elisofon's Canonflex, Kodachrome. The "savage," to take one of the most strenuous physiognomic characters of them all, was significantly kept alive through the centuries. He will resurge, perchance a last time, now employed as a voyeuristic Cold War spectacle of propaganda in the Elisofon photo essay "A Writer's Land of Primitive, Eloquent Beauty: Storied World of Africa" (Elisofon 1961), which I examine in depth. But before we meet "him," let me linger a moment in a specific section in my library to vindicate the generalist point made earlier about the Western homogenization of writing and visualizing Africa.

The twenty "Congo Calls" books were all written in the 1960s by journalists, travelers, adventurers, missionaries, and academic Europeans and Americans. Although highly disparate, the books abide (as they should) by an equivalent visual protocol, a montage of sorts, as if they had been choreographed by a mastermind with the whole world as his stage. It is a blend of antithetical viewpoints, similar to those in operation in the *LIFE* magazine about Nigeria. The viewpoints differ, of necessity, depending upon the topics of the books. A typical two-page or two-panel narrative of a "Congo Call" travelogue, for example, contains photos displaying Lumumba dead and old, defunct ritual practices, adjoined by photos of modern buildings, factories, and a university that all are there to stay, the assumption is. In other words, photos replete with inaction are juxtaposed to masculine action, embodying modernity. In ideological terms, the old world stands for weakening Communism, the new for Western and capitalist strength—a trope of female-male discrepancy that Kozol found characteristic of *LIFE*'s anti-Communist rhetoric in general.[2] The book selection of anti-Communist Congo montages advocate uninterrupted Western tenancy. The Congo should prevail as property, is the message. What is best for Africa is better for us.

What this preamble about my library demonstrates is the century-long Western obscuration and belittling of Africa. My small library may be biased, as I may be, but the individuality that rests within each single volume cannot be discarded, nor its partnership with the others confronting the same visual language of appropriation. In Elisofon's company, we will extend this argument.

## Elisofon's Storied World of Africa in Images and Words

An ongoing lament by Elisofon about his own photography was its (or his) incapacity to produce what he could do in painting: to achieve an "image organic to the nature of the material . . . [which] is a basic concept common to all art" (Elisofon 1961b, 10). He tried engineering his photographic craftsmanship into absorbing both technical and aesthetic devices and modes. We have followed him long-windedly juxtaposing photographs for contrasting and conflicting purposes. He would experiment with similar ruses when painting, applying colors to "convey a feeling of conflict or tranquility, evil or well-being, happiness or sadness . . . masculinity or femininity" (12).

Elisofon's experimental multitalent, his desire to crosscut genres and conventions, writing, painting, and photographing, were definitely timely and applicable. Photojournalism was challenged from different quarters. With the postwar expansion of the *LIFE* readership reaching its peak in 1956 with 5.8 million subscribers, the advertising revenues doubling between 1946 and 1955, and, of course, the rivalries from other periodicals, as well as the advent of TV, the magazine needed to reboot and in particular modernize its visual formats of narration. Philip Wootton, then an assistant managing editor at *LIFE*, has been credited for introducing two such readably interacting publishing methods, those of the special issue and the series. He invited reporters to present him with suggestions. Elisofon was quick to respond. Out of their cooperation emerged the massive *LIFE* cultural artifact, "Africa: A Continent in Ferment," and Elisofon's two literary photo journeys: the one on the South Seas, "Voyages to Paradise: A Camera in South Seas Seeks Famous Scenes in Literature" (*LIFE*, 24 January 1955, 60–77), and the second, the "Storied World of Africa."[3]

The two essays were a success; here Elisofon could apply what he burned for, the multiform of presentation, and *LIFE* would prove to be in tune with the upturn of the media. Yet the essays were ambiguously at odds with the magazine's programmatic placard of modernism that Erika Doss has described as "aimed at a synthesis of seeing with belief, combining visuality with consumerism and nationalism, and attempting to diffuse, or efface, the tensions of class, race, and social conflict in America."[4] The essays encouraged the consumers to lift their eyes momentarily from the domestic narrative of the white nuclear family in exchange for outdoor exoticism, foreign cultures, and "uncivilized" people. Would that boost nationalism? And furthermore they defied another *LIFE* educational imperative: the visual rhetoric of manifesting "to see and be instructed." In indulging in Elisofon's literary-visual landscapes, the *LIFE* consumer had to touch base with the dynamism of a juxtaposition that was complex, not simple or binary. They contained an intellectual dialogue between, on the one hand, sensual and irrational images and, and on the other, quotations from the Western literary canon that it required almost an educational background to master. The exercise was academic, seminar-like.

The literary essay placed itself, it seemed, among those who dropped critical commentaries on *LIFE*'s monolithic photo-vision. Elisofon adjured: you cannot learn about the world only from ogling it, at least not when the subject matter is Africa; you have to reflect too. The problem was that Elisofon did not explain why he engaged his viewers/readers in a commensurate aesthetic game that anesthetized reflections rather than opening them up for debate or questioning them.

Lastly, with reference to *LIFE*'s alleged objective of striving for national consensus, coherence, and integrity, the question is: how did Literary Africa address itself to relevant political perspectives? As scholars have pointed out, the magazine's struggle for democratic rights was partisan, a chimera; its grand vision did not encompass all people and classes. "The magazine never championed more radical civil-rights demands, let alone political movements or racial images that might seriously disturb its liberal vision of an integrated middle-class American democracy," explains Doss.[5] Elisofon's essays were no exception. This is why the two essays are clear as dishwater.

Elisofon's idea of creating an allegorical conjunction by espousing literature and photography, juxtaposing literary and photographic landscape paintings on the same pages, was received, as I have said, with acclaim by his colleagues and with as much kudos by consumers. The crowd-pleasing belle, the "Tahitian Girl Bathing" on the front cover of his first literary photo essay (Elisofon 1956), who poses even more seductively inside the essay (63), would be as energizing as the threatening Savage on that of the "Storied World of Africa" essay, only differently.[6] The Tahitian girl was detached from the American domain of racial purity, servicing mainly the outsider. She was an object for male pleasure, as were most portraits of naked African women in Elisofon's photo essays. Occasionally, they were presented, and then apologized for, under the cover of their ethnographic functionality.[7] Ironically, the Savage was to engage male resourcefulness of another normative kind, as a buttress for the neocolonial nation-building à la the "Congo Call" books.

The cover page title of the South Seas essay, the "Storied Isles of Romance in the South Seas," launched a journey into a paradisiacal other-world that *LIFE* typecast as "Elisofon's literary South Seas with each picture captioned by the quotation that inspired it" (61).[8] So the ideal viewer/reader of the essay would need to be familiar not only with works by writers such as Herman Melville, Robert Louis Stevenson, W. Somerset Maugham, Paul Gauguin, Jack London, and Pierre Loti but also be engaged in the aesthetic mechanisms of Elisofon's paralleling of two artistic modes. Only that the South Seas with *Moby Dick*, *The Black of Falesá*, and *The Pool* had not asked to be retranslated into amorous advances by another white man. The romance was a fake, as many romances are, and when religion or politics penetrates them, they get even worse. This commentary is developed in my reading of its far more advanced follow-up, Literary Africa.

The journey to Africa with literary extracts as guidelines was planned to take place in 1957, but another serial feature, the fourth segment in Great Adventures, "Helicopter Safari in Africa" (*LIFE*, 10 June 1957), was considered too much in the ballpark, and Elisofon's was deferred.[9] In a memorandum to Wootton (2 October 1958, HRC 29.16), Elisofon impatiently wrote: "I believe that Literary Africa is perhaps the most poetic way to approach this area, and we have a great script that is far more varied and exciting than the successful literary South Seas." In another letter a year later he returned to the topic of aestheticism as a clinching agent to encapsulate Africa (to Phil Wootton, 22 November 1959, EEPA, file S-2.6), also explaining what he meant by the poetic approach:

> I would like to finally say that the Literary Africa essay must be primarily one of beautiful pictures, although I do not hope to reduce the entire continent and its entire quality to poetry and I may be capable of it, it is my hope that these pictures will not only be beautiful but at the same time make Africa come alive to the public.—This will not be an essay depending for its excitement and quality on animal pictures, dancers and naked girls. However, I make no promise to leave them out and have hopes of photographing these old subjects in a new way!

By mid-August 1959, he was ready to go—via Brussels and negotiations with Belgian authorities—to Nairobi to start his three-month itinerary. He was privileged as few, if any, travelers to Africa were, and now too. A small squad of stringers had been recruited by *LIFE-Time* Curtis Pendergast to service him en route. The Kenyan government had a car waiting for him, and tourist associations had arranged the local itineraries. Embassy personnel and chiefs of information at various places, from Kenya through southern Sudan, Uganda, Rhodesia, the Union of South Africa, the Belgian Congo, the French Congo, Liberia, Sierra Leone, and Nigeria, had been notified about his coming, and a few of them had received the script that detailed the individual quotes on which he would annex his photos. The whole continent lay outstretched, as it were, passively biding its time in anticipation of the magic carpet and the cameraman to pass. It is from this distance the shooting started. It is pertinent to recollect Enwezor and Zaya's terse statement: "Photography remains one of the most enduring and focused instruments of documentation, regardless of its fragmentary constitution, falsehoods, and *mise-en-scènes*."[10] The shooting that followed was based on a parody of documentation; it was a counterfeit. It was not Africa that was under the lens; it was an iconic reflection imposed by another colonial outsider. Elisofon's imagology was a converted duplication extending disassociation and racialized estrangement farther away from its imagined base.

The essay contains eighteen color photos, including the cover image. Four of them are spread across two pages, and another three extend across a space of a little less than two; six are designed for one page, and the remaining five fill 60–70 percent of a single page space. Their visual content engages the eye and alerts us to the same engrossing power that so many of *LIFE*'s photographic pages do. But as we saw with the South Seas photos, they require more from the viewer than an ogling, appreciating browse. For a full appraisal of them, the ideal reader was expected to be familiar with the Western canon of literature about Africa, which had a risk. This reader would find the context out of which the single extract had been kidnapped in total disharmony, intellectually and aesthetically, with Elisofon's visual and ideological creation. Each photograph (except the cover image) was not only appended by the traditional captive one-liner but with a literary extract of fifty to two hundred words. In other words, each photo has its own literary emissary or the other way around. Elisofon's select group of writers was: Joyce Cary* (two works), Winston Churchill, Stuart Cloete*, Joseph Conrad*, Andre Gide, Geoffrey Gorer, Ernest Hemingway* (two works), Rudyard Kipling*, Vachel Lindsay*, Alan Moorehead, Alan Paton*, Theodore Roosevelt, Stanley, and Laurens van der Post (the asterisk signifies "fiction"). Of these fourteen writers, three were born in southern Africa (Cloete, Paton, and van der Post); the others (except Lindsay) had spent some quality time, or had traveled, in Africa.

The itinerary narrative of his Literary Africa trip is littered with annotations page-up-and-page-down of where and what African "body," spectacle, animal, and piece of land to photograph and how to manipulate the objects for them to harmonize with the select literary extracts. How should, for instance, flamingos, zebras, or the baby elephant be shot, from up in the air or on foot, for them to agree with Julian Huxley's, Ernest Hemingway's, and Karen Blixen's perspectives? How would visual interpretation, coming second, add depth to the texts? It was a challenge, Elisofon thought, merely on a logistic, artistic, and technical basis; he was never close to pondering the project's treacherous dimensions. So he emulated, copied, reproduced, and "illustrated"—the word he used himself—the texts in this way and this order. The African book selection that he traveled with was imposing, including (apart from the ones he used in his essay) writers such as Karen Blixen (*Out of Africa* [1938]), C. S. Forster (*The African Queen* [1935]), Julian Huxley (*Africa View* [1931]), Aldous Huxley (*The Sorcerer's Apprentice: A Journey through Africa* [1948]), Robert Ruark (*Something of Value* [1955]), Osa Johnson (*I Married Adventure: The Lives of Osa and Martin Johnson* [1940]), Emil Ludwig (*The Nile: The Life Story of a River* [1937]), Peter Abrahams (*Mine Boy* [1946]), and a whole set by H. Rider Haggard. Abrahams, Kwame Nkrumah, and Mbonu Ojike were the only black writers listed in the whole collection of 150 writers, each allotted from a single quote to eighty. A thick Western filter shrouded Elisofon's Literary Africa.

## Eden's East Africa

Elisofon's second stop in Kenya-Uganda was a logistical copy of the 1947 one. In a letter from Nairobi (31 March 1947) to his boss in New York, he had outlined his photographic East African venture: "we have to include," he wrote, "the physical features of the country, its inhabitants both Africans and wild animals." There have to be pictures of mountains, plains, rivers, lakes, the Great Rift Valley, and the Indian Ocean port of Mombasa. Interesting animals, he added, were giraffes, buffaloes, zebras, flamingos, rhinos, and elephants. His taxonomy of "original" specimens must include, he specified, "the native African who still lives in Kenya" [*sic*][11] and, naturally, portraits of the white settler (about whom the conditional clause "who still lives" would have been more appropriate) (HRC 10.5). So closing in on Karen Blixen's perceptions in *Out of Africa*, his camera tried to emulate her simile "giraffes as rare flowers," Julian Huxley's "volcanoes like ripples" (at Lake Navasha) in *Africa View*, and a scene depicting the Maasai bloodletting cows in Robert Ruark's *Something of Value*. Blixen and Hemingway were his favorites. But Blixen was not to be one of the holy eighteen who were sanctioned a place in the essay.

Of the six East Africa images in the *LIFE* photo essay, two relate to humans, three to animals, and one to a natural site (Murchison Falls). Two were taken from a helicopter. As we saw, Elisofon, by conventional automation, verbal/visual lassitude, or exclusionary racism, synthesized animals and "native Africans" into the imaginary of one. His amalgamation seemed to be a rational assumption. He was absorbed (as were his times) with the "noble savage" romance that the pastoral Maasai, in a bloodline conjunction with their cattle, embodied par excellence. Photographing the singularity of the Maasai was a must, he wrote to his New

York office, "which every writer on East Africa describes so glowingly" (10 August 1959, EEPA, S-3.15). So he was obliged. He took hundreds of photos of bloodletting Maasai warriors and blood-eating Maasai girls during his trips to the Kilimanjaro region. The picture in the *LIFE* essay of a young couple, captioned as "Young Maasai warrior in Kenya talks with village girl" (EEPA EECL 3339), connoted the myth's primeval bliss and peace, here, demonstratively, in stark conflict with the unnamed violence of the Mau revolt that had been fought not far away from the Olengaitoli village, where this picture was taken. Its serenity would not be fully dressed without its biblical innuendos, generic Adam and Eve communing in a paradisiacal flirtation.

The photo was backed up by President Theodore Roosevelt's almost half-a-century-old anthropological description of men and women in a Maasai kraal with its "fine shaped savages" ("The men were tall . . . Thotmes or Rameses").[12] In this travelogue, Roosevelt thanked Christian mission work for opening up the East African "paradise" and propagated that "in these parts every effort should be made to favor the growth of a large and prosperous white population" (102). The annexed lines in the *LIFE* essay from Roosevelt were metonymically controlled by their ideological and textual provenance, impregnating Elisofon's picture further. Its innocence was as false as Blixen's lyrical savanna epiphanies that Elisofon referred to frequently in his field-notes. In a paper called "Literature and Society," read at a teachers' conference in Nairobi in 1973, Ngugi wa Thiong'o castigated Blixen, "a writer in the racist tradition," for construing in *Out of Africa* a cosmos with "God at the top followed by the white aristocracy, ordinary whites, domestic animals, wild animals who are all in 'direct contact' with God" and leaving Africans "as parts of wood and stones" outside of her creation.[13] He could have attacked Elisofon's wildlife Eden with the same fiery ammunition had he read these lines.

Kikuyu people were excommunicated from Elisofon's gallery of deified types, disqualified probably as being brutal freedom fighters ("terrorists," in today's parlance), humiliated loyalists, or simply not enough original.[14] Settlers were more than welcome. In 1947, he spent a week with the Pitt-Moores, a British coffee plantation family in the Kambu district. This time he hung around Erik Rundgren, a professional "White Hunter" with Ker & Downey Safaris, Ltd. (a company that still exists), and took pictures of a taxidermy outside Nairobi (EEPA EECL 7492), which was mounting and selling poached elephant feet to serve for waste baskets and buffalo skulls for ash trays (an activity that he did not sympathize with). It was the wild game reserve's dirty backyard. Rundgren was the photo essay's prototype of a British (Swedish?) settler entrepreneur. "Tough 'white hunter' Erik Rundgren scans Kenya bush" read the caption, contrasting his masculine authority with the Maasai couple's feminine laid-back chatting. Rundgren surveyed the landscape, controlling it, as it were, in a posture of appropriation that the generic African would not be permitted to adopt by the colonial photographer (EEPA EECL 777). The anonymous African's look was absorbed by the colonial camera or lost in predetermined activity.

Arriving in Nairobi in late August 1959, Elisofon confronted a country four months ahead of the clubbing of eleven detainees in the Hola concentration camp and only two months ahead of the closing of all the Mau camps. Kenya was approaching the end of a British terror regime, the worst in the empire's colonial history; however, the state of emergency was still in operation (until November of the same year). Meeting Tom Mboya, the devout Pan-Africanist in Nairobi, and photographing him at lengthy sessions, Elisofon was naturally at the intellectual forefront of the situation in the country. Yet this momentous time of transition right in front of his camera seemed to have left him cold as ice. Not a word in his field-notes, not a picture taken in clear support of the British withdrawal to come. His loyalty was chained to the nature of his *LIFE* commission, which jarred resolutely with the political development in the country and on the continent. Elisofon hardly invited Hemingway's antihero Francis Macomber in the short story "The Short Happy Life of Francis Macomber" ("You can drive . . . I'm so expensive") to dismember the tough white hunter Rundgren or forecast his precipitant exit from the land that he had no right to.[15] On the contrary, the extract extolled manhood in the embodiment of big-game fiction's Robert Wilson and safari tourism's authentic Rundgren.[16] "The European improving eye," writes Mary Louise Pratt in a much-cited sentence, "produces subsistence habitats as 'empty' landscapes, meaningful only in terms of a capitalist future."[17] Rundgren's "scouting" eye of the Edenic "Kenya bush" forecast a very near future when Roosevelt's elite hunting with four hundred African porters was to be replaced by exploitative international tourism.[18]

Obviously, Elisofon failed to organize (or rather his stringers did), another Hemingway scenario that he thought was indispensable. The quote entraps the famous death drumming lines from "The Snows of Kilimanjaro" about the vultures "squatting obscenely" ("The cot the man lay on . . . moving shadows as they passed").[19] I add a quote from Elisofon's August New York letter (EEPA, S-3.15) to demonstrate not only how far he was prepared to go to achieve a photographic goal but, more important, as an example of a regular make-believe stunt he practiced.

> One problem on the Kilimanjaro trip will be a photograph of three vultures "squatting obscenely" which Hemingway describes in the "Snows of Kilimanjaro." It is probable that we will have to kill an animal in order to attract the vultures and this cannot be done too near Kilimanjaro since it is a Preserve. It would be wise to inform [Henry] Reuter [official tourist guide to East Africa] of this problem, so that the itinerary can include a detour into non-protected country in order to get the cultures with Kilimanjaro as a background. Since Hemingway describes so little and is so important in the Literary Africa script, I feel this is absolutely essential to plan for.

Elisofon's East Africa photo gallery included three mammals: the zebra, the leopard, and the elephant, with their literary appendages. His field-notes almost never invoked religious references. Yet here, notwithstanding his secular thought base, in scrambling for the perfect match of the animals and the textual worlds and the urge to fill their "emptiness," tradition's biblical fantasies formatted an African safari narrative of innocence—innocence meaning contentment and its biblical opposite, knowledge meaning the good or the bad. "A zebra herd races across a grassy plain in the shadow of Ngong hills near Nairobi," ran the *LIFE* zebra caption. Its literary counterpart had dislocated the scene, evoking running zebras in Nyika National Park in northern Malawi instead. Laurens van der Post's sensuous captivating description of "the drumming of the hooves . . . the rhythm of their speed moving in waves across their shining flanks, charged over the crest and made for the pool where the leopard lay" tapped into Elisofon's pictorial representation that was neither good nor bad, only—natural.[20]

The connection between the ingredients that were contained in his photograph of "Leopard snarls in Ubangi-Shari [Central African Republic] jungle," the second photo, formulated another Jungian reflex of the primeval unconscious.[21] Alan Moorehead's adjoined lines about his first sighting of African "wild animals in their natural surroundings [*sic*]," the "tense vitality in their movements, an element of challenge in their glance, that immediately diminishes you" also played with the wilderness theme, allegorically attesting to the game park's (or the colony's) sovereignty as allegorical safe haven (for the white man).[22] Also, here, Elisofon had manipulated the geographical provenances, Eden's borders being eclectic. Moorehead did not watch leopards from the inside of his car in a central African jungle. He did not watch leopards at all. The animals that he had run into were indolent kudu bull browsers in Kruger Park (Johannesburg). The "challenge" against his manhood that he talked about was as hypocritical as Hemingway's.

Elisofon's third animal session depicted "A young elephant in Kenya game sanctuary [Aboseli] helps nudge a baby to his feet." (Note the religious connotations of "sanctuary.") Pictorial anthropomorphism found an outlet in Elisofon's choice of Rudyard Kipling's creation fable of "The Elephant Child," another interlineation of the theme of Maasai innocence and immaturity.[23] Fundamentalist Eurocentrism ousted no doubt any errant thought the American might have had about the possibility of engaging with an African creation myth instead of Kipling's.

The last photograph in this section related to the landscape category of the visual sublime, one of Elisofon's favored photographic genres, and more directly to the noun "beauty" in the essay's title. I have already paid tribute to his stunning color pictures of the "Mountain of the Moon." Other celebrities that he could not resist were sites such Victoria Falls and Murchison Falls near Victoria Nile in Uganda.[24] Certain features in the African landscape were more important than others for the Western photographer. Mountains, confluences of rivers, waterfalls, cataracts, panoramas, the profiling of the shores, savannas, and the jungle had been the given constituents of Western observation of Africa for centuries (see Luig; Staples 2006). Elisofon fell into the Victorian stereotyping of the African landscape with a light heart. He was particularly enthused to be able to reinterpret with his camera visual comments by the greats, John Speke, David Livingstone, and, in particular, Stanley. His choice of Winston Churchill, another giant, as his voice-over for Murchison was self-evident.[25] The visual impact resulting from the power of the bursting water masses in Elisofon's photograph and the word "roar" of its caption matched Churchill's depiction of the falls exploding in "magnificent fury." The two merged in the artistic convention of the sublime excess. The opposite page in the *LIFE* essay contrasted the Murchison fury with a somnolent gliding boat on the "peaceful" Congo River.

Anne Morrow Lindbergh's travel sketch of "A Safari Back to Innocence,"[26] apart from integrating four of Elisofon's safari photographs, sums up, handsomely, I propose, most of the aspects that I have discussed in this chapter thus far.[27] This is her homily for *LIFE*:

> Meeting great flocks of Masai cattle grazing dry hills one slips further back to biblical days of Abraham and his descendants, counting their wealth in cows.

> Here a herdsman—some Masai David his staff erect, in his earth-red robe—stands ready to defend his flock from lions. Down inside the enormous extinct crater of Ngorongoro guarded by its arm of mountain walls, one stands like Adam among animals fresh from the Creator's hand in the Garden of Eden [94]. . . . In Africa one sees it as if for the first time, like a child or an artist. Perhaps, ever, like a saint, one focuses with that "absolutely unmixed attention" that Simone Weil equates with a prayer. (98)

An innocence of cultural callousness, blindness, and denial. What sexy "lions" did she and *LIFE* magazine fear, I wonder.

## Apartheid's South Africa

The double-page that harbors the two South Africa photographs was gracefully organized with the first photo taking in the visual representation of a man with a rope leading eight oxen and wagon in a single file. Behind the retinue was another man on horseback. The sun was setting (we know this also from the field-notes); the distinct contours of the equipage were black as sin and the horizon lightly encouragingly brown. It was: "Century-old voortrekker wagon recrosses Transvaal veldt." The image extends across the upper one-fifth of the two pages like the movement of the caravan that it simulates. We know that Elisofon took the photo on 29 September 1959 in Potchefstroom, a city 120 km north–southwest of Johannesburg, during a historical reenactment commemoration of the 1838 extension of trekking. The second photo that covers four-fifths of the two pages, with the exclusion of a half-page spaced for the literary extracts, depicted another masculine progression, less optimistic and spirited, against the background of an enormous and bulky pile of quartzite rock: "Johannesburg miners walk back to compound after day's work." He took this picture at Daggafontein Mines, an Anglo-American corporation, one of many gold mines in the area at that time. It was in the city of Springs, 50 km east of Johannesburg.

The visual narrative of the two pages connotes movement, contrariness (the upper procession is to the right; the one beneath to the left), power, organization, time, nostalgia, and dreariness. How does the literary material, lines from Stuart Cloete's *The Turning Wheels*[28] and Alan Paton's *Cry, the Beloved Country*,[29] interact with the two photos?

In contrast to Elisofon's peregrinations in East Africa, his South African travel was straightforward. His travel plan incorporated the topics that eventually materialized on the *LIFE* pages. First, Eliot and Joan met a trekker veteran, Pieter L. Ferreira, ninety-one years old, at Enkeldoorn (now Chivhu), a small city in Mashonaland, 146 km south of Harare; the first white settlement in Zimbabwe. Ferreira was "a lieutenant in the Rhodesia Horse during the battle of Chigarra,[30] which was fought a few miles from Enkeldoorn in 1896 against the natives in revolt," Elisofon wrote in his notebook, and continued:

> We shot him for quote about Boer necessity for space and freedom, from Cloete's *Turning Wheels*, and quote about "the whole of Africa was theirs while their wheels would roll." There are not many around who made the trek . . . so we shot this old man wearing his medals [one given him by Cecil Rhodes]. (HRC 26.4, travel itinerary)

This portrait-picture did not do.[31] In Potchefstroom, a week later, Elisofon was fortunate in running into the event that provided him with a series of photographs of historical trek enactments. "The whole of Africa was theirs," wrote Cloete, and nothing in his twenty-eight-line extract ("Rootless, the whole of Africa . . . between their big cloven hoofs") modified Elisofon's initial statement of faith. On the contrary, the celebration of the Boer "ties of kinship; religion and war their bond" received the American stamp of approval. Elisofon's or *LIFE*'s snap adoption of the nostalgic trekking image, with the eight oxen and the two men facing the sunset, had rebounded. The "white" frontier myth of penetration, idealized by Elisofon as the "necessity for space and freedom," has always had many admirers and was irresistibly American.[32] He liked the Boers, and perhaps he was right: the "South African government" was pleased with its visual framing of the Cloete quote.[33]

The second photograph has a far more somber setting. He photographed "machine boys" drilling blast holes in quartzite rock two thousand feet down in Daggafontein mines, "shoveling boys, winch drivers, tram boys, haulage boys." He would also take pictures of coal miners in Enugu (Nigeria) the next month. He had Peter Abrahams's *Mine Boy* in his pocket, quoted from the novel in his field-notes, and must have considered using him but opted for the more conciliatory Paton in the end. The quote ("We come from Transkei, and from Basutoland . . . for all South Africa is built on mines") did tell what it all was about, but candidly. *LIFE* did not mediate to its readers—with *Mine Boy* as a vehicle—the hard facts that black labor and American money were the backbone of mining in apartheid's South Africa.

In all, the narration of South Africa in the photo essay was ambiguous: an endorsement of racist Boer political ethics and criticism of the apartheid state's exploitation of black Africans in the mines, or, differently argued, each storyline eroded that of the other, as if conclusions were left open for the viewer/reader to consider.

## Savagery's Congo

No epistemological concept is richer in the meaning-production of cultural degradation and Eurocentric self-reflection than "savage/savagery." The sum of its shifting applications reads like a condensed history book of the Western view of the Other in its thousands of costumes, from military uniforms to the harlequin's motley rags. My intention here is to deconstruct its historical specificity as a visual marker in Elisofon's dual narration of "Congo" and perhaps add another garb to the term's crowded wardrobe.

The six photographs that formulated his Congo narration consisted of four images that overtly characterize masculine aggression and humiliation of the Other; the two remaining, in contrast, conjure sensations of rest, beauty, and harmony (the sublime). The first three that I discuss emanated from a single photographic session of around ninety-nine shots in a village in Legaland (Wageraland), near Shabunda, in eastern Democratic Republic of the Congo (DRC), organized in advance by Elisofon's major Congo stringer, Jean Labrique, press attaché of the governor-general and a writer whose colonial days were running out (May 1960) (EEPA, S-3.9). The Kalimba photo session was videotaped by Joan for *LIFE* to warrant Eliot's way of working, which was demonstratively as aggressive and physical as the "savage-look-alike" group of men was inspired to be. He was choreographing them as if they were members of a vaudeville theater group (video HRC EEL004 Time) practicing for a performance on "savage behavior." A number of the shots were focused on a single, not identifiable, individual who readily came to typify a "race," a "tribe," or an "African savage." On the cover page of the *LIFE* magazine edition, this man was initially tagged as a threat: a "Wild Warega Warrior poised for attack." Grim-faced and dotted, he was caught in a posture of pointing his spear at the camera, or rather he was directed to do so (EEPA EECL 5284). The same man reappeared on the last page of the essay. Now he posed in a close-up of a facial paroxysm, intimating staggering fury at the Other/the viewer. The caption is repeated: "An exited battle-prepared Warega tribesman prepares to hurl his spear." He is "wild" no longer but ready to commit the bloody act. Rightly I mused, contrapuntally, am I being threatened for trying to name the lacunae of the *LIFE* essay? The reading of the sixteen appended lines from Vachel Lindsay's racist poem "The Congo" (176) ("Then along that riverbank . . . To the Mountains of the Moon") brings, of course, no solace. "'Blood' screamed the skull-faced, lean witch-doctors."[34] Elisofon had choreographed this photo session with Lindsay's horrible lines as his prompts. What naïveté of reader response did *LIFE* count on?

In the EEPA data with regard to these pictures, a passage from Daniel P. Biebuyck's *Lega Culture* had been invoked to explain their cultural frame of a Lega initiation act called *lutumbo lwa kindi*. It may generally be applicable, only that the sequence of Elisofon's mass shooting, with its persistent focusing on the dancer's mimics and movements, is more in communion with the dominant cameraman than absorbed by the demands of a cultural rite-system. The choleric aggression à la Lindsay that the pictures expressed was in perfect conjunction with the fantasy of what "savagery" might hold, but they seemed to be out of tune with what Biebuyck understood as the main ethical principles of Lega culture. Lega men did not hurl spears at strangers; they pointed with the walking stick, a gesture of friendship.

> The society safeguards the moral and social code necessary for the Lega to live together in harmony. For example, it teaches filial respect, marital fidelity, nonviolence, and cooperation. Bwami is also the political power that allows the Lega to live at peace with their neighbors.[35] (Biebuyck 1973, 68, also 155, 195)[36]

The next photo-making séance was captioned "An old Warega tribesman of Congo [who] squats under a tree" (EEPA EECL 267), which was only spatially true, as the photographer's guidance of him was more than that. The portrait of the Lega man was taken at Kabila, a village between Mindu and Pangi in the Maniema district. Elisofon's script, a collage of lines from Conrad's *Heart of Darkness* ("They were not enemies . . . this bit of white thread from beyond the seas"), highlighted the mythic riddle of the "startling" white thread against the black skin.[37] Following the Conradian script, Elisofon had theatrically wrapped a strip of white cloth around the anonymous Lega man's neck.

Anonymity is legion for the many thousands of Africans that Elisofon photographed during his travels, with the exception of men with power, political leaders, both within and outside the colonial cadres; famous artists; and a few others. In other words, only men who had stepped out of "savagery," as it were, were honored by being identified and recognized as individuals. This was a journalistic ethical principle that he would never have accepted for Americans and Europeans (including the "Boers" he had met at Potchefstroom). For women, anonymity was a rule; EEPA classifies them simply (and lazily) as "ethnic." What is "ethnic"? A young Lega woman, from the same village as the Conradian man, fell out as a person with a name, Manganza, but was instead discredited, being photographed by Elisofon in anthropometrical poses, from the front and in profile (EEPA EECL 252). The Victorian visual representation of Africans, derived from physiognomy and phrenology, was in practice as late as the 1960s.

What was the codified meaning of the white thread that many Conrad scholars also have struggled to decipher? Within the frame of the same quotation and (rhetorical) question hides the complimentary anecdote of Marlow offering the dying slave "one of my good Swede's ship's biscuits" (Granqvist 2003), which lines (and story) Elisofon had omitted, I assume, not to dismantle the unity of his storyline. We can, again, follow Elisofon's directions in his step-by-step shooting of the genuinely miserable-looking man, creeping in and out of his nest (EEPA). Elisofon's photograph emits strong feelings of abandonment, and, for me, knowing its manipulation, also feelings of disgust.[38]

So also the next image, "Men of the Wagenia paddle in the rapids of the Congo" (EEPA EECL 9603), a hymn to muscular manhood as exhibited by a crew of "fishermen" at the Boyoma Falls near Kisangani.[39] It is not the backwash of its powerful visual language of body and muscles that troubles me but rather the catastrophic theme Elisofon loaded it with. Its hermeneutic key was Stanley. The annexed quotation from his *The Congo* ("Whatever interest we may profess . . . the muscles of whose members have a more immediate and practical value to us . . . the tropical world must ever remain worthless to them and to ourselves") was an unfinished explication de texte.[40] Metonymically, men's muscles in Stanley's vision were not there for some tea (like the paddlers'), they were to be exploited to the full; otherwise, Africa would remain unproductive and sterile. At this nebulous point of exposition, at the very word "ourselves," Stanley was interrupted. Elisofon did not let him finish the argument that he was developing, as if its outspokenness would have spoiled the aesthetics of the photo's masculine self-consciousness. This is what the bodyscape of the playful muscles in the Wagenia canoe predicated:

> In every cordial-faced aborigine whom I met I see a promise of assistance to me in the redemption of himself from the state of unproductiveness in which he at present lives. I look upon him with much of the same regard that an agriculturalist views his strong-limbed child; he is the future recruit to the ranks of soldier-labourers. The Congo-basin, could I have but enough of his class, would become a productive garden. (Stanley 1886, 93–94)

So rationally argued the engineer of King Leopold II's African real estate in 1884. In the end, the forced labor economy would result in a death toll estimated to be as high as ten million people. Elisofon's appreciation of Stanley was astonishingly myopic.

The last two Congo pictures are "A boat glides on Congo before Stanleyville" and "Butterflies congregate on floor of Congo jungle." The first is a panoramic, esoteric river landscape lacking in cultural specificity; the second is an explosion of butterfly colors in a close-up, imposing and wondrous. Geary characterizes Elisofon's Congo photographs (in general) as "stunning" (2002c, 51). They are, but as I have said, even a photo of Victoria Falls can contain its own disproof. At least here the grand craftsmanship of the two photos, of their making and their visual impact, can be disentangled through the text-image coalition. For the production of the first image, Elisofon had returned to Conrad's novella (38) and one of its many epiphanies of a Garden of Eden in a state of decay, similar to his trope of the undergrowth of rottenness swallowing the slave/the old Lega man. The short passage ("the smell of mud, by Jove! was in my nostrils . . . high stillness of primeval forest . . . as it flowed broadly by without a murmur") and phrases like "black creek," "rank grass," "mud," and "sombre gap" deflect the emblematic sublime of its visual companion. Second, André Gide was invited to scribble a melancholic note about a lost butterfly. His writing occurred during a tour outside Brazzaville, at the confluence of the Congo and the Djoué Rivers (Livingstone Falls). It reads: "There was a little path, almost along the river's edge, and a shady creek where a canoe was lying moored; a great number of butterflies of a great many different kinds; but . . . the finest got away."[41] Here, too, fake discolored Elisofon's picture. In a letter to Pierre Carton in Brazzaville from Entebbe (Uganda), he (then accompanied by Judson Gooding, who would work with him in Nigeria) wrote:

> For the Gide butterfly picture, could you arrange for some local butterfly expert to catch several large brilliantly colored butterflies and to mount them in natural positions, rather than in the flat position in which they are usually mounted? We

> may want to place them on the ground or on a bush and produce a posed but beautiful picture, and will need them in life-like attitudes if the picture is to be successful. (9 September 1959, EEPA, S. 3.23)

The "stunning" butterfly image was fractured, as horror and deprivation defied life on the Congo river (Conrad).

## Sexuality's West Africa

It sounds like voyeuristic agitprop when the editor, in the introductory passage of the "Storied World of Africa," lowered himself to using one of the most well known sex-addicted lines in Hemingway's writings on Africa to represent the *LIFE* essay as a sum total. Reading it "to its startling end," the editor confessed, "one is reminded of what Ernest Hemingway wrote in the sensitive *Green Hills of Africa*: "I loved the country so I was happy as you are after you have been with a woman that you really love. . . . Now, being in Africa, I was hungry for more of it" (Hemingway 1935, 72). *LIFE*'s call for pornographic viewing, as it proved to be, was rationalized and normalized by the two interacting Western myth systems of machismo/patriarchal primitive masculinity (of which Hemingway was the authorized prototype[42]) and the sexualizing of Africa, a vital product of which was the denigration of the female body (see Armengol-Carrera 2011; Hyam 1992). We will see how the last four photographs conform to these myths.

The emblematic photograph taken in Mali of "the woman bathing at the sunset in the Niger, near ancient Timbuktu" (which was the excited editor's informal caption) was one out of a series of seven (EEPA) that Elisofon took at the same spot, within a time span of a couple minutes. Within this period of time a second woman, in the immediate background inside her boat, was maneuvering it toward the riverbank, thus adding dramatic space, action, and depth to the main event. This was the bare-breasted woman in the front washing herself, intermittently splashing water on her breasts, while in a dialogue with the woman behind her. In one of the photographs the woman with the bare breasts turned her face toward the photographer as if responding to the "male gaze" or his directional guidance (EEPA EECL 7874). Being the first image-text in the photo essay, and, what's more, rewarded with the editor's prefatory enthusiasm plucked from Hemingway about female sexual submission, its gendered iconography pressed hard on all the others. It saturated, in fact, the essay as a whole.

The story of the juxtaposed extract from Joyce Cary's *The African Witch* ("The two girls loved the glittering river. . . . It was like greenish glass, glistening where the film of the thinner liquid rested upon its surface")[43] was true in the sense that the image and the text shared a social encounter between two women friends at a riverside, idealized in Cary's "glittering river" and Elisofon's sunset across the Niger. The fact that Cary's fictional protagonists lived at the small Rimi River in Katsina state (in northern Nigeria) may be of minor significance. But the ethical-cultural discordance, between the essay image's immersion in eroticism and Cary's religious (Muslim versus Christian) contemplations in *The African Witch*, is immense. The Cary overwriting does not salvage the photo; it lends names to the hypocritical and sexist intention that backs it.

It is not surprising that one of the two-page photos in the essay was a dance scene whose major attraction was centered on nudity and the dancers' breasts. Colonial photography overflowed in pictures of women's breasts where a clear duality was upheld between what was considered beautiful and what was considered ugly. Elisofon's choices of female objects were generally guided by "beauty" and "youth," and we remember his comment having photographed a dancing session visiting the king of Bakuba in 1947: "I got tired of photographing old hags with horrible figures: and picked out a nice young one with a fine figure, only she said she couldn't dance."[44]The one photograph that the *LIFE* essay picked from the twenty-odd that Elisofon took of the Liberian National Dance Troupe, who were apparently performing for him, fulfilled his "aesthetic" standards.[45] The dangling breasts of the two young women of the essay photo, vertically and horizontally centered for absolute attention, were "cannibalized" (to use Lucy Lippard's term) (EEPA EECL 5076). Its caption, "Liberian girls near Monrovia do a dance of celebration," lied. It was the white man with his horny camera who was the subject of the "celebration." The supportive lines culled from amateur anthropologist Geoffrey Gorer's travelogue *Africa Dances* ("Africans dance. . . . The West African negro is not so much the blackish man or the cannibal man or the primitive man as he is the man who expresses every emotion with rhythmical bodily movements")[46] generalized and idealized the dance as orgasmic, conforming it to Hemingway's metonymic reductions of Africa and Africans as sexual objects for copulation ("you feel it welling up again") (Hemingway 1935, 76). The stereotypes of the hyperemotional, irrational, and childlike African were also played out in the narrative of the last two photographs in this section.

These two photographs were placed side by side on opposite pages. The picture on the left-hand page portrays the torso of a young coquettish woman, smiling, with closed eyes, looking down, with a headscarf and a dress in the same brown colors. The caption reads: "A Vai girl smiles in the market in Monrovia" (EEPA EECL 212). The picture to the right is another torso portrayal of a young "woman," hardly more than a child of twelve to fourteen, naked, her face and upper body covered with white ritual chalk. She smiles broadly and looks straight into the camera. The caption is "Liberian girl giggles at her chalky ritual make-up" (EEPA EECL 4749). Neither of the women was named, another instance of how visual de-individualization configured representativeness. The stylish market woman with the alluring smile stands for the modern world, and her naked partner with the demonic grin for outmoded and outgoing "savagery." The visual dichotomy founded on shifting material codes (such as clothing) of course has a long tradition in colonial and missionary photography (Granqvist 2002). It had a renaissance in the 1960s when a gigantic Western picture industry construed various modalities of "Africa in transition." The nostalgic hinterland of female nakedness that the *LIFE* essay clung to did not signify a threat. It sustained a world of myths, a replaceable world of opportunities to be embarked upon with Western help. The second caption was misleading. According to the EEPA data catalog about the series of the photographs that Elisofon took, the "giggling girl" was one of six or seven Bassa who, having returned from the prescribed time of training after circumcision, were performing a dance for elders and women in their village. In the photograph that was picked for the essay, the girl returned a warm scoffing smile at the cameraman, amazed, I guess, at his persisting comic bouncing and twitching around the small group.[47] He, in his turn, wanted the viewer/reader to understand that she was already on "his" side, disaffiliated from her culture, soon another translated, replaced woman with Western makeup and Western self-indulgence. This is why she was captioned to giggle at herself. It is as if Mr. Johnson's sweet-talk with the village belle Bamu has been rewarded: "Oh, Bamu, you are my savage girl here—you do not know how happy I will make you. I will turn you to a civilized lady and we shall not do any work at all."[48]

As a photo appendage in Elisofon's service, Mister Johnson, the polyglot and trickster, code-switched from Standard English into rotten English. He spoke a Hausa version of Pidgin English ("I got a lil girl, she roun' like de worl.' She smoot like de water. . . . Why you 'fraid for me? I no got nuttin, no stick, no knife.") (19–20), an example of childish bantering that Chantal Zabus has called Cary's dependence on the "double [colonial] heritage of levity and barbaric primitivism."[49] The returning candid smile of the Liberian girls on the two *LIFE* pages had been appropriated to reduce them as cultural personae and delete them as gendered individuals.

The *LIFE* essay portrayed, let us recollect, twelve individuals, eleven of whom were nameless black Africans, stereotyped, categorized, and debased. One was white—a colonialist, hunter, tourist guide, and the only one in Elisofon's African gallery who was identified with a name. Seven of the black Africans were women. Four of them were depicted naked; one was a Maasai, the second a "modern woman," the third a silhouette. Three of the men were wild "savages" and the fourth a Maasai with a spear. There were three photographs of groups. In the two with black Africans, the camera perspective was on the men's backs; the white group was a stylized romance of voortrekker penetration. There were four pictures of animals; two of "sublime" landscapes. Were it not for the improved equipment and technique, and Elisofon's skill, all of these images could have been produced as sketches or photographs by Charles and David Livingstone or Stanley almost a hundred years earlier, so little did they depart from the Victorian conventions of visualizing the "dark continent" (see Koivunen 2006, 61–72).

## Politics

The temporal gap between Elisofon's in situ photographing and travel and the publication date of the essay was as long as two years. It was not any two years in the political history of the African continent; they may well be its two most decisive ones after the Berlin Conference years (1884–1885). I use the word "politics" here to mean: first, the politics of Elisofon's travel (1959) and its connections with the literary project; second, the politics of the *LIFE* essay genesis (1959–1961) and its connections with the development in Africa in general. The two fields overlapped in many ways. In the year 1960, twenty new African states saw the light. Among them were the DRC, Nigeria, and Mali, which Elisofon visited in 1959. Kenya, we saw, was under a state of emergency until November 1959, with Kenyatta under house arrest and freed to become president of Kenya African National Union (KANU) in 1961. Patrice Lumumba, president of the DRC, was murdered with American and Belgian assistance in January 1961, less than a year after independence. Apartheid's South Africa staged the Sharpeville Massacre on 21 March 1960 with sixty-nine dead and

180 injured and the Pan Africanist Congress (PAC) and Armée Nationale Congolaise (ANC) banned, turning apartheid into a tragedy with global dimensions. This is just a partial list of a few major events during these years that were to shape African futures and that of the world.

The "Storied World of Africa" essay's option for the outer-world was a hiding-place. Its editorial preface with the Hemingway *Green Hills* quote demanded a response other than erotic titillations. In this enigmatic manner, the magazine positioned its role vis-à-vis Africa:

> Its [Africa's] struggle to emerge into the harsh modern world makes daily headlines. But much of the truth of Africa, of the forces that stir in its heartland, are illuminated by the memorable writings about it.

The first sentence acknowledged that the "struggle" for "harsh" modernity, euphony for the unutterable and the unexpected, was inevitable. The winning of freedom from decades of colonial superimposition and degradation, the magazine made it clear, was not a matter for elation only. Modernity, "freedom" in Western parlance, was conditional. It benefited Africa as long as it greased the Western wheels. The "Nigerianization" that we saw Elisofon hesitantly give a nod to, and other moderate turns in the postcolonial process, had to be matched by Britain and the United States pronouncing in a seasoned and resolute language the way to proceed. *LIFE*'s Nigeria essay was exemplary of such an accommodating strategy. When it came to the "forces that stir in its hinterland," the fractious forces of digestion and commotion, Cold War rhetoric turned out to be the only plausible outlet. The vagrant headline news from Africa in American media was not worth taking seriously, the *LIFE* editorial touted. In other words, the "stirring" revolts in Kenya, Congo, and South Africa, *LIFE* proposed, could be dampened by a dose of Western cultural know-how and strengthened hinterland American Cold War politics. In his book chapter "Transculture: From Kongo to the Congo," Nicholas Mirzoeff writes:

> Now the fear was that African nationalism could spread to African diaspora peoples in the West, especially the United States. Just as the Belgians interpreted anti-colonial activism as genocidal war against the whites, so the *Life* photo-essays presented the protests surrounding Lumumba's death as a global African-Communist conspiracy against white people.[50]

It might seem as if Elisofon's Nigeria essay with its documentary photography and the travel-shooting with the canon of Western literature as his compass was its own enemy—one based on reality, the other on fiction-mongering. But they were not. They were part of the same agenda. The racist sketch of Africa as an outer-world was as factual, political, and conclusive as the neocolonial documentation of Nigeria. The savage narrative was only different. Taking a literary quote out of its context (only that an abuse); adjusting it to arranged histrionics, manipulated landscape, and animal mise en scènes; and naming the project an exposition of African "savage beauty" was racism. It was not a savage fool's lost paradise. The myths of Africa were real in the sense that the vacuity, tenaciousness, and perversity that they inhabited would appeal to a political trickster like Elisofon. He could handle hardcore political and social issues, such as election campaigns and aerial expeditions, but also racist colonial storytelling—if it was purposeful. He could help demonize Africa and adjust to the holes it left. That the double entendre of his photography was ambivalent and ambiguous (Staples 2007, 183) is recognizing what it is. It is halfway, recognizing that it was a subsidiary of *LIFE* patriotism and American Cold War African politics is saying what has not been said and what needs to be said.

CHAPTER 6

# The American Broadcasting Company's *Africa*, 1966–1967

## A Shock of Change and an Updated Safari

The American Broadcasting Company (ABC) project was about altruism and pedagogy; its method was onslaught. "The biggest television audiences in history watched the longest, costliest, and possibly the most ambitious documentary production ever shown," blazoned James Fleming, the executive producer, throughout 1967. From six to nine producers with separate camera crews crisscrossed 85 percent of the African continent or thirty-nine countries during a 300-day shooting schedule (thirteen months) and produced in the end 600,000 feet of color film, the equivalent of 278 viewing hours. Equally heroic was the three-month editing process, whereby several crews transformed a copious amount of footage into a three-hour-and-twenty-four-minute television show. It included the recording of Gregory Peck's narration and the musical score by Alex North. "As a result," said Aram Boyajian, senior associate producer, "many beautiful and exciting sequences were ruthlessly cut down or eliminated entirely, simply because they took the film down a dead-end road. We had to do our best to keep the film moving."[1]

From its initiation in April 1966, ABC's *Africa* project was locked into the rhetoric of the blockbuster, in the sense of "a high-explosive bomb used for demolition purposes," compared intermittently with the budget race of the filming of David Lean's *The Bridge on the River Kwai* ten years back that would be telecast on 25

September 1966 as a three-hour ABC Movie Special. The cost of the four prime-time hours *Africa: A Journey to Discover the People and the Land That Are Africa Today* that went on air a year later on Sunday night, 10 September 1967, would amount to $2 million that, interestingly, was registered as a pseudopatriotic feat analogous to Muhammad Ali refusing to go to war: "No Viet Cong ever called me nigger."[2] Compare one hundred peaceful ABC filmmakers dropping a "bomb" about Africa over America with the simultaneous invasion of 486,600 U.S. military personnel in Vietnam. If Lean's epic war movie was schizophrenic, as has been argued, ABC's *Africa*, a crazy docu-reality show with hidden Cold War tendencies, was at least honest.[3]

## How and Why *Africa* Was Initiated

The $2 million ABC documentary *Africa* was launched with education as its prime goal, not Kwai entertainment, and with Cold War politics and the Vietnam War as its engaged neighbors. The United Nations General Assembly proclaimed 21 March 1966 as the International Day for the Elimination of Racial Discrimination, and in June Senator Robert Kennedy visited South Africa. These two events affected the world. ABC's *Africa* was bound to be different. Leonard Goldenson, president of ABC-TV and its overseer, called the show a "communication of multiple dimensions . . . [that went] far beyond the coverage designed for television presentation," presenting "raw materials for extensive educational series."[4] The envisioned program would entail knowledge, education, and entertainment. It was to be a multimedia probe never tested before in the history of television—strong words. At least this is how it was hyped.

What would the documentary do? Money was ready; expertise was needed from the outside. James Fleming, the man picked for the job by Elmer Lower, the ABC president of news, special events, started recruiting. The first two to be ushered in for a preliminary palaver were Blaine Littell and Elisofon, with whom Robert Ardrey, living in Rome, was also lined up. Fleming's knowledge of Africa was that of a cultivated *LIFE* magazine reader's, no more, no less. The rather unfortunate pick of Ardrey, as it proved to be, was on Elisofon's recommendation. He knew Ardrey from the shooting of *Khartoum* in Egypt in 1965, which would premier in Britain in June and in the United States three months later. Ardrey was the movie's scriptwriter, and Elisofon had photographed the still pictures in color for the prologue.

These three men, all reputed Africanists in one way or another, together with Fleming and his ABC associates, lay the ideational ground for the production crews that would crisscross the continent. Ardrey went on board leading eight-hour seminars at ABC about his particular role as a consultant for the project, and Littell and Elisofon directed courses about Africa to the "non-Africanists" that were employed in a number of offices. Littell would be coordinator of the marathon project; a guarantee for a happy conclusion and a commercial success, it was rightly thought. Twelve years with CBS News as a writer, editor, and foreign correspondent; author of a book about Stanley;[5] and two-and-a-half years in Africa were his impressive assets. Elisofon, named director of Creative Production, was to be another trump card, given his Hollywood fame, resourcefulness, and large African network; Ardrey, screenplay and science writer, the third boon, was hired no doubt for his timely and controversial books, *African Genesis* and *Territorial Imperative*. The three men would not, however, pull together even if they tried (with the exception of Ardrey and Fleming, as we will see); their individual talents and gifts never converged. This was a discrepancy that impinged on the Africa project as a whole, fractured as it was from the start by its megalomaniac objective of saying it all, which paradoxically, it needs to be emphasized, also contributed to opening up new avenues in the visualizing of the continent.

In the course of the following months ABC would sign a number of contracts with producers who in their turn recruited camerapeople and assistants. A large conclave of well-known media people, documentary filmmakers, photographers, journalists, and writers positioned themselves around Fleming, each ready for their brief or longer assignments, and some of them with more specialized engagements than others. Elisofon's unclear function as creative director was certified on 6 June and Ardrey's as consultant about the same time. These were also the weeks when Fleming and his aides started to launch press releases and give interviews about the intents and the rationales of the *Africa* program. Lower's description of it was as brisk and sweeping as Goldenson's: its intention was to "make a lasting a contribution in conveying knowledge and thereby fostering international understanding"; "to convey a comprehensive view of the lives, customs and the heritage of the people"; and to "shape the best zoological and historical travelogue of Africa in television history" (HRC 48.8).

Those formulated by Fleming were more complex, both down-to-earth and muddy, pragmatic and abstract, intuitive as he was to the multiform reactions he received on a daily basis from the crews in the field: "We agreed that through a comprehensive look at the politics, sport, culture, economics, nations, animals and people, that our basic aim would be to say what makes Africa tick" (HRC 48.8–9); Africa is "in a shock of change," "ABC's story is not about emerging Africa but new Africa"; "the modern world [Africa] and its technology works irrevocably." That Africa was undergoing a "change" was a truism of no news-breaking impact, that a metamorphosis, a process of self-reflective literacy, had gripped Fleming—and should grip the Americans—was the point: "It was only when we forgot conventional Africa and began to turn the cameras on people in agony, triumph and repose that the cheers began in our screening rooms." The "tick" and "shock" metaphors that he uses and which surfaced frequently in his letters and interviews were replications of Littell's impact on him and on the project, his, in Fleming's words, "talent for bombing sentimental nonsense." "I second," Fleming continued, "his impatience with the self-serving African communication that romantics persist in sending out to the world" that ABC calls "the bush jacket syndrome" (Fleming, 20 August 1967, HRC 48.8). Littell was *Africa*'s wise man.

Half a year later when the fieldwork was well under way, Boyajian, the person who was also in charge of the seven-team (each team involved two persons) final countdown of *Africa* in July–August 1967, commented on it, quoting Fleming's project rhetoric in a letter to Elisofon (6 December 1966, EEPA, V-3, 37), which is worth discussing further for the light it sheds on the complexities and contradictions that illumined *Africa*. The Fleming quote with Boyajian's authored exegesis that he wanted to share with Elisofon and all the other *Africa* producers for them to consider and act along reads as follows:

> "Our central theme is THE SHOCK OF CHANGE in Africa today. It is a seismic change. The giant awakens, not through his own desires or actions, but because the outside, represented by the main forces of the modern industrial, technical world, pushed and shoves and thrusts at this continent. It is the human result of these changes, particularly as they are acting on the heart of Africa that is revelatory."
>
> I [Fleming] have written all the producers—with Jim's ok—that we need stories about the modern push and shove and thrust. Not government people or students in a campus situation—but Africans who have taken over modern jobs, students outside campus and their activities, artists and writers with original thoughts. The man can be living in a hut—but if he is believable as a possible future leader ten years from now, he would do for us. My point is that a shock is one thing into another—and right now we have the "native bit" and enough of what it is going

> to bump into. The modern people would be taken straight—not that they are behind the times and trying to catch up—but in their own rights they are in the modern world. There must be an IBM machine or a birth pill factory somewhere in the Congo.

The "very idea of 'backwardness,'" writes John Gabriel, "commonly associated with the Third World, in contrast to the cultural and technological advances in the West, makes the Third World appear closer to nature."[6] The assumptions that the push of modernity affects the African and the American differently lurk behind Boyajian's words. For the African, it is a "naturalizing" process, a "seismic change," outside of her or his control; for the American, it is homemade individual enactment. The pseudo-scientific terminology used here (seismology, biology, Darwinism) defines the continent and its people as passive, ignorant "hut-dwellers" taken as it were by surprise, right in the middle of their sleep, by an outside world bringing fascinating modernity and superb technology, from IBM machines to birth pill factories (in the "Congo" at the time these commodities would have been paid for and installed by the United States). The ABC proposal to their fieldworkers to go for stories that captured their ideal "African" who is imagined in transition between the hut and the office, fumbling, hesitating, murmuring, was racist in its mollified condescension. Gabriel's imposition that "the intellectual hegemony of the West . . . re-imposes itself in the West's ability to define and control the world's problems" (Gabriel 1994, 154) also applies to the formalistic ABC agenda of this kind.

Far from all of the *Africa* project's producers complied with this regime. Strangely enough, Fleming challenged and queried his own incentives. Translating contemporary democratic liberalism into applicable formats to go with visions for the *Africa* project gave him butterflies. "Africa-watching is no longer a spectator sport for the west. As we watch Africa, we watch ourselves" and "what is Africa doing about the west." These could be significant self-reflections by any Westerner, even today.[7] The "shock" was personal. The absence of the ticking Mau warrior—not a seismic phenomenon—in Elisofon's 1950 and 1960 media world of Africa was his and *LIFE*'s choice.[8] Fleming's choice was adamantly different.

Let's follow the project's intellectual but weird genius, Robert Ardrey (EEPA EECL 861). He was contiguously close to Fleming and Elisofon from the beginning of the process, and more anxiously at Elisofon's side or rather at his knees. Filming animal societies in Kenya and Tanzania was one of his urgent wishes that Elisofon had no problem acquiescing with. The other wish was far more complex, so delicate that it eventually pushed Ardrey away from the program. Two interrelated coincidences shape the background: Robert Kennedy's Affirmation Day Speech in Cape Town on 6 June, two years before he was killed, and ABC's frantic efforts to procure permission to film in the Union (it was granted after four months of negotiations). Kennedy's rock-bottom juxtaposing of the "black and white" situations in the two countries resonated, as it became clear to anyone affiliated with the Africa project, in a most tantalizing way. Kennedy said: "But the help and the leadership of South Africa or of the United States cannot be accepted if we, within our own country or in our relationships with others, deny individual integrity, human dignity, and the common humanity of man."[9] A week after Kennedy's speech, Ardrey wrote a letter to Fleming, upset to say the least. It must have become clear at this point to Fleming, if not before, that selecting Ardrey as consultant for his darling media venture was a fundamental mistake. The realization that Elisofon was to be a lame icon grew stronger in the process. Ardrey wrote:

> Bobby Kennedy has set back US-South African relations by God knows how far. He has deepened the fallacy that the American Negro and the South African Bantu are equivalent problems; worse, he has taken advantage of South Africa to give out campaign speeches in New York State and the future presidential horizon. This at least is how the South Africans look at it and they are polite and grim. And we must face it; it hasn't helped us, not one bit. And I'd be too curious to know what would have happened in the US if a foreigner had come to us, and done the equivalent. Even the Kremlin knows better. . . . The Afrikaner is proud, proud of their culture, deeply hurt by the image which he and the world have managed to combine to produce. It's 50–50, the Afrikaner's fault and the world's. But however one may feel about their particular social experiment, they are right in believing that they have created a culture of a sort, at the far end of the world, which the Australians for example have never attempted or accomplished. (EEPA, V-3, 11, 1)

Ardrey mistakenly believed, I think, that it was his popularity as scriptwriter and playwright that made him invulnerable for critique. His false renown culminated in *LIFE*'s generous offer of providing him affluent space to introduce his own book *Territorial Imperative*, a "smart aleck" extrapolation of studies of animal aggressive reserve and fascistic human segregation, inferred as a universal principle. In his pseudoscientific logic apartheid becomes a "culture of a sort." The "tribe" is the ultimate development of the welfare state, he preached whenever he had a chance.

Knowing your place, where you belong, was an evolutionary invention. "The first thing a man had to do was to learn to work." That is what the South African has done. Study their success. Ardrey was talking about the Boers. Assertions such as "patriotism is a calculable territorial force" and the appended rhetorical question, "Why did Finland fight?,"[10] and his even more dysfunctional charade, "all forces in a society of inward antagonism work for division and emotional mayhem,"[11] must have repelled and alienated, one would think, many of those who worked with him in Kenya throughout June and most of July. One in particular, as we will see, was William "Bill" Peters (1921–2007), a human rights activist, friend of Martin Luther King Jr., and producer of "Storm Over the Supreme Court," for which he earned a George Foster Peabody Award (1963).

But the main reason for his writing this letter was not to bash Kennedy and endorse apartheid; it was: who would travel to South Africa to film for ABC and whom would they/he meet? Fleming was working on it, Ardrey knew, and he saw this moment of friction opportune for him to intervene.

> If anybody's going into South Africa grinding an American axe of self-righteousness . . . include me out. I've seen no evidence that anybody connected with this project has such inclination. But I MUST restate my position. Under the circumstance it becomes all the more important that you and if possible Eliot come down far ahead of shooting, look about, make up your own minds, and meet a few people. What's happened is this. Berdine [Berdine Grünewald, South African actress, married Ardrey in 1960] has returned [the couple lived in Rome]; it was to be her last year in the theater] to receive a kind of prodigal's welcome. You should see the press. In Afrikaans, South Africa's "darling" is back. . . . She is tribal, like a Zulu. (EEPA, V-3, 11 2)

In other words, Ardrey wanted not only to prepare the ideological ground for the entrance of the ABC team, which he thought he could do by creating a public encounter of reconnaissance between the two celebrities Elisofon and Berdine Ardrey, but also be involved in the decision making about which the ABC team would be in South Africa. The animalistic wife-as-decoy tactics did not work. Even his last dallying appeal to the two Americans, Elisofon and Fleming, at least one of them bearing the brilliant plumage, the fancy mane, the handsome marking, Ardrey's farce of conjoining the animal sexual conquest, the masculine power game with the battlefield of Afrikaans-American humans, fell flat. This epistolary section is a goofy facsimile translation of the equally love-sick chapter 5, "Love's Antique Hand," in Ardrey's *African Genesis*.[12]

> The Afrikaner is a Texan, with all the limitations and far horizons that the word implies. But above all he is male. An Afrikaner female, like Berdine, is the ultimate female; the Afrikaner male is the ultimate male. Even as I equate him with the Texan, I acknowledge his limitation. But he has another streak. There is something deeply Irish in him. It has nothing to do with culture or ancestry. The Afrikaner is two thirds Dutch, one third French, and totally Protestant. Nevertheless, peculiar tides have produced in the Afrikaner black emotions, dark moods, poetic streams not unlike the Irish. That's why so unlike the Texan he's so proud of his theatre, his poets. . . . One must approach the Afrikaner like the Texan, ready for the worst and the best. But one must also sense in him the Irishman, and never forget it. . . . The question mark that overhangs South Africa is different in no least degree from the question mark that overhangs the Congo, or Uganda, or Nigeria, or Kenya. Who'll survive? It's the same simple question that we ask of the animal society. And we have no answer. History must provide that. (EEPA, V-3, 11 3)

"Ardrey had expatriated himself to Kalk Bay [a suburb of Greater Cape Town] and was deeply into bloodthirsty hominids and the evolution of territoriality in Western aggression, and so, posing as a paleoanthropologist," writes the South African literary critic Stephen Gray in a frenzied review of Eugène Marais, to whom Ardrey had dedicated his "fulminous hooey in *African Genesis* . . . with cute illustrations by Ardrey's wife."[13] Marais's "*Soul of Ape* is bogus," was Gray's ruthless verdict. The same could be said about Ardrey's attempts at producing a film about "animal society" not as an adjunct to Elisofon's and Newman's ABC photo book *African Animals* but as a visual takeoff of the TV documentary as a whole. It would be about "fear; the inseparable relationship of man and his environment; the never-ending sense of struggle for survival; the Sameness and continuity of Africa yesterday, today and tomorrow" (EEPA, V-9, 8, 1). Here is the racist imaginary of the first scene in his (never produced) ABC Africa film, a slim changeover of *Territorial Imperative* ethics:

> Against a background of rolling grassland plain, we see a circle of thirty Masai warriors, bodies daubed with ochre, robes draped from one shoulder, spears at the ready. Close, we see through a frame of two tall Masai bodies a black-maned lion,

> tail lashing angrily, coughing defiance, crouched in the center of the circle. The lion turns slowly, eyes alert, body tensed to spring, as the circle draws in on him. Suddenly, a single Masai jumps toward the lion. The animal charges, leaps, falls onto the Masai's up-ended spear, braced now against the ground. The warrior is badly mauled, but the others leap to the attack with spears and swords. The lion fights fiercely, mauling several others before he dies.

The nineteen-page film script modulated "the beginnings of life" and "the beginnings of animal life" with images of monkeys, "Pygmies," and a close-up of a "bushman gnawing of [*sic*] a bone," cutting to a "white hand holding" that belonged to L. S. B. Leakey at a table of fossils (EEPA, V-9, 8, 4–5).[14] The Serengeti Maasai that inhabited the outlined screenplay of Ardrey's *Africa* fable "linked with the hyena in death, his life is so intertwined with the lives of animals that it is natural that he should return to animals in death" (EEPA, V-9, 8, 12).[15]

Ardrey's carnivore evolution doctrine, in combination with his unconditional view of Man as a predator "whose natural instinct is to kill with a weapon" (1966c, 353), beleaguered his palavers with a choleric repetition and energy. He "promulgated [Raymond] Dart's message that violence lay at the root of human evolution," writes Carmel Schrire in her study of carnivore evolution's part in apartheid.[16] Ardrey's film script for *Khartoum*, with blackface Lawrence Olivier as the Mahdi and Charlton Heston as Gordon the colonizer, followed the same ethics of the struggle for the territory as evolution's ultimate solution. Now he was up to fabricating another bloody script. The ABC producers did not unequivocally support his battle cry "Might Makes Right," in particular when Lyndon B. Johnson the same year authorized the dispatch of one hundred thousand troops to the Vietnam War. Neither were they happy with Ardrey's ongoing (July) campaign for Elisofon to head the production team to South Africa, nor when this would not happen that Peters, whom he disliked, would not be critiqued for bad manners. Ardrey realized that the ABC staff was tired of him.

What remained for Ardrey was an honorable exit. In his resignation letter to Fleming of 25 July 1966 (EEPA, V-3, 21), he claimed that the reasons for it were problems of cooperation, his disapproval of the support of Peters, who was, in his mind, a troublemaker, biased, and incompetent as a non-Africanist. But above all, there was ABC's lack of "capacity to deal with the supreme delicacies of the South African situation" and his disappointment with the World Court's decision about Liberia and Ethiopia that went against South Africa,[17] due to, according to him, the pressure of world opinion, and newspapers such as the *New York Times* and London's *The Economist* (HRC 48.8–9). With Ardrey back in Rome, this meant that ABC could send its best film crew(s) to South Africa and that the *Africa* TV documentary could develop in a nondirectional manner in the hands of a number of skilled freelance producers and cameramen. But Ardrey was right about the disorganization. The ABC invasion in East Africa was chaotic. Littell made decisions that were at variance with those being made in New York; the film crews were too many in situ at the same time; there were complaints about miserable working conditions; quarrels were legion.

The cameramen and the producers that ABC had hired, among them writers, journalists, photographers, filmmakers, producers of TV documentaries, and bold adventurers, formed a highly competent class of professionals who dedicated, some of them, more than a year to the project. Many of them were familiar with Africa from earlier travels with their cameras. Among them were Gerald Feil (Kenya, Tanzania, Ethiopia, Nigeria, South Africa),[18] Marvin E. Newman (Ghana, Kenya, Tanzania, Angola, South Africa), William "Bill" Peters (Kenya, Tanzania), Richard Swicker (Kenya, Tanzania), Tim Knight (Ivory Coast, Guinea), Robert Campbell (Kenya, Tanzania), Eliot Elisofon (Kenya, Tanzania, the DRC), Johnny Coquillon (Kenya, Tanzania), H. J. Smith (Kenya, Tanzania), Pierre and Peggy Streit (Angola, Botswana, South Africa), Carole Marner and Gene Marner (Senegal, Mauritania, Mali, Cameroon, French Africa, the Niger River), Edward Magruder Jones (Nigeria), Tad Danielewski (Nigeria), Skeets Kelly (Egypt, Ethiopia, Sudan, Uganda, South Africa, Rhodesia/Zimbabwe), Leon Gluckman, the music, dance, and drama producer (Nigeria, Tanzania, Kenya), and Richard F. Siemanowski, Littell, and Fleming, scriptwriters.[19]

## *Africa*: Instruction or Propaganda?

Between February and August 1967 the producers and the cameramen were returning from their assignments, carrying with them an enormous load of audiovisual material that was to be cut, shortened, and organized into a format that would be persuasive and tell the grand narrative—or better, omit/refuse to tell such a story. The challenge was twofold. First, how to transform the 278 viewing hours into the final four; second, how to attune to the revisions that had been made during the process of filming, the "case of Ardrey" being one of them, and a number of other shifts, both unexpected and expected. The memo that Fleming wrote to the project staff about "the projected structure, scope, narrative pattern of AFRICA" (31 January 1967) listed sixteen segments in the order they were to be organized but were reduced in the final subject-by-subject rundown for the four hours of *Africa*.[20] At this point Jan Fleming made a pitch for an album that he called the "pictorial action," out of which the visuals, such as the non-British-flag and the non-French-flag, surfaced to describe places, personalities, and themes, but he would or could not distinguish the individual visual language they were wrapped in. The three rivers, the Niger, Congo, and Nile, promoted visual geographies with discrepant narratives. The multiform aspects involving the three major themes of education, sports, and health were particularized likewise in visual terms of vigorous impact. The portraits or the interviews of political leaders, politicians, and writers, in Fleming's presentation, were calibrated to adjust the rising or the falling trajectory of "freedom," or his version of it. "The current success story" of Kenyatta (1964–1978)[21] "with [his] narrative moving from Mombasa to Nairobi catching the reality of black, white and Indian human relations in this multi-racial society," spearheaded, it seems, the media-set of ABC *Africa*, the Kenyan leader stepping past less successful presidents like Guinea's Ahmed Sékou Touré (1958–1984), the Ivory Coast's Félix Houphouet-Boigny (1960–1993), and the Congo-Kinshasa's Joseph-Désiré Mobutu (1965–1994), the Washington star.

The album was divided along a "tension line with Tanzania, Zambia, and Malawi, as the front line of Black Africa directly resisting the policies of Ian Smith's Rhodesia, Portuguese Angola and Mozambique, and finally the Republic of South Africa." On the "good guys" side were the three presidents Julius Nyerere (1962–1985), Kenneth Kaunda (1964–1991), and Hastings Banda (1966–1999), and the real "bad guys" (B. J. Forster and his gang) and their opponents (Nadine Gordimer, Helen Suzman, and Alan Paton) occupied the album's lower part. Four countries formed *Africa*'s visual centerpiece—Kenya, Nigeria, Ghana, and the Republic of South Africa—each of which was traversed by more than one film crew. By the time Fleming produced his midway analysis, the "shock of change" was not efficient enough to shake his archaic view of postcolonial Kenya as a Karen Blixen land of Maasai persisting "in a changeless way of life" and Yoruba in "magic and witchcraft" ceremonies, while Nigeria was being torn apart before it even had started.

By August 1967, with the rough editing of the material at its absolute end,[22] the filming of Gregory Peck's voice-over and ABC News commentator Howard K. Smith's question "What's ahead for Africa?" hitched on to it, the reality specials went on air.

The subject-by-subject rubrics were advertised with the addenda that the early hour show featuring animals had been scheduled to attract young viewers to tune in.[23]

- FIRST HOUR: African animals and the land; Window on the past—Bushman; Civilization comes to Africa—Ethiopia; another new nation is born—Botswana.
- SECOND HOUR: The internal conflict—tribalism; Disease, scourge of the continent; Education, the hope of the continent; Ambition humbled—Ghana and Nkrumah; Makers and shakers.
- THIRD HOUR: The universality—sports; Africa's lively arts—Folk opera[24] to Miriam Makeba; Civilization's black mark—slavery; Kenya—a multiracial success; The Congo—divided riches.
- FOURTH HOUR: The "overseas provinces"—Angola and Mozambique; Colonialism—a controversial point of view; Apartheid—a moral dilemma.[25]

A prowling apologetic hesitation imbricates words like "civilization," "conflict," "divided riches," "controversial point of view" (colonialism), and "moral dilemma" (apartheid), as if to say "we (ABC) do not take a stand, it is up to you to do it." The Trendex overnight report covering the twenty-six major market cities found that 31.3 percent of the available audience was viewing (the average rating was 16.5; NBC did slightly better, 32.4, measuring simultaneously its season premieres of returning shows).[26] The reviewers, a large majority of them, rehearsed, duplicated, and rehashed ABC's advertisements and Fleming's pronouncements culled from within the one-year media archive about "Africa-in-formation." They were not only indistinguishably reenacting the ABC press-media's self-indulgent narrative of the production's infrastructure but also varieties of their sweeping textures of the intents: "we all worked hard against myth and misconception to discover the truth and tell it" (HRC 48.9). The hesitations and the self-reflections that we discovered among the same journalists and producers were demonstratively, as it seems, absent.

The reviews of ABC's *Africa* are a most boring reading. It is as if their hype and high-pitched tone signaled a religious alternative: Africa yes, Vietnam maybe not. A few representative examples: the *Houston Chronicle* (11 September 1967) considered the show "an awesome undertaking . . . an unprecedented tour of the fascinating and forbidding continent of Africa"; the *Miami Herald* (12 September 1967) wrote that the "great barbaric, troubled continent of Africa was given an unprecedented, hypnotically fascinating television scrutiny;" and the *Sunday News* (10 September 1967) that it "was the disservice performed to the once Dark Continent by the bushleague Hemingway's and the patronizing sensation-seekers that Fleming and his crew of knowledgeable newsmen . . . correct with a more illuminating view of Africa today" (HRC 48. 9).

But there was an individual voice or two. Jack Gould of the *New York Times* and Ben Gross of *New York Daily News* touched issues that dig more deeply into the annotated problematics of the *Africa* project and, as such, will, I hope, vitalized the discussion of the camera work and Elisofon's part in the project. Gross juxtaposed critically two aspects: South Africa on one side and the Other Africa on the other. ABC's vigorous and focused treatment of apartheid, a single inclusive topic, he said, was "the best I ever saw on TV." Its contrast was the "gigantic cornucopia of facts, figures, entertainment, and human interest sidelights gleaned from an entire continent" that challenged "the average viewer's derrière." It was a criticism of *Africa* that would grow from day to day. Totalizing narration or holism was a relentless point of departure for Elisofon's encapsulated visual attraction, be it a landscape scene or an African mask. It never left him. Gould took another direction, reviewing *Africa* for his Sunday afternoon *New York Times* edition:

> The brilliant and imaginative photography, a product of Eliot Elisofon's role as the project's director of creative production, had often the appeal of a pure travelogue, yet time and again, the camera and the microphone were instruments of incisive editorial comment, particularly in the concluding chilling analysis of South Africa. The ability of the reportorial staff led by Richard Siemanowski to visit seldom-pictured scenes and individuals was a first-rate tool.[27]

Gould's observation contains two topics: his views about the functions of the camera, the microphone, and the site as organic "instruments of incisive editorial comment" and his thoughts of preferring candid photography as it was executed at the sites in South Africa ahead of controlled "pure travelogue" photography, however brilliant or imaginative it could be. The changes in documentary filmmaking, working in smaller crews, rejecting scripts, and turning the liberated cameras on the individual or the drama of a situation, surfaced now and then in differing shapes in Fleming's talks and interviews and also in Ardrey's texts but never as an explicit subject. Naturally, there were differences among the crews and cameramen, some loyal with the old school, and some loyal with the advisory script, but there were one or two who invited the camera to define and explore African reality. Gould also misjudged Elisofon's part in the project.

## Style as Statement: The Camera in *Africa*

Cinema verité, the use of a direct-address style and the presence of an on-camera narrator without direction capturing events as they happened, had its U.S. origin in the multifaceted collective that consolidated around the two cinematographers Robert Drew and Richard Leacock, who from the early 1960s (as Drew Associates) would make a number of films that changed documentary filmmaking history, in providing the viewer with—to use a much-quoted expression—fly-on-the-wall perspectives.[28] Interestingly, two of them, *Land of the White Ghost* and the *Land of the Black Ghost*, dichotomously and antagonistically interdependent, dealt with Kenya and its first election before independence in early 1961, with KANU gaining two thirds of the votes. The first thirty-minute program portrayed (interviewed) the big-mouthed colonialist Jim Hughes and the second centered on Kenyatta, the leader of the independence movement, who was out of the reach for the camera, being in detention in Lodwar.[29] This was very far from the popular depiction of Kenyatta in the United States as a Communist agent and a Mau fanatic. Drew had earlier made it clear to Goldenson, who wanted him to make a visibility document for ABC about a continent, that this would not happen—and for this reason: "What I would do is find a story within a continent which in the telling would reveal something about the continent . . . that's the way . . . television ought to work" (O'Connell 2010, 87). So he and Leacock went for the snapping of the Kenyan fly. And neither of them would have taken on the ABC documentary *Africa* five years later; those who shared their radical rethinking and joined the "army" were marginalized.[30]

Departing from the etymology of "territory" as deriving from *terra* (earth) and *terrere* (frighten), hence "a place from which people are frightened off," Bhabha postulates a paranoiac situation of the colonizer asking two self-centered questions: first, "Tell us why you, the native, are there," expressing disgust and threat; their "there" will soon be our "here"; second, "Tell us why we are here" addresses the Other, insinuating interest, demanding subservience, requiring civilization.[31] Both signify fear. Surveying the canvas that the ABC documentary *Africa* filled with tropes familiar from Elisofon's remapping of the continent and the colonial discourse of repulsion and conquest that, in Bhabha's view, operates as a symbolic reality enfolding the colonizer as well as the colonized, I can hardly see the in-between space, any interaction, and any reciprocity of ambivalence even. There is *one* subject; *Africa* is a monologue with a few uncontrolled voices leaking out at instances when the master's scrutiny is either inattentive or replaced by a hand-held camera. Bhabha's two questions prompted ABC to revisit panoptically (via aerials) the sites of Kilimanjaro, Victoria Falls, Murchison Falls, the Niger, the Nile, the Congo, and the coastline at Mombasa. ABC's target was to fashion imaginaries of military parades and exalting pageantries, the mythic enclaves of the Ethiopian monarch and the warfaring northern Kano emir. The spectacles refer also, compulsively as it were, to the safari culture icon Hemingway's *Green Hills of Africa* ("I was hungry . . .") and the spear-bearing aristocratic bodies of the Maasai in Blixen's *Out of Africa*. "Tell us why you are there," the Maasai are asked, and Signe Hasso, the Swedish-born actress, reads a paragraph from the colonial autobiography rebounding their response in Bhabha's double and duplicitous meaning. "The Maasai were ruled as 'wild' and relocated when European ranchers wanted their land, while the Kikuyu were ruled as servants and ironically assimilated to the indispensable yet despised 'lower orders' of European society," writes Shaw.[32] The ABC interview done with Kenyatta ("Kenyatta does not like Americans," was Fleming's injured comment, having had to wait for his "yes" for six months) reverberates with the same patronizing airs of meeting a reformed loyalist cum nationalist.

Were it not for hour four of *Africa* about southern Africa and individual cinema verité segments intersecting, it would be another, albeit more combative and updated, version of the *LIFE* Africa archive. So similar are the administrative portrait shots, the visualscapes, and the scientific racism that plagued these perspectives. What differs has more to do with the medium. The interviewees speaking back, the synchronized image-sound system, sound mixing, and montage, gave the viewer a chance for the object-subject interchange that at best invited pondering, not only revering. However, the *LIFE* or the *National Geographic* print conventions held on to their control of the aesthetics and techniques used by most camera crews that were operating for ABC in Africa in 1966–1967. The voice from South Africa, "the world listens but from a great distance," brings home the gap that made *Africa* problematic, and this did not mean the miles separating New York and Cape Town.

The ABC visual-narrative rally across southern Africa was as speedy, conscientious, and say-it-all as the other crisscrossing pedagogical tours. It started with highlighting the racism governing the Portuguese "provinces" (ABC's terminology), the Angolan refugees in Zambia, a panorama of Victoria Falls with the obligatory allusions to David Livingstone and Cecil Rhodes, and the interview with Ian Smith as self-ordained watchdog of "Christian civilization." These fifteen minutes served as a prologue to ABC's predestined assignment, an inside view of apartheid of the kind that American TV consumers had not witnessed before. The many interviews that were produced were not at all conventional stiff portraits. Irrespective of whether the persons were Boers, Afrikaner Calvinists, or anti-apartheid activists such as Albert John Luthuli, Alan Paton, Harry Oppenheimer, and Helen Suzman, the interviewees enjoyed the same "right" of returning unrehearsed answers. "Leave us alone," bawled the separate development enthusiasts with the camera as a witness and another as actively present reviving Luthuli's meeting with Robert Kennedy half a year earlier and Helen Suzman's rallying for the Progressive Party, as the only true parliamentary opponent of the apartheid state.

The footage was part of the dramatic logic in which things happened according to a script that was dictated by everybody else but the ABC producers. This also pertained to the many encounters with South Africans ABC registered, each of them filmed from within a correlating context of "now" and "here." However, nowhere was the observational camera more active as during Gerald Feil's filming of the Cape Town Coon Carnival at the festivities of the New Year in shabby Hanover street, working class District six, that was to be demolished and declared a whites only area only two months after this happening; in 1968 about forty thousand people from there were removed into shanties. His camera authored the story of an absurd and disjointed blockage. On one side of the Cape were the Coloured minstrels and a black-faced white, on the other side racist white policemen. The minstrels advertised themselves in synchronous sound and ironic visual graphics as "irrevocable coloureds," "men between," the police not at all, unseen or not by the candid camera, until the same camera overtly dived down in a bold close-up on a police dog. In a consecutive segment we could see an aerial (also with Feil as filmmaker) of Robben Island with Nelson Mandela held captive.[33] The story had reached its logical closure: apartheid unfolded in front of the camera. Here are two local voices talking about this very spectacle on 2 January 1967, both resounding the duplicity of racial segregation that the film ethics of these segments succeeded in transporting. "Can it be that the whole Coon Carnival is one big mass display of emotion-packed people finding relief in a gigantic explosion of pent-up desires and frustrations?"[34] And the question is answered in the next comment:

> The Coon Carnival also sets off the Cape Coloured Community from the Whites. The White community will never be able to put up a carnival as bright as the Cape Coon Carnival. The reason for this . . . is because the basis of the Coons is giving vent to feelings which for 51 weeks of the year have been repressed. The Whites has [*sic*] not been repressed, so that there can be no wild burst of feeling.[35]

The *New York Times*' Jack Gould picked up the racial theme: "The destruction of Negro family life under apartheid . . . was set forth with rare eloquence in both picture and Mr. Peck's firmly stated delivery of the accompanying commentary" (*New York Times*, 11 September 1967); a statement that was backed up by Ben Gross, as we saw. It is the picture that expedites vocal confirmation, and not the other way around. The Southern Africa part of ABC *Africa* and apartheid was revolutionary.[36]

To move from southern Africa to Nigeria in early 1967 the ABC film teams would apprehend was to move from one control center to another, from racial discrimination to a civil war. Soyinka, walking down a street in Lagos, opened the political segment of the second hour of *Africa* with satiric banter about Africa's new nations, such as Nigeria, acting as a clown, stupendously selling cocoa and peanuts for nothing to the West, caught in a hook-up of certifying the colonial legacy of power that the Biafran "war mongers," he insinuated prophetically, were profiteering from. He said:

> Most nations hide their agonies and their crises, and try to protect their deepest values, in essence by wearing for the foreign intruder a clown's face; and for an international port especially, such a mask is inevitably a composite of the circus hats, the scars and other profanities of the nations who congregate in it. Lagos is the comedian's mask of Nigeria.

And Littell and Robins, who followed up with him, citing him in situ: "There is much that strikes Soyinka . . . as profane: the huge American cars wedged like ships in drydock in the narrow lanes of the city; air-conditioned skyscrapers; women's European-style wigs, and even the schools and hospitals which . . . seem to have been put there not to benefit Nigerians but to enrich the publishers of textbooks and the manufacturers of medical equipment."[37] So too does Feil's situational camera accompany him on walks, turning its eye and ours on the dried-up fountain, on the half-empty skyscrapers, on the face of an angry man making statements about misuse, misapplication, and danger.[38] In its final version, the special segment was about four minutes long, but in hindsight taking into account the massacres of Igbo of 1966, Yakubu Gowon's retaliatory measures of 1967, and the more than two-year-long imprisonment of Soyinka for his antiwar struggle in August, the segment was momentous to say the least.[39] Tad Danielewski's filmed drama juxtaposing two antithetical scenes each subsuming life or death added to Soyinka's pessimism about Nigeria. The first was a court scene in Kano with Emir Elhaja Ado Boyeso, face veiled, eyes cold, facing the man to be judged; and the second, the story about the escape from the north told by a wounded refugee in a hospital bed in Enugu. Cyprian Ekwensi, the novelist, was, with Gabriel Okara and Achebe, "a roving ambassador for Biafra" and spoke to the camera "for the people of the enclave."[40] Danielewski's footage was filmed in the direct cinema style by a nervous camera that let "things happen in a natural way" (Feil). While filming the emir, war activities went on in the street outside. There were reasons for his shaky hands.

## What was Elisofon's Function?

ABC's choice of multiplex Elisofon was a given. He was a reputed Africanist, he had a wide network, and he was a traveler. They needed him and could use him. But under what label? As Ardrey fan, animal society photographer, Congo River traveler, Mobutu allied, or color expert? Any of these features were justifiable as distinctive credentials. The *Africa* project's animation emanated at least theoretically from the politics of doubt and inquiry that Littell's punctuating rhetoric of "Africa-sentimentality" represented. This was not Elisofon's domain. On the contrary, his concept of Africa was rightly deemed the traditional old-time school of representation: mountains, masks, leaders, naked women. His consumable specialty had to be collected from elsewhere. For his pioneering work in the field of color control and, more important, on the admirable use he had made of it for films such as John Huston's *Moulin Rouge* (1952) and Basil Dearden's *Khartoum*, he was made director of Creative Productions. Officially, he was expected to help the photographers add an artistic, "pictorial style," to their work.[41] In more practical terms, he was supposed to coordinate film techniques in an effort to minimize photographic differences, especially in regards to lighting, camera manipulations, and lens usage. This never happened for two very obvious reasons: one, neither group nor individual coaching was organizationally possible; second, most of the photographers were experienced, immersed in their individual craftsmanship. Looking back, he admitted: "I was given kudos for color photography—too many kudos, since I didn't do too much more than select the film we all used, a new high-speed Kodak film that was still unproved, and help to pick some of the camera crews" [such as Gerald Feil's].[42]

As he admitted, during the post-September review session Elisofon was unfairly credited with being responsible for the high-quality color aesthetics of *Africa*. But more flawed was the media's focus on his presumed administrative and logistical part in *Africa*, which was zero. Here is a typical tall story about his delivery: "It was first-rate—the narration, the commentary, the filming and the editing. . . . Elisofon must have been behind many of the sensitive hunches." This misrepresentation of him was not his fault, nor was he responsible for its ongoing actualization, except that he enjoyed, I am sure, the accolade, invalid or not. With his friend Ardrey on board in the first week of June 1966, and with Littell at their side to spearhead the project, he did what was expected from him, gave a seminar to the *Africa* staff, both cinematographers and administrators, on the topic "The Making of Color" (9 June 1966; HRC 58.51), as did Ardrey on his specialty.[43] Elisofon started his lecture with the no-news information: "I am a talker," and went on making statements such as: "Pseudo-realism is photography's enemy"; "no color photograph should be a facsimile of nature"; and "the photographer has to feel as well as to see." "My friend Ardrey" was not only provided to ensure the realization of what Elisofon thought he could accomplish within the *Africa* program (apart from what ABC had in mind), Ardrey was to be Elisofon's spiritual supervisor, and at least at the beginning also that of the project. Elisofon put it like this:

> To begin with, Ardrey and I urged them to do a sequence on nature, and when our plans were finalized I took off for Africa to direct that part of the program. . . . Now I have done a lot of animal photography in Africa and I am sick and tired of what I call cute animal pictures. So I directed a segment on animal behavior, showing the family life of an elephant, lion and hyena; how they live, survive and the relationship to the land. (HRC 15.8)

Out of their cooperation and with ABC's backing evolved a two-dimensional scheme centered on animals: the ABC book *Animals* (1967) with Elisofon and Marvin Newman[44] and the filming in the Kilimanjaro area (with the coproducers William Peters and Richard Swicker) and the two scientists Hans Kruuk (the hyena) and George Shaller (the lion) focusing on the ecological basis of animal social behavior. Revisiting Serengeti in the company of Ardrey and the scientists, mediating the evolutionary interludes and interactions they were absorbed by, he recollected the aesthetic animal quotations he had selected for the Literary Africa essay (1961).[45] The Serengeti plains shooting in July involved at most four intercrossing crews, and intersecting with them were Ardrey and Richard Leakey. One of the teams produced the cinema verité sequence, with Feil's camera sound-tracking a gazelle killed by a hungry lion that came to illustrate—without his cognizance, I believe—Ardrey's concept of carnivore evolution.[46] The field was chaotic, with too many crews competing with each other, stepping on each other's toes, and getting frustrated.

The sequences on the Maasai were linked with his shooting of the animals, as they always had been with Elisofon, only now with pseudoscientific signatures. "There is a tremendous drama built in Africa, as far as the *people and natural elements* are concerned; and this offered a challenge and opportunity for all of us to do something extraordinary," he said in the interview with Stan Mayys [my emphasis].[47] Describing the project, as the panoptical photographer he was, he used a historical metaphor of surveillance to encapsulate it. It had, he said, "the effect of viewing a great canvas or the acropolis at Athens, from a great distance" (EEPA, 9, 4). The extraordinary for him might have been the challenge of the comprehensiveness of the project, its totalizing solicitations, or it could have been the argumentative sustenance of Ardrey's evolutionary holism that he embraced without, I think, considering its political spin-off. Ardrey's dramatic metaphors of premise, intrusion, and denouement, when boiled down, stood for the evolutionary beginning, a natural but ever-changing commotion between humankind, the animals, and the land; "intrusion an act of either 'rape or love'; the solution, the denouement, to be found deep in the distant past, in the 'dark heart of Africa,' or in the 'dark heart of ourselves.'" Ardrey continued:

> There is a strange unity that runs through Africa. No matter where you start—fear. Tribalism, ecology, disease, sex, nationalism, racial relations or whatever—the thread runs from north to south and east to west. Also what unifies Africa tends to destroy, to pull it apart . . . everything seems to cut both ways.

Translated into the typology of Serengeti, the animal-man interaction, a bloody scene of the Maasai and the lion, was scripted by Ardrey, as we saw earlier, into a foray for an ABC film, but was never realized. Fear was the bulwark for self-defense, killing, and territorial safekeeping.

> I am alone in the African street, lost, afraid, and without allies. I understand nothing. . . . *Australopithecus africanus* lies buried not in limey caves, but in my heart and your heart, and in the black man's down the street. We are all Cain's children, all of us. (Ardrey 1961, 356–57)

"One should read Louis Leakey, who found man's earliest remains in the Olduvai Gorge . . . and one should certainly read Ardrey in *African Genesis*," Elisofon recommended his followers (Elisofon 1969, 177). Inspired by Ardrey, he formulated his own version of an evolutionary dogma for Africa, drawing a pencil sketch of a tree depicting the continent from "Plant life-Kilimanjaro" at the trunk to "Egyptian art" at the top of one of the three major branches (EEPA, V-12, 10). Why? For fun or more plausibly to visualize a synopsis for an imagined future book on the "whole of Africa," on holism's Africa, which did not progress further than the sketch. The *Animal* book came closest. "Africa is a treasure land," declared the preface, rich in diamonds, spaces that stretch forever, mountains lost in clouds, forests, and animals. Were it not for man "with his civilization," the territory would be the perfect Adam and Eve idyll, he ironically points out. "The animals of the African wild are in danger," we learn, but the good thing is that "man has at least awakened to the need to save them" (EEPA, V-12, 3), which the first TV hour of *Africa* was to be demonstrating. The picture book, with its biblical innuendos, contained twenty-one animal portraits, as individuals and in groups or "families," many of which have been republished in books and articles over the years.[48] Some of them interfaced with the theistic essays about the "wisdom of wildness" by Anne Morrow Lindbergh and her husband, aviator Charles A. Lindbergh.[49] The ABC *Africa* book followed suit; it was both a transcendental statement of belief and a missionary appeal for animal protection and international support for it. The fifteen "sanctuaries" in the six countries that did exist were far too few.[50] Ardrey's impact on Elisofon was manifest.

Before leaving for New York on 13 August to return to Kinshasa in December, Elisofon made two aerials. The first proved to be another of his many near-death experiences, this time while taking a few still photographs of snow-rimmed craters of Kilimanjaro.[51] The second was a tour of Mombasa and the coastline in connection with the documentation of the reelection campaign for Kenyatta, through which he moved Kenya further into the one-party state—backed by the United States. ABC's commitment to American Cold War tactics was just as predisposed: by focusing on the Maasai and not the Kikuyu; by photographing Tom Mboya, nicknamed the

"American ambassador," and spear-less Kenyatta rather than Oginga Odinga, the KPU opponent and the socialist.

Elisofon's second Africa section—the first being Kenya-Tanzania—grew out of his two-month sojourn in the DRC, in December and January 1966–1967. This trip to the Congo was Elisofon's fourth, and there would be others coming up in the 1970s, all accredited by Mobutu's and the American embassies' goodwill. His two segments, the Congo River steamer route from Kisangani to Kinshasa and the American relationship with Mobutu, were incorporated in the TV program.

Before closing in on these two points, let us follow Elisofon's peregrinations *before* he boarded the steamer with his crew. They traveled east and south of Kisangani, which was practically a "military zone" controlled by the Armée Nationale Congolaise (ANC) and in reach for them too, if needed for protection. This was the time of the first (July 1966) of two mutinies in the northeast, called the Kisanagani or the Mercenaries' mutinies. Some two thousand Katangese gendarmes and foreign mercenaries loyal to Moïse Tshombe mutinied in Kisangani but were crushed. The second took place a year later, which allowed ABC's *Africa* to incorporate the two of them in its review of the "Congo Crisis," with a note about the Belgian Jean Schramme, who led the second, also failed, mutiny.

The film crew visited an Eastern Rebellion refugee camp at Wanie Rukula, south of Kisangani, and took a slew of photos; also of a military patrol at Bukavu, at the southwestern edge of Lake Kivu, where they met Colonel Kakudji; of tin mine workers near Kalima in Kindu Maniema district; of White Fathers Mission station at Shabunda, in South Kivu;[52] and of "Lega people" in two Shabunda villages, most likely the same he had visited in 1959 for his "savage man" hunt. Elisofon took aerials of the villages, staged and produced images of initiation ceremonies and dances, and photographed women with facial and torso scarifications and thread-wrapped hairstyles. It was a compendium of a photo habitat, with which we are familiar (EEPA EECL 9344). The most spectacular individual photos, in all their conventionality, are the sixteen portraits Elisofon took of Colonel Eustache Kakudji at Bukavu. The colonel led the ANC recapturing of Albertville (today Kalemie)[53] from the Simba rebellions on 29–30 August 1964, taking, it has been alleged, four hundred Katangese rebels prisoner, then torturing and killing them.[54] I find it hard to believe that the ABC group was not cognizant of what had happened two years earlier where they were and the degree of atrocities that were committed on both, or all, sides. And if they knew the details, they should also have realized that they were facing a war criminal. Maybe they did. Elisofon's series of photos of Kakudji balance between innocence and culpability (EEPA EECL 460). What about the then CIA station chief Larry Devlin saying, and Michela Wrong quoting him: "He [Mobutu] was right for Congo at that time . . . in blocking Khrushchev."[55] But Mobutu's "peaceful revolution," as his phlegmatic 1965 ascent into autocracy has been called (in contrast to the previous five years), was in reality a reconstitution of well-known colonial structures, amenable to and applicable for Western discourses, a transitory Cold War tool, to distract another tyrant. Both Levin and, it seems to me, Wrong were wrong. As the title of their Africa book chapter indicates, "Congo-Kinshasa: Light in the Dark Heart," with twenty-three of Elisofon's photographs, Littell and Robins were, too, beating around the bush, but hesitantly: "Gradually, and with a firmness that often has amounted to ruthlessness, General Mobutu has brought order to the Congo. No human obstacles have been allowed to block the tasks of reconstruction . . . a neo-colonialist, a cynic paying no more than lips service to the martyred Lumumba."[56] Shadowing the story that hung to Colonel Kakudji was not an enlightened act.

The ABC film crew's two- or three-week river trip from Kisangani to Kinshasa in January 1967 flung Elisofon into a photographic frenzy that generated almost five hundred documents. Behind not only the mere volume of the shots but their disciplined organization along the narrative structure of a travelogue with its formulaic segments of departure, passage, and arrival, I believe that he had in mind the Congo-Stanley book he was planning to do, and not the special for ABC. On the other hand, as the film that the crew made and he directed became a postcard of a limpid lame duck, it was a pity as the material carried visual storytelling potential, in fact insinuated it by the camera stills' unwillingness to ignore the regime of filmic conventions. Life on deck was an unruly visual medley of fish and wild animals, soldiers of the UN peacekeeping forces, Congolese war veterans, scarified women doing elaborate hairstyles, and a man with a monkey. Life outside the deck invited Elisofon's regularized camera to shoot riverbank scenes, steamers, barges, tugboats, and dugout canoes going up and down the river. The ABC crew must have stalled the steamer for a while to allow the photographer to accompany a group of fishermen on joint canoe trips to the fish-traps in the cataracts and take at least one hundred pictures of the same kind as he took in 1959 of the Wagenia paddlers. The third segment of the travelogue depicted the dramas of embarkation and disembarkation, stoppages, the handling of river port facilities, and welcomes and good-byes. In all, it was a Congo River trip full of "real" life, right in the middle of the Western clown Mobutu's hell, of which no one wanted to be reminded, not even formatted as a neutralized Elisofon special. So it did not come to pass.

The reason for filming the Congo River with a filter of escape, silence, and oblivion attached to the camera lens was complicity of a graver kind.

> I [Elisofon] asked Fleming for one piece of Africa for myself with nobody crawling around me. So with just my team I went into the Congo. We took a fascinating steamer trip from Kisangani to Kinshasa to film life along the river: the feeling of the Congo. I don't think it's ever been filmed this way before. It was very beautiful and very moving. (Mayys 1967)

In other words, we are supposed to share with Elisofon his "feeling of the Congo," an "obtuse" meaning that defies communicative logic. Martin Jay's discussion of Roland Barthes's twofold impact of the photograph on the beholder, it "being an illogical conjunction between the *here-now* and the *there-then*," I find relevant here.[57] "For denotation, instead of being a straightforward analogical representation of nature, turns out to point to a traumatic reality that is no longer there, a fragment of a whole that can never be revealed" (Jay 1994, 445). Elisofon's catchword "beautiful" was not a cover-up for either nostalgia or a traumatic memory, as its time and space pointers were deleted. So also historicity that takes us again to the aesthetic breathing hole of the sublime. If the sublime for postmodernism, according to Jay, is its willingness to "live with the pain of unrepresentability" and for modernism solace and pleasure about something lost (583), it is in the latter dark hole that Elisofon lands. Had he been concerned about the discrepancy between Conrad's *Heart of Darkness* that was referred to in the *Africa* segment on the Congo and his production of the four five-minute-long visual "moving" requiem of the river, the most inappropriate word to characterize it would have been "beautiful," unless it was, as I believe, a narcissistic replication of his 1959 staging of the "Conrad man" with the white thread around his neck. Elisofon's filming of the river was one of the many Western paradisiacal romances of oblivion it has been shrouded in. It had not "been filmed this way before," he claimed; true, at least not with a Mobutu soldier, Sgt. Major Sylvestre Bambula, at the cinematographer's side throughout his "fascinating" but stymied trip. The Cold War scenario, here the "Congo Crisis," sculpted the events right in the midst of ABC's *Africa*, "the most ambitious documentary production ever shown."[58] What got lost, what was gained?

Upon arrival in Kinshasa, Elisofon and his associates stepped right down into Mobutu's private territory, Mont Ngaliema, the hill that overlooked the Livingstone Falls and housed his palace with the barracks of the presidential guard. Elisofon was quick to establish contact with his entourage, and took his first photos of the ruler in one of his many exhibitionist poses pointing with his fetishist staff to a map or a design of some kind. All the other two hundred shots can be divided into two groups: one is about a press conference and the second about the parade of the Corps des Volontaires de la République (CVR), Mobutu majestically controlling each or rather the cameraman acclimatizing to the icon god as he was to the mythology of the Congo River.

The atmosphere of the press conference was antagonistic, even hostile (EEPA EECL 2430). Mobutu waved a Belgian newspaper, citing Associated Press journalist John Latz, who accused him of bamboozling and fraud, of turning the country into a police state.[59] A man in the audience, in a harsh dialogue with Mobutu, argued that the country was starving, so "what do you do about it?" Mobutu played intimidated, furious, convinced of his infallibility, made a snap royal resolution, and his handymen took notes: "First I will start right off by saying that from today . . . imperialism has no place in the Congo" (EEPA V-12, 1). But the real grounds for meeting the press was far more serious than this sour colloquy, although his ad hoc resolution was part of his large scheme to expunge remnants of colonialism, as later on changing the name of the country (1971), its cities, down to the names of people in his own household (including himself). The big issue that day, with Elisofon taking photos of the people in the room, was Mobutu's decision to nationalize Union Minière du Haut-Katanga, to be renamed Société Générale Congolaise des Minerais (now Gécamines), as of 1 February 1967, and doing this without any negotiations with the company or the majority Belgian owners. He was on the warpath to form a totalitarian political system, having abolished the national constitution, banned the political parties, and piece by piece taken full control of the mass media and the military. The only party he tolerated was his own Mouvement Populaire de la Revolution (MPR). His killing was motivated by politics. On 2 June 1966 he hanged four opposition politicians at a public execution on trumped-up charges, without defense. In the years to come, slaughter and assassinations were everyday crimes. If the air in the pressroom that day was stifling, it was an omen of what would happen. There was fear even among the Mobutu Cold War supporters. Mobutu was imagined (and would paralyze the Congolese because of this) as Conrad's Kurtz, who, in Mayer's words, "embodies both master and servant, god and fetish, paradoxically collating the function of the agent and the function of the instrument, aspiring to the pleasure of control and of submission, and ultimately suffering nothing but the painful implication of both states."[60] This is a memorandum from Sherman

Kent of the Board of National Estimates (a group of senior experts) to director of Central Intelligence McCone, dated 27 January 1967, almost synchronous with the press conference.

> We believe the chances are increasing that anti-Belgian or antiwhite incidents will lead to a situation wherein the lives of many Europeans in Katanga, and perhaps in the rest of the Congo, would be in danger. There are some 40,000 Belgians in the Congo (including about 15,000 in Katanga); there are also some 40,000 other whites, including 1,000 to 1,500 US citizens, most of whom are scattered in other parts of the country. Clearly, a rescue operation to evacuate even US nationals would be very difficult, and an effort to remove all Europeans vastly more so. The situation may not deteriorate this far; it is impossible to predict Congolese events with confidence. But in view of the recent turbulent history of the country and the critical nature of the present troubles, such a contingency should be kept in mind. For the Board of National Estimates: Sherman Kent, Chairman.[61]

The parade on one of the next days was a first-year celebration of CVR, which at its start (9 January 1966) consisted of hopeful students dreaming about a life of intellectual freedom. Their vanguard radicalism became a threat for Mobutu, and the parade that the Americans were to witness and that Elisofon photographed was far from a jubilant, rollicking walk along the Kinshasa streets. With the international press along the sidewalks, it was orchestrated to be a demonstration of CVR's evolution from its identification as an avant-garde movement to Mobutu's own MPR party, which was established on 20 May 1967. The march we will follow via Elisofon's photographs was staged as a mock funeral (EEPA EECL 2366) to aggrandize in a cultlike fashion the unilateral personality of the president and to celebrate his brave expropriation of the "Mining Union of Upper Katanga." Elisofon's camera wandered with little enthusiasm between the different charters of CVR, each with its own authenticated dressing insignia, posters, musical instruments, T-shirts of Mobutu, and nationalistic banners with rough depictions of Lumumba and Mobutu. Passing the emperor and his entourage—including his wife, the government, foreign diplomats, and his medical doctor, William T. Close, father of actress Glenn Close (EEPA EECL 2396)[62]—and the coffin, the mock protocol required the youths to show stern and deadpan faces, no smiles, and their right hands raised above their heads in Hitler-Jugend-like salutes. The end of the drilled performance in front of Mobutu was the culmination of the liturgy. The spectacle was not hilarious, as it may appear. Instead, it can be seen, metaphorically, as a deplorable first scene in a five-act tragedy. As such, it embodied a visual roundup of how the United States and Belgium, in exchange for Mobutu's servitude as the West's prime Cold War ally, were to keep the *abacost*-dressed tyrant in power with economic and military assistance for thirty-two years, allowing him systematically to loot and oppress his country. But what did it tell us about Elisofon's photography that my narrative is dependent on?

"The outstanding event of the parade was a mock funeral of the Union Minière Haute Katanga," wrote also Elisofon in a note (EEPA, V-12, 1)—without irony. This is the problem. If a photograph by Barthes's definition is the "perfect analogon" of reality, a "message without a code" (Jay 1994, 442), Elisofon's photographs of the parade, despite their overt laid-back drabness and analogon neutrality, were impregnated with a second-order capacity of loyalty. Elisofon pictured what Mobutu wanted him to depict: the iconography of the ruler, his portrait, his staff, his *abacost*, his gestures, his anger, his votaries, the T-shirt, the mock funeral, the genuflection. The script was monologist; it was Mobutu's. Elisofon's camera never slipped, never talked back, never saw what Feil or better what Feil's camera would have seen. This also means that the two narratives of the Congo special part of ABC's *Africa* are Cold War accessories, the first through the passive myth of the mesmerized Congo River, the second through the invisible equivocation of the "Congo Crisis" happenings in 1966–1967. Elisofon, the trickster, connived other plans. The one closest in time was his intention to produce the book about Stanley with the Congo River as the visual leitmotif. For this to happen, he would need to win over Bill Close, the American doctor, to help him deal with the dictator. There was no room for a radical American camera.

CHAPTER 7

# The Cold War Affinity between Zaire's Mobutu Sese Seko and the United States' Eliot Elisofon

It was mythmaking as dynamism that haunted Elisofon. It was activated by a mix of bewildering colonial self-assurance and laid-back irony that he never really came to terms with. The American media has consistently toughened and corroborated this complex imaginary, allowing it to take on iconic dimensions that misrepresent Elisofon's role in "writing or viewing Africa." We have studied power interventions, real, fragmented, or illusory, that propagated from within the coloniality of *LIFE* magazine and ABC frameworks; Edward Said, thrashing out the classical colonial texts (Hemingway and Blixen), defined their injunction as an "imperialist system of representation,"[1] and Caren Kaplan discussed masculinist travelogue discourses as "instrumental in the construction of rationales for imperialism" (53).

The beginning of the 1970s was not only the height of the Vietnam War, with President Richard Nixon expanding it in April by invading Cambodia and, four months later, on 4 August, rewarding his Cold War ally Mobutu hosting him in the White House. It was also Elisofon's finale in several ways, the most tragic aspect of which was his untimely death. Of the thirty-six months that constitute the years 1970–1972, he spent twenty-three at home (basically in New York and at Vindelhaven in Maine) and the remaining thirteen traveling in West Africa, particularly in the DRC, topping his "Congolese" shooting by 50 percent of the thirty-seven thousand

Elisofon documents held at the EEPA. The DRC was a special site in Elisofon's world; it had been so from the start of his traveling. His interventions were not only his excessive photographic demonstrations (1967, 1970, 1971–1972) of Mobutu's military power and his totalitarian regime. They leak into simultaneous projecteering involving an African art book, the *National Geographic*–sponsored Stanley book, children's books, and diverse travelogue productions that all were refashioned, canceled, or abandoned. More felicitous and finished projects were an article on Akan gold, the filming of African sculpture for CBS television, and Elisofon's bitter oeuvre and farewell, the four one-hour programs in the documentary series *Black African Heritage* (*BAH*) (for Westinghouse Broadcasting Company).[2]

## Elisofon in the Footsteps of Stanley

We remember Elisofon climbing the Rwenzori Mountains in 1951 with a Swiss Alpinist and "the only porter with shoes," taking a series of photographs that were the very first and best color pictures ever taken of the wet fauna in the heath region, of the wind-bared rocks and Mount Stanley. And that the "Mountain of the Moon" pictures and those of animal life in adjacent Virunga National Park were his contributions to the *LIFE* special issue on "Africa, a Continent in Ferment" (1953) and the *Nile* book (1964). Stanley had climbed the heights in 1889 and had his illustrator make images of what he saw. Elisofon's expedition was number six, a figure that he never missed mentioning in his cataloging of Stanley's and his mutual crossings on the African paths. Stanley's bravado appealed to him, as did Stanley's illustrations and books, which he had been reading since childhood. Here we will follow him in his documentary pursuit of the God-Father Pursuer, armchair traveling in the footsteps of both men, with the younger explorer taking all kinds of personal risks crossing rivers, hitting bumpy roads, and photographing buildings, factories, and animals from precarious or dangerous aerial angles (if not hunting).[3] Leopold annexed the Congo with Stanley as his assistant; Elisofon appropriated Stanley.

Elisofon's admiration for Stanley was not only lifelong, it was, as I have mentioned a number of times already, total and incontestable, taking in not only Stanley's self-centered conclusiveness, enticing visual imaginary, and journalese curtness (talents that Elisofon himself for better and worse sized up to) but also Stanley's rough colonial logistics in opening up "Africa for the world," without Elisofon acknowledging, or choosing not to, the paranoid barbarity of Stanley's entrepreneurship as King Leopold's traveling agent. The samples that Elisofon selected for his Literary Africa travel in 1959 and the 1961 *LIFE* "savage" essay from Stanley's 999-day-long search for the course of the Congo River to its mouth (1879–1884) and from the second, the west to the east journey (1887–1889), were codified along the lines of goading the reader/viewer to stop at his observations of the simulacra. The stimulants could be a kinglike cloud hiding Rwenzori, tapestries of mosses and lichens covering the mountain slopes, a Pwoom Itok mask, an African dress, or a riverside bustle.

Up to this period, Stanley beguiled many other travelers and journalists in Africa, not only the visual copyist Elisofon. One of them was his partner from ABC's *Africa* trekking years, Blaine Littell, who had written a travelogue about Stanley only four years earlier principally along the same "stragglelogue" concept as Elisofon and the *National Geographic* planned to do, but with a more focused lens.[4] Littell's objective, he explained, was a whim. "Following Stanley within a fixed period of time would give me a goal to shoot for, a sense of mission," such as when children play a game following a line that takes them through hedges, out along rooftops, and into bathroom windows. So, he continued, if "Stanley had mapped the contours of lakes, measured the heights of mountains and traced the rivers [exactly as Elisofon would do]," he, contrarily, would map "the terrain features of the 'African personality.'"[5] But like Ardrey, Littell landed in a similar cul-de-sac. On the last page of his book, he writes: "I cannot continue my search for answers by following the African into the bush. . . . Of the African mind and personality, of the African heart and soul, I know no more now than when I started. . . . There is a secret in the African bush. I have not found it" (292–93). Ardrey's commiseration, we remember, landed in the South African street as an urban pitiful metaphor for division and segregation. Littell's three-month pilgrimage in Stanley's footsteps in the 1964 Congo rebel area, with a rifle on his back, was first of all a misfortunate homage to himself, identified, as he was en route, like a despairing mercenary longing for home. His book proved to have little to do with Stanley who—in contrast to him—had "found it." His nineteen quotes from *Through the Dark Continent*, in addition to the slick title of the book, served as no more than lifeless epiphanies and commercial riders. Stanley was popular in the Cold War West, but Littell did not know what to do with him. Stanley remained ambiguous, and five years later, writing about him in his (and Eric Robins's) *Africa: Images and Realities*, Littell described him as an arduous explorer, a subtle colonial broker who had been foresighted enough to buttress Leopold's claim to territory "with a sheaf of treaties arranged with Congo chieftains" that he had acquired long before Leopold hired him.[6] He reflected: "the footprints of the colonial explorers who trod yesterday's 'Dark Continent' . . . have grown faint in the African dust" (Littell and Robins 1971, 15). He contravened himself or he debunked, telling the world that "I trod them and that is enough." But Littell's hopeful wish was definitely out of keeping with Elisofon's.

Elisofon's dream of producing a book about Stanley did not lack either aspirational insight or logistical authority. He had all that a magazine such as the *National Geographic* might look for in an informed associate and photographer. He had traveled in the Congo four times since 1947, and what was even more salutary for the coverage were Elisofon's close contacts with both the Mobutu regime and the agents of the United States Information Agency's (USIA) propaganda efforts. In December 1969, Elisofon made it happen. The picture editor of the *National Geographic*, David H. McCuen, and Elisofon agreed on initiating a photographic tour that would land, they planned, in an Africa book alternatively called "In the Footsteps of Stanley" or "Stanley and the Congo," with Stanley as its fixed star and the Congo River and Mobutu as its tributaries.[7] Conrad's *Heart of Darkness* was the book fantasy's generic subtitle and Mobutu, as god and fetish, its Kurtz. Along the *National Geographic* "Stanley route" Elisofon kept the two iconic Western texts close at hand, consulting them for directions and emulative quotes. This is how he anticipated his shooting in a letter to the *National Geographic* staff:

> There is bound to be some repetition [in the shooting], but I have done my best to touch on as much as we can illustrate Stanley's difficulties in opening the Congo as well as to give the reader the greatest possible participation in this extraordinary adventure as well as subject material which will make a contribution to the information about Africa.[8]

We notice three objectives that Elisofon had in mind for his travels: one of a more general nature of improving the reader's knowledge of Africa, and the two others celebrating unequivocally Stanley, the bold adventurer and explorer. He was not what Mayer calls him: "a true-blood adventurer [who] set the basis for Leopold's international campaign, which led to diplomatic recognition for a system of colonial rule that would be characterized by previously unknown methods of exploitation and cruelty" (163). Such notions were foreign to Elisofon and his colleagues. Stanley's narrative of invoking stereotypes portraying African "tribes" in terms of the exotic racialized Other[9] were also Elisofon's, down to his paranoid photographing of hairstyles, facial markings, and tattoos. He admired Stanley for his intrepidity, copied the aesthetics of his expressiveness, and, again, turned a blind eye to his murderous descent into the Congo. But most of all he admired himself for doing just this.

> Hopefully, we will capture the mood of Stanley's adventures with photos of huge dugout canoes manned by Congo tribesmen, primitive villages along the river, the dense rain forest, the magnificent falls, and the abundant wildlife. We also want to look at the modern cities and the industry that supports them; at Africans who are becoming westernized and at those who are not: in short, we want to capture the essence of central Africa in the Congo. . . .
>
> En route, our photographer should constantly be on the lookout for African art and handicrafts. Pottery, basketry, weaving, carving, and ironworks are highly developed. In the southern provinces especially, one can find mask carving, statues, ceremonial axes, etc., in wood, ivory, and bone. (EEPA, W-1, 11.1)

The last segment could be read as a programmatic description of his scrambling for African art that was an ongoing occupation of his ever since he stepped onto African soil in October 1942, when assigned *LIFE* pool photographer with the Atlantic Fleet in North Africa (Morocco and Tunisia).[10] In addition, addressing himself lavishly as "our photographer" and an explorer "on the lookout," he took up the mantle of another Stanley obsessed, with home as a marketplace and an arena for recognition.[11]

Elisofon divided the shooting itinerary (J1) in two geographical zones of operation, Kinshasa (Leopoldville) and Kisangani (Stanleyville), within and between which he traveled in planes that Mobutu provided him with. The Kinshasa zone of his logistical shooting arrangement incorporated the Congo River up to the left bank tributary of the Kasai with the transboundary (Angola) Rio Cwango and the adjoining Kwilu River, the stretch of land connecting the Stanley (Malebo) Pool at Kinshasa and the city of Matadi at the Congo River estuary, and, as if this were not large enough, he added the Katanga Province in the southeast as big as Spain to his Western program. In a single week (18–23 March 1970), he and his camera traversed this enormous landscape, touching on sites that related to his flawed discourse of Stanley's "opening up of Africa." The Kisangani zone covered the DRC parts of the African Great Lakes—Lake Albert, Lake (Edward) Rutanzige, Lake Kivu, Lake Tanganyika, Lake Mweru—their immediate environs, and the "Pygmies" in the northeast and southeast of Ituri Rainforest (an area larger than Ireland). By 28 April he was back in Kinshasa, and his four-week Stanley expedition was at an end, supplemented surreptitiously by a photographic "art" rush through villages between Ilebo and Mweka in the Kuba region in the south-central Congo (places he knew from earlier travels and which he would return to in 1971 and 1972). On 4 May he received a letter from the *National Geographic* that there would be no book on Africa nor on Stanley, either as an attachment to the Congo River or separately. Let's examine in more detail what happened during these four weeks, and why this photographic drudgery ended in naught.

Elisofon's aerial photography was of long standing. His very first *LIFE* job outside the United States, documenting Finland in 1939 preparing for war, employed the panoptical perspective of narrative reduction and centrification. Selecting iconic sites for shooting, although beclouding and forbearing, cannot compete in colonial preponderance with Elisofon's attempt at construing the heroism of Stanley's African travels from the air. That he could use a Grumman 6-seater Widgeon amphibious aircraft belonging to Mobutu (and paid for by the Americans) skyrocketed and eased his photography tremendously (EEPA EENG 08485), but it was as much smudged by the vehicle it depended on and its Western gaze shortsightedness. In his study of panopticism in aerial war photography, Nicholas S. Saunders writes: "Aerial photography (and maps) present a bird' eye view of the world—a view which registers a palimpsest of past activities, a narrative of action and event."[12] What these layers may contain is bound to differ. The non-Western conception of the landscape has more to do with "memory, kinship, physical experience, and social process than with producing drawings or photographs of three dimensional physical spaces on two dimensional media" (Saunders, 33). Elisofon's reproduction of the Stanley geography, we will see, was a colonial blueprint of Selfhood, avoiding, like the narrators of Conrad's *Heart of Darkness*, any recognition of what the "jungle" said about Stanley the "businessman explorer's" achievements and the methods he used. I will organize my analysis of his air and foot tours around Stanley's Africa along the parameters of its uses of waterscapes, the cities, the landscape, technology, architecture, and the "Pygmies."

In a pertinent passage about gendered landscape photography, Lucy L. Lippard notes that women's landscape is "acculturated . . . , a critique of landscape altogether by being more attuned to the local/ personal/ political than to the godlike Big Picture." "If men find the unknown irresistible," she continues, citing Susan Griffin, "many women feel the same way about the known."[13] If we transport this snap argumentation about landscape as an artificial male construction to Elisofon's ideologically overdetermined African topography, the result would be devastatingly definitive. The "known" landscape, the one lacking in sensual pleasure and unworthy of his framing control, did not qualify to be one of the many thousands of Big Pictures that he took of rivers, estuaries, mountains, canyons, valleys, deserts, and their typological and social spin-offs. Gillian Rose's historicizing observation that the "techniques of perspective used to record landscapes were also used to map female nudes . . . the art genre of naked women [emerging] in the same period as did landscape painting,"[14] could have been made with the same bearing on the parallel aesthetics of Elisofon's artwork (mainly flowers and nudes) and his landscape photography. As he himself repeatedly reassured, the "camera is my pencil." The fact that neither Lippard nor Rose was discussing gendered photography in Africa is irrelevant here. The politics of Elisofon's African scenes, their authoring and designing, were impacted by the same gender asymmetries they discuss along the line of colonial and racial decorum. His framing of the landscapes as either sublime-awesome, picturesque-disorderly, or a combination of Western romantic art conventions pushed them outside their natural space-time habitats into a no-man's-land ready for possession.

Elisofon drew a grandiose panorama of Stanley's travelogue, omitting its memory bank, its stories, and the mercantile plans for rapacious grasping. His imagery of air power formulated picturesque postcards of a landscape with a meaning only for "an era in which international associations and global corporations would rule the day, and takeovers would be enacted not by means of military interventions but by contracts and agreements—even if the contracts, like Stanley's treaties [with chiefs], might be enforced, the agreements forged, the mutual benefit made up" (Mayer 2002, 164). Elisofon's first aerial loop encapsulated Stanley's trade stations and his momentous building of the road from Matadi to Kinshasa, taking a series of photographs of the ocean shore and the river ports (Boma, Banana, Matadi), of the Inga (hydroelectric) Dams below the lake called Pool (Stanley) Malebo, part of the Livingstone Falls' series of rapids, and of Zongo Falls and its hydroelectric power plant on the Inkisi River, a south-bank tributary near Kinshasa. His second first zone loop took its ascent from Lubumbashi, the Katanga "capital," in the southeast of the DRC, which he inspected for its industrial assets, city market activity, and the National Museum. He went on photographing still from the air an open pit copper mine and another hydroelectric plant near Kolwezi, on the Lualaba (Cambeshi) River, the major headstream of the Congo, which he followed, passing the city of

Ubundu, up to the spectacular Tschopo River Falls, to disembark his Widgeon at Stanley (Boyoma) Falls (Kisangani), the station that Stanley founded in December 1883. At Boyoma, he would take hundreds of pictures, now on foot, of the Wagenia fisheries. Kisangani was a base for his northeastern trips.

The second zone aerials centered on Virunga National Park, the Aruwimi River, and the Great Lakes. As he did with the Congo port cities, he surveyed meticulously the cities and the waterscapes of the lakes, photographing the city of Bunia at Lake Albert and Beni northwest of Lake Edward–Rutanzige, and hovered over Mount Stanley in the Rwenzori mountain range that is located on the CDR side in between the two lakes. "We climbed part of Rwenzori with Joan in 1951. I am glad that the *National Geographic* team in Uganda is coping with Rwenzori, I had nine days of hell on the mountain," he reminisced (HRC 37.5).[15] Lake Edward–Rutanzige, we were taught, is fed by Rwindi River and empties to the north into Lake Albert via the Semliki River. The Ruzizi River trades water with Lake Kivu and Lake Tanganyika in a north–south direction. Elisofon took us also via air to the cityscape of Kalemie (Albertsville), which we visited in the company of Littell in 1964. Lake Mweru was also pictured. What his patterned topology, created from a height of 500 m, simulated is an attempt by the *National Geographic* and Elisofon to demonstrate where Stanley's confused but determined feet took him, what waters he had to cross in order to see the light. And also to do it with an aesthetic care for the finesse that only skilled aerial shooting can produce.

Virunga National Park, north and northwest of Lake Edward, was his next panoramic target. He scanned large chunks of the park, taking aerials of buffaloes and egrets, a herd of topi antelopes, and white pelicans on the Rwindi plains; shooting segments of the Semliki River at Ishango; and getting glimpses of Rwenzori Mountains and farther north of Mangbetu villages, two of which—Medje and Mongomasi—he had visited on the very first days after his arrival at Isiro (25–27 March) and where he produced at least five hundred photographs. But to collect the Stanley storyline of the Aruwimi River (the extension of the Ituri River), he had to return to the elevated vantage point of "his" Grumman. He was thrilled viewing the cataract area at Yambuya (the base for the Emin Pasha "Relief Expedition"), where (at Panga) Stanley was stopped because of the rapids and had to struggle by land to reach Basoko and the Congo River.[16] The three book engravings of Stanley ascending the Aruwimi to the base served Elisofon as aerial take-offs. The pilot was instructed to navigate the aircraft for the "right" shooting angles. Elevation is a complex position we need to be reminded of. It also "suggests the power to process and understand that which is seen, and it objectifies and interpolates the colonized subject in a way that fixes its identity in relation to the surveyor."[17]

Elisofon's diehard surveying of confluences during these hours over the Congolese water systems departed from a simulative instinct of participation and affiliation with Stanley's systematic and grand slam approach, neglecting its racism. Ever since the 1890s, when the London Aborigines Protection Society condemned the expedition for atrocities, Stanley's reputation has been a shaky one, but superimposed miraculously until, if you like, the very day when the *National Geographic* sent out Elisofon for, it thought to begin with, a technically and visually more advanced reconnaissance. In its preliminaries, it was perhaps the very last homage of Stanley coverage in Western media, here bolstered and apologized for by Cold War pragmatism.

We will now accompany Elisofon on foot in his ongoing quest of Stanley (J1), with his 1959 notebook of literary quotes as his chaperone. From Bukavu on the shores of Lake Kivu, where he had flown from Kisangani, he drove to Goma in a car at the other end of Lake Kivu to check on, as his plan was, the Nyiragonga Virunga Mountain, the active stratovolcano close to the city,[18] and from there he continued via Rindi into the Virunga Park to photograph wildlife. The crater was not of interest this time (it would be at his next trip with the Brachers—J2—in November–December 1970), so he did not stop for it, and went for a massive shooting of buffaloes, elephants, and fish. Stanley, he commented in his notes, lived off game and shot species such as rhinos for food. "There is a wonderful description of a baby rhino in *The Darkest Africa* and I intend to do a rhino in Albert Park [the old name of the park]" (EEPA, W-1, 14). But he did not find any rhinos and decided to embark on his "Pygmy" project instead, again inspired by his master:

> The pygmies who have never been successfully photographed in color. The Ituri forest where they live is one of the darkest and gloomiest places in the world. . . . Stanley took several pygmies with him during the Emin Pasha expedition. (EEPA, W-1, 14; HRC 37.15)

Elisofon was referring to and authorizing Stanley's description of a "Pygmy" brought to him as part of a pillaging raid for food in the farms in their frantic search for the beleaguered and dehumanized "rear column." Stanley speaks:

> Not one London editor could guess the feelings with which I regarded this manikin from the solitudes of the vast central African forest. To me he was far more venerable than the Memnonium of Thebes. That little body of his represented the oldest types of primeval man, descended from the outcasts of the earliest ages, the Ishmaels of the primitive race, forever shunning the haunts of the workers, deprived of the joy and delight of the home hearth, eternally exiled by their vice, to live the life of human beasts in morass and fen.[19]

In a commentary on this passage with a bearing on Elisofon's "ethnographic" mission of improving the conventional portrait of a "Pygmy" by adding color to the classification, Michel Tavel Clarke notes:

> The denial of coevalness which allows Stanley to construct the Pygmy as primeval man is of course related to evolutionary models of progress but it also involves an affective engagement with ideas of history, memory and recognition.[20]

Elisofon was not overwhelmed by any feelings seeing the Mbuti, in contrast to Stanley. It was the body—its signatures, movements, and eroticism—that occupied him. What moved him was the allusion of the ethnographer's objectivity, hence his competitive ambition also to be the first to use color for registering clarity. It was not merely a traveler's subjectivity. The Mbuti, the Mangbetu, and the six Kuba villages he visited a couple of weeks later were positioned along the parameters of what Clarke calls a post-Darwinian scientific racism that centers on deviance and Otherness, embodying (also in Clarke's words) a shift from a "theological regard for the deviant body to the contemporary pathological or teratological view." Elisofon drove to Kanya-Bayonga and continued to a village near Beni, on the edge of the Ituri forest, where he could stay for a day or less photographing Mbuti people, classified, both then and now, as "Pygmy, hunter-gatherers," a group representing half of the molested Okapi Wildlife Reserve (twenty thousand inhabitants).[21] He focused on men hunting (EEPA EECL 10028), men dancing, and a nude portrait of a young woman with facial paint, choreographed to pose from the front and both sides while the camera sneaked around her bare torso. Fear, abjection, and disassociation characterize ordinarily, as here, the men and the women who met Elisofon's consuming camera. The "Pygmies at the edge of the forest near Beni," as one caption reads, protested in the only way they could—by being absent in front of the camera (EEPA EECL 5474). "Will try for better pygmies in Bunia" (200 km north of Beni) (HRC 37.15, 7), he complained in his notebook. But what is a "better pygmy"?[22] He found what he wanted among the Mangbetu (not in Bunia), southwest (80 km) of the northeastern city of Isiro.

Among the Mangbetu there were people, he expected, "who still bind children's' heads to elongate them, and where the women wear decorated small boards to preserve the modesty of their derrières. The houses are colorful too" (HRC 27.15). His stay with two separate groups of villagers in Medje and Mongomasi was more rewarding—at least from his point of view. But not fully. "Not much of their old culture remains," was his reflection, observing that "heads are no longer bound [the practice was outlawed by the Belgians] [and] houses are no longer painted in interesting patterns." So "whatever was left I tried to capture in these few days," he muttered. Assisted by a loyal military entourage, credited as he was by Mobutu, the chiefs of the two villages, Christopher Mogendo of Medje and Victor Teingu of Mongomasi, had no other choice than to mobilize ad hoc their musicians, artists, and dancers to execute what was required from them. Elisofon was absolute and abrupt: "I insisted on that." Mogendo's court orchestra musicians had to dress up and collect their talking drums and rattle; the handful of women dancers had to smarten up in barkcloth garments ("nogetwe"); and the Medje woodcarver and the blacksmith set out to work. The Medje marketplace was transformed by the Armée Nationale Congolaise (ANC), and the American guest was taken into a Victorian wonderland stage whose major object/subject was Mbombio, chief Mogendo's "principal wife" (as the EEPA curators register her). She was subjected to a photographic onrush (in 126 documents) acquiescing to two disparaging roles of what Veit Erlmann calls "spectatorial lust."[23] One such chore was sitting perseveringly for the two days it lasted while an elderly woman did her hair-do, creating an exotic, high-status, and Mobutu-ordered "funnel-shaped coiffure" and posing from different angles when the work was done (EEPA EECL 2986). Elisofon's animation for this "Pygmy" coup was deepened by the fact that the hairdresser had an elongated skull ("lipombo"). One of the photos of the couple he had cropped to include only the woman's skull. The nameless woman had been collected from a neighboring village in their rented Ford pick-up truck. Both Mbombio and her husband in addition had to dress up for the performative dance, with the men wearing basketry hats and the few women, bare-breasted, the "negbe" and the "nogetwe," clothing that Elisofon found rousing.[24] Mbombio, photographed in a dance posture in close-ups from the side, exudes humiliation, anger, and defiance (EEPA EECL 5662).[25] To finish the days with "Africans on stage," Elisofon ran into a final successful photographic session. "I . . . noticed some well-carved stools and made some pictures of a man making one [a stool called 'Nobala']." He had eventually come across a "better pygmy," a man safeguarding culture. "Whenever I noticed a long head among these people, I tried to use it in a picture," he writes home (HRC 37.15). After having taken pictures of Victor Teingu's (in Mongomasi) three younger wives (one of them was Sabina Abirangomo) and a group picture of half the family—thirty-six wives and twenty-five children—Elisofon's meeting with Teingu turned out be short, effective, and one-dimensional. It was all about the chief, who not only manifested patriarchal cupidity and power of an impressive kind but also a talent for dancing to the joy of Elisofon's camera and loyalty to the country's landlord and despot. Teingu then switched costumes and sat for a portraiture personifying the double-edged chief wearing the national costume to which were stitched three medals, a badge cheering Movement Populaire de la Revolution (MPR); the only political party in the country, a church medal, and an insignia of his status as village "member" of the Congolese government (EEPA EECL 2242).[26]

The Stanley documentary was completed. Elisofon could pride himself on having pointed at the sites through his camera that were paramount for Stanley's resolutions, such as his proving that the Ruzizi River flowed into Lake Tanganyika and was not the source of the Nile, that he had discovered the Congo by sailing it and thereby opening the interior for European trade, that his remarkable entrepreneurship of building the road between Matadi and Kinshasa was revolutionary, and that he had discovered the "Mountains of the Moon" and Lake Edward. Second, Elisofon, with as much smugness, pointed to the heritage of Stanley, the sure-enough results of his explorations: modern Africa, modern CDR. And third, the tracking after the "mood of Stanley's adventures" had resulted in photos of "primitive" villages along the rivers, dense rainforest, magnificent falls and rapids, abundant wildlife, Wagenia fishermen, and exotic "Pygmies."

Upon Elisofon's landing in Kinshasa at the end of April, the *National Geographic* editors had changed their minds: they would not do a book on Africa, there would be no chapter on the Congo, and no chapter on Stanley (or a mix of the two). Eight weeks' work was, to all appearances, it seemed at least for the *National Geographic*, of no value.[27] What had happened? Let me hypothesize. Elisofon's lack of contextualization or refusal to historicize Stanley, his penchant for aestheticizing Africa, and his unwillingness to question his own presumptions were irksome issues that made any attempt at producing a semiacademic text impossible. This had become clear for the *National Geographic* photo editors in the course of the two months.

Another problematic issue would have been the difficulty to recruit a writer willing to cooperate with Elisofon on producing lengthy prose passages tributary to the photographs (one candidate had already run away). The chances were a hundred to one that they could find such a person, given that the photo material consisted mainly of postcard aerials and retakes of Elisofon's earlier motifs from sites he had visited before. But I think what hurt him, and was the major reason for the abrupt relocation of the agreements, was Elisofon's clinching to the Stanley-Mobutu analogue.

Before I examine Mobutu's role in Elisofon's photography during his last two years in Africa (1970–1972), we will accompany him on a brief off-Stanley's tracks expedition (J1) that he pursued as if he could not stop or rest for a while, the spasmodic traveler he was. Continuing by air to Kananga and from there by car to Mweke and nearby Luebo (Kasaï Occidental Province), he turned up on trodden paths known to him from earlier travels (1947 and 1951). For a few days, he moved in and out of four Kubaland villages in the area, to stop more resolutely in Bungamba (between the Mweka and Luebo). The second part of this trip brought him for the first time in contact with the Pende people and a village close to Gungu in the Kwilu district (Bandunda), where he stayed for a day photographing Minganji masqueraders (EEPA EECL 4353), the "mungonge" ceremony, and Pende men with filed teeth. Again, his photographic offensive was hectic (508 documents).

Of course, the southwestern expedition provided for its own objectives. In Kananga, as part of his Mobutu observance, Elisofon photographed military training at École Formation d'officiers. The other sessions come very close to contemporary visual anthropological fieldwork in Elisofon's recalibrating closeness and distance with different lenses and angles. Through this technique he could produce varying close-up perspectives of the object, of, say, the details of the Minganji mask or of the Kuba warrior's costume (performing at the state visit of the Nyim Kot a Mbweeky III at Bungamba) and at a distance frame group photos of the musicians, the dancers, and the warriors. These theatricals, as well as the ones we witnessed southwest of Isiro, among the "Pygmies," were choreographed (and paid). They served the guest (Elisofon) uniquely and under the surveillance of members of his state entourage. This meant absolute subservience on the part of the entertainers and the audience. Elisofon's close-up of an individual titled warrior wearing "the elaborate headdress" was a preposterous photographic copy of the Lega "savage man" published on the front page of the *LIFE* magazine edition of "The Storied World of Africa"; here a Kuba man was acting out the white man's stereotype on the white man's bidding (EEPA

EECL 5260). The group photos of Nyim Kot a Mbweeky III's female entourage (J2) and of his spectacular "warriors" (J1), similar to the framed photos he took of his predecessor's "harem of wives" in 1947 and more recently of the more modern Victor Teingu's family at Mongomasi, were part of Elisofon's collections of the anomalous and gross. The photo of Pende men with filed teeth would fit this category as well.

The next subject, a Bungamba woman in the crowd, was picked out by the photographer for the scarifications on her stomach. Elisofon has cropped the upper part of one of the two close-up photographs, the unwanted section of her body, her head, to change its aspect ratio, in this way accentuating the body modification and neutralizing her. In the second medium close-up photo of the same woman we are invited to see her stomach, torso, and face, including the faces of a few of the villagers surrounding her (EEPA EENG 09006, EEPA EENG 08607). What we see is embodied anger, contempt, humiliation, and resistance both from the woman and the others. "Who gives you the right?" they seem to be thinking. The photographing of this woman, the villagers, and Mbombio, the harnessed wife in Medje village, is a representative example of Elisofon's routines in Africa of simply taking it for granted that it was all right to approach women's body parts, motivated and legitimized by his voyeuristic-racial gaze in the name of pseudoscientific or liberal curiosity.

## Mobutu, Elisofon, and the *National Geographic*, 1970 and 1972

Reading Michela Wrong's book *In the Footsteps of Mr. Kurtz* and a passage like the one that follows, the first question that started nagging me was where complicity starts and if it ever ends:

> No man is a caricature, no individual can alone bear responsibility for a nation's collapse. The disaster Zaire became, the dull political acquiescence of its people, had its roots in a history of extraordinary outside interference, as basic in motivation as it was elevated in rhetoric. The momentum behind Zaire's free-fall was generated not by one man [Mobutu] but thousands of compliant collaborators at home and abroad. (11–12)

She draws a constructionist axis that combines Stanley, Leopold, the Congo Free State, Force Publique, Mobutu, the Cold War, and the Central Intelligence Agency

(CIA) (to which list one could add Swedish missionaries during Leopold in the Congo delta) as an operational perpetrators' family, but, more remonstratively, she alludes to and puts the blame on a far more diagnostic and individualized category that she calls "compliant collaborators." So, since my first question cannot be answered in this circumscribed context, my second will best be considered a cautious pondering upon what the interactions of William T. Close (Mobutu's personal American doctor), Elisofon, and President Richard Nixon have meant for the imagining of the people of Congo and what their reciprocate impact on the United States has been? So were the trio collaborators, and the rest of us in the West lame spectators? My discussion next works along that tentative parameter.

Elisofon's talent for finding middlepersons, or rather delegates, to speak in his favor was exceptional, bordering on a dauntless impertinence, that he camouflaged (as the best journalists do) under a rhetoric of knowing all (about Africa) or at least aspiring to know all (about Africa). And in most situations few would resist his boyish frankness; if they hesitated, he listed his accomplishments (true or not), and if this did not work, he picked up one or two of his books, commonly the ones on the Nile and African sculpture. Exactly what happened next?

We are now going back to the first week of his arrival in Kinshasa from New York (J1) when he starting to organize his work, "getting squared away," as he phrased it (letter 29 March 1970 from Isiro; HRC 17.15). His was a formidable success. U.S. ambassador Sheldon Vance, whose friendship with Mobutu culminated in his refusal to transmit negative summaries about the regime to Washington and to recommend the United States sell the jungle rifle M16 to Mobutu, introduced him to unwilling Close, who warmed up after having been acquainted with Elisofon's books.[28] Close promised, Elisofon explains, to show them to Mobutu, and concludes his heroics: "This led to complete co-operation including the use of a Grumman 6-seater Widgeon, an amphibian plane belonging to the President."

Another triumphant stroke was his acquaintance with the Belgian Lt. Col. John Powis de Tenbossche, the president's financial adviser ("l'aide de camp"), who whipped into shape a document signed by the office of the president "commanding the government, army, and others to co-operate with the *National Geographic* project." In addition and along the same governmental goodwill boulevard, he acquired a letter of accreditation from the minister of information, Jean-Jacques Kande, and from another middleperson, M. F. Busschots (Compagnie Cotonnière Congolaise), who in his turn recommended Elisofon, in his capacity as a favored guest of Mobutu, to M. Belina, the director of COMACO ("community market for conservation"), and suggested that the American be provided with every kind of assistance while visiting Isiro and the Mangbetu people (EEPA W-1). I doubt that any journalist, ever, has been so rigorously and coercively embedded in a state system than Elisofon was for the two years it lasted, while he reciprocally profited from a number of privileges concerning logistics (access to a private airplane; access to SODEMAC's services [a governmental aircraft company that served the army]; radio network services), MPR leaders, and local contact persons (soldiers, government administrators) to help him with the travel arrangements and organize the entertainment.

The Congolese whom he encountered were those whom the chiefs or the USIA had drafted to perform for him—on orders—both professional and semi-professional artists, dancers, singers, and persons with specific skills such as the Wagenia fishermen at Stanley Falls. They were less of a problem—now. Elisofon remembered: "When I tried to do the Wagenia in 1959, they demanded exorbitant fees—and held me up for more by stopping right in the middle of my take." Now, the circumstances being different, he hoped "to avoid this by having an official with me." This is genuine power-talk. A second group he met were individuals whom he rushed at to make what he called candid pictures and who did not live up to his expectations, which were to ignore the searching camera. Instead, as "soon as you arrive people either leave or stop what they are doing normally" and trying to "arrange them usually result in posed-looking pictures" (letter 29 March 1970, HRC 37.15). What Elisofon describes indirectly are communities and people living in a police state, hounded by fear and disgrace. The individuals he photographed, like the two women I discussed who expressed raw body language of unwelcoming defiance (Elisofon stopped the retakes), like the performers who formatted a posed conscience of control, like the Mbuti forest dancers and the Kuba warriors, and like those who withdrew into what Elisofon discreditably called posing, while making a travesty of the cameraman's pretensions, were all part of a vocabulary belonging to communality under siege. Mobutu's and Elisofon's views on "authenticity," "Mobutism" ("Authenticité" or "Zairianisation") and "traditional authentic" were idealistic and political false fronts of delusion and power.

Elisofon's photographing in the DRC was embedded (for lack of a better term) in the sense that it conceded both to Mobutu's military control and Washington's oversight. The American supervision was staged by the intensive and active presence of the Kinshasa embassy in Elisofon's doings and his close contact with Frank Shakespeare, the "zealous anti-communist"[29] and director of the USIA. A couple of weeks before Mobutu, accompanied by his doctor, met Nixon at the White House, the director of Central Intelligence Agency declared as follows:

> Much of the credit for the Congo's recovery and relative stability in recent years is due to Mobutu. He has managed to concentrate authority in his own hands and remove from power everyone [but how?] who could have posed a threat to his control.[30]

Elisofon could without blushing crown himself "Lord of Photography." The credentials and the documents that the Mobutu regime showered over him opened up not only the roads to his selected sites but also made the passages smooth and fast,[31] which his daughter Elin has corroborated on several occasions.[32]

Thus far we have studied Elisofon's March–April docu-photography that focused on the generalities of the "Congo-Stanley" book and not the state accessories of Mobutu that Elisofon reached by air only. He took pictures of the commander in chief's "model farm" (Nsele), his mansion, his steamer, and the guest quarters for international gatherings (the former multimillion dollar "OAU Village" built for the summit of 1967) on Mont Ngaliema (Mount Stanley). The footage he made before he left for Mali was a portrait of Andre Mambu, a first-year cadet at the military training center in Kananga (EEPA EECL 12684), and the one hundred pictures he took of the soldiers in simulated smoky combat training. With the same intensity he documented female paratroopers trained by an Israeli mission outside Kinshasa and was permitted—another remarkable privilege bequeathed an American journalist—to take pictures from the cargo aircraft cockpit of soldiers jumping using round parachutes.[33]

On 18 June King Baudouin and Queen Fabiola paid a visit to Mobutu. They exchanged rhetorical flatteries or flat hypocrisies, each of them blowing their horn about the legacy of Leopold, the king humbugging: "au-delà des souvenirs, ce qui demeure, c'est une grande œuvre, qui se poursuit aujourd'hui dans des circonstances nouvelles" and Mobutu nodding regally.[34] The White House transcribed a conversation on 4 August, a couple of months later, between Nixon, Henry Kissinger, and Mobutu dealing with political facts of a kind, and not gentlemanly screwed-up African history. It concerned the threats of Communism, and more precisely Nixon and Mobutu fretting about "infiltration" of students, both entering the Congo and leaving, and Mobutu craving more military aid.[35] Mobutu was accompanied by William Close and his wife, Tine, who sat next to Donald Rumsfeld during Mobutu's official party at the White House, he remembered, as he did the noisy "interaction between Mobutu and these captains of industry seeking American investment in the Congo for their own gain."[36] The historians are right. This was the year (1970) that marked the apex of Mobutu's legitimacy and power. For America, he was the best option there was in his role as a bulwark against Communism in Africa, a lesser evil it was thought than Soviet-style dictatorship. The American newspapers (most of them) followed suit.

As Mobutu and his family (with the Closes) toured Disneyland, Hollywood, and Beverly Hills, relaxing from politics, Elisofon was resting after the four months of work in Africa in his summerhouse on the island of Vinalhaven, writing a number of letters discussing the logistics and the desiderata for his next travels to Africa, which was a return to the Mobutu-inherited enclave. In a letter to Close (27 July 1970) he explained: "I am sorry that I missed King Baudouin's visit to the Congo, but I felt that the fifth anniversary of President Mobutu should be included in my book I am planning to do on the Congo," adding that his hope was that an airplane would be available for him and that "local authorities" were solicited to assist the film team's (*BAH*) travels to and fro. A couple of months later, in another letter (19 September) to Close, he wrote that the *National Geographic* had given him permission to do a portfolio of pictures for Mobutu, querying whether he could assist him to select the best of them, when he visited in Kinshasa at the end of October for the Mobutu five-year anniversary. In a third letter (19 September 1970), he detailed that his needs for air transportation were: to Goma for filming in Albert Park, to Kisangati for the Wagenia, to Paulis (today Isiro) for the Mangbetu, to Port Francqui (today Ilebo) for the Bakuba, to Gungu for the Bapende (the Pende), and to Kasongo-Lunda (in Bandunda) for the Bayaka ("Pygmies"), and he wrapped up by fishing for an invitation to "catch rides with the Sodemac" and use "your Beachcraft" (the president's amphibious vehicle). He knew what he wanted, and went for it, without stuttering (EEPA W-1.19).

On 19 January 1972 (J4), Elisofon was back in the Kinshasa, to set in motion his second assignment for the *National Geographic* Film, this time with the main focus on the recent achievements of the DRC in the economic and social spheres that would encapsulate industry, communications, education, public health, and public welfare. The country's beauty, natural resources, and rich cultural heritage, reflected in sculpture and handicrafts, in music and dance, would be written about in depth and authenticated with Elisofon's best photographs. The *National Geographic* writer Peter T. White,[37] a member of the magazine's Foreign Editorial staff, and Elisofon had agreed on a project description for their work. In a letter (29 November 1971) to His Excellency Dominique Sakombi, Mobutu's young minister of information and engineer of the Mobutu personality cult, they emphasized that the prospected story would be read by at least 7,250,000 readers (an alluring argument for a personality cult expert). The emphasis, White and Elisofon wrote, was on

> the most dynamic aspects of modern life in Zaire. We hope to focus on outstanding manifestations of economic development. On the hydroelectric project at Inga and on light industry. On the new automobile assembly plants and the new tire factory. On the progress of the national airline. On new achievements in the mining industry in Katanga. And on the remarkable work of the [diamond] Mining Company of Bakwanga [in Kasai-Oriental Province in south-central DRC]. I daresay that few among our many millions of readers are aware of the enormous utility of boart, and of your country's role in its production; for a vivid description of this activity, we hope to see the technical advances at Disele. . . . In the course of our travels we shall seek to meet some of your country's outstanding personalities. Most important among these . . . will be His Excellency Joseph Désiré Mobuto, President of the Republic of Zaire, who has played such a prominent part in making Zaire what it is today. Mr. Elisofon and I hope to be able to spend a part of a day with the President and his family, on his model farm as well as at his residence on Mount Stanley. (HRC 37.16; EEPA W-1; see a draft of Elisofon's letter to Ursula Mahoney and William Holden (?), *National Geographic*, 28 March 1971)

But White did not turn up in Kinshasa. He had been replaced for unknown reasons by another *National Geographic* writer, John J. Putnam, and without Elisofon's knowledge, a laxness that annoyed him. This turnabout resulted in a letter to Putnam (on 6 January) where he simply stated what he planned to do, as there was no time or place for consultations of the kind he had had with White. In other words, Putnam had to acculturate his Congo-Zaire story along Elisofon's visual perspectivity, and he'd better do so, was the photographer's prenotice. The letter put on ice what he would do: go to Bakuba to "complete what I have missed of [Mushenge] village life," do pics of a 'Pygmy' family [the Mbuti], of rare [white] rhinos, of "antediluvian animals" such as the okapi, of the volcano Mount Nyiragongo surrounding Lake Kivu, and add to his Congo River life album. On modern Congo, he would focus on Kinshasa with its busy streets, outdoor cafés, art market, fountains, flags, and the residence of Mobutu, and cover "a well-off government official and his family" (which was to be former Congolese government minister Paul Mushiete Mahema Mpala with his family) and document education at Université Lovanium and the Beaux arts school. Industry would be represented by the Goodyear tire plant, the huge Lubumbashi copper smelter, and the process of pouring molten metal diamonds "that had never been photographed." And finally he would photograph the Inga dam, the hydroelectric dam on the Zaire River at Inga Falls, and on the top of everything, as it sounds, do a portrait of "Dr William Close an American Mobuto's private doctor."[38] For better or worse, there were to be no portrait-makings of either Mobutu or Close.[39]

More than a decade had passed since the photographic *LIFE* essay "The Hopeful Launching of Proud and Free Nigeria" appeared, but juxtaposed with the *National Geographic*'s on the Congo, both engineered by Elisofon, the time gap is invisible. It is as if nothing had happened, and what had happened was foreseeable, controlled, scheduled even. It was Africa as a still-life painting, a replica of one of Elisofon's thousands of photographs of gaping rhinos or profiled torsos of African women. Nigeria and the DRC were changing; *LIFE*, *National Geographic*, and Elisofon were not. The Nigeria article, we saw, was formulated within the rhetorical discourse of contrasts of the old–the new, the malleable–the absolute, the plural–the conclusive, simple categorizations that soak the irrevocable doctrines and practices of the Abrahamic monotheistic religions. "Yesterday's Congo, Today's Zaire," we will see, speaks the same imperious language, now with two interactive agents at its head (see appendix).

Putnam and Elisofon, although widely at odds about its presentation, were in agreement upon the basic theses of the article. The first one was the overly simplified conjecture that the Congolese "yesterday" included unqualified slaving, intermittent warfare, colonial rule, and half a decade (1960) of "chaos and slaughter," and that the "today," antithetically, was all peace and stability, duality of narration that also the *National Geographic* practiced (Langford and Langford 2011, 42). Each side neglected any references, ancillaries, even the tiniest dependent clause, to African voices telling alternative stories, such as that of Patrice Lumumba. The second premise outlined, with as much sweetening of the Stanley–Leopold II–Mobutu saga that terminated, as sagas do, in a bonanza, a "huge and varied treasury of minerals . . . copper, tin, zinc, and the world's largest reserves of cobalt and industrial diamonds" (407). The third contained the magazine's evangelizing pamphleteering: keep Mobutu warm and alive so you can go and get it, Zaire's natural wealth is waiting for capitalism, and American industrialists. Mobutu's anti-Communism, the magazine innuendo hinted, postulated the shipping out of both American military aid and Western civilization. The Nigerian *LIFE* essay concluded with the same ideological overtures, only that the alleged postcolonial consumers of "new" industrial Nigeria were Europeans.

Putnam-Elisofon's Congo/Zaire travelogue was divided into ten segments, each in its genre a minitravelogue that can be organized along the parameters of temporality as codes of both experience and concept. This is how the then-now experience challenged Putnam right from the beginning of his travels:

> I decided, before searching for the future, to journey into the interior to learn something of the past. And so I boarded a plane for Mai Ndombe, formerly Lake Leopold II. . . . There, I was told the lives of the people are guided both by the government and by the god of the lake—and the present is still the past. (401)

Reading Conrad's novella as a guide book, as it seems, and citing here the canonical passage with Marlowe "travelling back to the earliest beginnings of the world" engulfing in the shibboleth "I had no time," Putnam embarked on the same imaginary trip into Conrad's double-edged "interior" to find that the people whom he encountered at Inongo on the lake had attuned their memory-bound conventions to Mobutu's despotic rules of the day. That was modernity for them, not Putnam's and Elisofon's peregrine project of keeping the time-geographies apart.

> Time has dimmed the memory of slave caravans, but Mobutu's powerful one-party system must deal with other problems created during a convulsive past. Zaire's diverse peoples . . . have only recently come to accept the concept of nationalism. Mobutu's determined administration seeks to forge Zaire into a strong, modern, and economically sound nation. (401, caption for a picture of "Shackles that once bound Congolese slaves")

Putnam's concept of a future for the Congo/Zaire as emptied of its shackled past dimmed his cognizance of what was taking place in the country while he was talking/writing. Traveling upstream on the steamer *Col. Ebeya* for Kisangani, he took pictures of the riverside activities, three of which were published, none of which met either the technical or the aesthetic qualities of Elisofon's pictures of the same trip, which he had done a couple of times already. Also Elisofon would travel on the same boat but in the opposite direction between 15 and 23 March taking a couple thousand pictures of women's hairstyles, people bargaining on the deck and the deck-side, the making of dugout canoes in the river villages, and whatever he considered either temptingly bizarre or so recognizable and well known that it provoked a modifying retake. The two-page Congo River spread (414–15) contained the three Putnam photos (an upper part double-page spread of pirogue traffic and two single-page touristy shots of life on the deck replaced Elisofon's picture of the steamer at anchor). To be upstaged as a prime photographer of the Congo River by an amateur must have been a shock, and understood as a purposefully insulting move. But now back to Putnam's river passage with its Conradian allusions. Nighttime Africa, now even darker, took hold of him.

> At night only the beams of the *Col. Ebeya's* two great searchlights cut the darkness, sweeping this way and that, now catching an island, now the river—its surface dotted with clumps of water hyacinths that seemed to race towards us. (410)

The searchlights penetrating the dead of night could not prevent the unknown agitating him, to the point of the hyacinths whizzing toward the bewildered journalist. A menace it was. In Kisangani, as if absorbed by another cautionary tale than Conrad's hallucinations, he met Dr. Alexander Barlowatz, who told him about the 1964 Eastern Rebellion that had plagued the city and the "magic water" the soldiers and the rebels were using to protect themselves from the enemies' bullets. The "winds of freedom buffeted all Africa at gale force," pondered Putnam as a deduction translating the human pursuance of freedom into the unintentional brutal power of nature (410). The accompanying two-page photo spread to illustrate Putnam's epiphany is the photo of the Belgian doctor examining a child and a second of another doctor performing a hernia operation. The theater is the Presbyterian Medical Center at Pulape, and the photos were taken by Elisofon.[40] The third picture, taken by Putnam, represents the negativism of the West-Africa binarism: the Mampuyu Mpesa, a self-ordained "Prophet of God," diagnosing a mother with metal keys. The caption clarifies the ideological thematics of the two pages: "Medicine and witch doctors compete in a land where protein-deficient diets render even measles a major child killer" (417).

Putnam's next territorial escapade into the "interior" took him to the Ituri forest, this time in the company of Elisofon. For the latter, these were familiar paths. Here too Putnam collapsed into the Conradian colonial jargon of Africa as prehistoric earth with prehistoric men, from the "earliest beginnings of the world" (Conrad

[1902] 1994, 33). Putnam "marched into the forest from Epulu [to Eboyo village]" to discover "the last domain of Zaire's pure pygmies, the country's earliest inhabitants." "Their future is uncertain," he prognosticated (419). This is one of the two events where Elisofon's extended photographing of Mbuti net-hunting antelopes, dancing, and celebrating (422) synchronizes with Putnam's minitravelogue of the two days among these people (420–21).[41] Elisofon repeated his photography from April 1970 done in the same village and among the same individuals. In a letter home (Isiro, February 1972), Elisofon wrote:

> The Mangbetu are one of the oldest kingdoms in the Congo, along with the Bakuba and Bakongo. They are called the "long heads" because they used to bind the heads of their children to elongate them. The form of the head is very beautiful, like a Modigliani painting. I photographed several people who still have these long heads. These pictures will fulfill the National Geographic's request to add some everyday pictures to my previous take.[42]

Elisofon's photo taken in March 1970, near Gungu, of Pende men who, the caption reads, "seemingly skewer their cheeks with thorny sticks and arrows [which] they remove [after a brief dance and] then return to the clearing—mysteriously free of wounds and scars," wound up, as it were, the jungle miracle world of the Congo.[43]

Putnam's last trip into the "interior" was by car from Kinshasa to Kasango Lunda (in southwestern Kwango), picked for its backwardness and lassitude. "It is a poor and isolated region, lacking development and still bound by ancient custom," he explained, a perfect target for authenticity scavengers. Here he encountered Kiamfu (king) Panzu Nzama Fumukulu, who held royal sway over forty thousand square miles and some four hundred thousand Yakas and, at Putnam's prodding, cast a tailor-made spotlight on his twenty wives and seventy children. The Kiamfu's son had been seized by "development," carrying, Putnam noticed, a "transistor radio to hear the day's soccer game in Kinshasa" (429, 432). To orchestrate the extravaganza of the polygamous African family, the magazine chose a double-spread picture of Mangbetu chief Teingu and his thirty-six wives and twenty-five children (426–27), a photo that Elisofon, we saw, took in spring 1970 (EEPA EECL 2242). The fact that thousands of kilometers and two years separated the two sites and cultures of Kasango Lunda and the Mangbetu village of Mongomasi had no real importance; their positioning as mathematical nomenclatures of disparagement, absurdity, and procrastination did. Elisofon's three photos of former government minister Paul Mushiete Mahema Mpale in Kinshasa, and his Belgian wife and three children, placed suitably on the magazine's next two pages, were barefaced signs of Western-infested normalcy that Elisofon's caption checked off: "The family enjoys the luxuries of a new home and swimming pool, and riding at a nearby club" (428–29) (EEPA EECL 2416). Conversion or change—religious, ethical, and cultural—remained fundamental risk-takings for the Africans that Putnam and Elisofon either ridiculed or celebrated, only that the stepping-over, however genuine and successful it was, fostered traits of evolutionary stigmas. Seen in the light of the Congo-Zaire magazine's dialectics of dubious equivocation, Elisofon's photo of family members of the Kimbanguist Church in a street in Kinshasa, an anticolonial, Bible-inspired, Mobutiste straw-boss organization, fell into the same trap of the country fostering magicians, witches, healers, and prophets, mixing their fluids senselessly but creatively. Their moral code of foregoing "tobacco, alcohol, and 'licentious' African dances," Elisofon remarked, did not speak in their favor either (*Tribute to Africa* 1974, 9).

Before we leave Putnam's travelogue, we will accompany him and Elisofon on their second joint journalistic session, their visiting the diamond country, the mine Societé Minière de Bakwanga, in the city of Mbuji Mayi (before 1966, Bakwanga, southeast of Kananga) in Kasai-Oriental, and Elisofon on his own also Shaba (now Katanga Province), the land of copper; the Gecamines Shituru refinery in Likasi (between Kolwezi and Lubumbashi); and the open Kamoto copper mine (west of Kolwezi). At least as far as Elisofon was concerned, his photo work of the diamond and copper sites was eager-beaver frenetic in documenting the activities both from the air and on foot. His three photos dominating the two-page spread are out of sync with Putnam's brief and cursory text about the Mbuji Mayi diamond smuggling and the swelling foreign-exchange earnings. Summarily, Putnam's writing about the DRC was geared toward a populist overview of the descent of colonialism, Mobutu's vigorous seizing of the country, the lionization of him in Kinshasa streets and clubs with the "authenticity" campaign in full bloom, and his coquetting with primitivism as a racial agent for oddity and deviation. As regards Elisofon, it was all this, too, but in contrast to Putnam he was also engaged in completing the job he considered to be his national duty as well as that of the *National Geographic*: to provide a dualistic view of the DRC, not a warped one that ignored and minimized the country's riches and potentials. The two Americans were part of the same Cold War media branch, but their approaches differed in emphasis and insight; the two were also out of earshot of each other during the whole commission except for the "Pygmy" visit and the diamond site documentary.

In fact, "Yesterday's Congo, Today's Zaire" was embedded in two narratives and two visuals, the journalist and the photographer fashioning their own individual story versions. Putnam the writer took pictures of the Congo River landscape, village people, a "witch doctor," and portraits of an anonymous Kitombe fisherman and famous songwriter, Luambo Makiadi (who was given a state funeral on 17 October 1989 by Mobutu's government), and Elisofon the photographer, in his turn, produced more than twenty-six word captions, each a far more illustrative abstract of Congolese realities than Putnam's segmented pussycat travelogue. In addition to the photos I have already discussed, Elisofon had republished in his repetitive theme-bound style an aestheticized two-page-spread picture he had taken in 1970 of Wagenia fishermen at the Stanley Falls rapids; made a two-page collage of seven headshots of girls with "hair-raising coiffures";[44] recorded an ensemble of hippos and a solitary elephant at Virunga National Park; and had two of his aerials published, one of Lubumbashi and the other a remarkable photomosaic of the Congo riverscape at Kisangani. The caption under the last picture, "Watery fingers of the Zaire," points to another example of Elisofon's sacrosanct admiration of Stanley's performative travel method:

> In his travels on the river, explorer Stanley found it howling with "the insensate furies of the savageland." Fighting cannibals, hunger, and disease, he became the first to follow the mighty Congo's course. (425)

This was the theme for the Congo book that Elisofon dreamed about writing and which the *National Geographic* had given him an assignment (1970) to write a chapter about, only to pull out in the end without explanation. Elisofon's life, condensed and keyed up, ran out without warning, and the Stanley-Mobutu book that he talked about right up to the very end of it was to remain one of his many unfulfilled dreams.

The only aerial of Kinshasa printed in the magazine article had been taken by Putnam, which might seem provocatively odd, to say the least. Elisofon's elevated album of Kinshasa contains thirteen titles holding about thirty pictures each. They were taken (in 1970 and 1972) from varying altitudes and obtuse angles, each representing different segmented views (urban housing quarters, the downtown area, the city market, Boulevard du 30 juin), important buildings and sites (the

Parliament, Mobutu's mansion and steamer, Hotel Inter-Continental and its guest quarters), and the Kinshasa river port facilities. That none of these hefty scenes, instead of Putnam's bleak postcard simulacrum, was selected to represent the "non-jungle Zaire" side of the project illustrates the conflict that separated the two men. The cleft between them did not originate in ideological disparities about how to configure the Congo, as we have seen. The two shared the basic agenda for shepherding and manipulating it for the American readers, now also bereft of *LIFE*, which had published its last issue on 29 December 1972. As he frankly admitted on a number of occasions, Elisofon worked with energetic patience as a subordinate but would not transact in situations—with anybody—where equilibrium as a work ethic required untold and endless palavers. As a jack-of-all-trades he abided by the rules, was loyal to the regime (colonial and noncolonial), and was equally, or even more, gratified with putting his foot down if the system proscribed it. For these reasons, too, he was unhappy being one of many in the ABC hierarchy shooting in Africa in 1966–1967, and worse so as his title, "Director of Creative Productions," proved to be a commercial fleshing out. In the 1970–1971 *BAH* series production and its five-month filming, his thirst was quenched: he was the boss, the one and only, controlling the camera work of John Smith and Maya and Georges Bracher during the five months of shooting.

Although the outcome of the *National Geographic* Congo documentary resulted in a disorganized and muddled story, it achieved what it was designed to achieve, to praise the metamorphic Cold War route with the American puppet Mobutu in the lead. His Grumman 6 aircraft hovering over his mansion with Elisofon photographing the scene is a perfect Cold War image of their gullible partnership (EEPA EECL 15718). In this sense, the Putnam-Elisofon melodrama did what it was meant to do, misrepresent Africans. The two white men were in the forefront as players in a political farce in which photojournalism had lost its ethical bearings and legitimacy. Whose camera, if any, can tell the truth about Africa?

CHAPTER 8

# The Politics of the *Black African Heritage* Series, 1970–1972

The 1966–1967 ABC documentary *Africa*, this gigantic effort of domesticating another continent by encapsulating it in (mostly) stand-still images and Cold War rhetoric, and in whose production Elisofon played an unsatisfactory role, not up to par in his mind, nonetheless broke ground for his idea to produce a TV film of equal national grandeur that would carry his signature. It would be a work that he was to control from beginning to end, organize the sites and the events for filming in five countries, edit the script, supervise the filming, write the manuscripts, and select and employ the introducers, Julian Bond, Ossie Davis, Maya Angelou, and Gordon Parks.[1] He would do all this, and, in addition, chaperone the postproduction activity, lecture, and give interviews. He would logistically own the oeuvre in the manner only he could. The *Black African Heritage* series for Group W (Westinghouse Broadcasting Company) (*BAH*) adopted the down-home epic approach of the ABC *Africa* story, only its regional locus was minor (West Africa and the Democratic Republic of the Congo) and its focus specific. But these were relative transitions. Elisofon's ownership of *BAH* was contingent on Washington and Richard Nixon as its major promoters.

## The USIA and Elisofon in Africa, 1970–1971

The USIA in Africa was restructured in two major ways. There was an increase from thirty-three posts in thirteen African countries to fifty-five in thirty-three, which involved a more intensive circulation of magazines, books, news pamphlets, exhibits, manuals for teachers, and films about American life and the American lifestyle. But the change was contrapuntal. The fervid attempts at producing cautionary national tales transfused and manipulated information. In the *Boston Globe*'s feature article (9 January 1972), "USIA's Right-wing Bias: Director Frank Shakespeare's Missionary Zeal Is Directed at Stopping Communism," Stanley Karnow (of the *Washington Post*) excoriated the agency for "displaying the good side of the United States to offset the image of poverty, violence, racial tension and other shabbiness in commercial American films and novels." Overseas USIA libraries had been recommended—and this is one example of this—by Shakespeare to purchase books by Barry Goldwater and, in the same vein, paradoxically as it may seem, drop the long blacklisting of Ralph Ellison's *Invisible Man*. The upgrading of Ellison's novel was not the result of reconsideration of its literary values. In Shakespeare's thinking, it was a conservative action to demonstrate domestic progress with regard to racial justice and respect for civil rights, a Cold War gesture to counter Soviet accusations of ongoing oppression of blacks in the United States. Oppression had long been so flagrant that, by the 1970s, doubt remained as to whether mainline liberalism, however enlightening for whites, had much promise for blacks. One way to provoke the white American establishment was, if not wholly to discredit it, to challenge Americans' claim to moral superiority over the Soviet Union. Ushering in Goldwater's *Conscience of a Majority* (1971) and *Invisible Man* for African consumption was an anti-Communist flag-waving presentation of the "good sides" of American life serving the fiction of national unity.[2] So what was there in *BAH* that enthused an unabashed advocate of ultra-conservative beliefs, such as Shakespeare, a man who "wanted to destroy liberals,"[3] to engage in the production of *BAH* and with such an enthusiasm? Let's study the correspondence between Elisofon and the Washington political elite that took place during the first months of the filming in Africa.

On 11 March 1970, a week before Elisofon left for Kinshasa to start photographing for the *National Geographic* book on Africa (J1), he wrote a letter to Shakespeare—with a copy to Assistant Secretary of State for East Asian and Pacific Affairs Marshall Green[4]—where he listed the projects that he was engaged in, highlighting the two CBS Camera Three shows on African sculpture, and—which was his major alert—describing in crisp words his agreement with Westinghouse[5] to shoot in the Congo, Mali, Niger, and Guinea "where black Americans came from and get their cultural heritage." He finished with the plug: "I am becoming more involved in Africa than before" (HRC 44.1). A couple of weeks later Shakespeare circulated Elisofon's schedule for filming to USIA Public Affairs Officers in Kinshasa, Lagos, and Kano (Nigeria), Bamako (Mali), Niamey (Niger), Yaoundé (Cameroon), Cotonou (Benin), and Abidjan (Ivory Coast). The impact of Shakespeare's letter was profound. Elisofon got what he wanted. His specifications would concern everything from assistance with changing schedules; storing film rolls or masks that he had procured for his collection; visa problems for Nigeria; negotiations with dance groups, artists, and artisans; and qualified assistance with local background research. Again, it is difficult to imagine that there was any Western photographer in postwar Africa gratified by such a lordly backing by his country and its African allies. For the six the months of filming, Elisofon was pampered like a touring visiting film star and treated like a state employee, a court photographer, and expert African mask collector, in the service of one of President Nixon's most creative and powerful magicians, Frank Shakespeare.[6]

The USIA Public Affairs Officers whom Elisofon and his first cameraman, John Smith (whom he worked with in Kenya in 1966), met during the six weeks of reconnaissance (J1) for the *BAH* were quick to identify what Elisofon and his partner considered hot and where and how to acquire it, and at what local price. The American embassy or legation officials would direct Elisofon's film team to the cutting-edge within the field of art and culture of the particular territory they represented. As his leads thematically pointed to the already-there, "tribal" groups with specific uncommon rites, masquerade dancers, mask-makers, long-heads, scarified bodies, African leaders, and so forth, his long-standing colonial albums only needed updating and regional touches for them to requalify, now with the thematic of black heritage as a state-sanctioned objective, and not another magazine article. The USIA station missionaries in Abidjan, Bamako, Niamey, Lagos, Ibadan, Kano, Accra, Cotonou, Douala, and Kinshasa had been alerted by Washington and were prepared for Elisofon's arrival.

The material proceedings were straightforward. Here are some insights into his game plan. Besides the information he had culled from conventional sources about the regions that he was visiting and about what they could offer in terms of the "authentic aberrant" and in situ artwork, Elisofon depended on rumors, newspaper cuttings, and his traveler's intuition. "I once saw a photo of men in very short colorful skirts doing [ritual] wrestling and the caption mentioned the Cameroons," he wrote an inquiry to John E. Garner at the American embassy in Yaounde, whose curt answer was that it is not a "popular sport here" but it can be arranged for nothing.[7] He did not go; Elisofon never photographed in the Republic of Cameroon. Similarly and equally ad hoc, the idea cropped up to "film the tribe at Lake Chad [Buduma] (called Boudoumas in the Niger) who make the papyrus canoes and have cattle with huge horns that serve as floats when they swim out to the island pastures."[8] Once in Maiduguri, he could, he suggested, hire or borrow a Land Rover to take him to the site for the Buduma. The answer from the USIA officer was that there was no car for rent, "for any purpose." However, John H. Thompson, the USIA Branch Public Affairs Officer in Kano who had been contacted by John Shellenberger, came up with a brilliant tip. He would make a formal request for the transport to the governor of the North Eastern State, Colonel Musa Usman and to the governor of Kano State, Alhaji Audu Bako, who both were avid USIA film viewers. But Elisofon failed them; he never turned up in Maiduguri (where he took photos, we remember, in 1959, of the building of the railway extension Kuru-Maiduguri).[9] Neither the "ritual wrestlers" in Cameroon nor the Buduma "tribe" at Lake Chad with Kuri cattle bulbous horns and the papyrus reed boats was visited by the high-ranking USIA photographer that Elisofon to all appearances could have been designated. He was more successful with a number of other eye-catching events, two of which I will stay with to further characterize his hectic, demanding style. In a letter to the embassy in Abidjan, typical of this kind question, he wrote:

> I am particularly interested in filming a group of acrobatic dancers who employ little girls in their performance. One of the groups made a sensation during the Dakar Festival. Could you find out exactly where I can film them, how many hours' drive from Abidjan and the approximate cost?[10]

The response from F. Wenston Fenhagen (who had replaced Alpern) was fortuitous, in consonance with the USIA sense of the political import that this outwardly simple request had for both sides. Fenhagen had been in contact with Minister of Tourism J. B. Gbohou, who revealed that the girls were of the "Yacouba tribe" at Zouan-Houien, a village outside Danané (70 km west of Man), that the folklore region par excellence was the Man region (where his home village was located), "particularly in the field of picturesque housing, local dances and sculpture," and that he would personally provide an escort. Fenhagen also enlightened the visitor by intimating that the minister would expect a tip of 5,000 CFA to cover the dance performances, a good offer as the "going rate" was known to be 25,000 CFA. To justify his special arrangements for Elisofon, Gbohou wished to receive from the American a letter with a paragraph about his career as a *LIFE* photographer.[11] Half a year later, the deal was clocked in, the footage taken (also of another tourist trap, the bush expansion bridge at Yacouba on Fenhagen's advice), and Elisofon probably wrote a jubilant letter to match the minister's[12] and to enhance the minister's career.

The two officers in Niamey, Vincent Hovanec and Marilyn P. Johnson, acted on the same tourist-related premises as all the other USIA staff throughout Elisofon's West African cum Congo route 1970–1971. Only that he was not an ordinary lost traveler with a hungry camera. Johnson seconded the proposal that the Elisofon team document the celebration of the tenth anniversary of Independence Day in the capital, organizing and paying (between 300,000 and 150,000 CFA) to the Tuareg men riding dromedary camels and the Djerma horsemen in quilted armor during performances. Hovanec had extended his service during the spring shooting in an exceptional manner that made Elisofon call him the "hero" of his four-month 1970 African trip—a salvo to add to a young man's CV. Elisofon wrote in a letter to Shakespeare: Hovanec traveled

> with me into the edge of the Sahara desert where I wanted to do some preliminary filming [he did not return to them while revisiting Niger in December] of a rare group of Nomads, the Bororos [also called Wodaabe by Elisofon]. We found and lived with them for several days. We ate sardines, slept on the desert sand, worked in a 1400 temperature in the sun, drank boiled water and had a rather rough time. Vince not only proved his durability and eagerness to help, whether it was carrying equipment or directing background action, but he kept his cool throughout. He has a sense of humor and an ability to adjust to extraordinary circumstances which should be of great value to the U.S.I.A.[13]

The meddling or mediation between Elisofon and Africans and Americans was not always happy-go-lucky. In the letters he wrote to the USIA officers (with whom he had worked and often also stayed) upon his return to Maine after the first four months of filming, he apologized for his irritability and tension. He did it as routinely as if the amends were an introductory epistolary phrase. The most problematic case of irritability was his post–May 1970 Nigeria mission. The mishaps of lagging visas and refusal to allow the photographing of Nigerian antiquities dragged at least two USIA men, John Shellenberger in Lagos and Philip Cohen in Ibadan, into Elisofon's world of appeals, exhortations, and hubris. Telegrams and letters were sent to ministers in the two countries pointing out that the project was in jeopardy as were also the Brachers, who were bunking in Abidjan because they were still unwelcome in Nigeria. Elisofon bombarded the Nigerian minister of information, Sam Epelle, with letters—directly and via Shellenberger (HRC 50.1-2). After half a year's procrastination, in February 1971, the visa applications were given the go-ahead and the filming in Yoruba land could start.

Elisofon's struggle with the Antiquities Commission of Nigeria was not a successful one. Seconded by the informal agreement he had procured on the spot, he photographed in the Lagos museum in the spring. It started out well. In a letter to Ekpo P. Eyo, the Nigerian director of the Federal Department of Antiquities (1968–1979) (written on 12 December 1970, but left with the Lagos USIA office for them to route to the addressee), Elisofon decided to apply for "extension of the permission" to include not only the Lagos but also the Benin and Jos museums, reminding Eyo of the check of $100 he had sent him as "a fee for the privilege" and the additional $100 that he was ready to pay for each day of the photography sessions. But the exchange of "tea" stopped here. He did not receive the permission during the time at his disposal, and the consequence was that Elisofon's planned shooting of Nok, Ife, Igbo, and Benin artworks remained undone.[14] Wilbur Petty at the USIA Lagos office, Elisofon assumed, must have got it wrong hearing Eyo explaining to him that "foreign photographers [were] persona non grata with the Antiquities department" and that therefore "Eyo was adamant in his refusal to give permission."[15] Petty, it would prove, quoted Eyo accurately. Meeting Eyo in May at a Harvard conference on African art, Elisofon confronted him about the dismissal and questioned him about the reasons. Eyo told him that he had never received the letter, which was correct, that he only received a phone call from Petty about Elisofon being on his way to Lagos. For, Eyo explained, had the request been submitted to the commission with a list of what objects Elisofon wished to shoot and for what purpose, "the permission would have been given gladly." So Elisofon probed what had happened, who was right? Shellenberger's reply to Elisofon (26 May 1971) was of no help in deciding the moral dilemma (HRC 49.1-2; see also 50.1). Shellenberger admitted, hesitantly but still, that the 12 December letter never was communicated to Eyo. USIA was to be blamed in that sense. Yet something else went awry.

> I talked with Eyo this morning. In contrast to what he told you, he stated that there was *absolutely no certainty* [original emphasis] that your request to photograph would have been approved even if the letter had been received. He added that in his telephone conversation with Wil [Petty], he, Eyo, made no mention of a need for a letter of request and did in fact say that photography by foreigners of Nigerian antiquities was a matter of considerable concern for the Commission (he said to me that a court case is currently pending). Wil apparently assumed Eyo's remarks foreclosed everything.

I have stayed with an episode that might seem trivial. But it casts light on the history of Elisofon's imperious attitudes toward the ethical positioning of himself as a photographer and collector in Africa. Even if permission was granted a few months later, the cumbersome tardiness perhaps demonstrated a dimension of "Africa speaking back."

During the summer, in July, now back from the four months in Africa, having visited the USIA officers in at least ten African countries, on the varying and intersecting commissions for the three agencies of Macmillan (the children's book *Five Faces of Africa*), the *National Geographic* society (chapter on the Congo river; alternatively the book on Stanley), and the West Africa reconnaissance for Westinghouse Television, he wrote only now one of the many synopses, "Focus on Africa," of the *BAH* project. He enclosed this rambling proviso with his letters of thanks to the Public Affairs Officers whom he had met during jaunt 1. The first paragraph reads:

> The origin and cultural heritage of black America is a subject of increasing importance each day. Articles in newspapers and magazines continue to increase and almost every American university has begun courses in African studies. The television media has made some sporadic attempts to cover this vast subject, but many of these can only be described as travelogues. There has been one major exception, the ABC four-hour special in September 1967. Without questioning its worth, it must be pointed out that too much was covered, and that there was no specific focus.[16]

The film, he asserted, will be interactive, "so that they [black Americans] can better understand themselves, [and] we them." This was a topic that the film did not address more than in its promotional rhetoric. His assertion that, in contrast to the ABC special, the structure of the series would be precise, cover less of the continent, and be less totalitarian, was problematic too. Through his frequent commentaries about the differences between the two projects, his and the ABC's, Elisofon unknowingly invited the viewers/readers to focus on the correlations. Those who compared the two would not see any strategic improvements, except that *BAH* did not attempt at devouring the whole of a continent. But it was equally bombastic. The geography, Elisofon explained in the synopsis, would include the coastal zones from where the "black slaves came from to the United States," the Niger basin, the Guinea Coast, and the Congo. The film on the Niger basin was to be a story about the variety of peoples clinging to the river bank, from the northern part of Guinea, through Mali, touching on the Sahara, and down through Nigeria to the sea. The presentation of the Congo was buried in the platitudes and puzzling assumptions that we are all familiar with.[17] The film, called *Africa's Gift*, done in Africa and in the United States, was to examine the "effect Africa has had on the Western world" from within the three fields of painting, music, and dance. At this point he was not aware that *Africa's Gift* would immerse the three other films, making *BAH* a documentation about the scramble for art in Africa and a propaganda film for the Museum of African Art.

Another outline called "In search of soul" began with this self-homage:

> I know where the heart of this subject beats. I have made seven expeditions in Africa. . . . I drove from Cape Town to Cairo as long ago as 1947. In 1951 and 1959 I crisscrossed the entire continent by plane, truck, jeep, canoe and on foot. In 1966 and 1967 I produced and directed two large parts of the four-hour ABC Africa Show. Our goal then was too general. . . . The black American has a feeling for life not based on material gain or comfort, but on what we call soul. We will search for this priceless ingredient in our film. The major part of our film would examine the heritage—sculpture and soul—that was left behind. [The film] intends to show our debt to Africa and especially the fight of soul. . . . [On the animal-human leap, he returns to the "Pygmies" in the Ituri forest and "three other tribes from the Congo."] Physical coordination and prowess are part of the black Americans' heritage from Africa. Nowhere in the world are there more beautiful bodies and we intend to show this when possible. . . . When I visited the Bapende earlier this year. I witnessed a ceremony that comes under the heading of magic or sorcery.[18]

About Elisofon's genuine commitment to the making of *BAH*, his enthusiasm about its thematic undertaking, and his big-hearted energy, there were no doubts, nor that he was right observing that the new interests about Africa in the West required updated educational materials. Africa needed to be (re)written. The questions were how, what, by whom, for whom? Those have also been my questions digging into the Elisofon archives.

On 5 October Elisofon met Shakespeare and John N. Hutchison in Washington, who by then had had feedback from their Africa USIA officers in the field about their work contacts with Elisofon. They were content. In a letter to Shellenberger in Lagos, Elisofon wrote that in all likelihood the organization would pick up the film for African distribution and that Shakespeare, he had also learned, would recommend to his staff that the 16mm black-and-white prints of the two half-hour African sculpture TV shows for CBS would be shown in "each African capital to some selected VIPS."[19] A week later, Shakespeare distributed a ponderous telegram to the African offices that verifies what was said at the meeting in Washington.

> Tentative plans call for travel by train Dakar to Bamako, Land Rover travel across southern Niger or northern Nigeria to Lake Chad, with side trips to Cameroon and other coastal areas. He will provide PAOs as far in advance as possible. . . . Film series of interest for Agency. . . . PAOs requested to provide such facilitative assistance as possible.[20]

Elisofon had become an instrumental voice in the USIA propaganda library. The agency successfully exploited his triumphs as a photographer and a well-known media personality.

## Elisofon's Manner of Filming and Photographing the Sculpture and the Soul

The technical level of the filming equipment, the movie cameras Eclair and Bodex, Ingenue zoom lenses, tripods, MST motors for the sync sound, generators, 7,244 feet Ektachrome, recording tapes, and other devices that filled Elisofon's Land Rover hung upon the camerapersons, whether it was low-budget Smith or less-so Georges Bracher. With Westinghouse's approval, Elisofon was allowed to employ Smith for six weeks starting mid-May (J1). By then Elisofon had finished his footage in the Congo for the *National Geographic*. With him acting storyboard artist and director and Smith prefilming, they would rush through five West African countries (Senegal, Ghana, Mali, Niger, and Nigeria), identifying and planning the topics (sites, characters to shoot, events to visit, masqueraders and entertainers to hire). The rest of the footage period (J2 and J3), from the end of October to the end of March 1971, now with Bracher holding the camera, was one of reparation, addition, and completion. So were the museum filming or the filming of fixed art objects. A lot of Smith's prefilming segments proved, however, to be propitious enough to survive the final screening. The intercrossing of Elisofon's second objective, photographing simultaneously the Niger riverside for one of his children's books in the Macmillan series "Five Faces of Africa" (never published),[21] while directing the filming for Westinghouse, impacted in several ways on the *BAH* "sculpture-soul" thematic.

The Niger River theme inscribed and particularized the geography of the filming for economical and logistical reasons. Being "one of the most fascinating Rivers in Africa, rising in Guinea, flowing through Mali as it curves near Timbuctoo [*sic*] and the wonderful country of the Tuaregs and then goes southward through almost all of Nigeria," the Inner Niger Delta and the cities Bamako, Segou, Mopti, Goudan, Timbuktu and Niamey, the Fulani and the Dogon, were to be places and people Elisofon came back to at least three times during these years. A concentration of his photographs and film segments emerged out of these visits, with as much determination as the cursed River Niger Delta was expunged from his visual narrative. "Unfortunately part of its delta empties into the sea through Biafra, but I have no intention of photographing the war as I feel that this will soon be over and will destroy the timelessness of the film."[22] "Timelessness" is a key concept in his "black heritage" exposition. The riverside pictures that he took during his Literary Africa journey (1959) in Onitsha and upstream were not revised. The photography for the fourth children's book, the "Yoruba tribe," also coalesced with the filming project, and so did the fifth on that of Ghana. The Yoruba filmic and photographic sessions took place in and outside the cities of Ibadan, Ife, Ogbomosho, Ede, and Benin City, and the Asante story in and in the surroundings of Besease, Kumasi, and Elmina.

Elisofon's parallel photographs taken during the *BAH* filming in the West African countries are naturally interesting in their own right but also for how they correlate with the semantics of the filming with Smith and with Maya Bracher and Georges Bracher. During the relative short time of six weeks, traversing with Smith five countries, the Smithsonian Collections Research Center registers 1,451 albums taken by Elisofon. The figure for the much longer period and four more countries (Burkino Faso, Benin, Ivory Coast, DRC), in the company of the Brachers, is much smaller, or 917, a difference of 534. The obvious reason for the lopsidedness of the two portfolios of photos and the overweight paradoxically of the one obtained during a much shorter time is the different work characters of the two shooting periods. The May–June travel (J1) was similar to Elisofon's surveillance trip for his Nigerian article, "The Hopeful Launching of Proud and Free Nigeria," in 1959. It was not only their cicerone, the Niger River, that triggered their Land Rover to indulge in a heated up, crazy, and hazardous peregrination to collect the material for the Macmillan books. It was also, and more importantly, due to Elisofon's aspirations to meet face to face with as many of the USIA staff as possible. He had realized that without their assistance, he would fail to organize all the nearly one hundred staged performances and portrait shootings that he did later on, as well as to find time to catch up with the settled cultural events that he was anxious to film. It was a dramatically split venture. His camera went hot, and so did Smith's Bodex, and Georges's and Maya's.

During the second period (J2 and J3), Elisofon's photography was an accessory pursuit mainly. In particular, after February 1971, when filming was abruptly interrupted and Elisofon was solicited to return to New York for a week, photographing was minimal. Having scrutinized his filming up until then, Westinghouse editors gave him a talking-to for poor footage and advice on how to proceed by improving not only the technique but also clarifying his approach to his narration. From now on and for the rest of the time that Westinghouse explored Africa, candid photography was close to nil. Elisofon pooled all his attention and time to improve directing Georges Bracher. But it was too late, or rather he did not want to.

To be able to discuss the interaction between his photography and the filming as two synchronous activities, I have thematized the photos that Elisofon took in West Africa 1970–1971 for *BAH* (J2–J3).[23] Where did they land? The Niger River world was represented in a multiform of varieties, even aerials from the Inner Delta archipelago in the Sahel. Any reader of this book with a weakness for writing a river travelogue is welcome to step in and finish Elisofon's amputated children's story about the Niger (and why not also those on the Nile and the Congo?) on the basis of his photographs that move us tardily from Bamako to the Niger's meeting point with the Benué, its largest tributary (at Lokoja). He pictured the river market at Mopti, on foot and in a helicopter; dromedary camels resting under a tree at the river, near Timbuktu; a domestic scene outside Niamey (71); and boats on the bank of the Benué. The other photos effused other sensibilities and precepts, and, more succinctly, were far from open-ended. The following are the major tangible clusters of his portfolio: staged masqueraders, dancers, performers; carnivals; male and female body-dress as signatures; ethnic categorizations; portraits of particular individuals; artisans at work; architecture.

The staged masqueraders, dancers, musicians, and performers whom Elisofon sought out were well known to him already, as they were to the cultural attachés of the Western embassies and the tourists who visited their regions. Elisofon had photographed many of the groups several times. In most respects these groups were as professional as any European cultural dance group. They knew their prices, and many of them also knew Elisofon's appetite and impudence to manipulate, choreograph, fashion them into his imaginary. I introduce an insider here, Pascal Imperato, an American doctor, who had been sent to Mali to direct smallpox eradication and a measles control program by the United States Agency for International Development and who was to meet Elisofon all the three times he traveled in the Dogon land 1970–1972. Acting as his consultant and guide during his work around Bamako in 1970 and 1971, he had this to say all in all:

> The artist in Eliot drove him to create and he always tried to create on film Africa as he wished to see it and in so doing often missed documenting the Africa that was there. He and I were always in hot dispute over this matter and it brought him into continual conflict with the Africans. The way he wanted masked dances performed for his cameras was the way he would have painted them on his own canvas. But it was usually at variance with how they were actually performed. Eliot wanted the dancers out in the sun and against an acceptable background. But they were accustomed to dancing in the shade next to a dense background of onlookers wearing T-shirts, sun glasses and wrist watches and leaning on bicycles. Eliot wanted nothing of T-shirts, sun glasses and wrist watches in his creations and off they came and out went the bicycles. The polite tolerance of Africa permitted this once in a village, but not a second time.[24]

Fragments of the reality of now, whether it was reminiscences of the Biafra war or a flap of T-shirt, sullied the aesthetics of his vision of what he considered the "timeless," and it postulated, as we see here, not only his proverbial right to correct its "deviances" but with the same kind of imperiousness bring it home for acclamation. Many would say that it was worse than a stealing.

The sessions of Elisofon photographing masked performers wearing Chi wara headdresses in the Bamana region were split in diverse visual thematics: focus on their cultural and material differences, male or female, vertical or horizontal, single or double; on their production, the carving out of a solid tree; and the dancing that took place on two sites, Bougouni village and Bakamo national district (70 and 71). Most of these hundreds of photographs were close-ups of the particular mask or the performer's dance. The documentation omits the context, the audience, and the musicians. Single black-and-white photos sneak in as if by mistake, providing the observer of them the chance to study the context that Imperato was concerned with.[25]

The first three pictures illustrate the Chi discourse: the audience, the masquerader, and the carving of the mask (EEPA EENG 01618, EEPA EECL 3367, EEPA EECL 6751). The second group is a visual arrangement of an N'tomo society initiation masquerade, also photographed in the Bamako district, with an audience surrounding the performer wearing an N'tomo mask. In each case, the attention of all and everybody, even the carver having had to invade, for him, an uncommon workplace, is sucked in by the white man's inquisitive camera. But summoned and wangled attention defies presence and empathy. The passive clapping of hands, the stiff faces, and the resolute bearing of the bodies that the photos manifest speak their own language of distrust. The communal masks did not speak English; the camera was not let in. There were very good reasons for the mistrust.

Elisofon visited the villages around Bamako three times during his *BAH* shooting period: in June 1970 with the Londoner Smith as cameraman, in December with the Brachers, and in March 1971 with Georges Bracher and Joelle Dorval as operators (Maya had had to return to Dakar for family reasons, and Dorval replaced her). Imperato, his helper, in his turn, as we saw, was getting progressively more frustrated with Elisofon's desiderata, and so were the masquerade leaders, many of whom Imperato knew. Geary, whose account of Elisofon's three-act filming in Bamanaland that the following passage is based on, identifies two major obstacles that he encountered and had to confront. One was the ethnic compulsion to adjust to the communal labor timing of the masquerade (late April and early May); the other to travel east, to another village and lose time, if his plan was to photograph the vertical chi wara (the most popular headdress among the New York art dealers). But none of these tangible cultural norms would quell his restlessness, adjust his tight schedule, and mellow his by now dependable operative effrontery. Geary records several reenactments that he manipulated—in one way or another—during his degrading encounters with the Bamana. There was on one occasion his asking the dancers to retreat to a more fashionable part of the village, as well as bidding the drummers to remove their Western shirts; there was his commanding the dancers at another event to mix a chi wara vertical headdress with an incorrect (*n'tomo*) costume; there was his recruiting two out-of-village dancers and their three accompanying drummers to replace the dancers whom Imperato knew and had hired but who refused to accommodate Elisofon's whims (EEPA EECL 3370). The photo of these five makes evident their mortification and anger; they wanted to run away, which they tried to do (Geary 1995).

It is along these parameters of invasion, coercion, and nervousness that Elisofon and his camera team, all of them immersed by the best intentions in the world, rushed in and out of people's lives with or without understandable forewarnings. To this one could add his obsessive repetitive ritual of returning to the same physical object and the same site for their charged personified meanings. Imperato characterized Elisofon's energetic pulse as a "crashing tornado." "The kinetic drive and ambition charged up inside of him were enormous and in the quiet somnolence of Africa he was like high voltage electricity rushing down the fragile wires of a pocket transistor radio . . . He burned everything up in his paths" (Imperato 1976, 315). "A hell," exclaimed Georges Bracher, in an interview on 28–29 May 1992, to peg the speed and the intensity of the filming with Elisofon.

> It was passionate. Eliot knew his subject to the bottom, he had made the local preparations, when we had finished a segment, and he knew exactly where to go next and what to film. Madness! We had a Land Rover with which we drove 13,000 kilometers within four weeks. I was the driver. I drive, we stop, I install the material, I film, a hell! . . . We climbed Rwenzori in the fogs . . . the sun emerges for three minutes, I filmed, we got the three minutes! Physically, I like this kind of situation![26] (My translation)

The attempt at organizing another recurring "expedition" up the western part of Rwenzori, with the Brachers for *BAH* (12–18 November 1970) was more than anything else a ceremonial Stanley-act of self-glorification. His amputated Kevin fantasy about revisiting Kilimanjaro in 1973 was another. For the six-day trekking the group reaching a height of 4,463 meters, Elisofon had hired seventeen carriers that in the end were twenty-seven, plus a guide with a rifle. With Maya as travel writer, we are taken into a taxing ascent through the bamboo forest, grand heather plants, lichens, mosses, and swamps. And fog. At last, between 5 and 6 p.m. on 15 November, "the whole mountain range was in front of us against a blue sky . . . it was unexpected and beautiful," she wrote in a letter to her parents.[27] Georges's luxuriant "three minutes," a metaphor embodying the mélange of horror and fascination that he felt it was to work for Elisofon, equaled one hour for Maya. This was real-time. The still pictures that were taken (many of them by Maya) focused on Elisofon, the pilgrimage's godfather, medicine man, and mental guide, only extempore on objects that might have been the targets of the expedition (EEPA EENG 09464). It was an expedition that had no other objective than itself. For Elisofon, another climbing of the Rwenzori confirmed the self-made myth of omniscience (he had the images). The self-made myth craved constant nourishment. No wonder that he identified himself with the "stone crusher" and that he, at the level of climbing where Maya saw the fascinating variety in the scenery, registered the five peaks around him, the "tallest [of which] is Mount Stanley, named after the first European to discover the range in 1889."[28] The masqueraders, the dancing women with painted faces and scarifications, the ethnic unorthodoxies in dressing and architecture threatened to burst Elisofon's ever-expanding "cultural heritage" cabinet. Rwenzori, his fetish king of kings, helped him on, helped him finish his *BAH* mission.[29]

Elisofon's visiting the Dama rituals in a few villages, lying east of Bandiagara in Sanga (Mali) at the top of an escarpment, exploded into another "tornado." During these many sessions, he photographed, wildly, the Stilt (both in 1970 and 1971), the Kanaga (also in 1959), the Sirige (1959 and 1971), and the Dyomo masquerades (and took pictures from a helicopter of the Bandiagara escarpment).[30] In Niamey, Niger, as we have seen, he attended the hunters' festival, the Hausa horsemen show, and Tuareg noblemen riding dromedary camels, all executed during the celebration of the tenth anniversary of the nation (1971). Here too his footage was excessive. Of the staged masked performances that Elisofon documented in Nigeria, the Egungun in Ede, the Gelede in Meko, and the Ighogho in Benin City (1971), the first two attracted an audience that neither interacted with the masqueraders nor with the photographer in other ways than posing at his bidding; the third was a private show for Elisofon alone without an audience.

Equally formalized and individualized were the five performances (four of them with masks) organized for Elisofon by the Ivorian minister of tourism, J. B. Gbohou, via the USIA man Fenhagen in Abidjan. Two of them, the Ge Gblin stilt masker dance and the Dan acrobatic dancers with the young girls, were more than local village entertainers from the Man region; they had obtained a reputation outside the country, and Elisofon did in-depth stories of individuals in each group (EEPA EECL 4791). The three masks, Wanyugo used at funerals, for and against witchcraft (the dancer was also called the Senufo fire-spitter), the Fibre and cloth mask, and the Nufori acrobat-mask who performed the final rituals of a Senufo funeral, were all exhibited for Elisofon, exclusively, at village squares outside Korhogo, where any informal member of an audience was pushed outside the framing of the scene.[31] The mask in a brown costume "made from mud-dyed ritual cloth designed to terrify the women and children in the audience . . . normally excluded from masked rituals" (EEPA staff comment) must have lost his hideousness since the audience hunching in the background of Elisofon's photos were mainly women and children (EEPA EENG 09790).

There is a richness of detailed documentations of African men in Elisofon's 1970–1971 photographic targets, mostly in artwork situations, from wood-carvers, blacksmiths, sculptors, weavers, to businessmen (many of them named), and, more conventionally, of traditional mug shot portraits of men with power: the paramount aristocratic chiefs of Kumasi and Dagomba (Ghana) with sword bearers and gilt-edged regalia, and again of both Adesoji Aderemi, the Ono of Ife, and John Adetoyese Laoye I, the Timi of Ede whom he had photographed in 1959 for *LIFE*. It is an African "men's world" that fits Elisofon's gender construct of masculine finesse and power: the paradoxical partnership of jazzy handicraft and extravagant authoritarianism. Elisofon was a sexist man of opposites.

It is definitely sexism that inscribes his visual thoughtlessness of endlessly, year in and year out, categorizing women along a curvature of normalcy that was restricted to youth, beauty, and body. His 1970–1971 collection of women recoils in bounds of this kind, and coheres largely with my "women walking" analysis. The visual differences between women's dancing oftentimes show up in nothing else but that of bare torsos versus covered torsos. The two women's dance groups, for instance, he had mobilized to perform in Bamako (J1) demonstrate this (EEPA EENG 0195; EEPA EENG 02038).[32] The centrifugation of the pictorial parts (in the latter series of pictures) of the dancers, the musicians, the audience, is self-reflexive, as if the camera or the cameraman watched it/him/self. It is narcissism or myopism that feeds on the woman's body, breasts, face, hair, and clothing. Elisofon has beaten the bushes, and African women with four-lobed silver and gold earrings, beaded necklaces, facial paint and scarifications, elaborate hairstyles and headdresses emerge—as if awaiting his bid. In Bamako, Bokoto, Mopti, Chadavanka-Abouza,[33] Mossi, Ibadan, Accra, and their rural environs, Elisofon's camera curled around the woman's body, clicked and licked customarily. Every twenty seconds there is a new anthropological—or is it sensual?—angle of her head and torso, never to bow out. There are even more photos in the

1970–1971 *BAH* collection of the stereotype of African women's heads used for the single purpose of carrying burdens: the "Zarma" woman, near Niamey, carrying a decorated water pot, the "Fulbe" woman in the Sanga region carrying calabashes, and endless series of shots of women on their way to a market. Maya Bracher's eight portraits of "Young woman with lobed gold earrings, locally as 'kwottenai,' near Bamako, Mali" and the two of "Wives of Nyim Kot-a-Mbueceky III," and the many others she took, working side by side with Elisofon and photographing the same topics, produced an original presence and sensibility, a touchstone of another kind than that of her boss.

Contradictorily, given the colonial backsliding tendencies that I have been problematizing here, my view is that his study of women's pot-making takes on the dimension of Elisofon's photography at its best. That is when it engages in visual memorizing of the fine-spun operations of creative fingers. He excels in his own photographic artistry when describing the methods, the tools, and the progress of the artisan's work, male or female. There are many examples of this throughout his career, from his study of freezing hands of the Finnish composer Jean Sibelius during a cold October photo-interview at his home in Ainola in 1944, intimating the elegiac, mournful sentiment of the Finnish wars (interestingly, the Finnish noun for "hand" is "*käsi*"; the Finnish verb for "understand" is "*käsittää*") and of the ethnography-rich visual details of how African carvers use their tools to produce masks: the Dogon carver and blacksmith; the Bamana weaver in Senou village; Lamidi Olonade Fakeye, a sculptor in Ibadan (*BAH*, EEPA 3:5); and Kouakou Yao, a Baule sculptor, Yagolikro village, Ivory Coast (1972). And they multiplied during the last years of his life, when appropriating also women artisans. This can be seen in three documentary photo sessions: Lulua women burnishing pottery at Bakwa Balaie village, near Kananga; the Asante women shaping clay pots, near Kumasi (71); and a Kuba woman decorating woven cloth at Mushenge.

The final audit of the 1970–1971 West African still photos, before we turn to the ongoing directing and shooting of the *BAH* film, relates to "architecture," an umbrella concept that I use to cover all kinds of shots of buildings or static entities that Elisofon was inspired and provoked to document. His work on them resembles what he had been doing all his life: photographing sculpture, masks on stools, sitting still on a chair painting flowers. An ostentatious gallery of human artifacts built for meditation, prayer, sleeping, eating, communing come on the scene when I have explored the photos Elisofon took during his months in West Africa 1970–1971. More than anything else these photos exude his passion for geometrical symmetries, color mixtures, anesthetized overviews, and bizarre—in his view—details. "Anything else" suggests his exclusion or negligence of what happened or may not have happened inside the edifices and domiciles. The people who moved in and out, worked on location, or just hung around were either refused participation or formatted to coalesce with the ambience of the sacrosanct, the "timelessness" of the site. They were immersed in a past that had no present.

Nonsecular milieus[34] that Elisofon photographed were "ancestral shrines" such as the Palace of the Oba in Benin city; the Yoruba Shango shrine of the Timi of Ede; the Djinguere Ber mosque in Timbuktu, with its entrance door (with a man) and minaret (71); the Great Mosque of Mopti; the Asante shrine house near Besease, with priestess Okomfoyaa Anosua, attendants, musicians, and a dancer (71); and a village sanctuary near Korhogo (Ivory Coast) (71). The few people who as if by mistake sneaked into these photos were either marginalized or invited to melt into the walls. The architectural construct that appealed to him most, and which he treated as benevolently as an old African mask stored in a museum, was the Dogon granary, its size and usage differing from village to village but still preserving an aesthetic and ideology of Sameness. Elisofon's familiarity with the "Granary land" descends from his first visit to the area in 1959; he would be returning three times after this crisscrossing the landscape for the treasures I have identified. The villages and the regions in Mali that he visited were "of a piece": in 1959, it was Bin village, near Bamako, where he photographed; in 1970, it was mainly the villages of Ogol-du-Haut (Sanga region)[35] and Bougouni (Bamana region); in 1971, Ireli and the Senou village, along the Bandiagara escarpment (Bamana, in Imperato's company); in 1972, the village of Banani Kokoro and other villages in the Sanga region. In Niger, the granary pictures were taken in Chadawanka village (71)[36] south of Niamey, and others east of Zinder city (which is across the border, northeast of the Nigerian city of Katsina). In the Niger granary picture albums, we can follow a segment of the construction process of a granary. Passing into the Ivory Coast, reaching the Senufo village, near Korhogo (71), we have also moved far away from aesthetics, cosmology, and family ethics that the Dogon granaries were embedded in to challenge granaries of a more mundane fashion, made of mud and topped by a thatched roof. Not even Elisofon can make the last granary photos glimmer. The one I have chosen was photographed in Tano Sakassou village (1972) in the eastern part of the Ivory Coast. It is a picture of a small, insignificant vehicle storing only food. For it to take shape, Elisofon had arranged a "Baule" (Baoulé) woman to lean alluringly against it (EEPA EECL 7906). Needless to say, she almost overwhelms the granary. No human (not even a Wodaabe male or female beauty) would outshine a Dogon granary. Or maybe?

## The *BAH* Series of Four Films and Their Manuscripts: Films or Camera Albums?

In letters to two USIA agents, Weston Fenhagen (Abidjan) and Phil Cohen (Ibadan), on 9 and 10 February 1971, respectively, from Lagos, Elisofon explains, frustrated, that he had been summoned by his employers to return to New York for a ten-day palaver about the deficiencies in the *BAH* shooting—with only a month remaining of the filming. In the letter to Cohen he tells him that he will return to Lagos on 19 February to reshoot in Ibadan and Ife related to the Yoruba material, anticipating having an agency car available for him, as film time will be brief. He needs to collect an American cameraman, Joseph ("Joe") King, in Cotonou on 23 February. More than anything, his letter instigates a nervous turmoil, bureaucratically effective, no doubt, but annoying.

In the synchronic letter to Fenhagen in Abidjan, he explained that he will continue his Ashanti coverage in Ghana and, then, about mid-March, return to the Man region in the Ivory Coast. There is no mention of Joe King in this letter. With Fenhagen, he was more open about the intellectual critique that antagonized him: "I . . . had to fly back to New York to review everything . . . all shots until now. It was the only way to plug the holes and do a decent completion of the project." "One of the faults of my work so far has been coverage in width instead of in depth." And "to remedy this I am planning to spend more time in Man." Yet there was no restorative remedy available. Neither "plugging the holes" nor recruiting a new cameraman would salvage *BAH*. The multichrome American aggrandizement impregnating the project, its own enemy, crippled it.[37] Elisofon fell into his narcissistic trap by juxtaposing width and depth as bilateral contrasts. Depth, in this semantics, requires the exploratory and analytical context for the object to shine and width generality for it to be understood and accommodated by a broad audience. At best, the two concepts interact; they are not venomous antitheses. Second, and he was the first to admit it: "I am not a cinematographer; I am a photographer." So for lacking know-how in shooting, directing, and screenwriting, you could not fault him. For not providing creative space for the Brachers he could, Maya a multitalented photographer cum camerawoman and Georges a partisan cinema verité cameraman.[38] It was also Georges's freewheeling style and the observational camera eye that would make *Touki-Bouki* "one of the most important African films ever made."[39] Had Georges Bracher been entreated to help Elisofon for a minute or two to let go of his fascination with the stereotype, whether it was of his own making or inherited, and let Bracher's hand-held camera act with less control, without a scriptwriter and director literally hanging over his shoulders,[40] the *BAH* films might have become a doctored up, although smaller, variant of ABC *Africa*. Depth and width would not find each other.

What triggered the dramatic intervention pulling Elisofon first to New York for consultations and then to new location filming in the Ivory Coast was a rather scathing letter on the style of filming from William L. Browning, the Westinghouse director of films, who, with the film editor, director, and screenwriter Muriel Balash,[41] had reviewed two versions of his footage and were "still concerned about quality and content of the material."[42]

> Taking the most important consideration first, I must question whether or not the footage you are getting will be adequate in substance for achievement of your original concept. Generally speaking, I see a collection of "still" shots with very little filmic story line. Specifically, my opinion is that the great number of isolated sequences such as coverage of various craftsmen, fishermen, dances, foliage etc., will leave us wanting in the development of an interesting and contemporary motion picture presentation. Somehow I have the feeling that we are in danger of winding up with just another National Geographic lecture that relates to this place, that place and the other place without much of any true feeling for culture, heritage and people under discussion. As an example, I was disappointed in not being able to see more of the woodcarver than just a bland and static posed collection of shots showing him seated in front of a dwelling and working on his sculpture. I wanted to see more of how he loved his family, his pleasures, etc. What I did see appeared to be somewhat honky rather than a comprehensive presentation of a heritage that Black Americans and others still relate to. I do think that more coverage of these people in different living situations rather than reams of footage on the same man carving, weaving, fishing, etc., will be more meaningful to your original story concept. (EEPA, x-3, 17)

Browning and Balash did not stop there. They pointed out that the footage was unprofessional, technically and organizationally. "A great percentage of the material is still almost a full stop underexposed . . . long shots seem to be the predominant offender"; "composition seems to be quite sloppy and unprofessional throughout"; so, for instance, in a dance sequence, "a dancer's arm is dangling in the frame prematurely and confusing the viewer." "Almost everything seems to have been shot from eye level . . . more imagination in camera placement would be helpful" (Browning). Balash continued:

> Landscape and fauna must be shot for a purpose. Broad pans of large, general indistinguishable vistas are a waste, unless specifically significant (such as desert shots of skeletons, rugged terrain, or very lush foliage. Some flower and leaf designs could relate texturally to mask and material design. . . . The camera must be used more imaginatively. Meaningful camera movement, interesting angles, possible wide-angle distortion (for a purpose). . . . Develop drama wherever possible.

These were harsh words that Elisofon took seriously, on the face of it. The doer in him was at beck and call to execute what he considered was expected from him and how the scenes of the kind that Browning and Balash were unhappy with could be refashioned. In the letter to Fenhagen, he wrote, desperately, as if landing on a passing thought about approaching again the acrobatic girls he had met in the village of Zouan-Houien, outside the city of Man.

> My idea is to choose one of the small girls who is thrown by the dancer and film her daily life. As you know girls about ten years of age in West Africa are very responsible people. They help a great deal in family life, carrying loads of wood and water on their heads, even a baby sister or brother on their back and so on. I want to show this aspect of African life and choose the right village for this important segment of the film.

His other idea was to create another in-depth story of individual members of the Ge Gblin-tilt-dancer mask group in the same Man region. But this was all talk. None of these segments in the final text read by Angelou came close to what we normally understand by depth. What we learn from Angelou's reading of the section related to the small acrobatic face-painted girls is that they undergo heavy physical training to strengthen their neck muscles, part of which is accomplished through carrying bulky pots from the forest in a particular manner and being isolated from the rest of humankind. The last sentence of the eighteen-line and six filmic shots of the child-abusing segment reads: "The Dan continue to make and use masks and figures as part of their tribal traditions." A highly disputable sentence, both for its simplistic ethnographic bearing and the ethically speaking bad vibes it sends out. The Dan minstrels' stilt "walk through the rain forest to perform in a small village celebration," and the second tourist show that Gbohou, the Ivorian minister of tourism, and Fenhagen had recommended, manifested as twelve graphic lines and came into view in four shots. The last sentence about the stilt-walker in Elisofon's original manuscript reads: "Drums have been added to a Kora [a string instrument] to provide the music for his antics which are more acrobatic than dancing (EEPA, F-2, 2). In reading it, Angelou has replaced "antics" with "performance" and omitted the auxiliary. Or a Westinghouse editor did.

Browning must have realized that this criticism could only be a demonstration of an editorial point of view and remain an internal cliffhanger. There was no chance that Elisofon would or could (perhaps also should) alter the narrative and ideological structures of his oeuvre. To even suggest this, given the little time left, was absurd. Westinghouse would need to promote the series on the bases of the mythology that Elisofon was entrapped in and not on the films in their own rights. And they would proceed to do this, we will see, in a most convincing way. Muriel Balash's advice to Elisofon must have sounded to him, also, like another voice from the outer world: "Think in terms of developing major thread—not much per tribe, as per ideological and human behavior in dealing with their environment and each other, and the forms that were developed to cope with them" (EEPA, X-3, 17). He did the opposite. And what about Balash's general note to Elisofon: "Beauty shots do not a TV show make!" We will see if she was right.

The presenters of the four films were well-known and highly regarded African Americans. Apart from those selected in the end, Bond, Davis, Angelou, and Parks, other names had been polled, among them Marcia Gillespie, Marquita Jones, Barbara Minstrell, and Bill Cosby. On 18 November Elisofon signed the $1,000 contracts with the four presenters, and the final voice-over shooting was done in January.[43] Elisofon's manuscripts, revised only on a small scale by the presenter and/or a Westinghouse editor, remain (with the visual) a most transparent graphic testimonial of the emptiness of the *BAH* catchwords of "heritage" and "soul."

Each film documents piece by piece an endless row of artifacts, where the particular object, whether it is a Senou dance, a Tuareg sword, a Basonge mask, or Bambara drums, takes on metonymic functions incorporating ethnicity, landscape, history; history also in its less heroic tall tale meaning of having been encapsulated by the Western "explorer," contemporary or not. The films are sped-up collages of visual snapshots and vocal one-line captions. Watching the films or reading the manuscripts is like following a time-pressed guide in an ethnographic museum. Here are some examples (the figures in parentheses denote the films in which order they were broadcast in April–May 1972):

> The Watusi, like all Africans, express themselves completely in dance (1); Bapende are among the few tribes in the Congo who still continue their traditional ceremonies (1); Every man ["Tuareg"] still wears a long sword (2); British carried away precious objects from the Ashanti during their wars at the turn of the century. A gold pendant 4¼" is now part of the Tishman Collection in New York (3); The Yoruba are the largest tribe in West Africa. They have maintained most of their tribal traditions. One of them is called Gelede, a ceremony to drive witchcraft out of a village (4); Pictured for us now are eighteen masks. They are all from central and West Africa, the major zones many American forefathers came from. (4)

Through an all-embracing and exclusive focus on "modernity" or colonial ethnography, the *BAH* narration was catastrophic. The survey documentation aggregates African peoples into a homogeneity that is both misleading and demeaning. There are no efforts in the footage to explore the intriguing relationships between art, social organization, and the rituals that link peoples across regions. "Its [modernity] systems of naming and incorporating the world into its dominant logics and 'truths' produced epistemologies that posited Africa as a monolithic place where oldness begs newness, the less developed solicits evolution, and simplicity beckons the benevolence of the cultured" (Amkpa on colonial photography, 4). In all the four films, there is only one single narrative that can be said to communicate with an audience, a lack that also Browning and Balash pointed at. This is the elusive story of the Dolo, the blacksmith and his son Samuel, of Ogol-du-Haut village in Dogon land, and their production of the mask from tree to initiation (3). It stands out in its own right.[44] Most of the other minuscule filming stubs were carriers of epistemological and burdening overtones that crushed them. They were "carried away" (to use Elisofon's own term about the one-way transatlantic trade) to become another analog metonymy for greed and brutality that impregnated the complex discourse of being both the "black" American identity booster and "white power" magnifier. Elisofon's goodwill stumbled on his myopism and the politics of Westinghouse lobbying. *BAH* was edited to serve the progression of Warren Robbins's lifetime project, the establishment of the Museum of African Art (MAFA). And here it did well. But what happened to Africa?

The films were about themselves, about the provincial process of the producer and his camera engaged in a selection process of deciding which artifact or mask was worthy of his attention. When it had been provisionally endorsed, that is registered, provided with a name, a lineage, an affiliation, and evaluated by the yardstick sophisticated enough to synchronize economic and aesthetic values, only then was it declared ready for the shipping. But the fact is that each of the four films exhibits about fifty sculptures and masks, photographed or filmed in situ and in collections, exhibitions, and museums in the United States. For filming the sculptures for *Africa's Gift*, number four in the series, eleven collectors (including Elisofon) in New York were invited to open their doors. The series exhibits in all about two hundred masks and sculptures, eighty portraits, sites, animals, and five fragments of stories (such stories that Browning failed to persuade Elisofon to do). Two-thirds of *BAH* stagger along as a reenactment of a tour, we saw, in a Western art museum with bored college students in a throng, who during the breaks would be taught, as extras, that "dancing with colorful masks is part of a Gelede ritual to protect the community from witchcraft and evil spirits" (3:3), that the "Cape Buffalo was made famous for his tenacity and fierceness in a story by Ernest Hemingway, 'The Short Happy Life of Francis Macomber'" (1:3), that "neither the African nor Western artist believed in naturalistic art" (4:7). Yet it could well be that the following wide-eyed remarks prompted some students to engage in African studies, questioning the assumptions of these statements.

> Sculptures such as these from the Basonge in the Congo were brought to Europe by explorers, missionaries and government officials who regarded them as curios (4, 6); it was not until the early 1900's that these objects (Bakuba) were appreciated by the Western world (1, 11); the objects we are seeing now are in museums and collections where they have been preserved from damage by termites and the climate (1, 12); only recently have African governments begun to appreciate their own art and protect it from being sent out of the country (2, 6).

Angelou, the presenter of "The Slave Coast," as we will see, was regretful about her participation in it.

## The Reception of *BAH*: African American Critique

Apart from the in-house reservations about Elisofon's *BAH* that hardly attenuated at its windup in February, when it was officially launched with a hurrah that was meant to swing Capitol Hill, its less enthusiastic facade as represented by the section vignette was to be voiced during the fall. The lines from Connie Perdreau's letter to the editor for a student magazine at Ohio University were provoked by Elisofon's complaint in an interview in the same paper that all too few African Americans had turned up to his lectures about *BAH*.[45] It is in the interface of these two perspectives that the American reception *of BAH* took form.

To start from the top. On 29 February the U.S. Mission to the United Nations (UN) and Group W sponsored a joint screening and a reception of *BAH* at 799 UN Plaza, New York.[46] The premiere was attended by ambassadors from the five continents and George H. W. Bush, then U.S. ambassador to the UN. Present was also Elisofon's secretary, Dotty Scherf, who in a letter to Elisofon, then photographing for the *National Geographic* in the Democratic Republic of the Congo, had the following setback to communicate to him in Kinshasa:

> As for George Bush, he mentioned you as the instigator behind the project, but his remarks were only about two minutes long. . . . I don't know who was responsible for the cutting of the film to this type of presentation but I thought it pretty bad . . . no matter what professionals or blacks with emotions think. There were quite a few blacks. I believe George was responsible and after seeing those oval cutouts that introduce the programs . . . I believe anything of him. (10 March, HRC 42.12)[47]

The next larger event in the launching ritual took place at Warren's MAFA on Capitol Hill a month later. For this purpose, Elisofon had had an exhibition of sixty artifacts from his own home collection organized to "salute the four TV programs," honoring his own entrepreneurship. But more importantly, the salute concerned the unilateral ethics of *BAH*, the difference of African art "as distinguished from African artifacts and cultural sociological objects."[48] This was politics. It was the promulgation of "difference" that the Westinghouse Broadcasting Company, Robbins, and Elisofon now officially proclaimed to be *BAH*'s role. It was a plot to further the aesthetic-political evolution of MAFA with the discourse of "black heritage" as its hammering tool. Opening the exhibition, Donald McGannon, the

Group W chairman, spoke on cultural reciprocity, on the new identity formation, on "black pride," which also was, he intimated, "white pride": "'Black African Heritage' goes to the source. It returns to the parent continent in quest of—only to bring back—the history, traditions, culture and beauty of Africa and its people which are blood and sinew of our spiritual inheritance in America" (HRC 52.10). With the same evangelist pathos, Robbins concurred, rehearsing the homily he had used at the exhibition of the reopened museum a year earlier, on 20 May 1971.[49]

By April–May, when the four films were being broadcast by about forty stations across the country (two in South Carolina: Charleston and Spartansburg, and one in North Carolina: Charlotte), a large album featuring the mythic career of Elisofon, with samples from the films and printed feature material, was distributed to national newspapers located in every corner of the United States.[50] Georges Bracher's unique role as cameraman was officially credited, but that was all; Maya Bracher's work as scriptwriter was not even noted. The Westinghouse promotional campaign was opinionated and culture-based, but it was equally, or foremost, concerned with budget.[51] The films were, indeed, fortuitous: notwithstanding expenditures, they turned a profit, but this did not inspire them to acquiesce to Elisofon's renewed proposal to do another four-part film about Africa (on art), finding themselves, they thought, in another risk-taking situation. Despite the voluminous promotional campaign for *BAH*, the media reception was lukewarm, offensively indifferent. Among the forty-odd newspaper reviews that I have examined, extremely few prove to be based on an individual critic's experiences of having viewed the shows. The great majority of notices about *BAH* were refashioned clips from the feature text material[52] and loyal restatements of the official Westinghouse *BAH* doctrine. The majority of them simply ignored the programs by presenting them in two or three lines. Bob Foster, the media reporter and columnist for *San Mateo Times*, belonged to the minority that was affected, for one reason or another. A few others, we will see, were openly antagonistic. Meeting Elisofon en route between the two California stations KPIX and Oakland KDIA, Foster asked him: "What is the reaction of blacks when they find a white man doing a comprehensive cultural history of races?" Elisofon admitted that it was mixed. "Some of them resent me, others feel I am a hero for bringing the history of the black man's heritage to the attention . . . of . . . the blacks as well."[53] This seems to have been the crux of the issue that brought Angelou to write the article "'For Years, We Hated Ourselves,'" which appeared in the *New York Times* on the very same day as the airing of "The Slave Coast" took place on WCBS-TV (16 April 1972), for which film she was the duplicitous, self-castigating, and corporate rebel narrator. Her two seemingly contrapuntal acts—participation and rebellion—made her article even more naked. "The culture of Africa," she wrote, "is not caught only in masks and dances, tribal chiefs and musical instruments . . . in the recording of tangible Africana . . . a perfect photography of a much-photographed Benin mask." It is sad, too, she continued, that the "matrilineal inheritance[54] which exists in many African cultures could not be caught on the ephemeral film." But why not make an attempt at trying? Elisofon's response in the *New York Times* (14 May) to Angelou's criticism was partly nominal ("no program can do everything"), partly evasive (a visual discourse of matrilineality is for the university, not "for a general television audience"), but what triggered the formulation of his TV mailbag reaction "Being White, Do I Love Africa Less?" was Angelou's comment: "And yet the photographer is not as committed to the subject as a Black American must be." For Africa, she stressed, is "more than a glamorous fact, [it] is a historical truth" and this demands the "insider-witness." Elisofon's *BAH* is lacking in "depth," "explanation," and "soul." It is not truthful, it is flawed, ignoring the specifics of the history, social structure, and economy of the people portrayed. Angelou's concluding "White Hunter" simile, more than anything else, explained not only her view of the intricateness and asymmetries of Elisofon's imagining of Africa but of Western photography of the continent at large. She wrote:

> There is a Kenyan story which says that a child complained to its mother that he saw only photos of men killing lions and asked why he didn't see photos of lions killing men, since he knew that happened too. The mother responded, "Wait, my child, until the lion takes the photo."[55]

Three of the movie critics and reviewers who were openly negative, pointing to Elisofon's reactionary and exclusionary representations of Africa, were Lou Cedrone (*Baltimore Evening Sun*, 15 March 1972), Rex Polier (*Philadelphia Evening Bulletin*, 31 March 1972), and George Tashman (*The Independent*, 16 May 1972) (HRC 51.9). Tashman also met and interviewed Elisofon, accompanied by Tetsuko Kuroyanagi the future Japanese celebrity. In their talk, Elisofon again criticized Angelou and defended his bravado objective to show African Americans what Africa is and has been, "to give them pride." Tashman was skeptical. More so after Elisofon's inventory of his accidents in Africa, the many diseases he had suffered—from amoebic dysentery, jungle rot, to worms three inches long—and his naive idolization of Mobutu. Polier's verdict was unequivocal:

> [*Black African Heritage*] produced the same stereotypical views of Africa that we have been seeing since the days of Osa and Martin Johnson and their little African spectaculars. . . . The dancing tribes (one had to be filmed on tour in America) reminded one of years of looking through *National Geographic* magazines. . . . I think that the museum only perpetuates the old trappings of a civilization that has discarded them except for the theater, museum, and history texts.

More disturbing than these individual media voices was the combination of reticence and contention that he ran into during his tour of American universities, summer and fall 1972 and the beginning of 1973. Here I will stop at Elisofon's reactions after his stint of lectures and discussions with students at the Columbus Gallery of Fine Arts (Columbus Museum of Art) and Ohio State University on 16–19 October 1972, lecturing on "Sculpture of Black Africa" at the Paul Tishman Collection Exhibition at the gallery and presenting the *BAH* films for the African Studies Program and Kennedy Lecture series at the university. This pattern of combining African art lectures and the *BAH* films characterized the organization of his remaining public performances; *BAH* and art were one.[56] Interviewed for the student-run newspaper, the *Post*, by its assistant editor, film critic, and future science-fiction novelist Dave Skal about the backlash Elisofon thought he had had among the black Americans, he was both disappointed and angry.

> So here I am with four films on the roots of the black experience on a campus with a potential black audience of almost 1200, and how many do I draw with any presentation? Six. Out of an audience of three hundred, six are black. . . . I don't understand why they are not showing up. . . . Haven't they had any interest in the culture from whence they came? . . . The black revolution, and its roots in African culture, is important to all of us. . . . Americans have been given very little exposure to African culture. What they've seen mostly are Tarzan movies and white hunters shooting elephants.[57]

One of the six in the audience was Perdreau, whose direct address to "Mr. Elisofon" prefaced this section. Her full note to the editor reads:

> Africa depicted in his presentation on Tuesday reeked of the underlying colonial spirit: the myth of the happy native, the exoticism of the so-called primitive life and customs on the "dark continent" and the exploration of the indigenous population

> for the financial benefit of the "bwana," in this case Elisofon and Time-Life. Moreover, the fact that Elisofon paid these Africans for their services, makes one seriously doubt the verisimilitude of the entire production. . . . It is apparent that you took much from the great continent of Africa, Mr Elisofon. What, in turn, did you give them? More importantly, what have you given us?

Perdreau and many others not only understood the populist linguistic smokescreen of relating to African Americans "coming from Africa" but were cognizant—some of them to the radical extent of not "showing up" at the screenings—of the gruesome reality embedded in the "White Hunter metaphor," whether the object-subject was a lion or Elisofon's elephant. Equally informed were the audiences across the United States about Elisofon's lifelong collusion in the arbitrary media fabrication of Africa. His crediting (also in the Skal interview) of John Huston's colonial *The African Queen*—indirectly—for his achievements in the colonialist documentary film on Africa (and it is not sarcasm on his part) would hardly have been taken seriously, no more than the discrepancy he moots, in the same talk, between *The African Queen* and the Tarzan movies (another cherished mythological Smithsonian Elisofon quote). The two were as consanguine and as kindred as can be.[58]

CHAPTER 9

# Elisofon Collecting Artifacts and Elisofon Curated

## Colonialist Power

The word or concept of "museum" had a special ring for Elisofon, whether it designated an art museum or an ethnographic museum. The museum ring he harkened to announced the primacy of a Western epistemology, a canonical hierarchy of aesthetics that separated the bad from the good along imaginary borderlines. A "mythic steady-state universe" (Kasfir 1992) (which Elisofon called "timeless") superseded the interacting, hybridizing, creative chaos this museum credo was. Once inside the circulating exhibition, its unpretentious anteroom, or the museum, the object had been metamorphosed. It had undergone taxonomic shifts from being the invisible trophy or curio mask to being a history-bearing artifact in the ethnographic museum, and, at best, to being a canonized piece of African art (in that order). For this to happen, the system of appropriation required a mediator, a connoisseur, a traveling, self-ordained doctor collector, such as an Eliot Elisofon. The skillfully carved mask I bought in a market in Calabar in 1982 will never be converted, barring a miracle in the form of an African art connoisseur entering my home one day uninvited. It is these sides of the museum—the art tabernacle, the secular everyday storage house, and the courtroom—that fascinated Elisofon. It is in the courtroom aspect of it, where decisions were taken on questions of authenticity and valorization and the Kevin boy in him could reach out for confirmation. In 1958, his position as judge or "expert" on "African art" was made official. He was nominated for a Research Fellow in Primitive Art at the Peabody Museum of Archeology and Ethnology of Harvard University, and in the same year he published the book *The Sculpture of Africa*. He became a recognized arbiter of "African art," a public appreciation that he enjoyed for the rest of his life.

As Elisofon himself recalled, and we remember, his fascination with African art was set in motion when visiting one of the very first U.S. exhibitions of African sculptures as works of art and not as "mere" artifacts: Walker Evans's "The African Negro Art" show in 1935.[1] What he could see was not only more than six hundred sculptures but also portfolios of photographs that Evans had taken of them. As I see it, the exhibition triggered in him three different and life-lauding modus operandi: first, sketching and photographing objects, people, and landscapes, and on the top of that, sending these works home for a national ovation. These were events and activities that his idolized explorers since childhood, Stanley and Speke, had been engaged in—why not he as well? Second, his desire of photographing art objects as Evans did—but much better—was probably another provocative correlation that inspired him. Third, the formal "beauty" of the African sculptures on display that he fell for was to turn into an aesthetic devotion and principle that lasted for life. In an article many years later he wrote: "We did not appreciate the artistic quality of African sculpture until the painters of the Paris School discovered it, among them Picasso, Braque, Derain, Vlaminck, and Matisse" (Elisofon 1959, 48). He was one of those who was influenced. His own watercolor style, with the jagged, cubist vignettes of nudes and flowers, admittedly bears engaged resemblances.[2] Citing a passage out of James Johnson Sweeney's *African Folk Tales and Sculpture*, he further tries to clarify his aesthetic allegiance:

> Since their time European artists in each generation have been able to find in or another aspect of Negro art something that seemed to justify their own theories: the expressionists found an emotional use of color and distortion of shape, the cubists found "structure," the surrealists found fantasy, mystery—even a pathological inspiration.[3]

So there it was, an "African art" to be desired, mainly because it was recognizable to us, could be imagined by us, and reconstructed to be our own. "Negro art" justified our own aesthetics; we take it, as it were, and reincorporate it within our safe museums where the wooden masks never rot or lose their memory banks. "In other words, the act of ascribing identity simultaneously erases mystery" (Kasfir 1992). Through our cameras, our Cold War greed, our green dollars, Africa came closer, we imagined. "Aesthetics and politics mesh," says Johannes Fabian in discussing the object-collecting of Leo Frobenius and Emil Torday in *The Scramble for Art in Central Africa*. "The transformation from curio to object of art began . . . when the mechanism of distinction mobilized political and ethnic categories: that is, when the products of certain groups (people near the court, or certain ethnic groups of 'nobility') were praised as pure and refined."[4] With Elisofon, the two categories backed up each other. His "intrusive curiosity," as with the two ethnographers, was not "sanctioned by science" (Fabian 1998, 97); it was motivated by what he would have defined, if asked, as his inalienable right as a practicing commissioned photojournalist. His joint methods of photographing and collecting dovetail effortlessly, however, into the composite noun-verb dictum—appropriating these objects—which more than anything else characterizes the operation of Elisofon's magazine photojournalism and filming in Africa. But not throughout. Transactions did occur. His liberty suspended the liberties of the Other on a number of levels. Those who owned the artifacts or used them for cultural practices were not granted the same inalienable rights.

I will return to a couple of examples to counter his "intrusive curiosity" policy as it materialized in his 1947 and 1951 travels in the Belgian Congo and then briefly annotate his more sophisticated methodological strategy in West Africa and the DRC in 1970–1972. Needless to say, Elisofon, the collector, as I have noted, was one of many desirous Westerners in the African art-scraping business during his time. He was no doubt more informed than many of them about Africa, but before all else he was an armchair collector, an armchair ethnographer, a global gentleman-traveler, and a muscle person photographer. He was the all-around lucky amateur, in the best sense of the phrase. His production of "knowledge" from Africa was "ecstatic," to use Fabian's term related to "less somber mediations of knowledge" involving in particular his infatuation with the body (dance, music, performances). In what sense, then, were Elisofon's thousands of portraits of bare-breasted African women "ecstatic"? Was it a residue of a surrealist's "pathological inspiration" (80–81, 100)?

Elisofon's first peacetime fieldwork photography (an offshoot of his 1947 canonical Cape Town—Cairo journey) took place in Mushenge, in the Kuba Kingdom (Kaṣai), where we accompanied him earlier for his two-day meeting (the second occurred in 1951) with Mbop Mabiinc maMbeky, the indirect-colonial ruler between

1939 and 1969. This time I discuss this prototypical encounter from a theoretical point of view, addressing how the dialectics of, on the one side, ethnography and aestheticism and, on the other, collecting and photography formatted the encounter in a fashion it would principally impact on all his photographic sessions in Africa involving people. The ethnographic context included doing his homework and browsing the historic study of the Bakuba and Bushongo by Emil Torday and T. A. Joyce based on their expedition in 1907–1909,[5] the two days spent in photographing objects in La Musée de la Vie Indigène (the Native Art Museum) located at that time in the former Stanley Hotel in Leopoldville/Kinshasa, and another two days photographing and collecting at Bushenge. Anne Maxwell notes how the managers for the Great Exhibition employed photographers to "document anthropological exhibits, thereby transforming the fleeting spectacles of racial and cultural difference into permanent portable objects that could function as memorabilia and collectors' item."[6] Elisofon's practice, as it is demonstrated here, could be compared with a more advanced kind of, as Maxwell puts it, "fleeting spectacle." It is an array of coalesced ethnographic representations (in Torday and Joyce's book), the complementary photos he took in the Leopoldville museum, his fieldwork photos in Mushenge, and the objects he collected. Elisofon's visual storyline is further backed up by the sequential utilization of the "performative-permanent" expressiveness of their Other for his book *The Sculpture of Africa*, in his magazine article "African Sculpture" in the *Atlantic*, in the 1952 *LIFE* article "Mystic Art of Tribal Africa," and for the identification of the items transferred to his private collection in New York.[7] All were part of a narrative and visual spectacle in which Elisofon was at its sui generis midst.

> The so-called fetish figures were also magical. They were made to act for the owner. To protect him and his family, to propitiate spirits, or to harm enemies. . . . I collected among the Basonge small fetishes less than six inches high, each of which had a specific function against evils such as thieves, lightning, and sickness. There were also larger fetishes which protected an entire village.[8]

He organized the artifacts that he acquired along two major rule systems: one, so that they met the standards of the Western museum, naturally a very eclectic and subjective judgment; and two, so that they were commensurate with Western art conventions. In other words, the integration of Elisofon's collection of African objects was as culturally preconceived and predisposed as were his African photos.

The tomfool concept such as "magic," a dubious term to qualify any circumstance or condition, has always been a run-of-the-mill attendant attached to African art works. Is the visual effect of African art on the Western viewer per se "magical," producing an impact of illusion, incantation, or simply a kick of the supernatural? I don't think so. As preponderantly "magical" in its function as a hideout for the supernatural are the apprehensions of the religious rituals governed and legitimized by theology, an exclusive Western discipline. The word "fetish" or the phrase the "devil's hand" belonged as much to a monotheistic denomination as to the secular world of "civilized" art, the confederate of the "primitive."

To move from statuettes and images to sculptures (masks), for them to be authenticated, they had to engender thrills in Elisofon of another kind besides their monetary-worth museum values. For him, as with most Western collectors, the most popular artifacts were the ones about which he was ready to exclaim: "Here the fantasy of the African knows no bounds." It was the one swerving "from almost simple, realistic portraiture to the wildest flight of imagination, in which the face is part human, part animal, or almost entirely cubistic." This "magic" resonated inventiveness, newness, and "anticlassical appeal to modern art," which the two from his own collection, the Bambara Headdress (Elisofon 1959, fig. 12)[9] and the Bateke Ancestor Figure (fig. 5), represented. They were published in his *Atlantic* article. During the 1950s and the 1960s, due to the flexibility for export of these masks, too, American museums became increasingly crowded with African masks and naturally scrupulous about purchasing them, since specialized "African art" institutions were also being established in New York and Chicago.

For Elisofon, the otherworldly fixtures fetched out of initiation ceremonies or secret society séances, in particular those that he himself had both choreographed and photographed, were manna from heaven. As their accretion was tough, heroically tough, bordering on the risk-takings of Stanley, it was even more all the worth of it. Just imagine being one of the few who had snapped a picture of the white rhino or discovered a $2,000 unique precolonial mask? On the route to the Kuba king in the Luluwa area, in January 1947, between Kananga and Lwebo, he was

> fortunate enough once to see part of such a ceremony [circumcision ceremony, or "tundandi"] in the Belgian Congo, when I came across a clearing in the jungle where young boys of the village had been taken away from their parents for several months to undergo the coming manhood with their teachers. Here the boys had been circumcised and taught the folklore of their tribe. I was able to see twenty

> boys dancing in a snakelike line under the rigid tutelage of a weirdly masked teacher carrying a small whip, before I was invited to leave.[10]

In another delayed reflection, from 1957, about the same event, the topic of dances he had witnessed during his by then rather short globetrotting career comes up: "In a hidden clearing . . . [were] Basonge boys, being whipped by a horribly masked leader teaching the dance of manhood, their naked swollen bellies thrust out from loose hips in a flow of movement as interwoven as a cubistic painting."[11] He catalogued these boys rightly as Luluwa (Lulua) people, Bashila Kasanga (Kasonge), undergoing the ritual finale of the not-public *mukanda*, with the "Chokwe-like dancer"[12] firmly guiding the youths, but the incident, as we see, involved more than documentation of an ethnographic dance in a Kasai forest clearing (EEPA EENG 01900). Elisofon's intrusion into the cultural space of the *mukanda*, with the camera observing the mask and the boys, turns into a happening of multiple meanings. The acknowledgment that he was "invited to leave"—an understatement for "stop and go"—was first of all a defiance of the well-known fact also, I am sure, known to Elisofon: no outsiders were entitled to be present at the "hidden" ceremony of male initiation. The photo also evidences that there were no other onlookers than the three drummers to the left of the boys. The villagers resisted his transgression; it was as simple as that: he had no business being there. Apart from Elisofon's official registration of the Luluwa mask dancer, for which Constantine Petridis, curator of African art at the Cleveland Museum of Art, has credited him as the only photographer who has "documented the use of the masks in the relation to the *mukanda*" (1999, 43), the photographic circumstance it involved must have left Elisofon with a sense of humiliation rather than thrills. The frustrated versions of the photography published ten years later were reconstructions of a dismissed ego.[13] Out of them emerges a psychic mise en scène embodying cultural Chokwe tutelage, adult abuse of children, and the image of a cubistic painting, a linear dramaturgy of the hunger-stricken bellies of the kids and their rotating hips. It is not a tale of a "horribly masked teacher" with a whip that Petridis related when commenting on Elisofon's achievement. This single photograph, the single second of its making that encapsulated a white man's point of view and a specificity of its cultural background, migrated or was compelled to migrate to take on new (two of them author-appropriated) meanings from within three American magazines, spread out over time (1957, 1959, 1999) and thematics (dancing, two on African arts, one academic). Was the photo emptied of Africa before it left the continent? Can the earlier discussion—or similar photo diggings—be one way of complicating it, renovating it, bringing it back (at least halfway)?

Clashes with the locals such as the one that took place in Luluwaland, one of Elisofon's very first, were to be more a matter of course than exceptions. His self-ordained mental guide from 1947 to 1972 was a gospel truth—what I have called his autonomous "American mission"—the unequivocal journalistic duty and right of his to shoot the object planned, do it quickly, collect the necessary data, disappear for a new venture, and by swift mail post it to the United States, its foster home. The law and its ethics were unconditional and supreme. Like so many Western photographers, he repeatedly violated African cultural and ethical conventions, with or without knowing or caring about them. He thought that it was unavoidable, deplorable, the rich man's educational obligation. Very few Africans would or could stop him, often afraid to do so, surrounded as he was by local politicians, colonial officers, army soldiers, or USIA staff. For the record: there were hundreds of significant Africans who gladly posed for him, Africans who in their turn used him, took advantage of the exposure, and enjoyed the limelight.

We will stay with another prime example of African artifact hoarding, mainly for what it may tell us about Elisofon's tricks and practice of piling up his New York home collection. The looting interlude took place during 12–13 May 1951 while Eliot and Joan were revisiting Mbop Mabinc Kyeen in Mushenge and a neighboring village. They were stalled at Kananga, on their way to Kinshasa from Kisangani, after finishing the heroic trek of climbing part of Rwenzori.[14] "We jumped off the train with the bag and baggage on the spur of the moment, hired ourselves a car, and promptly went on safari to visit the King of the Bakuba at Mushenge."[15] But the safari was nothing but a collector's raid. Passing Zappo Zap, for Eliot the second time, they discovered that "all the fetishes were picked out by others." In a village close to Bulape outside the city of Mweka, where they spent the night in an American Presbyterian mission, they were more fortunate.[16] They ran into a "mad funeral dance" where they eyed among the "drunken" mourners and musicians wearing "feathers, animal teeth, beads with knives and spears,"

> a very old Bakuma drum with a marvelous head and hand carved on it. Tactless as it was, we asked if they would care to sell it. We almost started a minor riot asking for it while they were using it and in spite of the fabulous price we got nothing but growls and yells and smears. (Letter 3, HRC 61.5–6)

Instead, they bought an alternative, less fabulous, drum from a visiting chief for 500 francs. By then they had recruited a certain Jimmy to serve as their purchasing agent, a "real bargainer," Joan commented. The next morning they met Bope, ill, "near death," they thought, which was a mistaken assumption: he would live until 1969. The verbal depiction of him, although lacking the sumptuousness of the official 1947 photography, oozed the same derogatory extravaganza of excess. This did not prevent the curators of the 2014 Elisofon celebratory exhibition from providing the 1947 phantasmagoria of an African king a central position. Elisofon did not take another picture of Bope, the "fetish king," in 1951. This might have belittled, not the king necessarily, but the photographer's iconic representation of him. Here is what they saw at the time:

> He was lying down wrapped in blankets with all his fetishes, mostly animal tails and bones and things, hanging around him. He looked awful and like any big black negro with a hangover or something. Around him were a few of his 350 wives. No one can talk to the king except thru his noblemen, who are fine looking men wearing the Bakuba outfit. (Letter 3, HRC 61.5–6)

He gave Eliot a "very old, very fine dance mask, Pwoom Itok" (EEPA EENG 08931), and Eliot responded by pallidly offering him an 11 x 14 *LIFE* picture of himself and a bell he had bought in Bukavu (at the southwestern edge of Lake Kivu). So undramatic and barren was Eliot's second meeting with the Kuba king, compared with the first. Elisofon was disappointed at learning that Bope had not taken any photos of his village with the camera he gave him in 1947 that "could have made a really funny article for the magazine" [*LIFE*]. Pejorative ridicule is the chronic leitmotif of Elisofon's viewing and many reprintings of Mbop Mabinc Kyeen.[17]

The day of collecting (or shall we call it looting?) culminated in Jimmy's rushing into the neighboring villages for artifacts to enrich the American couple, referred to in the letter as "his trying to scare up objects for us to buy." He was even successful in persuading the angry, resisting, and mourning villagers to abandon their drum as well as to sell almost "every box [that] exists in the village." "Our Bakuba collection," summarized Joan proudly in her letter home, "is one of the best anywhere." At their lodging, the American mission house at Bulape, the Elisofons had to be silent about their own project-mission, collecting similar "devil's hands" that the missionaries were demonstratively and energetically burning in the courtyard or sending to their congregations as trophies. Paradoxically, some of these artifacts may have ended up, through antagonistic channels, in the same Western museum to be retranslated and alienated. As newborn trophies of another kind, the artifacts confiscated in Africa were reappropriated by magicians as honorary specimens of African art. Colonialist power politics serves the West's Mammon or the West's God. It is a long, semisecular process. We have seen one segment of it. "Naming and categorizing are interventions as important as connoisseurship," observes Kasfir (1992, 44), identifying the two major agents in action, the curator/anthropologist and the fieldwork collector, but for the artifact to land it needs several hands. I solicit the following critique by Kasfir to provide an intellectual frame for the "art quest activity" we have witnessed and to help interpret the next phase in Elisofon's collecting, his fantastic entrepreneurship in shifting and translating the objects into their new habitat of recessiveness and spectacularity.

> Seen from an anticolonial ideological perspective, collecting African art is a hegemonic activity, and act of appropriation; seen historically, it is a largely colonial enterprise; and seen anthropologically, it is the logical outcome of the social-evolutionary view of the Other: the collecting of specimens as a corollary of "discovery." . . . Omniscient curatorial authority has the power to flatten out these hills and valleys [the artifact standing for a whole culture], but should it? Is the public really incapable of understanding that African cultures and the arts they produce, are not monolithic? Do we really want a text "without a shadow?" (2007b, 7–8)

Elisofon saw, but his "magic carpet," the camera, was not allowed to reproduce his field of vision[18] or collect it. If the museum was an institutional yardstick for the terminus of the object he re/acquired, the Western art canon was the prescriptive archive for its ranking. The camouflaging of the essentialness of African cultural products under the custodial Western canon, be it familiar tags like "magic" and "primitive," or allegations of dependability, analogousness, and secondariness, was meaningless. Elisofon beginning his *Atlantic* article with this art history gloss is not different.

Having said this, it is refreshing to come upon a review in the *Boston Sunday Herald* on 26 October 1958 of "Primitive Masterpieces on View" exhibited at the Boston Museum of Fine Arts from 16 October to 23 November. Half of the artifacts had been borrowed from Harvard's Peabody Museum and the rest from private collections such as Elisofon's. The critic, Robert Taylor, takes on a hedonistic attitude toward the objects, far from the common reverence in the saluting of ancestral African objects. Number 43 in the catalog, listed as "a typical Bushongo cap covered with a chicken feather" (an object that Elisofon had acquired in 1947), he depicts as "a wonderfully compelling piece of carving and design but I also derive pleasure from knowing that it was an actual sorcerer's mask confiscated by a Belgian officer in the 30's." And, summarily, in a reference to African sculpture, he makes a comment that Elisofon would hardly have endorsed, the conservative purist that he was: "It expresses the ferment of natures' forces, fertility, wars, the surge of supernatural influences constantly affecting man in a thousand ways, but at ways in changing, prodigal abundance."[19] Its "changing, prodigal abundance," Taylor suggests, also makes room for its colonial history and, furthermore, his subsequent reflection on it from a viewer's outward perspective.

Among the thousands of photographs and artifacts that Elisofon took and collected during his many travels in the West Kasai villages, you will not find (or I have not turned up) a photograph, a sculpture, or a mask of any accompanying item that is not designed to stay rigorously within the Elisofon canon of authenticity, timelessness, and anonymity, turning its face away from what he deemed to be aberrant details. As an example, he would not, I believe, go for the shrine for "Miko miYool [wearing] a long pole with a rope attached to it, signifying the magic telephone line used by the spirit to send dreams to his devotees." Why did he not, as Jan Vansina might have asked (but it is I), also reproduce those "Kuba [who] were also eager to ride bicycles, use mirrors, operate sewing machines, or play gramophones" or who "imagined that their spirits also made use of technological innovations" as did Miko miYool?[20] Elisofon's art world of Africa's culture was an imaginary that only existed in sterile museums.

Elisofon's collecting up to his last *LIFE* consignment, the arduous literary cum Nigeria coverage in 1959, although profiled to prioritize what he judged to be orthodox and authentic, was a concoction of artifacts, copper earrings, pipes, bows and arrows, textiles, instruments, and what he desired most, masks and sculptures. He was an ardent and omnivorous collector but not necessarily different from so many other traveling narcissists who scraped Africa for "art" in the 1940s and 1950s. From 1960 onward, within the commotions of the time, African de-colonization, the Cold War, and the engagement with Africanness in the United States, his collection build-up took on a dedicated, almost what I would call jingoistic direction. It became an American statement about art. The artifacts he had shipped across the waters from West Africa and the DRC were symbolically imbricated with the evangelizing enthusiasm that defined, as we recall, the *Black African Heritage* (*BAH*) project. The *BAH* project was a political megaphone for America, African art the gospel. The first phase, we saw, was the rough fieldwork; the second was the logistics of the transatlantic transfer in which the mediating assistance by the American embassy staff, USIA officers, and State Department personnel was crucial. At this point, the individual artifact became, as it were, U.S.-sponsored African art. During his lengthy stints of shooting with the Brachers in 1970–1971, in particular, many of his objects were stored at the homes or the offices of U.S. staff either waiting for shipment or to be used by the agencies for local educational events. Marilyn Johnson at the U.S. Foreign Office in Niamey (Niger) was one of those who stored Elisofon's material. Eventually, she appealed to him to request a formal authorization from the Department of State, through Warren Robbins, the D.C. political charmer, to ease the grand exit for a sculpture that Elisofon had left behind, surely for it to acclimatize.[21] Wenston Fenhagen in Abidjan (Ivory Coast), on the other hand, would bide his time: "we have now learned to roll with the punch and every day we safeguard all that lovely African art of yours."[22] But the major outpost for Elisofon's export of the major base artifacts of his collection was the American embassy in Kinshasa, the home of his trading partner, and a collector himself, deputy chief of mission Bayard King. He was Elisofon's most energetic proxy, buying for him objects he missed (such as the "Batshick and Balega masks"), transferring others stored at the embassy (such as "the Bayaka masks [that] were in perfect condition"; the "Bakone stone figures suffered but can be mended"[23]), providing Elisofon accommodation while in transit in Kinshasa (one of Elisofon's many hosts who received a letter of excuse for his irritability), and his networking partner in staying alert about the African art sales market.

The previous paragraph dealt with a few African migratory artifacts. Their American waiting rooms, frustrated departures from Africa, and celebratory arrivals right at the footsteps of the White House guaranteed those long lives in the service of the new country. A few of them reached the rank of emblematic ascendancy. Those were the African artifacts that the two presidents, Lower at ABC and George E. Moynihan of Westinghouse Broadcasting Company, requested or solicited directly from Elisofon. In a letter to Elisofon while staying at the Stanley Hotel, Nairobi, ABC president Leonard H. Goldenson wrote that he wanted the object "to be a handsome display in the window of our new building at 1330 Avenue of the Americas."[24] Moynihan shyly advocated that he wanted something to enhance his own "collection."[25] He was fortunate (he paid) in acquiring a Bakuba mask called

"Mashamboy," cowries, and beads, in addition to Elisofon's instructive note that "Stanley brought a million of them to the Congo to exchange for food."[26] What Lower got, the story does not tell.

It was during the period of his filming and photographing for ABC, the *National Geographic*, and Westinghouse (1966–1972) that Elisofon slowly turned into a practicing art dealer from a frantic on-the-ground collector, both in Africa and in the United States, and developed more and more into a political aesthete. In her qualified study of how African art (Kuba) promoted African American identity in the 1960s, the scholar Sarah van Beurden suggests that a "further investigation of the circumstances that led to the founding of [the Museum of African Art, now part of the Smithsonian, and the Museum of Primitive Art, now the Rockefeller Wing of the Metropolitan], the ways in which they collected and displayed African art, will add to the transnational analysis of postcolonialism."[27] The next segment of such a transnational analysis takes us to the study of Elisofon's homework: his different approaches to promoting the artifacts for public displays, his subtle experimentations with combining photography and the exhibits, and African American politics in response to his appropriation of African artwork.

## From African Artifact to African Art: Eliot Elisofon's Ways of Doing It

A comment Elisofon made in a traveler's letter to his editor Hicks in 1947 has loyally followed me ever since I came upon it a few years ago. Elisofon was en route from Cape Town to Cairo, in Kenya at Karatina market on the Nairobi–Nyeri highway, south of Nyeri town, missing Mount Kenya for the fog but compensating this with the great pleasure he took in photographing women squatting near their woven baskets. This is his intriguing comment: "Their postures and natural positions made picture after picture as easy as copying old masters in the museum. . . . They hadn't the faintest idea that I was shooting then and were very unconscious of the camera." There are two sides that I find interesting in Elisofon's observation. One is his notification of banding together the two contrary, almost dissonant, sites, the museum and, as here, the marketplace—one the holder of deadpan material objects, the other in itself a bounteous field of human shebang. Compressing these sites into an idealistic photographic concept, we recognize and recollect its presence from a number of photo sessions (in this book) where Elisofon captured the single moment with his pictographic paintbrush, transferring it into the still-life art form.

Divining that the object did not fulfill his aesthetic principles (the "unconscious" Kikuyu market women did), we have revealed him over and over again arranging or propping the picture rather than taking it for what it was, at that moment, in that place. His pictures of sculptures, whether they were the few that were held by African museums or the thousands that had been integrated into Western museums since the 1870s, were refined by his eye for composition and a sense of lighting, of which the 405 pictures, taken between 1947 and 1952, that were printed in his book *African Sculpture* bear witness. They too were manipulated or refined, about which stewardly method William Fagg, the longtime curator at the British Museum and coproducer of the *Sculpture* book, and Elisofon were to quarrel in the mid-1960s.

Painting and photographing, Elisofon repeatedly explained, enriched each other. From his own painting he drew the color scheme sensibility, the symmetries of lines, the solitary craftsmanship of slowness; from photography its opposite, speed, the unexpected, the abrupt. "It took 20 years to learn that pictures are at their best when conditions are absolutely at their worst."[28] Paradoxically, at the moment of being trapped in this happenstance, his concern turned into another craftsmanship, another technique, that of designing. "We are dealing with photography as one of many visual arts along with lithography, easel painting and even architecture." Once landed in the happenstance of the Karatina market, his imaginary fractures evolved into other terrain, the visual curating of the museum artwork. This is what he said about his fluctuating moods at a conference on photojournalism in 1966:

> So I've confessed that I'm unhappy with my photography and am not satisfied with what I've done, even though I have been a successful photographer. I cannot get everything I want from the photographic medium, which may be an insufficiency on my part. I find myself groping now in many directions for self-expression. It has occurred to me that maybe I ought to look around a bit to discover whether or not it was entirely my fault that I reached this position in life after 30 years as a photographer.[29]

Photography, for Elisofon, had parallel concurring vectors. We remember his gigantic project in 1959 to do a visual pageant through the literary device of two hundred quotations from fifty authors. For this he took one thousand pictures, of which eighteen were published in 1961 in *LIFE*'s most expensive effort ever to encapsulate Africa for export, the single largest in its publishing history, and a last-minute attempt at fogging the continent. Here Elisofon's photography acted as a visual codification of the West's supremacy over writing Africa, a double-layered political certification.

In each case, the *LIFE* essay and the art book, Elisofon's photography serves a confirmatory additive medium of aestheticizing the objects of the Other, pushing them into a postmodern iconographic trap that makes him uncomfortable with his own oscillating avocation, charging him to ponder "an insufficiency on my part," his restlessness, indecision, and subjectivity. These phantoms can best be illustrated by a paragraph in a review he wrote of the Italian Mirella Ricciardi's book *Vanishing Africa* (1971). Commenting on her explaining that "I was committed to photograph [the vanishing 'tribes' of Kenya] a whole way of life that's changing and slowly dying, to be replaced for better or for worse, by a Westernized civilization and culture," he responded by totally misrepresenting her intention: "The author has accomplished this objective within her own limits, producing a highly personal book which is devoted almost entirely to beauty. The volume is a visual feast for everyone lover of Africa or not."[30] Elisofon's constant invocations and applications of "beauty" as benchmark, standard, and canon risked alienating everybody and everything. And it often did. His cosmos was populated by one sensibility. His unwillingness to see what Ricciardi was trying to do is the same elusive phantom of blind beauty that turned his 1961 postcolonial *LIFE* essay into phantasmagoria. The thesis of Ricciardi's book is the dialectics of societal change. The technical abilities needed for it to produce visual poetry can be registered, but whether they can organize a "visual feast of beauty" depends ultimately on the individual viewer.

Amy J. Staples has elegantly summarized what I call the fragmentation and self-absorption of Elisofon's photography. "In the case of the Elisofon collection, his photographs can be used as a lens to examine historical relationships between Africa and the West, the invention of indigenous contexts of object use and meaning, and the key role that photography plays in the interpretation of museum collection and exhibition practices."[31] We saw all these operations in function, simultaneously, creatively, exasperatingly, designing them to educate the United States about Africa with the loudest hullabaloo in *LIFE*'s history. This was achieved by selecting a fragment from a book on Africa by a white male writer (American, British, French) by another white man, using the literary expression as a conductor's searchlight to identify a piece of African land, and finally translating the object into its visual Other as in a children's game. Elisofon's experimentations with photography and collected artifacts started much earlier. Or rather the two were never either separate artistic intuitions or different crafts. They interacted restlessly, which he diagnosed as a failing. It was not so. His photography, in my view, was at its most critical, energizing, and intriguing peak when provoked by its own invalidity or the competing incentives that Elisofon owned. Having seen the already domesticated and the desired, leaving the museum for the bush, returning to it having captivated the Other, was Elisofon's way of upholding his lifelong struggle with the fallacies and demons of authenticity. The refashioning of the original, whether it happened by the transactions of the camera work in situ (the staged photographic reenactment of a ritual taken outside the initiation context) or the designing after its removal into the Western marketplace arenas, private collections, galleries, and museums, was sanctioned by—to use Elisofon's own word of elevation—the soul of his mission. It was his soul that made him produce "Africa's Savage Beauty," the *Sculpture*, the *Nile*, and the *Color* books, and would set forth his multilayered museum work and teaching circuit with his own collection as its base.

Back from his second African trip in 1951, with his collection taking form, he initiated a traveling exhibition called "Understanding African Negro Sculpture," which circulated among twelve institutions from 1952 through 1954, starting at the Art Institute's Gallery of Photography, the Chicago Museum of Modern Art from 15 January to 1 March 1952. It visited the Museum of Modern Art in New York from 2 July to 14 September the same year.[32] It is these two exhibitions I will visit too. The Chicago exhibit included ten objects, the one in New York only seven, all loans from his own collection.[33] A much larger space was provided Elisofon's photographs, whose only function was, we are informed, "to point up details in the sculpture which might elsewhere be overlooked by the spectator." The "interpretive photographs," affirms the Chicago reviewer further, "add considerably to the interest of the display and to the understanding of Mr. Elisofon's objectives." And that is to educate the ignorant viewer to understand what he or she sees. "By using light and enlargement it is possible to greatly increase the visual impact, and to point out details not ordinarily seen by the naked eye." The five photos of a Dogon figure show its symmetry both from the side and from the back, and in silhouette. The multiple exposures permit the observer to see around the object, "thereby treating the African sculpture, which led to Cubism in the Western world, in a cubistic manner," teaches Elisofon.[34] But what has his lesson to do with Africa?[35] What did the gallery visitors learn about the *nkisi nkondi* figure, the "spirit holder," or, as the artifact in the *Sculpture* book captioned it, the "Bakongo (the Congo river) fetish figure, mirror on the stomach, necklace, banana formed objects around the neck," one of the ten exhibited artifacts (registered "Eliot Elisofon bequest 73-7-297")?

Nothing. The New York reviewer was equally receptive, ready to ring the doorbells for Elisofon's crusade: "modern art . . . has opened our eyes to the bold structure and expressive force of African art and brought it out of the ethnologist's cabinet and into the art museum." In the New York exhibit, Elisofon profiled thirty-two photographs to, among other things, "make an extreme enlargement of a head . . . in order to facilitate the study of the facial expression . . . in another case . . . three studies . . . a close-up of the head . . . a profile photograph of the head and shoulders to demonstrate the balance of the chin with headdress and breasts with shoulders."[36]

Elisofon's cabinet was an artsy-craftsy sweatbox. The same sweatbox fascinated not only Elisofon and the cultural elites of the American East Coast, it snatched the West at the same speed as Africa was throwing out its occupiers. So you'd better go for what was left—now. This was roughly what Elisofon recommended J. O. Brew, director at Harvard's Peabody Museum of Archeology and Ethnology, do. A number of liberated Nimba masks, he wrote in a letter to Brew, had "recently been placed on the market which may never again be available." They were used by the Baga in the coastal lowlands of Guinea who had "converted to Islam and as a result have been giving up their pagan idols." Brew listened. Peabody exchanged pieces of Mimbres pottery for a Nimba mask with the New York art dealer J. J. Klejman.[37] As he did also, when Elisofon with little or no demur told Brew that he, instead of being nominated a Research Fellow in Oceanic Art, would be better served by an assignment as a Research Fellow in Primitive Art and, even more, would appreciate that if such an appointment was plausible, it happened before the publishing of his and Fagg's *Sculpture* book. A perfectly rational suggestion. On his side, he declared he would contribute to the Peabody's collections by trying "to obtain donations of pieces from collectors I know;" donate contact prints of (some of) the twenty-five thousand African sculpture photographs he had taken; and donate prints from his collection of photographs of "primitive peoples in the Pacific and Africa and Peru" and of "important ruins and objects of those areas." He wrote this letter of intent on 30 December 1957; only a few days later, on 11 January, Brew recommended Elisofon's application for the Peabody board, and on 20 February 1958 he was appointed. There were two hotshot men all set to utilize each other's knowledge, contacts, and positions. And they did. For Elisofon, the nomination was a sobriquet that he took advantage of whenever there was need for self-acclamation, pairing it with other accomplishments such as surviving Nazi Stuka bombs in Finland, climbing Rwenzori, and writing two books about Africa.

This year 1958 was a year of miracles for Elisofon, besides its coordination with his book and the academic cheering.[38] It was the second beginning of a series of exhibitions of African art at which he would carry through his soul in his multiple offices of an alleged primitive art expert, reputed *LIFE* photographer, lecturer on (color) photography, and Africa traveler. His lectures at a few universities and meetings with students were additional, not always happy, backups to the exhibits and his connoisseurship in art. The two-channel geographical contribution to his collection, the African with its many handymen and agents and the American with its network of art enthusiasts and millionaires, became the more sophisticated and commercial the closer we got to 1973. In its appropriation and redefinition in a Western epistemological system, the discourse of Elisofon's African collecting/collection epitomized his American mission, becoming a historical artifact itself and grist for the mill of postcolonial criticism. I will stay with this miraculous year in his professional life, which also involved photographing a selfie of him and Kim Novak in Hollywood and the exhibition of his drawings of flowers in India ink and color washes at Durlacher Brothers in New York, 30 September–25 October.

Elisofon's exhibit in 1952, "Understanding African Negro Sculpture," told little about Africa and everything about himself, as we saw. The next mission, his curating of "Masterpieces of Primitive [alternatively African] Art" exhibitions at Harvard's Peabody Museum, the Boston Museum of Fine Arts, and the Brooklyn Museum, October–January the following year, was in contrast to the 1952 traveling exhibit grandiosely pompous, taking in three geographical areas (Africa south of the Sahara, Oceania, the Native Americas). Over half of the works had been selected from the Peabody Museum, others from public and private collections such as Elisofon's. Pompous, not small, but logistically the same. The trio, Brew, Perry Rathbone (director of the Boston Museum of Fine Arts) and Elisofon, at a meeting in June agreed upon designing the exhibition to emphasize the bond between the primitive and the modern artist in treasuring freedom from naturalism and the passion for fantasy by juxtaposing particular works, using the same dichotomous pedagogy that Elisofon did in his yearning for an understanding of what was at stake. In this manner, the trio convened, Picasso's *Les Demoiselles d'Avignon* would be accompanied by "a selection of Bakota funerary fetishes," Paul Klee's paintings of masks "with primitive African masks," and an Amedeo Modogliani sculpture and portrait painting with "African examples showing similar facial attenuation."[39] The *Boston Sunday Herald* reporter Robert Taylor, whose reaction to the "Bushongo cap" object I discussed earlier, thought that the "Primitive Show" was a "dazzling experience," "in the feeling of profound, ritualistic emotions expressed with shattering sincerity . . . in the virtues of a strangely baroque restraint in Africa." T. H. Parker of the *Hartford* (*Conn.*) *Courant*, another reporting visitor, referred to its liberatory function, quoting Rockefeller's speech at the opening of the Museum of African Art in New York in early 1957: "To this end our aim will always be to select objects of outstanding beauty whose rare quality is the equal of works shown in other museums of art and to exhibit them in the fullest measure." This is what the Boston Museum of Fine Arts was doing, Parker contended: the exhibition was emancipatory—long live art.[40] An apt comment relevant here is Schildkrout and Keim's: "The decontextualization, with all its problems of intellectual imperialism, nevertheless opened up the possibility of seeing and exhibiting African art and Western art together within the same museums and the same kinds of exhibition spaces" (34). As a quick response to my questioning: what "possibility," whose "possibility," they respond by offering but little more than another liberal apology: "a *trans*versal aesthetic that would require viewers to understand alternative worldviews and aesthetics" (35). An African sculpture collected is an act proffering a loss that cannot be repaired or saved.

A new decade was passing, with Elisofon constantly haggling, hammering out deals, bartering, in fieldwork in Africa (for ABC) and among New York art dealers (Brew, Klejman, de Havenon, Jacques Hautalet, Julius Carlebach, Peter Pollock, Everett P. Lesley, Walter A. Weiss, and others), acting as price setter of African objects, and lecturing as part of exhibitions and conferences on African sculpture and art, with a fervor as unstoppable as the theme was monophonic.[41] Some of them shared with him their experiences from traveling and collecting in Africa. One of them was the Freedom Rider activist from 1961–1962 Albert F. Gordon, who owned Tribal Arts Gallery in Manhattan (3 August 1972). Another was Anatole Yaron, a segment of whose letter to Elisofon, which communicates the collecting ethics at the time. Yaron tells him (9 June 1972) about his traveling "thousands of miles through the jungle and deserts of Africa" and how he had managed to find a handful of "primitive African sculptors whose work is completely uninfluenced by Western culture—about which they know nothing."[42] He continues:

> These artists are all genuine: they have never been bought and their skills come from their own innate talents. They live in a culture that is in the early iron-age, 3000–5000 B.C. They have never been to a city and have never seen sculptures or works of art created by modern Western man. They believe in spirits and witchcraft. (HRC 63.8)

The further we move into the American 1960s Africanness, Elisofon's aestheticism radicalized to provide space for his "black heritage" commitment spurred on also by Robbins, the pragmatist and the visionary in one, with whom he would establish a formal partnership, if not friendship. On 25 March 1963 Robbins, in the process of buying the house(s) that would become the Frederick Douglass Institute of Negro Arts and History, invited Elisofon to join him as an associate and "a trustee of the new Museum and help us build a first-class institution in Washington which the African Diplomatic Community can rally around consider to be 'their' center."[43] In the mid-1960s, the rhetoric of the primitive and its subtextual playmates started to cave in; "primitive" was turning into "traditional," another sinuous misnomer. By the end of the decade the museums were ready for another round of grand displays, pulled forward by a more self-reflecting language and a political stance hesitantly in tune with the American streets, but above all by Washington's and Robbins' forwardness.

The first to come out was the Peabody Museum exhibition "Masterpieces of Black African Art," which opened in November 1969. It drew, the press release announced, its objects exclusively from its own holdings of "sculptural art" (an alleged policy shift from "ethnographic materials") organized in the categories of "South African Rock Art, Bronzes from the former Kingdom of Benin, Brass and Iron work, Sculptures of West and Central Africa, Ceremonial Masks of Africa and Poro Society Masks from Liberia." Were it not for the reservations attached to the two words in the curator's writing of their acquisition history, it would read as a parody of a nineteenth-century British Museum handout: "Black Africa [*sic*], especially West and Central Africa, was the first tribal area of the world to be 'discovered' and recognized as having produced 'Art' by early 20th century European artists." The next note of information that interests me describes the criteria along which Elisofon's coastal artifacts have been arranged: "Sculptural styles are organized geometrically by tribal regions, moving from west to east from the great Niger River drainage to the Congo basin. Several of the finest pieces are from the Museum's Eliot Elisofon Collection of Primitive Art."[44] This is an acceptable, even laudable, representation of the artifacts. It combines ethnicity and place, and it could do no more. Elisofon's ethnic designations were as a rule handpicked with a journalist's nervous fingers: static, unconditional, and, by definition, not trustworthy. As Rosalinde G. Wilcox has shown, naming and designating cultural artifacts collected in regions characterized by cross-cultural exchanges, people floating in and out, and with a long history of European commercial activities has been particularly problematic.[45] These were, in other words, Elisofon's lifelong African hunting grounds. The Peabody Museum exhibition was a solid success. The concept and some of its material traveled south and reappeared under the new name of "African Sculpture" at the National Gallery (Washington, D.C., 28 January–February 1970) and in modified form at the Brooklyn Museum (New York, February–June), where Elisofon gave a lecture called "Black Soul," the manifesto of his *BAH* mission. The *New York Times* art critic, John Canaday, who was one of the 155,000 who had seen these, what he called "disappointing exhibitions," based his comparative judgment on what he experienced in Washington a year later. He had seen the groundbreaking exhibition "The Language of African Art" at the renovated Museum of African Art at the National Portrait Gallery that ran from 1 July to 7 September 1970 (HRC 58.22).

It was groundbreaking for the simple reason that it permitted the *New York Times* critic to walk around bewildered and confused, not knowing whether he was being pushed into a corner or liberated from others. At one moment he jubilantly exclaimed: "it is the only exhibition I have ever seen where African sculpture is allowed to speak for itself, although we have been putting words into its mouth for a long time now." And even more to the point: "it was good to see African sculpture attached to its own world, even to a remote and synthetic echo of its own world, after having seen it for so long exhibited as material for aesthetic consideration alone, extracted from all contexts that accounted for its creation." Then came the hesitations. Didactics was still there and perhaps should be. He concludes: "the Museum of African Art's show fuses the two opposing attitudes toward African sculpture to the advantage of both." The dichotomous subtext spells it out: the bilingual exhibition was an anachronism, the *New York Times* title for the feature, "In Its Own Language, For a Welcome Change," a Capitol Hill summer romance.[46]

As cruel fate would have it, this proved also to be groundbreaking time for Elisofon. In a letter he wrote to Beverly Carter, deputy assistant secretary of state reports about a meeting he had at Robbins's home that in many ways reflects in a nutshell the strategies of Elisofon's American mission. More specifically, he was making an attempt as a backup for Robbins to raise state money to fund the exhibition of Gaston de Havenon's collection of African art planned to feature as part of the reopening gala of the museum in May 1971 (through 3 October).

> This exhibition will serve not only to dramatize the opening of the new museum building, but will also demonstrate America's growing interest in Africa. This is important, not only to the Africans, but to all Americans and particularly those whose ancestry includes Africa. As you know, the four films I am making for Westinghouse

> Broadcasting, hope to dramatize this. The Museum of African Art is also performing this function in America's capital. I hope that you and the Department of State will do everything possible to make this exhibition most successful by giving it the support it deserves. (29 October 1970, HRC 68.12)

Here in highfalutin rhetoric, the two events of the opening of the Museum of African Art and Elisofon's all-purpose contribution to its collections and his filming for *BAH* are (to use his own word) "dramatized" to support a rather pedestrian application for dollars. That the plea was buttered up with the sentimental cliché of America's "growing interest in Africa" was Elisofon's way of warranting the writer's in-house position when addressing a secretary of state. A few months later, Robbins circulated a welcoming letter the "trustees and members of our National Council," detailing the program for a week in May 1971, in which the de Havenon African masterpiece exhibit from New York was the number one public drawing card, Senator Hubert Humphrey, chairman of the board of trustees, number two.

The programmatic politics that seeped into Elisofon's letter to Beverly Carter was definitely played out to the full during his last year (1972) as an activist, on all fronts. From 11 April to 14 May the "Permanent Collection Featuring Works Collected in Africa by Eliot Elisofon," an exhibition of sixty artifacts from his own home collection to "salute the four TV programs" (as it was announced), was exhibited at the Museum of African Art; from 29 September to 1 October he led a workshop on photography at the University Museum, Philadelphia; on 19 October at Columbus Gallery of Fine Arts, Ohio, he talked about his film *Africa's Gift*, in conjunction with the public viewing of the whole series and with the exhibition "Sculpture of Black Africa," featuring the New York Tishman collection; and on 25 October he gave the lecture "African Art in Tribal Society" with eighty color slides at the exhibition "African Art from the Museum of Primitive Art [New York]" at the Museum of Art, Rhode Island School of Design. This four-event concoction of photography, film, sculpture, and lecture summarizes well the essence of Elisofon's professional caliber as it crystallized during the last years of his life in the United States. During this year he was also occupied with the publishing of a book manuscript, "The Meaning of African Art" (an earlier version was called "Africa and Its Art"), for Harry N. Abrams, Inc., but his time ran out.

What stayed with him to the end was his irritation at whatever scraped his field of expertise, or what he reckoned was his area of expertise. On 11 October, having seen Roy Sieber's exhibition "African Textiles and Decorative Art" at the

Museum of Modern Art in New York,[47] Elisofon bubbled with resentment to the degree that he wrote Robbins a woeful letter, listing the mistakes and the lacunae that he considered undermined the exhibit. First of all, it made no attempt at showing "African art in its proper environment." Why did they not display a narrow weaving loom and heddle pulleys in the gallery, or, failing that, use photographs (his)? Why was Paul Tishman's gold collection not represented?[48] Why was there not a "single appliqué cloth panel from Abomey, not one painted cloth from the Senuto, no back side panel from the Mangboto"? More demonstratively, as Elisofon had "photographed all these which could have been used if the real objects were either unavailable, or if there was not enough room for a large display."[49] Elisofon's aggravation was partly personal, partly the pose of knowing one's stuff. Sieger, the first American with a Ph. D. in African art, had not consulted him. He was a scholar who, Elisofon knew, would tear his African art book manuscript into pieces if he were given a chance to examine it. Any ideas of installing or simulating a "proper environment" to enlarge the art objects, Sieger and, for that matter, Fagg would have rejected robustly and asked Elisofon to define what and whose environment he had in mind.

## William B. Fagg and Eliot Elisofon: One Sculpture, Two Shadows

Fagg and Elisofon were worlds apart: Fagg a descriptive, neutral documentarian also when taking field photographs, and there are 2,500 of them; Elisofon an aesthete always psyched-up to use the camera for flashy misquotations. That they landed in the same 1958 book was neither a mistake nor a studious design. What made their tie-in tolerable were two things. One, that the book in intellectual terms was two in one, Elisofon, the photographer responsible for the 405 photos; Fagg, the expert-scholar, the writer of the introduction, for the scholarly side. Their "mistake" was that each flimflammed in the other's area of mastership. Second, their misalliance animated—creatively—the bickering between them for the rest of their lives.

In *The African Sculpture*, photography's function resembled that of the ethnographic co-coadjutor, Western apologist/custodian of collected artifacts. It was a monumental, overpriced, and also much-criticized work, boosted by its double-crossing nature.[50] Right from the start, in his introductory essay, Fagg turned against the presumptions of "his own" book, pointing out that it presented a detailed analysis of the aesthetic philosophy of African sculpture, which it should not have done: "It is not the purpose of these brief notes to define, describe or analyze the qualities of negro art . . . indeed most of those who have written from the aesthetic point of view have succeeded only in interposing an opaque screen of largely irrelevant verbiage between it and the student" (23). This was a direct debunking of Elisofon. His reason was not that Elisofon had adopted the "museum object photography" conventions[51] by de-contextualizing or nullifying the setting (which Fagg himself also did) but by targeting each sculpture with a meticulous artistic mannerism through his camera. To listen to a contemporary outsider Gwilym Iwan "G.I." Jones, anthropologist, photographer, and writer of *The Ibo and Ibibio Peoples of Eastern Nigeria* (1950), is to stay next door to the in-group language speaker. Reviewing the book, he criticized both writers, in particular Fagg, for using defective attributions and classifications, taking it for granted that any reader would understand what was meant by "tribe" and "style."

> It is high time that producers of works on African Negro art made up their minds about the labels which they attach to their specimens. It is one thing to define a particular style and to call it by the name of the tribe in whose territory it was first discovered; it's another to call all carvings made by or obtained from the people of a particular tribe by the name of this tribe.

Elisofon's "overpowerful spotlight" was problematic, also the close-up distortions, whereas a number of plates taken from different angles were commendable, Jones concluded, hesitantly having picked a winner. "What more can we expect or ask for in these days when African Negro Art has ceased to interest the majority of anthropologists and has become the accepted domain of the art critic and the connoisseur."[52] Jones had circled in on the discrepancies that united the two.

In his publication *Nigerian Images*, Fagg collaborated with another famed photographer, the German Herbert List, who in Deborah Stoke's profiling of him comes out as "known for capturing transitory atmospheric effects."[53] His impact on Fagg was to bring out "the true nature" of African sculpture by the photographer employing "only natural daylight." It became Fagg's credo: "I find his photographs the truest I have ever seen. . . . [By] using dark backgrounds for dark objects, List softens the silhouette to a properly secondary status and so partly overcomes the limitations of the two-dimensional surface."[54] Another tributary aspect that Fagg incorporated in his directorial photography (his own and List's) via Arnold Newman (who also, we remember, took photos of the Congo Kuba King in 1958) was his gimmick to add emblematic props of all kinds around or on the poser.[55] His purpose was documentary, "to record the object," not to redesign it into a personality, Stoke asserts. Elisofon's letter to Fagg, with its takeoff in *Nigerian Images*, oozed like a snuffbox full of displeasure. "Great naturalness can be achieved with artificial light as well. . . . I think that the function of the photographer is to make a piece of sculpture readable; to translate into a two dimensional medium, a three dimensional work of widely diversified forms and textures."[56] Elisofon is here referring to his usage of multiple angles to highlight the sculpture. He is also skeptical toward Fagg's tolerance of not separating the context from the object, whether it is someone sitting for a portrait or a sculpture. "Unless the photographs are made of objects *in situ*, and seen by dim light filtered through thatch, or by torches . . . , any attempt to photograph the object away from its setting is being done to inform about the characteristics of the sculpture itself. . . . [It] should at least allow the object to be discernible from the background." At their next confrontation, Elisofon, the eclectic connoisseur, and Fagg, the dilatory scholar, clashed face to face, and in public. It was the photographer's duty and right to isolate the artifact from the background, Elisofon argued, it was an ideal way of collecting information and clarity about the object. Fagg thought as passionately that this was a faulty method, the opposite was right, object and context are one, and information is not tint and tone. Isolating the background is isolating Africa. The two men had known each other since 1953, now it was 1971.

The venue was Center for Afroamerican and African Studies (CAAS) symposium on "Traditional African Art," at the Peabody Museum, 4–7 May 1971. Among the speakers were Rosalyn Walker, Daniel Biebuyck, Philip Dark, David Fagg, David Crownover, and Elisofon. The last three were the main speakers of the conference: Fagg, "On the Meaning and Uses of Tribanality"; Crownover, "The Exhibition of African Art"; and Elisofon, "How to Photograph Primitive Art." Fagg spoke about the networks of artists of long African standing working in cast metal (Lower Niger area) and ivory carvings (the West Guinea Coast and the Kingdom of Kongo); Crownover, a Penn Museum authority on both African tribal art and preparations of exhibitions, about which he talked; Elisofon on his favorite topic—of all seasons.

Both Fagg and Crownover had participated in a similar conference in 1961 at the Royal Anthropological Institute, London, called "The Artist in Tribal Society." Fagg was reported by William Davenport to have had discussed "the possibility that a *horror vacui* and the extension of the use of an object might be bases for the so-called aesthetic or creative impulse . . . [and] points out the permissible scope of individual expression and explicit critical values toward sculpture in Africa," and Crownover, "the fallacy of presenting African art as pure art, yet he agrees that museum exhibitions can be used to reconstruct anonymous tribal artists, the best of whom can be placed among the greats in historical art."[57] Their Peabody talks a decade later addressed the same topics and points of view.

The provenance of Elisofon's paper (written after the Peabody conference; it contained comments on Fagg's presentation) "How to Photograph Primitive Art" had longitude, staunchness, and spin of a kind that one could, symbolically, nominate it, not a rubric, but a title to cover the whole spectrum of his African filming, whether it featured racialized African leaders, walking or dancing bare-breasted women, staged masks in motion, gaping hippos, wet Rwenzori panoramas, or dry museum artifacts.[58] The concepts of "primitive" and "art," historical carriers of umbrage of distortion, define and misrepresent their objects but do it openly, with their best intentions. Elisofon wanted us to see what he saw. That is the "how" in the title, which in its turn allows us—and me—to ask, "why/what?" He was the very last presenter at the four-day Peabody conference; it was Friday 3:30 p.m., and the closing dinner would start at 7:00 p.m. He showed eighteen slides and talked.

The first eight slides were all pictures taken in situ. They were portraits of leaders, pictures of ceremonial dancers and singers, and a single one on a site. The other eleven were of artifacts; six of them were photographed in situ, three in private collections in the United States, and the last two were made at the African Sculpture Exhibition in Washington, 1970. What is notable but also illuminative is that what concerns these eight specimens; he exclusively discussed the reasons why he chose to use a wide-angle 28mm lens and *not* "a normal lens." To include the entire bush expansion bridge on Cavally River near Danané with the "trees on both banks," it was necessary to go for the 28mm focal length. The same annotation governed the making of the image of "three Bambara [Bambana] dancers with Sogni [Sogoni] Koun antelope headdresses near Bamako."[59] For including the entire scene the wide-angle lens was a must. Only that any technical exposition about the usage of lens elements, long-range zooming, isolation, and magnifying in these examples, and in others, served a far more dignified purpose. The discussion about these eight pictures was a preamble for the crux of his lecture, which was to demonstrate that primitive art photography of purifying objects or scenes, that is to make them look-alikes of the idealized origins, was as much a routine as changing camera lenses for the image-making of sites and "types." This is what I meant by the word "illuminative." Elisofon did not talk about, nor did he as a rule register in his field-notes, the whys, whens, and hows he staged the objects. The word "authenticity" was for him ignis fatuus. The eight pieces from the Ivory Coast, Nigeria, Mali, and the Congo were a warming up expo of didactic juxtaposition.

Applying his method of administering the artifact-art process, his American mission, especially with William Fagg, the Brit in the room, his explanations of the "how" were to be adamant and contentious. Elisofon approached the multiple de-contextualized museum artifacts with committed fervor. The Ife brass head picture, he explained, was made "by placing the sculpture at the edge of the arcade inside the courtyard of the Ife Museum . . . set so that soft light from the sky but not sunlight illuminated the head from one side [and a] white cardboard was held near the shadow side to reflect light of the year"; the Igbo-Ukwu terracotta bowl at the Department of Antiquities, Ibadan, was shot by the same 55mm Micro-Nikker, but indoors, and with "simulated daylight and a roll of paper to simplify background"; the image of the ancestral shrine at House of Oba, Benin, was done with one "strobe light above and to left of camera"; the Ashanti stool at Prempeh II Jubilee Museum, Kumasi, required a "six foot wide roll of paper" and lamps "together with soft daylight" for it to materialize.[60] The artifacts that had been collected and found their way to the Unites States were treated in the same way, despite the additional layer of estrangement they had been subjected to. An intrusive material "layer" was the mending of the artifacts, a curative procedure that many of Elisofon's objects underwent on their arrival in New York. One of the "imported" images that he showed for the audience was of the Guro heddle pulleys in Mr. and Mrs. Harold Rome's collection, New York. (It was the one he referred to in the letter to Robbins [17 October 1972].) Another was of a small Dogon figure, "which resembles Cubistic painting," from his own collection. Both were taken by a "4×5 Linhof camera, 18cm Symmer lens" with multiple exposures and lighting "to achieve different effects" and highlight their modernity.[61] These two photos, and a third he had taken of a mask at the 1970 exhibition in Washington, D.C., whose original location was Museu Nacional de Antropologia, Luanda, Angola, were the soubrettes in his lecture about *how* primitive art photography can "analyze and demonstrate aesthetics in sculpture."[62]

One thing is missing. His brush-off of Fagg. It is as much depictive of Elisofon's mission—and as brutal. They were on the separate sides of the Niger River.

> William Fagg is an outstanding scholar in African art but anyone who has seen his photographs of the same subject knows his weakness. In his lecture at this

conference he showed slides of an Ife stool which had about ten loose sheets of writing paper scattered around the object. He also has some mistaken ideas about photographic lighting. He wrote in the Introduction to *Nigerian Images* that photographer Herbert List "employs only natural daylight. By this almost unheard-of-technique he achieves the closest sympathy with the original artists who were similarly limited by the light of the sun—and has, I believe, succeeded in preserving and liberating for us the real nature of these sculptures." Fagg concluded that "these are the truest photographs of African sculpture."

This is nonsense. No one can tell the difference between daylight and simulated daylight if it is carefully executed. It is easy to differentiate tricky spotlighting with multiple shadows. What does Fagg mean by real? If the objects were kept in a dark shrine where there is almost no light, is this the way it should be photographed?[63]

# Conclusion

> An alternate political culture is not simply something outside the system; it is first and foremost a domain from which a language and a dialogic can reveal eurocentrism in all its modes of thought control; yet not as polemic, which presumes a eurocentric subject-object relation to those it polemicizes. As a network, an alternate political culture would be a framework for political autonomy that speaks in terms that the eurocentric subject-object paradigm cannot hear. It needs to be a cultural framework in order to resist all efforts to reduce it to a subject-object paradigm again, and to commodify it. It has to be political in order to critically address the structures and ideological frameworks of the coloniality of power in opposition. And it has to be alternate to contest eurocentrism as the enemy without falling into the language of eurocentrism in doing so.
>
> —Steve Martinot, "The Coloniality of Power: Notes toward De-Colonization"

Having followed Eliot Elisofon step by step across the African continent for five-plus years and approaching the last paragraphs of this book, it would be otherworldly not to declare—if it does not stand out between the lines—my respect and admiration not only for Elisofon's enormous drive, inquisitiveness, and general know-how that kept provoking and stimulating him to add one photographic site, one new scheme, one particular portrait-making to endless others right to the end of his lifelong traveling in Africa, but with equal sincere esteem acknowledge his many gestures of carefulness and backing that he bestowed on people he met. One such a momentum was his assisting Priya Ramrakha (1935–1968) to move to the United States (1960) for an education in photography at the Art Center School of Los Angeles,[1] another his relief work custody of children at the French Moroccan concentration camp !Sidi El Agachei on 25 December 1942.[2] I have recognized such instances of Elisofon's altruism *passim*, not analyzed and valorized them in their own right, for no other reason than that the book is not a biographical coverage of Elisofon as person and traveler with Africa as his hinterland. It is an intellectual and critical study of the ideology of his photojournalistic imagining of Africa, its "eurocentric subject-object parameters" or "whiteness."[3]

However, two multifaceted parameters central to Elisofon's professional self-perception need to be reiterated. Early in his career, inspired by his unprivileged upbringing, he made it his task to "point his camera at things that needed attention." He started to roam the New York streets and poverty-stricken parts of the United States, documenting children in the slums of the Fourth Street in the Lower East Side of Manhattan (where he was born, "100 feet from the Bowery"); coal mining in Pennsylvania; the miserable education system in Georgia; the Ohio relief crisis; coal miners at Jenkins, Kentucky; and poor communities in the South.[4] He was one of the initiators of the Photo League (1936–1951), a school and salon formed by immigrants and children of immigrants that "would become a casualty of the McCarthy-era blacklists for leftist leanings." Periodically, he was its president (1939 and 1941). For this, he was publicly punished, as were many other members. As a consequence, he self-censured.

> Leaguers were inspired to make inequity and discrimination tangible in their work. Tenement facades, shoeshine boys, protests, and portraits of the poor all figured frequently in their work. Often, their empathy was suffused with playfulness and humor as in Eliot Elisofon's shot of children playing in an empty dirty lot behind a sign that reads "WPA Cleaned This Area . . . Keep it Clean."[5]

This is what he said in an interview apropos his share in the Photo League exhibition "Toward a Harlem Document" (which he preferred to call a "crusade") of forty prints at the New School of Social Research, where he also taught the subject (1938–1942): "To tell the whole story with a picture, you have to show both sides—how things are and how they ought to be."[6] What "they ought to be" would take on a different meaning in Africa.

Throughout Elisofon's wartime in Scandinavia, in the many interviews with him, he pointed out his commitment to "social issues," but without explaining what he had in mind and how and why the camera could be a tool of change. He spoke with hesitancy about it, referring vaguely to his prewar documentary work in the United States, almost as an excuse, citing simultaneously, and with far more vivacity, his secondary passion, that of his hunger for painting, making it sound as a competitive pitch, a winning corollary, as aesthetics also proved to be. His social agenda and artistic inspiration were the two criteria of his activist get-up-and-go. The two seemed to be incompatible programs that started to hound him at this time in his life, never to be brought to a halt.

It was not chance that fashioned Elisofon's trickster career. It was personal and timely arrivism, a hotpot of charm, creativity, intelligence, self-awareness, and planning. Having distributed work to *LIFE* since 1937, joining the staff in 1942 as a war correspondent, he was inch by inch closing in on *LIFE*'s "overt educational imperatives" (Doss 2001, 8) and masculinist dispensation.[7] His postwar material world, its mechanisms of restriction that he was answerable to, were to be configured by a number of circumstances: the colonial paradigms of repression and racism, the psychotic national "Red scare," and, increasingly, the reductive strings that the Cold War period brought with it. Elisofon's radical and free-speaking camera of the Depression and his combat camera of World War II metamorphosed in Africa into the programmed colonial and Cold War camera. It is his Third Camera that produced the grand majority of his photographs, both the well-known and the less-known, hiding in the archives. At the time of his second African travel (I count the 1947 trip as his first), an intrusive visitation of him occurred that conditioned Elisofon's freedom of expression as a photojournalist.

On 6 March 1951, the last year of the Photo League's sixteen-year lifetime, Elisofon received a letter from the FBI in which he was accused of being a Communist. The Department of State had found his name listed in the New York Police Department files in the suspect list, which notification in its turn was based on his name appearing in the 27 October 1941 issue of the "Communist" *Daily Worker*, where he had been introduced as writer of the article "Behind the Candid Camera Man, How the Job Is Learned in the Photo League" (HRC 69.2; 71.7–8). Or it could have been another article: "Camera-Eye on Southern Life in 1940. Elliot [*sic*] Elisofon's Remarkable Photo Exhibition of Dixies's Disinherited" also in the *Daily Worker* (29 March 1940). The U.S. attorney general blacklisting of the Photo League as "totalitarian, fascist, communist, or subversive" in 1947 would implicate a number of honorable World War II combatants, not only Elisofon. Elisofon was furious and self-righteous. In an affidavit to the State Department, he swore to and signed (10 March 1954) a statement that he was not a Communist Party member, never had been one, and that he had not been and was not connected with any Communist organization. As if this were not enough, he was constrained to cleanse himself, as it seems, from the allegations before his employers, although, by then, six years had passed since the FBI had contacted him. On 8 March 1957, in a ten-page-long affidavit for *Time* and *LIFE*, "for my accreditation as a press representative to the Defense Department and all branch of our Army, Navy and Marine Corp," he listed his World War II honorary exploits in Tunisia, Canada, Sweden, and Finland, and continued:

> In 1947, I drove from Capetown to Cairo and upon my return to America, was of assistance to the Combined Intelligence in selecting hundreds of my photographs, taken on *LIFE* assignment, for the purpose of documenting roads and topography. In 1948, again on *LIFE* assignment, I photographed the entire Atlantic coast of Europe. I deliberately made hundreds of photographs of docks, harbors and beaches. Of my volition, while I was in Oslo, I consulted with Commander Porter, the Naval Attaché of the American Embassy, and received instructions from him as to what was important. I executed these suggestions and the photographs which I took are now in Intelligence files. These photographs include fjords on the Atlantic coast nearest to Russia. (HRC 71.8. 9)

And he added that he had refrained from fraternizing with the crew of *Moulin Rouge* while working as a "special color consultant" for John Huston, 1952, "including the star José Ferrer," who had been questioned by the House Committee on Un-American Activities in 1951. One is pushed to query how many of the aerials that Elisofon took in 1959 of terrains such as the Mau Mau hideouts in the Aberdare Mountains and Mount Kenya, the Witwatersrand mining area in South Africa, and the industrial centers in northern and southeastern Nigeria and along the Atlantic coast (later on of Mobutu's enclaves) wound up in American military archives (and not—only—in EEPA).

Elisofon's second unfulfilled dream, the parameter that we have confronted on a number of occasions and in many variations in this book: his uninterrupted aspirations not only to integrate aesthetics with his documentary photography, whether it was a portrait of women working or of panoramas of the Congo River, but to make the aesthetic appeal (he called it beauty, the primitive, the true and pure, modernism) its essentialist or orthodox epicenter. Reality in Africa was his subjective engineered version of imperialist nostalgia; reality in the United States was separate from him, a photojournalist's free-standing object. For the former to emanate and qualify as a product and surface as an accomplished photography for sharing, it underwent a series of processual operations: it had to be authenticated and blessed, first of all, by the external regulating systems, at times outside of Elisofon's control (*LIFE*'s publishing ethics, the politics of American values, and laws) and by his normative imaginary of what constituted (or should constitute) the American public's expectations of what made an image of Africa click. The image was his artwork, the camera his brush. He was a virtuoso of handling it. The handicraft, the apex of the multifaceted creative process, turned out to be the embedded photograph of Africa that so many people have taken pleasure in, made use of, but also over and over again, been misinformed by. It is Africa beside its point.

Eliot Elisofon's photography in Africa is a product of a colonialist mission, a Eurocentric subject-object relation as commodified delusion.

# *LIFE* Photo Essays by or with Eliot Elisofon

The *LIFE* photo essays (most of them by Elisofon) that I discuss in more length in the book are listed here in the order they were published, followed by the chapter numbers in which they occur. The essays can be viewed online on *LIFE*'s Google Books page.

"Finland: Soviet Russia Crowds a Nation of Democrats." *LIFE*, 30 October 1939, 69–76. Chapter 1.

"Date in Casablanca." *LIFE*, 1 February 1943, 94–96, 99. Chapter 1.

"Morocco Feast: Potent Caid of Rehamna Tribe Entertains General Clark and Staff" [a subsection of the essay "Allies Overrun North Africa"]. *LIFE*, 17 May 1943, 15–21. Chapter 1.

"Swedish Glass." *LIFE*, 7 August 1944, 65–68. Chapter 1.

"Sweden's Model Apartments: 'Stockholm Building Is Wonderful for Wives Who Work.'" *LIFE*, 12 March 1945, 112–14. Chapter 1.

"England's King Visits South Africa." *LIFE*, 10 March 1947, 10, 27–32. Chapter 2.

"African Big Shot: A Fat Black Monarch of the Congo Rules His Tribe with a Heavy Hand." *LIFE*, 31 March 1947, 129–32. Chapters 2 and 9.

"The Coast of Europe: It Is a Bright Magnet for American Tourists." *LIFE*, 13 June 1949, 62–80. Chapter 1.

"The Nile: Its Course Unfolds Mighty Panorama of River People and Civilizations." *LIFE*, 20 November 1950, 118–29. Chapter 2.

"LIFE Goes on Location in Africa" [the making of *The African Queen*], *LIFE*, 17 September 1951, 173–79. Chapter 8.

"One Fifth of a Nation Celebrates [South Africa]." *LIFE*, 21 April 1952, 27–44. [David Douglas Duncan's photographs.] Chapter 4.

"Mystic Art of Tribal Africa: Images of Early Negro Culture Influence Native Life of Today." *LIFE*, 8 September 1952, 116–25. Chapter 2.

"Lost Peaks and Big Game: Albert Park Is Africa's Wild Paradise." *LIFE*, 4 May 1953, 75–86. Elisofon's photo essay is part of the *LIFE* special issue "Africa: A Continent in Ferment," ed. Alexander Campbell, *LIFE* 34.18 (1953): 9–178. Chapter 4.

"Voyages to Paradise: A Camera in South Seas Seeks Famous Scenes in Literature." *LIFE*, 24 January 1955, 60–77. Chapter 5.

"Black Africa Surges to Independence," part 1. *LIFE*, 26 January 1959, 100–110. Written by Robert Coughlan with photos by Eliot Elisofon. Chapter 4.

"Stormy Future for Africa. Eruption of Black Africa," part 2. *LIFE*, 2 February 1959, 82–104. Written by Robert Coughlan with photos by Eliot Elisofon. Chapter 4.

"The Hopeful Launching of a Proud and Free Nigeria: New Nation Is a Model of Preparation in a Turbulent Continent." *LIFE*, 26 September 1960, 54–68. Chapter 4.

"A Writer's Land of Primitive, Eloquent Beauty: Storied World of Africa." *LIFE*, 13 October 1961, 66–87. Chapter 5.

"A Safari Back to Innocence: Immersion in Life, Journey to East Africa." *LIFE*, 21 October 1966, 88–94, 97–98. Written by Anne Morrow Lindbergh with photos by Eliot Elisofon. Chapter 5.

"Yesterday's Congo, Today's Zaire." *National Geographic* 143.3 (1973): 398–432. Written by John P. Putman with photos by Putnam and Eliot Elisofon. Chapter 7.

# Notes

## Preface

1. Eliot Elisofon Photographic Archives, National Museum of African Art, Smithsonian Institution, Washington, D.C., http://africa.si.edu/collection/eliot-elisofon-photographic-archives/.
2. Harry Ransom Center, University of Texas at Austin, http://norman.hrc.utexas.edu/fasearch/findingAid.cfm?eadid=00146p1.
3. Ali Behdad, "On Globalization, Again!," in *Postcolonial Studies and Beyond*, ed. Ania Loomba, Suvir Kaul, Matti Bunzi, Antoinette Burton, and Jed Esty (Durham, NC: Duke University Press, 2006), 76.
4. Stephen Greenblatt, *Marvelous Possessions: The Wonder of the New World* (Chicago: University of Chicago Press, 1991), 122.
5. For a brief biographical overview of Elisofon, see Roy Flukinger, "'To Help the World to See': An Eliot Elisofon Retrospective" (booklet and web page), Harry Ransom Center, University of Texas at Austin, 2000, http://www.hrc.utexas.edu/exhibitions/2000/elisofon/elisofon2.html.
6. Robert Young, *Colonial Desire: Hybridity in Theory, Culture and Race* (New York: Routledge, 1995), 163; Robert Young, *White Mythologies: Writing History and the West* (New York: Routledge, 1992), 124.

7. Allan Sekula, *Photography against the Grain: Essays and Photowork, 1973–1983* (Halifax: The Press of the Nova Scotia College, 1984).
8. Ruth Mayer, *Artificial Africas: Colonial Images in the Times of Globalization* (Hanover, NH: University Press of New England, 2002), 76.
9. Loomba et al., *Postcolonial Studies and Beyond*, 34.
10. David Theo Goldberg and Ato Quayson, eds., *Relocating Postcolonialism* (Oxford: Blackwell, 2002), xii.
11. Anne McClintock, *Imperial Leather: Race, Gender, and Sexuality in the Colonial Contest* (New York: Routledge, 1995), 15.
12. Young, *White Mythologies*, 17.
13. "Beyond What? An Introduction," in Loomba et al., *Postcolonial Studies and Beyond*, 17–18.
14. Young invoking Emmanuel Levinas, in *White Mythologies*, 14.
15. Caren Kaplan, *Questions of Travel: Postmodern Discourses of Displacement* (Durham, NC: Duke University Press, 1996), 53.
16. See Beth Py-Lieberman, "Meet the Real 'Most Interesting Man in the World,'" Smithsonian.com, 6 December 2013, http://www.smithsonianmag.com/smithsonian-institution/meet-the-real-most-interesting-man-in-the-world-180949043/?no-ist.
17. For a discussion of the "gaze" and the "look," see Anne Maxwell, *Colonial Photography and Exhibitions* (London: Leicester University Press, 1999), 13–14; E. Ann Kaplan, *Looking for the Other: Feminism, Film and the Imperial Gaze* (London: Routledge, 1997), xi, xviii.
18. Frantz Fanon, *The Wretched of the Earth* (Harmondsworth: Penguin Books, 1967), 30.
19. Benita Parry, "Directions and Dead Ends in Postcolonial Studies," in Goldberg and Quayson, *Relocating Postcolonialism*, 68.
20. Peter Hulme, "Beyond the Straits: Postcolonial Allegories of the Globe," in Loomba et al., *Postcolonial Studies and Beyond*, 52.
21. Carolyn Martin Shaw, *Colonial Inscriptions: Race, Sex, and Class in Kenya* (Minneapolis: University of Minnesota Press, 1995), 181.
22. Lucy R. Lippard, *The Lure of the Local: Senses of Place in a Multicentered Society* (New York: New Press, 1997), 58. See the photo taken by Maya Bracher of the filming of wildlife on the Rwindi plains, EEPA EENG 08448.
23. Barnor Hesse, "Forgotten Like a Bad Dream: Atlantic Slavery and the Ethics of Postcolonial Memory," in Goldberg and Quayson, *Relocating Postcolonialism*, 161.
24. Okwu Enwezor, *Snap Judgments: New Positions in Contemporary African Photography* (New York: International Center of Photography, 2006), 11.
25. Christraud M. Geary, "A World of Images," in *In and Out of Focus: Images from Central*

*Africa, 1885–1960* (Washington, D.C.: Smithsonian National Museum of African Art, 2002), 15–22.

26. Philippa Levine, "Naked Truths: Bodies, Knowledge, and the Erotics of Colonial Power," *Journal of British Studies* 52.1 (2013): 5–25; Philippa Levine, "Studies of Undress: Nakedness and the Colonial Imagination," *Victorian Studies* 50 (2008): 189–218.
27. Martha G. Anderson and Philip M. Peek, "Ways of the Rivers: Arts and Environment of the Niger Delta," *African Arts* 35.1 (Spring 2002): 13.
28. Paul Gilroy, "The End of Antiracism," *'Race,' Culture and Difference*, ed. James Donald and Ali Rattansi (London: Sage Publications, 1992), 52, 53.
29. See Linda McDowell, *Gender, Identity and Place: Understanding Feminist Geographies* (Minneapolis: University of Minnesota Press, 1999), 34–70; and Sander L. Gilman, "Black Bodies, White Bodies: Toward an Iconography of Female Sexuality in Late Nineteenth-Century Art, Medicine and Literature," in Donald and Rattansi, *'Race,' Culture and Difference*, 171–97.
30. Simon Ryan, *The Cartographic Eye: How Explorers Saw Australia* (Cambridge: Cambridge University Press, 1996), 5.
31. Raoul J. Granqvist, "Fieldwork as Translation: Linnaeus' Apostle Anders Sparrman and the Hottentot Perspective," in *African Literatures and Beyond: A Florilegium*, ed. Bernth Lindfors and Geoffrey V. Davis (New York: Rodopi, 2013), 149–76.
32. Okwui Enwezor and Octavio Zaya, "Colonial Imagery, Tropes of Disruption: History, Culture, Representation in the Works of African Photographers," in *In/sight: African Photographers, 1940 to the Present*, ed. Thomas Kreis, Guggenheim Museum, 24 May–29 September 1996 (New York: Guggenheim Museum Publications, 1996), 21. See also Awam Amkpa, "Africa: Colonial Photography and Outlaws of History," https://www.academia.edu/4889353/Africa_Colonial_Photography_and_Outlaws_of_History.
33. Jordan G. Teicher, "Celebrating One Photographer's Rare 20th-Century Look Africa," *Behold: The Photo Blog* (blog), *Slate*, 4 February 2014, http://www.slate.com/blogs/behold/2014/02/04/national_museum_of_african_art_presents_the_exhibition_africa_reviewed_the.html.
34. Cf. Simon Gikandi: "The aesthetic derives much of its authority from its ability to claim autonomy from the historical, social, or cultural event and thus from the consciousness of a sovereign subject." In "Aesthetic Reflection and the Colonial Event: The Work of Art in the Age of Slavery," *Journal of the International Institute* 4.3 (Summer 1997): 2, http://quod.lib.umich.edu/j/jii/4750978.0004.306?rgn=main;view=fulltext.
35. Introduction to *African Material Culture*, ed. Mary Jo Arnoldi, Christraud M. Geary, and Kris L. Hardin (Bloomington: Indiana University Press, 1996), 19.

36. Sandra H. Dudley, "Museum Materialities: Objects, Sense and Feeling," in *Museum Materialities: Objects, Engagement, Interpretations*, ed. Sandra H. Dudley (New York: Routledge, 2010), 3.
37. Enid Schildkrout and Curtis A. Keim, "Objects and Agendas: Re-collecting the Congo," in *The Scramble of Art in Central Africa*, ed. Enid Schildkrout and Curtis A. Klein (Cambridge: Cambridge University Press, 1998), 28.
38. See Lisa Karlsson Blom and Mikela Lundahl, "Haunted Museums: Ethnography, Coloniality and Sore Points," *Glänta*, 18 December 2012, http://www.eurozine.com/pdf/2012-12-18-blom-en.pdf. See also Sidney Littlefield Kasfir, "African Art and Authenticity: A Text with a Shadow," *African Arts* 25.2 (April 1992): 40–53, 96–97.
39. For her discussion on similar aspects, see Annie E. Coombes, *Reinventing Africa: Museums, Material Culture and Popular Imagination in Late Victorian and Edwardian England* (New Haven, CT: Yale University Press, 1994), 127.
40. To view the photographs discussed in this book (noted with keywords such as EEPA EECL 252), visit the SIRIS website, http://collections.si.edu.

## Chapter 1. En Route from Scandinavia to Africa, 1942–1944: On Becoming a Trickster with a Hungry Camera and a Loud Mouth

1. His last military scene, the Pacific (1945), is not of relevance for my topic and will not be discussed.
2. Wilhelm Agrell, *Stockholm som spioncentral* [Stockholm as a Centre for Espionage] (Lund: Historiska Media, 2006), 85.
3. In a *LIFE* "Office Memorandum," dated 3 November 1939, in Eliot Elisofon Papers at Harry Ransom Humanities Research Center, the University of Texas at Austin, container 2.20 ("Finland"). The HRC Elisofon Papers are hereafter referred to as HRC, followed by the container number.
4. She worked for the Office of the Strategic Services (OSS), the U.S. intelligence agency preceding the CIA, undertaking trips to the Finnish-Russian front in 1942, writing an extensive report about her findings. Lauri Holmström, "Finland in American Intelligence 1941–1944," *Intelligence and National Security* 25.4 (2010): 490.
5. The choice of these two sites to represent the Other emanated not only from the metaphorical functions that Elisofon subtly ascribed to them but were also inspired by the contemporary Finnish political debate. The Valamo monastery (on an island in Lake Ladoga) was fought over in the war, and lost. Elisofon's blasphemous caption, "Here live 200 Russians in Byzantine splendor," was borrowed from the Finnish press.

His application of Fort Slava, a fortress built in the 1790s to defend St. Petersburg and destroyed by the British during the Crimean War (1855), was symbolic in two ways: as a historical monument of empires collapsing and thus as a twofold warning. The isle of Kukouri, the site of Fort Slava, was just a few miles away from the four Finnish islands in the Gulf of Finland that the Soviet Union claimed (Suursaaari, Lavansaari, Tytärsaaari, and Seiskar) and which the Soviet Union would have annexed by the end of the war in 1944. Kukouri or Finland might go the same way, was the implication.

6. One such example is his 1960 essay "The Hopeful Launching of a Proud and Free Nigeria," *LIFE*, 26 September 1960.
7. Eliot's report to the *LIFE* New York office (Wilson Hicks), "Finland—Oct, 1944—Elisofon—*LIFE*" (HRC 6.31), is a fourteen-page-long itinerary meant to serve at best as a resource bank for the edited version, a practice that the *LIFE* photojournalists in the field had to conform to. They had to accept that it could be rejected, which unfortunately happened to Eliot's "1944 Finland." The pictures he took of German mortars were sent to American intelligence, he explains in an affidavit to the FBI in 1957. In the same report there is a passport note that he had visited Finland in March 1944; if so, it must have been super secret as the trip has left no traces behind it.
8. A photograph in *Time* (25 September 1944) shows the minister to Finland, Hjalmar Procopé, leaving New Orleans. He has handed over his passport because his activities were "inimical to the welfare of the U.S."
9. Some seventy thousand Finnish children, most of them from Karelian families, were evacuated during the Continuation War to Sweden. It is supposed to have been the largest migration of children in the world. Eliot photographed some of these children in a hospital in Stockholm in May 1944, but he did not expand his pictures into an essay for *LIFE*.
10. In the field notes for his shooting travel of *LIFE* magazine's "The Coast of Europe: It Is a Bright Magnet for American Tourists," Elisofon recapitulates his averse standpoints of Finnish military command: "The complete military carelessness of the Finns at that time I will never forget," 13 June 1949, 62–80, all in color, HRC 11.7, 23.
11. Seven unedited quotes from Elisofon's meeting with Sibelius, extracted from his 1944 Finnish travel report, were published in "Sibelius Revisited," *Time*, 23 October 1944, 33. See Granqvist 2012a for an analysis of two of Elisofon's most famous photographs.
12. Elisofon had met Mannerheim in October 1939 for a photography session that turned out to be bothersome. Mannerheim refused to follow Elisofon's instructions about at which distance and altitude (Elisofon: "close" and "low") the photo should be taken, so Elisofon "fooled him with a telephoto lens" (HRC 6.10, 10). However, Mannerheim,

a skilled photographer himself, knew not only what posture he preferred but how to produce it. I find it is unclear who "fooled" whom. See Elisofon's photo in "The Liberator [Mannerheim] of Finland Mobilizes against Russia," *LIFE*, 23 October 1939, 22, to form your own opinion.

13. *Vecko-Tidningen Såningsmannen*, 16 September 1944, 20.
14. The fact that the ship and some of its crew were simultaneously engaged in the shooting of the semidocumentary war film *Western Approaches* (director Pat Jackson) in the Irish Sea increased the tension on board.
15. Eliot Elisofon, *Food Is a Four Letter Word* (New York: Lee Rinehart, 1948), 32–33. For the detailed report of his voyage, see "Number 41," HRC 5.13, 1–10.
16. John Scott, "U.S. Miscellany," *Time*, 13 March 1944.
17. Whether Eliot knew that Scott was a "double-agent," informing both the Russians and the Allies, I do not know for sure. I think he did. Scott traveled to an unbending Finland on 9 March and would return at least three times before the end of the year. He met Paasikivi on 8 May, a talk whose contents he would not disclose for anyone other than his bosses on each side of the Atlantic. The following articles, based on his travels in April–June, may contain cryptic, coded messages: "Finland: Death in an Empty Room," *Time*, 1 May 1944, and "Finland: Fateful Hour," *Time*, 3 July 1944. Lauri Holmström (2010, 497) calls him "the most significant unofficial actor on a personal level to the political intelligence of the United States in Finland."
18. He took a photograph of the ball-bearing negotiations between the two Americans and Marcus Wallenberg in the Skandinaviska Banken boardroom at the Gustaf Adolf's square.
19. See the menu in Elisofon, *Food Is a Four Letter Word*, 37–39.
20. "Globes of Steel," http://www.naderlibrary.com/hig.tradingwithenemy7.htm. See also "Foreign Trade: Backfire," *Time*, 29 May 1944. The reference to Bogart is based on Roger Wright, "Hitler, Bogart, and the Banker," *Chicago Guy's Blog* (blog), http://chicagoguy14.wordpress.com/.
21. None of his three photo travelogues were published by *LIFE* (individual photographs were published). He would also document the exchange of prisoners of war in the Gothenburg Harbor on 10 September 1944.
22. The Press Club of southern Sweden organized a three-day conference cum recreation for a group of thirty international journalists in the Malmö region on 23–25 July 1944, among them Nat Barrow, John Scott, Ossian Goulding, Denis Weaver, and Elisofon, all of whom also would participate in the tour of Finland in September–October. The article in the largest Swedish newspaper, *Dagens Nyheter* (30 April 1944), "An Increasingly Stronger Press Opinion in the U.S. against the Swedish Position" (vis-à-vis the export of ore [my

translation]), was one of many reporting about the American concern and double-talk. *Arbetet* published (24 July 1944) a review of the Skåne press meeting, with, typically, a photo of Elisofon taking a hot shot of a sunbathing female "beach motif" at Falsterbo.

23. The idea of the HRC holding Elisofon's selection of mutilated German soldiers to be used as a trophic propaganda resource is appalling; my browsing through it was worse. HRC 7.1–7.2.
24. This friend might have been either Valter Taub, a dramatist and actor, or Jan Brazda, a painter and sculptor. They were both Czechs and anti-German activists. Jan was the son of Amelie Posse, a Swedish writer and the founder of Tisdagsklubben (the Tuesday Club), a nucleus of a Swedish underground in case the Nazis took over. Taub, who fled to Stockholm in 1939, was writing for British and American newspapers during the war. He was imprisoned for a short time in Sweden for espionage.
25. These manuscript lines were deleted from the book and replaced by the innuendo "Through some heavy entertainment I was told about a very pretty redhead" (Elisofon, *Food Is a Four Letter Word*, 52). That a "friend" would have escorted her to his home without any advance notice is not plausible. Eliot knew who she was before indulging in his act of seduction.
26. A reference to the binding trade contract between Germany and Sweden.
27. But being banned by the head of the Swedish Sports Confederation, Major Bo Lindman, a reputed Nazi sympathizer, from the Stadion (the sports arena in Stockholm) to take photos of the middle-distance runners Gunder Hägg and Arne Andersson, the Swedish press reacted strongly and would use the same argument as Elisofon had about the Swedish loss of international recognition. Furthermore, the press pointed out that Lindman was incompetent and should go (Carl-Adam Nycop, "Svensk byråkrati" [Swedish Bureaucracy], *SE*, 25 July 1944: 24–31]. Elisofon had his revenge. In August, he could use his spectacular "robot camera" to take the well-known photographs of the two world-record runners when competing (in Stockholm and in Malmö), and, jubilantly, interview them in their homes and make a photo essay about them (*LIFE*, 30 October 1944; HRC 6.22).
28. This was a common practice in Finland up to the 1960s.
29. "Even in Lapland to run into that!" is the way he rephrased it a few years later (Elisofon, *Food Is a Four Letter Word*, 57): a formula of the civilized and the primitive.
30. His description of Finnish women takes on a similar patriarchal and sexist slant. "The blond Finnish girl with her blue eyes and high cheekbones is an extraordinary creature. Her legs are perhaps somewhat short and the general opinion favours long legs. And the Finnish wooden shoes do by no means help up the matter." In an interview in Helsinki,

October 1944, by Herman O. Gummerus, translated by "Eeva" (probably Scott's secretary) from Swedish into English. HRC 71.5. "Finland and Jean Sibelius" Container.

31. Hans Meyer, "Soldat med kamera" [A Soldier with a Camera], *Folket i bild*, 7 May 1944, 3–5, 24–25.
32. He nurtured the plan to produce a book—in line with his female portraits of Hollywood stars—about seven Swedish film actresses. It remained a dream.
33. "Sweden's Model Apartments: 'Stockholm Building Is Wonderful for Wives Who Work,'" *LIFE*, 12 March 1945, 112–14. Elisofon traveled from Helsinki to Stockholm in 1939 in the company of Wäinö Aalto, the famous Finnish architect whom he admired, and they met again on 10 October 1944 in Helsinki, discussing Aalto's "standardization plan" for postwar Finland, the main principles of which were "interchangeability and adaptability," similar concepts to pragmatism and functionalism that undercut Markelius's project.
34. *En amerikan ser på Norden: Fotografier från Sverige och Finland, akvareller och teckningar av Eliot Elisofon, Life Magazine* [An American's View of Scandinavia: Photographs from Sweden and Finland, Acquarelles and Paintings by Eliot Elisofon], *Life Magazine* (Stockholm: Svenska turistförbundet, 1944).
35. The exhibition organized by Gustaf Munthe, his passport to Sweden, displayed one hundred drawings (aquarelles, croquises), most of which were on sale. Elisofon had taken 106 photographs in Sweden (among them were fourteen photos of Finnish children at a hospital) and forty-three in Finland. The 150 "Scandinavian" photographs (and more) have remained basically unregistered. I have had the privilege to view them in a private collection.
36. "Date in Casablanca," *LIFE*, 1 February 1943, 94–96, 99. HRC 4.29. Elisofon's photo of the couple (with the story title) graces the cover of the edition.
37. "Morocco Feast: Potent Caid of Rehamna Tribe Entertains General Clark and Staff," a subsection of the essay "Allies Overrun of North Africa," *LIFE*, 17 May 1943, 20–21.
38. See "Venus on the Half Shell" (*LIFE*, 2 December 1946, 76) for a picture of her in a New York Diamond Horse Show.
39. In an interview for a Swedish newspaper: "Känd USA-fotograf: 'Sverige vackrast'" ["Famous U.S. Photographer: 'Sweden is the Most Beautiful'"], *Stockholms-Tidningen*, 23 July 1948.
40. The logical reason for his visit to Malmö on 23 September 1944 must have been to make a story about the inauguration of the new Malmö Stadsteater (Malmö City Theatre, today Malmö Opera), the largest theater in Europe at the time and still considered a masterpiece of functionalist architecture. It was also the first night of *En midsommarnattsdröm* [*The Midsummer Night's Dream*] and Vilhelm Moberg's *En mans*

*kvinna* ["A Man's Woman"]. But whatever happened, the report turned into an epicurean peregrination with Swedish smörgåsbord and fried eel as the main dishes. The story, a wisecrack about a pampered foreign tourist, was published much later (in *Sydsvenska Dagbladet*, 29 October, in Swedish) under the pseudonym "Elicif," during the weeks when he was on convalescence and organizing the exhibition "En amerikan ser på Norden."

## Chapter 2. Colonial Travel and Colonial Habits: Early Years, Elisofon in Africa, 1947 and 1951

1. Wendy Kozol, LIFE*'s America: Family and Nation in Postwar Photojournalism* (Philadelphia: Temple University Press, 1994), 56.
2. "Perhaps the most resonant object in the exhibit isn't even a photograph at all—it's a map showing the meandering route Elisofon traveled on a long assignment from Cape Town to Cairo. Judging by the accompanying photographs of minimally passable roads, one's tempted to say that for Elisofon, simply getting there was a large part of his accomplishment." Louis Jacobson, "Reviewed: Eliot Elisofon at the National Museum of African Art," *ArtsDesk* (blog), *Washington City Paper*, 27 November 2013, *Washington City Paper*, http://www.washingtoncitypaper.com/blogs/artsdesk/visual-arts/2013/11/27/reviewed-eliot-elisofon-at-the-national-museum-of-african-art/.
3. Caren Kaplan, *Questions of Travel: Postmodern Discourses of Displacement* (Durham, NC: Duke University Press, 1996), 61.
4. Elisofon's "Victoria Falls" story can be viewed in the online gallery "To the Victoria Falls," http://www.tothevictoriafalls.com/vfpages/tourism/lifegallery.html.
5. Elisofon's twelve-page essay "The Nile: Its Course Unfolds Mighty Panorama of River People and Civilizations" (*LIFE* 20 November 1950, 118–29) contains a number of his most well known photographs, exhibited and reprinted in many magazines, also abroad.
6. The photo of her is the one on the front cover of the Nile essay. EEPA EENG 09500.
7. The eights photos held by EEPA are tagged "Exorcism of Dwelling." EEPA EENG 02740.
8. In the graphic map of the third biggest basin of "cultures and racial stocks" in the Nile essay (119), the drawing of the Shilluk of the White Nile is modeled on Elisofon's photo of the "savage with the spear" on the next page. This photo/drawing is a forerunner of his cover image "Wild Warega Warrior Poised for Attack" (*LIFE*, 13 October 1961) that saluted the "Storied Word of Africa" edition. Eliot Elisofon, "A Writer's Land of Primitive, Eloquent Beauty: Storied World of Africa." *LIFE*, 13 October 1961, 66–87. EEPA EENG 00400.
9. Sabine Cornelis, "Culture coloniale, acteurs culturels et arts visuels au Congo

(1920–1950)," in *Aspects de la culture à l'époque coloniale en Afrique centrale: Le corps—L'image—L'espèce* (Paris: Harmattan, 2008), 166–67.

10. Full text of *The Belgian Congo at War*, published by the Belgian Information Center, https://archive.org/stream/BelgianCongoAtWar/BSW2_djvu.txt, http://www.congoforum.be/upldocs/BC%20at%20war%2011.pdf.
11. "More than 500 of them [Negro troops] died on the burning plateaus of the Gala Sidamo region, but they conquered Asosa, Gambela and Saio, took 15,000 prisoners and swept the enemy from the entire region." "A Primitive Mass of 'Natives' Become a Mass of Loyal Colonial Citizens," in *The Belgian Congo at War.*
12. Negro Art, "Genuine Congo Art Is Never Vulgar," in full text of "Belgian Congo at War," 5, published by the Belgian Information Center, https://archive.org/stream/BelgianCongoAtWar/BSW2_djvu.txt.
13. Dictator Mobutu Sese Seko closed the museum in 1971 as part of his "le recours à l'authenticité" project, and the 40,000 objects were kept behind closed doors in one of his palaces until 11 March 2010, when the Institute of the National Museums of Congo opened with help from the Royal Museum for Central Africa (RMCA) in Belgium, Tervuren.
14. Eliot Elisofon and William Fagg, *The Sculpture of Africa* (New York: Frederick A. Praeger, 1958).
15. Adrien Vandem Bossche, "Art Bakuba," *Brousse,* new series, no. 1 (1952): 11–26.
16. Jan Vansina, *Being Colonized: The Kuba Presence in Rural Congo, 1880–1960* (Madison: University of Wisconsin Press, 2010), 183–85.
17. Torday's collections (mainly) of Kuba art dwell in the British Museum and RMCA. The Belgian collection was continuously supplemented during the colony's lifetime.
18. Jan Vansina, "La survie du royaume kuba à l'époque colonial et les arts," *Annales Æquatoria* 28 (2007): 14.
19. He would be followed by Arnold Newman, another American photographer, about a decade later. "Bope Mabinsha King of the Bakubas Congo 1958," Arnold Newman website, http://www.arnoldnewmanarchive.com/media-gallery/detail/58/294. 2015.
20. Pictures of which, he explained, he found later in Emil Torday and T. A. Joyce's *Notes ethnographiques sur les peuples communement appelés Bakuba ainsi que sur les peuplades apparentées les Bushongo* (Brussels: Musée du Congo Belge, 1911).
21. Eliot Elisofon, "African Big Shot: A Fat Black Monarch of the Congo Rules His Tribe with a Heavy Hand," *LIFE,* 31 March 1947, 129–32.
22. Christraud Geary, "Two Days in Mushenge: Eliot Elisofon's Images of the Kuba (1947)," *African Arts* 26. 2 (April 1993): 72.

23. It is one of the photographs celebrated in the exhibition "Africa Reviewed. The Photographic Legacy of Eliot Elisofon" (November 2013–August 2014) at the Smithsonian National Museum of African Art.
24. Vansina, *Being Colonized*, 204.
25. In one of the many interviews with Elisofon where Bope surfaced, Elisofon depicted him as a monster culled out of a Nordic folktale. "While I was living with the Bushongo people, [I met the] Bushongo ruler [who] was a mountainous mass buried under an avalanche of plumage from which he stared out with heavy-lidded saurian eyes." Robert Taylor, "The Many Masks of Eliot Elisofon," *Boston Herald*, 7 November 1958.
26. Deborah Stokes, "Documentary Observations: The African Photographs of William B. Fagg, 1949–1959," *African Arts* 36.4 (2003): 65–69.
27. Elisofon's parading of "beautiful" women culminated in an essay in *LIFE* with portraits of Hollywood actresses ("Elisofon in Hollywood," *LIFE*, 11 November 1946, 85–88). About his portrait of Veronica Lake he wrote: "Hair like rolling waves on a dead smooth beach, deep blue eyes with endless depth. . . . She is so beautiful she reminds me of the sea which surrounds Vindelhaven where I live in the summer." The editor added: he photographed her "under a blue light with a double-exposure effect of the ocean in the foreground" (*LIFE*, 7 April 1947, 99). He uses the same blue color to frame his portrait of Ingrid Bergman (*LIFE*, 15 December 1947, 107), and the male editor is mesmerized almost into silence: "So struck with the beauty of Ingrid Bergman was *LIFE*."
28. She could be Kafinga Philonique, wife of an Nsapo chief who was photographed by Eliot (EEPA EENG 00349).
29. The Democratic Republic of the Congo, 1908–1960 (Zaire from 1971), remained Elisofon's and the United States' favored place throughout the 1960–1970s' Cold War against Communism. About half of Elisofon's thirty-seven thousand African photographs were shot in the Congo. Hundreds of artifacts were sent from Kinshasa to his home in New York (the transportation of a large number of which was paid for by the U.S. embassy in Kinshasa, as American embassies elsewhere in Africa did).
30. David Spurr, *The Rhetoric of Empire: Colonial Discourse in Journalism, Travel Writing, and Imperial Administration* (Durham, NC: Duke University Press, 1993), 93.
31. See the animated description of Nairobi affluence in Caroline Elkins, *Imperial Reckoning: The Untold Story of Britain's Gulag in Kenya* (New York: Henry Holt, 2006), 10–11, a sardonic foreword to the book's documentation of the gulag instigated or supported by, principally, the same social class.
32. In a parallel report he uses the phrase "the native African who still lives in Kenya." I think he is referring to the African who dresses according to the conventions of her or his

tradition.

33. His full name was Alexander Cambridge, First Earl of Athlone. He was governor-general of the Union of South Africa from 1923 to 1931 and is mentioned as "a sympathetic, tactful and popular governor-general, [who] even manages to get the British Union Flag included in the new South African flag, a move which has been opposed by many Afrikaaners" (http://homepages.warwick.ac.uk/~lysic/1920s/athlonelord.htm). Retired, he is in Nairobi, my guess is, as one of the traveling British royals with a cause.
34. See Paul Spicer, *The Temptress: The Scandalous Life of Alice de Janze and the Mysterious Death of Lord Erroll* (New York: St. Martin's Press, 2010).
35. Taylor, "The Many Masks of Eliot Elisofon."
36. Virginia-Lee Webb, *Perfect Documents: Walker Evans and African Art, 1935* (New York: Metropolitan Museum of Art, 2000), 13–22.
37. This is the EEPA's limpid representation of such an encounter: "In 1947 while on assignment for *LIFE* magazine, Eliot Elisofon photographed an older man along the road from Tanzania to Kenya. The man wore western clothes but with this Maasai earring." NMAfA object photography 73-7-784.
38. Taylor, "The Many Masks of Eliot Elisofon."
39. J. B. Harley, "Deconstructing the Map," in *Writing Worlds: Discourse, Text and Metaphor in the Representation of Landscape*, ed. Trevor J. Barnes and James S. Duncan (New York: Routledge, 1992), 237.
40. Renato Rosaldo, *Culture and Truth: The Remaking of Social Analysis* (Boston: Beacon Press, 1989), 69–70.

## Chapter 3. African Women Walk, African Men Sit, African Children Are: Gender as Difference, Exclusion, Segregation, and Passage

1. Simon Ryan, *The Cartographic Eye: How Explorers Saw Australia* (Cambridge: Cambridge University Press, 1996), 6.
2. Naturally, this figure is relative; there are photos by Eliot outside the dominion of the archives.
3. See "The Nigerian Electoral Process in Perspective," http://www.dawodu.com/elect1.pdf.
4. I am indebted to the feminist geographer Gillian Rose's chapter "Women and Everyday Spaces," in *Feminism and Geography: The Limits of Geographical Knowledge* (Cambridge: Polity Press, 1996), 17–40.
5. Michel Foucault, *Discipline and Punish: The Birth of the Prison*, trans. Alan Sheridan (New York: Knopf Doubleday, 1979), 109.

6. Similar albums of "women carrying" photos can be found in any of Elisofon's African footages. "Congolese women, with bunches of bananas on their heads, walking through manioc fields," Bunia, Congo (Democratic Republic), 1970, EEPA EECL 8699, is, with those discussed here, one of hundreds.
7. The EEPA archive contains two photos of "Habe men in the fields" (from the same Barhin village). The two men leading donkeys with firewood on their backs were equally submerged by the landscape (EEPA EECL 8440).
8. Following "Dogon women attending a funeral celebration, Sanga, Mali," Elisofon was sidetracked by nakedness, and twenty of his slides went astray (EEPA EECL 6234).
9. See also Linda McDowell, *Gender, Identity and Place: Understanding Feminist Geographies* (Minneapolis: University of Minnesota Press, 1999), 34–56.
10. The figures indicate the number of "documents" (photos) that are listed in SIRIS.
11. Given that there are about fifty ethnic groups in Plateau State, any classification of individual women performed at the marketplace and based merely on external characteristics must be highly capricious.
12. He also took a series of conventional anthropometrical photos of an "Izere woman with facial scarifications, near Jos" (9) and of the same woman "carrying basket on a wooden headboard" (3)—from front, back, and the sides.
13. In the 1930s, Swedish missionaries brought young "converted" Africans to Sweden for them to be displayed in the Swedish countryside and circulated between the congregations as propaganda tools.
14. John Loengard, LIFE *Photographers: What They Saw* (Boston: Little, Brown, 1998), 10.
15. See also a sequence of pictures he took earlier during this trip in Mombasa Harbor (Kenya) of workers building a spur line serving oil to tanker docks ("Workers on spur line of the railroad from Mombasa to Nairobi, near Mombasa, Kenya"). Railways as visual sites intrigued Elisofon. They appeared not only as themes in photo essay projects such as these but also as aesthetic background figures in many photographs depicting landscapes.
16. With a colonial history of exporting palm oil, ivory, and rubber, and importing gin as its brand, the original firm (John Holt) emerged to become one of the principal Liverpool firms trading on the coast of West Africa, with a branch in Lagos in 1899. P. S. Mandrides was a sister company. http://nigerianwiki.com/wiki/John_Holt.
17. In his series photos of "Hausa men at indigo dye pits, Kano," however, one single anonymous man, unconventionally, smiles into the camera. These men dyeing were complemented by pictures of tanners and leather workers, flaying and trimming the skin.
18. For the original company's beginning, see, for example, "On December 3, 1908, the

Governor of the Colony of Southern Nigeria acquired a lease of this land for a term of 99 years at an annual rental of 100 pounds from a Trader—Chief Dore Numa of Benin River, acting for and on behalf of the Chiefs and people of Sapele." http://www.pointblanknews.com/os2999.html.

19. The SIRIS naming is not correct. At the time when Elisofon took these pictures, the army was called the Nigerian Military Force (NMF). At the time of independence in 1960, it was changed to the Royal Nigerian Army. It became the Nigerian Army only when the country assumed the status of a republic in 1963.
20. The only political leader Elisofon met this year, except the Nigerians, was Tom Joseph Odhiambo Mboya (15 August 1930—5 July 1969), the Kenyan politician during Jomo Kenyatta's government and president of the People's Congress Party. Elisofon photographed him in Nairobi in June. Mboya was assassinated on 5 July 1969 in Nairobi.
21. Osei Boateng, "Nigeria: Squalid End of Empire," *New African*, 20 November 2008.
22. Martha G. Anderson and Lisa L. Aronson's photo essay of "Jonathan A. Greene: An African Photographer Hiding in Plain Sight" (*African Arts* 44.3 [Autumn 2011]: 38–49) demonstrates Greene's style of capturing the differences between European and African modes of self-presentation.
23. Oba Akenzua II (1899–1978), Oba of Benin (1933–1978), was not present when Elisofon visited. Instead, Elisofon took a couple of pictures of two of his boy servants and of the Benin palace ancestral altar. Oba Akenzua is famous for beginning the movement to return to Nigeria the Benin Bronzes stolen in the punitive Benin Expedition of 1897.
24. Eliot Elisofon, *Zaire: A Week in Joseph's World.* (New York: Crowell-Collier Press, 1973).
25. The two others were *A Week in Agatha's World: Poland* (1970) and *A Week in Leonora's World: Puerto Rico* (1971).
26. In letters to Hicks (24 and 29 December 1942), Elisofon told him about smuggling in Christmas gifts to children in Sidi El Agashei, a concentration camp populated with Central European Jews, Spanish Republicans, and French and Italian women who had relations with the German Armistice Commission. He had received a letter from the American Office of War Information (in French) that it was OK to distribute the gifts and also to take pictures. The Office thought that the pictures would be an excellent topic for the American press. So he kept them secret from the intelligence service and dispatched them to Hicks, with prints to his wife, Mavis Lyons. Eisenhower was angry about the leakage; Elisofon was reprimanded. They were not published but can be viewed in the HRC archive (HRC 4.21). See "Elisofon's Text and Images of Concentration Camp in French Morocco," http://gittermangallery.com/exhibition/67/press_release/.
27. "I Go Visit a Chief's Son: An American Boy's Storybook Adventure in Deepest Africa,"

photographed by Robert Halmi, *LIFE*, 13 April 1962, 74–87.

28. Elisofon in a letter to Robert Halmi, 5 December 1972, HRC 59.4, 68.8, 69.5.
29. A brilliant representation of this acquisitive syndrome is the Swedish writer, and Nadine Gordimer's friend, Sara Lidman's fictional biography, *Jag och min son* [I and My Son] (Stockholm: Albert Bonniers Förlag, 1963), written in Johannesburg in 1960, revised in Nyeri, Kenya, in 1963.

## Chapter 4. From Colony to Colonized: Elisofon Fashioning Nigeria

1. Quoted by John Loengard in the introduction to his LIFE *Photographers: What They Saw* (Boston: Little, Brown, 1998), 11.
2. Eliot Elisofon, "The Hopeful Launching of Proud and Free Nigeria," *LIFE*, 26 September 1960, 54–68. "A Writer's Land of Primitive, Eloquent Beauty, Storied World of Africa," *LIFE*, 13 October 1961, 66-87.
3. Alexander Campbell, "Africa, a Continent in Ferment: A Special Issue," *LIFE*, 4 May 1953, 1–179.
4. Campbell would publish a book about his African travels the coming year: *Heart of Africa* (New York: Alexander A. Knopf, 1954).
5. Duncan's unsentimental and straightforward story about Ducrest was cut down to a fragment only, in relation to his fieldwork. Duncan's Papers and Photographic Collection at HRC, series I, box 24.6 and container 307.11–12. The report is supported by sixty rolls of photographs.
6. Duncan's photo of Johannes Strydom (Strijdom), Malan's heir, as he was to be (1954–1958), was also published (Campbell, "Africa, a Continent in Ferment," 168).
7. "One Fifth of a Nation Celebrates," *LIFE*, 21 April 1952, 27–44. See the two-page note about Duncan stalking with a hidden camera a group of Russian Antarctic fleet sailors "on liberty" in Cape Town: "Reds on Liberty: Soviet Gobs Get Cape Town Leave but Freedom Does Not Relax Them," *LIFE*, 5 May 1952, 67–68.
8. Duncan's original caption shared with his New York staff read: "Ash-blonde Afrikaans boy playing with the baby Bushman was the result of good luck . . . and shows that at least at the infant level, at least, there is no 'color problem' in South Africa." He commented on his scoop: "I felt it was quite a show, watching them play together . . . with the backdrop of older Bushmen going about their tasks of weaving and making poisoned arrow" (HRC 22.8).
9. He took the photos of the demonstration (in a facsimile to me in April 2010 while working on this book at HRC, he explained that he took these pictures through a hole

in a book), of blacks marching with cardboard placards denouncing the "300 years of oppression," carrying the ANC flag, singing "Mayibuye Africa" to the tune of "Clementine," and of white girls from Witwatersrand soliciting money for the ANC. He took pictures of the speakers T. N. Dadoo, president of the South African Indian Congress; James S. Moroka, president general of the ANC; and people around the speakers raising their fists with the thumbs up. He shot the banner "Malan Remember How Hitler Fell." In David Douglas Duncan Papers and Photographic Collection, series I, box 22.9 at HRC. To my knowledge, this rich and unique material has remained unpublished, and Duncan, when I asked him about its history, did not recognize or remember it. He wrote two essays for *LIFE* in April–May 1952 on the subject of South Africa as a Nazi state in formation: "South Africa's Stormiest April" and "An Impartial View of South Africa's Crisis" (HRC 22.15).

10. Robert Ruark's essay appeared in *LIFE* on 16 February 1953 (120–35). His safari novel *Something of Value* (London: Doubleday, 1955) was one of the African novels that Elisofon shelved for his Literary Africa project. The publication dates for other *LIFE* contributions to the Mau Mau lore during the 1950s are: 3 November 1952; 13 April 1953; 3 November 1953; 16 November 1953; 1 March 1954; 24 May 1954; 8 October 1956; 12 November 1956; 22 July 1957.
11. Caroline Elkins, *Imperial Reckoning: The Untold Story of Britain's Gulag in Kenya* (New York: Henry Holt, 2006), 47.
12. However, one of Elisofon's photos of Ntore dancers performing the traditional Tutsi dance, on the shore of Lake Kivu, taken in 1951, was printed in the *LIFE* issue (EEPA EECL 6129), interrupting the Gatti collection (94–95). It was also published in Robert Coughlan's *Tropical Africa* (New York: Time, 1961), 38–39.
13. Cf. Bhabha's definition of the speaker's Other: An "otherness which is at once an object of desire and derision, and articulation of difference contained within the fantasy of origin and identity." Homi Bhabha, *The Location of Culture* (New York: Routledge, 1994), 67.
14. Hermann Wittenberg, "The Sublime, Imperialism and the African Landscape," dissertation for the degree of Doctor Litterarum in the Department of English at the University of the Western Cape. 2004, 93, http://etd.uwc.ac.za/xmlui/bitstream/handle/11394/1340/Wittenberg_DLIT_2004.pdf?sequence=1.
15. Henry M. Stanley, *In Darkest Africa: or, the Quest, Rescue, and Retreat of Emin, Governor of Equatoria* (London: Sampson, Low, Marston, 1890), 2:52.
16. Robert Coughlan, "Black Africa Surges to Independence," Part 1, *LIFE*, 26 January 1959, 100.
17. The statement in the editorial for the 1953 *LIFE* Africa issue did not dodge history: "If we were less ignorant, Americans might weep for the tragic land-love and fierce instinct of

survival that led the Boers to *apartheid*; but we could never approve it, even if it were not also a mask for brutality and greed" (178).

18. See Robert Coughlan, "Black Magic: Vital Force," *LIFE*, 21 April 1961, 118–21.
19. Robert Coughlan, "Stormy Future for Africa: Eruption of Black Africa," part 2, *LIFE*, 2 February 1959, 96. He summarized his observations in his book, *Tropical Africa* (New York: Time, Inc., 1962).
20. This was the same practice he used in April–May 1970 preparing for Georges Bracher's filming of the *Black African Heritage* Series (*BAH*).
21. The itinerary for the Nigerian trip, 29 October, 1959, was sent to the *LIFE* staff, George Caturani (photo editor), Gene Farmer, and Keith Wheeler, and to Foreign News. EEPA, S-1.1.
22. The figures inside the parentheses register the number of segments (the serial "thematic photo") that Elisofon shot at each location. As the 182 segments included 1,495 photographs (indexed by SIRIS statistics), the approximate number of shots for the single segment was around twenty-five, which is representative of Elisofon's shooting practice.
23. He photographed students at a town planning class at the institute.
24. He met him again in January 1971.
25. Rita Kiki Edozie, "Nigeria's 2007 Elections in Comparative Perspective: Democratic Capitalism and the Crisis of Democracy in Africa," in *Nigeria's Stumbling Democracy and Its Implications for Africa's Democratic Movement*, ed. Victor Oguejiofor Okafor (Westport, CT: Praeger Security International, 2008), 146.
26. It was a cherished photo, published not only in the *LIFE* essay and in Coughlan, "Black Magic," 57, but also in Elisofon's *Color Photography*, 74.
27. The photo was published in the Nigeria essay, as well as in Coughlan, *Tropical Africa*, 28, and Elisofon, *Color Photography*, 75.
28. Elisofon visited the same village again in January 1971, twelve years later. The women dancers were now fully dressed and unwillingly performed.
29. On the last page of the *LIFE* essay (Elisofon, "The Hopeful Launching of Proud and Free Nigeria").
30. Itinerary, 3.
31. Search results, EEPA, Nigeria 1959, on 8 October 2014. It needs to be added that this figure should be understood as indicatory.
32. Martha Langford and John Langford claim that this *LIFE* picture is a "'signature' look of Nigeria: seasoned photojournalist and African old hand Eliot Elisofon supplies a lead picture that is a study in cultural syncretism and Cold War technogratization," with one person wearing an antique gas mask, while the text exults Nigeria moving toward "a

modern world." Only that Elisofon's "signature look" is contradictorily complex. Martha Langford and John Langford, *A Cold War Tourist and His Camera* (Montreal: McGill-Queen's University Press, 2011), 27.

## Chapter 5. Elisofon's and *LIFE*'s Literary Africa: White Mythologies, Racism, and Cold War Politics

1. Jonathan Smith, "The Slightly Different Thing That Is Said: Writing Aesthetic Experience," in *Writing Worlds: Discourse, Text and Metaphor in the Representation of Landscape*, ed. Trevor J. Barnes and James S. Duncan (New York: Routledge, 1992), 79.
2. Wendy Kozol, LIFE*'s America: Family and Nation in Postwar Photojournalism* (Philadelphia: Temple University Press, 1994), 109–13.
3. Elisofon's proposals to the staffers included topics that were of a philosophical nature (Elisofon had a degree in philosophy at Fordham University): "Night Life in Japan [with sexist innuendos]," "The Divine Order Universe," "Peace," and "Longevity," and a few related to his nomadic lifestyle ("Travel," "Round the World," "Literary Russia," "The Islands of the Mediterranean").
4. Erika Doss, "Introduction: Looking at *LIFE*; Rethinking America's Favorite Magazine, 1936-1972," in *Looking at LIFE Magazine*, ed. Erika Doss (Washington, D.C.: Smithsonian Institution Press, 2001), 11.
5. Doss, "Visualizing Black America," 227. See Kozol, LIFE*'s America*, 46; and Kozol, "Gazing at Race in the Pages of *LIFE*," 159–75.
6. "The Tahitian girl" had a name: Mary Puaa. Elisofon paid her $10 for the posing.
7. "These images [of belles unattached from propriety, from men's control] in *LIFE* acknowledged that sexualized women were one important source of male power." Rickie Solinger, "The Smutty Side of *LIFE*: Picturing Babes as Icons of Gender Difference in the Early 1950s," in Doss, *Looking at* LIFE, 208–9.
8. In an introductory note about the South Seas issue, the story is drummed out of "paradise hunter" Elisofon, inspired by the extract he had selected from of Melville's *Typee* about "idolatrous altars of the savages." Elisofon went on a hunt for them, and, miraculously as it were (but note it was a pilgrimage), discovered a "Hoola Hoola" ground with nine "tikis." In front of one of them Elisofon posed for a picture taken by Joan, who accompanied him during part of the African literary excursion as well. He could now add "discoverer" to his list of sobriquets, a list that never came to an end.
9. It was photographed by Howard Sochurek. In its ravenous celebration of game hunting and "white" machismo, it is one the most hideous photo essays of Africa that I have ever

come across.

10. *In/sight: African Photographers, 1940 to the Present*, Suloman R. Guggenheim Museum, 24 May–29 September 1996 (New York: Guggenheim Museum Publications), 23.
11. What he means by "native Africa" is the African who clings to the "authentic way of life."
12. Theodore Roosevelt, *Africa Game Trails: An Account of the African Wanderings of an American Hunter-Naturalist* (London: John Murray, Albemarle Street, 1910), 167.
13. Ngugi wa Thiong'o, *Writers in Politics: Essays* (London: Heinemann, 1981), 17–19.
14. Elisofon met with the Kikuyu colonial chief Koinange Wa Mbiyu and his son Peter Mbiyu Koinange in 1947.
15. Ernest Hemingway, "The Short Happy Life of Francis Macomber," in *The Complete Short Stories of Ernest Hemingway*, The Finca Vigia Edition (New York: Charles Scribner's Sons, 1937), 15.
16. This is the convoluted ethics that backed up the *LIFE* Great Adventures photo essay "Helicopter Safari in Africa" (10 June 1957).
17. Mary Louise Pratt, *Imperial Eyes: Travel Writing and Transculturation* (London: Routledge, 1992), 60.
18. See John S. Akama, "Neocolonialism, Dependency and External Control of Africa's Tourism Industry: A Case Study of Wild Life Safari Tourism in Kenya," in *Tourism and Postcolonialism: Contested Discourses, Identities and Representations*, ed. C. Michael Hall and Hazel Tucker (London: Routledge, 2004), 140–52; Urte Undine Frömming, "Kilimanjaro's Melting Glaciers: On the Colonial and Postcolonial Perception and Appropriation of African Nature," *Ethnográfica* 13.2 (November 2009): 295–316. Also http://www.scielo.oces.mctes.pt/pdf/etn/v13n2/v13n2a07.pdf.
19. Ernest Hemingway, *Green Hills of Africa* (New York: Scribner, [1935] 1963), 3.
20. Laurens van der Post, *Venture to the Interior* (London: Hogarth Press, 1952), 236.
21. See Wole Soyinka, *Myth, Literature and the African World* (Cambridge: Cambridge University Press, 1976), 1–36.
22. Alan Moorehead, *No Room in the Ark* (New York: Harper and Brothers, [1957] 1959), 11–12.
23. Rudyard Kipling, "The Elephant Child," in *Just So Stories: For Little Children* (London: Macmillan, [1902] 1971), 71, 76.
24. Elisofon's photographs of Victoria Falls, taken in 1947, feature currently (20 March 2012) on Victoria Falls' website: http://www.tothevictoriafalls.com/vfpages/tourism/lifegallery.html.
25. Winston Churchill, *My African Journey with Illustrations from Photography by the Author and Lieutenant-Colonel Gordon Wilson, and Three Images* (London: Hodder and Stoughton, 1908), 165–68.

26. Anne Morrow Lindbergh, "A Safari Back to Innocence: Immersion in Life, Journey to East Africa," *LIFE*, 21 October 1966, 88–94, 97–98.
27. Elisofon's photographs featured a zebra on the cover of the edition, the same elephant family as in the 1961 *LIFE* essay, a sunset, and a group of gnus.
28. Stuart Cloete, *The Turning Wheels* (Leipzig: Albatross, 1938), 193–94.
29. Alan Paton, *Cry, the Beloved Country: A Story of Comfort and Desolation* (Harmondsworth: Penguin Books, [1948] 1974), 34.
30. See D. N. Beach, "Afrikaner and Shona Settlement in the Enkeldoorn Area, 1890–1900," *Zambezia* 1.2 (October 1970): 25–34.
31. "These quotations are excellent ones," wrote Elisofon in the August memorandum to Fran Glennon in the New York office, "to demonstrate the spirit of the Boers and should be some which the South African Government would be truly pleased with." He also listed a quote from Van der Post's *Venture to the Interior*: "Laughter matched the Sun" which Elisofon would translate into "A close-up of a number of black faces really laughing" (EEPA, S.3.15, 2). The latter was not published, although a large number of Elisofon's photos from South Africa would have matched.
32. A spread of it was published in Blaine Littell and Eric Robins, *Africa: Images and Realities* (New York: Ridge Press, 1971), 222–23.
33. In an interview with him—"The Man at the Barbecue Had a Magic Touch"—with Ernie Shirley in *The Star* (Johannesburg), 21 September 1959, Elisofon explained that he hoped to bring to life Cloete's description of the Voortrekkers' "love of freedom and the fact that as long as they had wheels and oxen they would constantly look for new horizons." It was more a Boer myth homage than a Cloete text simulation. EEPA S-27, 3.
34. Vachel Lindsay, "The Congo," in *Collected Poems*, rev. and illustrated edition (New York: Macmillan Edition, 1926), 176.
35. Daniel P. Biebuyck, *Lega Culture: Art, Initiation, and Moral Philosophy among a Central African People* (Berkeley: University of California Press, 1973), 68, see also 155, 195.
36. In connection with an exhibition of Lega art in the KBC Bank Gallery on Brussels' Grand Place, Jan-Jan-Lodewijk Grootaers wrote: "This society encouraged its members to develop self-knowledge and create harmonious relations with the family, society, nature, and the world of the ancestors. Membership for men and their wives was based on complex, secret initiation rites; it conferred status, power, and authority, as well as prestige and privileges." Jan-Lodewijk Grootaers, "Lega: Ethics and Beauty in the Heart of Africa," KBC Bank Gallery Brussels, 4 May–28 July 2002, http://findarticles.com/p/articles/mi_m0438/is_1_36/ai_n27670790/. See also Elisabeth L. Cameron, "Art of the Lega: Meaning and Metaphor in Central Africa," 2001, The Nelson-Atkins Museum of

Art in Kansas City and the UCLA Fowler Museum of Cultural History, http://academic.csuohio.edu/curnowk/curnowk/html/lega.html.

37. Joseph Conrad, *Heart of Darkness* (London: Penguin Books, [1902] 1994), 24–25.
38. Elisofon met Chinua Achebe in Enugu on 22 November and took a number of photographs of him sitting at a table with two editions of his fresh publication of *Things Fall Apart* (1958) in front of him (EEPA EECL 7041). Achebe's piercing eyes have followed my work throughout this book, reminding me of his words in his famous castigation of Conrad's *Heart of Darkness*: "Marlow comes through to us not only as a witness of truth, but one holding those advanced and humane views appropriate to the English liberal tradition which required all Englishmen of decency to be deeply shocked by atrocities in Bulgaria or the Congo of King Leopold of the Belgians or wherever." Achebe, "An Image of Africa: Racism in Conrad's 'Heart of Darkness.'" It was a liberalism that also haunted Elisofon. See Raoul J. Granqvist, "The Story of How the Most Famous Portrait of Young Chinua Achebe Was Taken," *Africa Is a Country* (blog), 18 September 2013, http://africasacountry.com/eliot-elisofons-famous-portrait-of-chinua-achebe/-.
39. It was a regatta. Elisofon accompanied the paddlers up and down the rapids, photographing them in the canoe from all angles. The process of the staging can be viewed in the same video that harbors the "savage" shooting (HRC, EEL004 Time). And, like this one, a whole day's work amassed 101 EEPA documents.
40. Henry M. Stanley, *The Congo and the Founding of the Free State: A Story of Work and Preparation* (London: Marston, Searle and Rivington, 1886), 2:93.
41. André Gide, *Travels in the Congo*, translated from the French by Dorothy Bussy Hopewell (Hopewell, NJ: Eco Press, [1927] 1994), 12–13.
42. Hemingway's writing about bull-fighting (his last before his death), "The Dangerous Summer," was published by *LIFE* in three consecutive installments during September 1960, one year before Elisofon's essay was printed.
43. Joyce Cary, *The African Witch* (London: Michael Joseph, [1936] 1951), 63.
44. Geary asks whether such photographs should be exhibited and republished at all. Christraud M. Geary, "A World of Images," in *In and Out of Focus: Images from Central Africa, 1885–1960* (Washington, D.C.: Smithsonian National Museum of African Art, 2002), 19.
45. The page with the two dancing women with dangling breasts was omitted from the second edition of *LIFE* (23 October 1961) and the twenty-three pages of color replaced by twenty. An alternative dance scene out of Blixen's *Out of Africa* was rejected, as Kenyan colonial authorities did not permit references to African women dancing to be published.
46. Geoffrey Gorer, *Africa Dances: A Book about West African Negroes* (London: Faber and

Faber, 1935), 63.

47. The staged photo session was filmed by Joan Elisofon (HRC EEL004 Time).
48. Joyce Cary, *Mister Johnson* (London: Michael Joseph, 1952), 12.
49. Chantal Zabus, *African Palimpsest: Indigenization of Language in the West African Europhone Novel* (Atlanta: Rodopi, 1991), 63.
50. Nicholas Mirzoeff, *An Introduction to Visual Culture* (New York: Routledge, 1999), 152–54.

### Chapter 6. The American Broadcasting Company's *Africa*, 1966–1967: A Shock of Change and an Updated Safari

1. In Edward Bliss Jr., *Now the News: The Story of Broadcast Journalism* (New York: Columbia University Press, 1991), 394–95.
2. A week later, ABC repeated the series in four weekly one-hour morning broadcasts. It was sponsored by the 3M Company World-Vision, which split the program into four one-hour segments. "I can only think," said one reviewer, "that the network's trying to reach an audience that wasn't available the previous Sunday night, offering the show to homemakers hungry for something more substantial than game shows, soap operas and Gypsy Rose Lee." HRC 29.18, 29.21.
3. Unfortunately, the ABC *Africa* show is extremely hard to research, restricted as it is by legal agreements with the donor that prohibit lending, duplicating, and viewing it off-site or digitally online. Also, if you can view it at The Paley Center for Media (New York and Los Angeles), the Center's restrictive and disciplinary manual makes it troublesome for a researcher. It is remarkable that ABC has not adjusted the regulations to permit a wider viewing of the documentation that surveys a dramatic period in the U.S.-Africa relationship and an emerging new era in a visual narration of the continent outside of the *LIFE* and the *National Geographic* conventions.
4. In James Fleming, "Four-Hour Long Telecast Will Introduce Africa," *Ogden-Standard Examiner*, 20 August 1967, 65.
5. Blaine Littell, *South of the Moon: On Stanley's Trail through the Dark Continent* (London: Weidenfield and Nicolson, 1966).
6. John Gabriel, *Racism, Culture, Markets* (New York: Routledge, 1994), 154.
7. The quotes come from Fleming's unpublished essay, dated 30 November 1966, titled "The Shock of Change." EEPA, V-7.
8. In a memo of 3 June 1966 to Elisofon, Tom Hopkinson, director of the International Press Institute in Nairobi, knowing Elisofon's traditional taste, puffs for a photo of Kikuyu women carrying burdens with an enormous sling suspended from their foreheads. EEPA, V-2.

9. Robert Kennedy's "Day of Affirmation Address" at Cape Town University on 6 June 1966, http://www.americanrhetoric.com/speeches/rfkcapetown.htm.
10. Robert Ardrey, "Man Is a Territorial Animal," *LIFE*, 2 September 1966, 52. The answer to the question about the Finns is: "For freedom only."
11. Robert Ardrey, "The Basic Drive—for Territory," *LIFE*, 26 August 1966, 58.
12. Robert Ardrey, *African Genesis: A Personal Investigation into the Animal Origins and Nature of Man*, drawings by Berdine Ardrey (New York: Atheneum, 1961), 117–42.
13. Stephen Gray, "Soul-Brother Eugène N. Marais: Some Notes towards a Re-edit of His Works," *Tydskrif vir Letterkunde* 50.2 (Pretoria 2013), http://www.scielo.org.za/scielo.php?pid=S0041-476X2013000200005&script=sci_arttext.
14. Richard Leakey and Robert Campbell from *National Geographic* joined the ABC team filming (Blaine Littell, William Peters, and Richard Swicker) to do a sequence on Maasai in Manyara, at Rift Valley Escarpment (Tanzania). On the basis of the footage that Campbell produced, ABC (New York) gave him a contract to continue doing wildlife filming on his own in Samburi and Serengeti for the project. As late as mid-May 1967, after a long wait for it to happen, Campbell sent his footage of the migration of wildebeest to the editors in New York for a last-minute revision.
15. It may well be that Ardrey's thesis about the Maasai-hyena linkage was confirmed by events that took place during the filming at Lake Natron in northern Tanzania. Littell wrote to Fleming in early June that the Maasai were dying of malaria and that the bodies were left for the hyenas. He asked that Elisofon and Peters bring medicine when coming a couple of weeks later. HRC 48.8–9.
16. Carmel Schrire, *Tigers in Africa: Stalking the Past at the Cape of Good Hope*, Third Glynn Isaac Memorial Lecture Cape Town 1999 (Charlottesville: University Press of Virginia, 2002), 40.
17. See Wiley Online Library, *American Business Law Journal* 6.3: 691–798, http://onlinelibrary.wiley.com/doi/10.1111/j.1744-1714.1968.tb00732.x/abstract; International Court of Justice, South-West Africa Cases, Judgement of July 1966, http://www.icj-cij.org/docket/index.php?sum=288&code=lsa&p1=3&p2=3&case=47&k=f2&p3=5.nternational.
18. I include in parentheses the countries where they worked—as far as I know.
19. An homage, on my part, to all the cinematographers, directors of photography, camera operators, and visual narrators whose ABC footage 1966–1967 lies hidden and unseen in archives, closed media centers, or private collections, waiting for the outside world's critical attention and undaunted appreciation.
20. EEPA, V-9, 7; "Conventional Africa Went by the Boards," *Sunday Post-Crescent* (Appleton, WI), 10 September 1967.

21. He was interviewed by former U.S. ambassador William Attwood, writer of the book with the self-descriptive title, *The Reds and the Blacks* (1967).
22. One of the ten editors was Elisofon's ex-wife, Mavis Lyons.
23. The program would be televised in four one-hour segments on successive Tuesdays, starting at 8:30 a.m. Schools across the country, ABC announced, would be informed of the program's educational value. Instructional material was distributed to twenty-three thousand schools.
24. Few knew that this was a reference to Gerald Feil's screening of a version of Amos Tutuola's novel *The Palm-Wine Drinkard*, as adapted and performed by Kola Ogunmola and his traveling opera company in a forest outside Ibadan.
25. The following is the summary of the four parts attached to *Africa* in its capacity as winner of the Peabody Award (1967): (1) The program opens with some facts on Africa and looks at Kilimanjaro in Tanzania, as well as Olduvai Gorge, where remains of early man have been discovered. In a look at Botswana, the lifestyle of the Bushmen in the Kalahari Desert is examined. In Ethiopia, architecture and history and Haile Selassie are discussed, and independence ceremonies are witnessed. (2) This part begins with a discussion of Nigeria and its modern capital, Lagos, and the tribalism that splits Nigeria. The program notes problems of health and education in Nigeria, and continues with an examination of Ghana, in debt because of the corrupt leadership of Nkrumah. Howard K. Smith analyzes new African leadership, including Tubman of Liberia, Nyerere of Tanzania, Nasser of the United Arab Republic (UAR), and Boumédiènne of Algeria. (3) This part opens with a look at sports and entertainment, including singer Miriam Makeba, and continues with an examination of the nineteenth-century slave trade off the African West Coast. The program looks at the multiracial state of Kenya, with Kikuyu tribesmen, the Masai, white farmers, city-dwellers, President Kenyatta, and the Republic of the Congo, where President Mobutu maintains an uneasy peace between the government army and mercenary soldiers. (4) This hour looks at the countries of southern Africa ruled by white colonists, beginning with Angola and Mozambique, where the Portuguese military force contains rebel activity. It continues with Rhodesia, where whites try to spread Western civilization, and South Africa, where cameras were not allowed, experiencing severe problems with its policy of racial apartheid. Smith concludes the broadcast, saying U.S. citizens know too little about Africa.
26. "*Africa* Show Called 'Landmark in TV,'" *Corpus Christi Caller-Times* (citing the *New York Times News Service*), 17 September 1967.
27. "*Africa* Show Called 'Landmark in TV.'"
28. Ian Aitken, ed., *The Concise Routledge Encyclopedia of the Documentary Film* (London:

Taylor and Francis, 2012), 844.

29. P. J. O'Connell, *Robert Drew and the Development of Cinema Verité in America* (Carbondale: Southern Illinois University Press, 2010), 109–10.
30. One of them was Gerald Fein, who worked with Albert Maysles in Kenya in 1961 on the shooting of the ten-minute-long black-and-white film *Safari Ya Gari* (*Africa Train Ride*). "This early travelogue film, made in a Kenyan train station, captures an impromptu musical performance. Some passengers eagerly join in while others sleep—blissfully unaware of the performance taking place around them." Joe McElhaney, *Albert Maysles* (*Contemporary Film Directors*), (Chicago: University Illinois Press, 2009), 182.
31. Homi K. Bhabha, *The Location of Culture* (New York: Routledge, 1994), 99–100. Compare Bhabha's commentary with Angelou's.
32. Carolyn Martin Shaw, *Colonial Inscriptions: Race, Sex, and Class in Kenya* (Minneapolis: University of Minnesota Press, 1995), 184. Cf. "In Karen Blixen's eyes, this [Europe and Africa] alleged contrast between the aristocrat and the peasant was played out in the Maasai and Kikuyu who were her neighbors." Sidney Littlefield Kasfir, *African Art and Colonial Encounter: Inventing Global Commodity* (Bloomington: Indiana University Press, 2007), 39.
33. Feil was convicted in absentia of committing a crime against the state for filming in South Africa. The record of the conviction has vanished. Source: a private letter to me dated 26 June 2013.
34. Jackie Heyns, "How to Cheat Fate—Be a Coon, Undercurrent Affairs," *Post*, 9 January 1966, in "Chronicle of the Kaapse Klopse with some documents on the sources of their music," compiled by Denis-Constant Martin, Fondation nationale des sciences politiques, Centre d'études et de recherches internationales, Paris (2007), 102.
35. Herman Arendse, "Like Snoek en Patats, the Coons Belong to Cape Town," *Cape Herald*, 31 December 1966, in "Chronicle of the Kaapse Klopse with some documents on the sources of their music," 103.
36. Feil: "The section about Southern Africa was the first ever strong and widely viewed discussion and condemnation of Apartheid on US network television" (private letter, 26 June 2013).
37. Blaine Littell and Eric Robins, *Africa: Images and Realities* (New York: Ridge Press, 1971), 69.
38. For Soyinka's reminiscences of Feil, see Wole Soyinka, *You Must Set Forth at Dawn: A Memoir* (New York: Random House, 2007), 24, 451, 462.
39. Soyinka was well known in the United States and Britain. His political speeches at that time criticized the cult of personality and government corruption in African

dictatorships. In June 1965, *The Lion and the Jewel* was produced for Hampstead Theatre Club, London, and during his imprisonment, it was played in September 1967, in Accra. *The Road* premiered (London) at the Commonwealth Arts Festival, opening on 14 September 1965 at the Theatre Royal. It was awarded the Grand Prix. In April 1966, his play *Kongi's Harvest* was produced in revival at the World Festival of Negro Arts in Dakar, Senegal. His first feature-length movie film, *Nigeria: Culture in Transition*, which included an abbreviated version of *The Strong Breed* and televised scenes from Amos Tutuola's *The Palm-Wine Drinkard*, was broadcast by American television stations on 16 October 1966. *The Trials of Brother Jero* and *The Strong Breed* were produced in November 1967 in the Greenwich Mews Theatre in New York.

40. Chinua Achebe, *There Was a Country: A Personal History of Biafra* (New York: Penguin, 2012), 109.
41. In an interview with Stan Mayys: "Dark Continent Also Long Continent," *North Adams Transcript*, 26 August 1967, 18.
42. Eliot Elisofon, *Java Diary* (London: Macmillan, 1969), 285.
43. Ardrey's was on the territorial imperative with allusions to animal and human segregation and war as a biological necessity (highly topical issues with both apartheid and the Vietnam War in sight from most angles of the ABC project).
44. Eliot Elisofon and Marvin Newman, *African Animals* (New York: Ridge Press, 1967).
45. He returned to choice quotes such as: "Elephants walking away as if they had an appointment at the end of the world" (Blixen, *Out of Africa*) and "Three big birds [vultures] squatted obscenely" (Hemingway, "The Snows of Kilimanjaro"). At this point in time, the Kenyan writer Ngugi wa Thiong'o's novels *Weep Not, Child* (1964) and *The River Between* (1965), as well as Achebe's *Things Fall Apart* (1958) and *A Man of the People* (1966), had been published. But literature on/about Kenya and Nigeria worthy to be acknowledged by Elisofon had to be written by Europeans and Americans, not by writers who lived in the countries. African writers as similar inspirational source banks were not on his radar.
46. It was, explained Fleming in a newspaper interview, a unique event, a rarity, "the complete record of a daylight kill by a lioness. Cameraman Gerald Feil never missed a move" (*Ogden Standard-Examiner*, 20 August 1967, 65). This is the only mention I have found of Feil by Fleming in ABC's extensive public material about the filming done in Africa. Fleming made a point of crediting his ABC filmmaking staff—but obviously not all. Elisofon agreed to this: "More credit should have gone to the men who were in the field—men like Jerry Field, one of America's most talented cameramen, who was never mentioned" (Elisofon, *Java Diary*, 285). The reason for nullifying Feil, who was first director of photography and director of filmed sequences on location in Africa

throughout the project's thirteen months, could have been Feil's unconventional and radical style of filming.

47. Mayys, "Dark Continent," 18.
48. See Raoul J. Granqvist, "Photojournalism's White Mythologies: Eliot Elisofon and *LIFE* in Africa, 1959–1961," *Research in African Literatures* 43.3 (2012): 92.
49. The special double issue "The Wild World," *LIFE*, 22 December 1967, published Charles A. Lindbergh's two essays "The Wisdom of Wildness" and "Timeless and Untamed: The World's Great Wildernesses and the Creatures [both 'savage' humans and animals] Still Found in Them."
50. The series of photos Elisofon took were of the elephant, the rhinoceros, the hippopotamus, the crocodile, and the baboon, each with a caption that dillydallies with anthropomorphism.
51. To take these pictures, in the company of three other cameramen, Johnny Coquillon, H. J. "Jim" Smith (who would work with him in West Africa in 1970), and Feil, Elisofon had hired the bush pilot Keith Mousely and a twin turbo–engine Piper Comanche (an alternatively named Piper Aztec). At eighteen thousand feet the tube to the oxygen mask got clogged, the pilot passed out, and the plane was falling fast toward a rock. Elisofon cut the line to the mask, with great composure, and put the tube in the pilot's mouth; the pilot recovered, and they continued flying and taking pictures. Ten days earlier, Smith and Elisofon had tried to climb it, but they got sick from the altitude, and gave up ("my heart began to palpitate too much," Elisofon remembered [Elisofon, *Java Diary*, 284]). ABC used the flight anecdote, variously retold and inflated, to describe what risks the filming crews, in general, submitted themselves to in the pursuit of the best footage, in terms similar to the patriotic wartime propaganda of the day. The American newspapers were quick to pick up this Kilimanjaro incident, with or without Elisofon's ready assistance. It was deified by being retold in the program for the "Memorial Exhibition at the Museum of African Art," *Tribute to Africa: The Photography and the Collection of Eliot Elisofon* (Washington, D.C.: Museum of African Art, 1974), 9.
52. While in Kinshasa in February, he visited the Baptist Mission Society, a camp of Angolan refugees at Kibentile near Mbanza-Ngungu, not far from the Angolan border. The newspaper *Somerset Daily America* (15 December 1966) reported that the American couple Rev. Daniel and Margaret Grenfell distributed lollipops to refugee children, who were pleased, the article noted. It also informed readers that ten children died every day. Elisofon sent malaria pills to the mission hospital when he was back in the United States after the visit.
53. Littell, who passed through the city in January 1965, only half a year after the killings,

depicted the city resembling "not so much a patient on the mend, bandaged but ambulatory, as a sick man in a coma." Littell, *South of the Moon*, 205–6.

54. "1966 30 Aug: During the recapture [July–August 1964] of Albertsville ANC forces commanded by Lieutenant Colonel Kakudji do not take prisoners. More than 400 rebels including many wounded are executed after having been tortured or crucified on the trunks of the palm trees that line the shopping street the length of the lake [Lake Tanganyika]." Archive-org-com. Chronology of the Democratic Republic of Congo/Zaire (1960–1997)—Online Encyclopedia of Mass Violence. http://archive-org.com/org/m/massviolence.org/2014-09-02_4514382_25/Chronology_of_the_Democratic_Republic_of_Congo_Zaire_1960_1997_Online_Encyclopedia_of_Mass_Violence/.
55. Michela Wrong, *In the Footsteps of Mr. Kurtz: Living on the Brink of Disaster in Mobutu's Congo* (New York: Harper/Perennial, 2000), 85.
56. Littell and Robins, *Africa*, 121, 124. Their selection of twenty-three photos by Elisofon for the book was a replication of his ABC Congo themes: a *Conrad literary river landscape* (crocodile spread, 112–13; rain forest spread, 115–16; river tributaries, hippo, 120); *old Congo* (billock livestock graze, 122–12; Shi woman pounding manioc with the caption "Balegas [Shi] are the only Congo tribe that does this chore with musical rhythm," 123); *new Congo* (tin mine near Kalima, 126; riveter repairs shipyard, harbor Kinshasa, 127); *Congo river life* (women traders, off-shore trading, 129; aboard life, 130–31); *Mobutu* (craftsman carving elephant group from ivory, 132; Mobutu in *abacost* [meaning à bas le costume, off with the Western coat], and admirers with emblazoned shirts, 133); *Congo "serenity"* (image spread, 134–35).
57. Martin Jay, *Downcast Eyes: The Denigration of Vision in Twentieth-Century French Thought* (Berkeley: University of California Press, 1994), 443.
58. Fleming, "Four-Hour Long Telecast Will Introduce Africa," 65.
59. EEPA, V-12, 3. See Latz's excruciating articles in the *Chicago Tribune*: on Mobutu (2 October 1966) and on the mercenaries (4 October 1966), http://archives.chicagotribune.com/1966/10/02/page/1/article/mobutu-turns-congo-into-a-police-stated/index.html. http://archives.chicagotribune.com/1966/10/04/page/55/article/white-mercenaries-calm-african-terror.
60. Ruth Mayer, *Artificial Africas: Colonial Images in the Times of Globalization* (Hanover, NH: University Press of New England, 2002), 172.
61. Foreign Relations of the United States, 1964–1968, vol. 23, Congo, 1960–1968, Department of State, Washington, D.C., 714–15. http://www.voltairenet.org/IMG/pdf/frus1964-68v23.pdf.
62. On the black-and-white photo of Mobutu published in *Africa: Images and Realities*, Bill Close can be seen in sunglasses in the upper right-hand corner of the photo.

## Chapter 7. The Cold War Affinity between Zaire's Mobutu Sese Seko and the United States' Eliot Elisofon

1. Edward Said, *The World, the Text, and the Critic* (Cambridge, MA: Harvard University Press, 1983), 77.
2. I have divided the shooting for the Stanley book project and the breakdown of the Elisofon-Mobutu partisanship with American coloniality into four jaunts: J1, March–April 1970, for the *National Geographic* and for Westinghouse Broadcasting Company with John Smith as cameraman; J2, 26 October–4 December 1970, for Westinghouse Broadcasting Company with Georges Bracher as cameraman and Maya Bracher as scriptgirl; J3, January–March 1971, for Westinghouse Broadcasting Company with the Brachers); and J4, 18 January–21 March 1972, for the National Geographic.
3. He was photographing a hunting expedition for capturing and killing gorillas during the latter part of June 1951 for American universities. See "LIFE Goes on a Gorilla Hunt," *LIFE*, 19 November 1951. See HRC 19.20 and 23.4. See his photos: http://life.time.com/culture/on-a-gorilla-hunt-striking-photos-from-a-1951-life-magazine-article/#1. In a coming issue of *LIFE* (10 December 1951, 16), a reader (Charles E. Spencer) wrote: "Sirs: Let me suggest we extend the Marshall Plan to the gorillas so that they may defend themselves against some of our inhuman humans."
4. I have borrowed the very apt genre title of "stragglelogue" for the "following-in-the-steps-of" narrative by Brian Kevin. "Notes on the 'Stragglelogue' as a Travel Book Genre, and How I Followed Hunter S. Thompson," *Matador Network*, 27 September 2013, http://matadornetwork.com/notebook/notes-on-the-stragglelogue-as-a-travel-book-genre-and-how-i-followed-hunter-s-thompson/.
5. Blaine Littell, *South of the Moon: On Stanley's Trail through the Dark Continent* (London: Weidenfield and Nicolson), 7.
6. Blaine Littell and Eric Robins, *Africa: Images and Realities* (New York: Ridge Press, 1971), 115.
7. The proposal was presented to Robert Gilka, the *National Geographic* director of photography, in December 1969 (HRC 42. 11; EEPA, W-1, 11; 16 December); on 20 February 1970, Elisofon signed the contract, and a week later he received an advance of $5,000.
8. 22 February 1970, EEPA, W 1–7.1.
9. Kevin C. Dunn, *Imagining the Congo: The International Relations of Identity* (New York: Macmillan, 2003), 29–32.
10. Here he started his lifelong traffic of transferring African artifacts to his home at 145 East 27th Street, New York, to the Harvard Peabody Museum and to various collectors for sale, and as gifts to colleagues and friends. The latter group consisted of individual

staff members of the Group W Productions (1971–1972), ABC (1966–1967), and *LIFE* (1942–1972). Wilson Hicks, his first *LIFE* editor, was a collector whom Elisofon served up to 1950. He supplied him also with Nazi memorabilia, both from North Africa and the Finnish war front in 1944.

11. See Peter Edgerly Firchow, *Envisioning Africa: Racism and Imperialism in Conrad's Heart of Darkness* (Lexington: University Press of Kentucky, 2000).
12. Nicholas Saunders, "Ulysses' Gaze: The Panoptic Premise in Aerial Photography and Great War Archeology," in *Images of Conflict: Military Aerial Photography and Archeology*, ed. Birger Stichelbaut, Jean Bourgeois, Nicholas Saunders, and Piet Chielens (Cambridge: Cambridge Scholars Publishing, 2009), 32.
13. Lucy R. Lippard, *The Lure of the Local: Senses of Place in a Multicentered Society* (New York: New Press, 1997), 58–59.
14. Gillian Rose, *Feminism and Geography: The Limits of Geographical Knowledge* (Cambridge: Polity Press, 1996), 97.
15. Lake Edward–Rutanzige, we learn, is fed by the Rwindi River and empties to the north into Lake Albert via the Semliki River. The Ruzizi River trades water with Lake Kivu and Lake Tanganyika in a north–south direction.
16. He also took aerial pictures of the INEAC (Institut national pour les études agronomiques du Congo belge) at Yangambi, south of Yambuya, an agricultural research station still in operation.
17. Bill Ashcroft, Gareth Griffiths, and Helen Tiffin, *Post-Colonial Studies: The Key Concepts* (New York: Routledge, 2000), 185.
18. See Brian H. Murray, "Henry Morton Stanley and the Pygmies of 'Darkest Africa,'" *Public Domain Review*, A Project of the Open Knowledge Foundations, http://publicdomainreview.org/2012/11/29/henry-morton-stanley-and-the-Pygmies-of-darkest-africa/.
19. Henry Morton Stanley, *In Darkest Africa: or, the Quest, Rescue, and Retreat of Emin, Governor of Equatoria* (London: Sampson, Low, Marston, 1890), 2:40–41.
20. Michael Tavel Clarke, *These Days of Large Things: The Culture of Size in America, 1865–1930* (Ann Arbor: University of Michigan Press, 2007), 28.
21. For the ongoing traumatization of this area, see Roberto Beneduce, Luca Jourdan, Timothy Raeymaekers, and KoenVlassenroot, "Violence with a Purpose: Exploring the Functions and Meaning of Violence in the Democratic Republic of Congo," *Intervention* 4.1 (2006): 32–46.
22. See the *New York Times* article entitled "Travel and Resorts—Albert National Park—Where Pygmies and the Wild Elephants Play," 27 February 1972, illustrated with Maya

Bracher's photographs. Note the title's merging of the "Pygmy" and the wild animal.

23. Veit Erlmann, "'Spectatorial Lust': The African Choir in England, 1891–1893," in *Africans on Stage: Studies in Ethnological Show Business*, ed. Bernth Lindfors (Bloomington: Indiana University Press, 1999), 126–33. Several chapters in this anthology are of relevance for an understanding of Elisofon's obsession with the African body, among them Jeffrey Green's "A Revelation in Strange Humanity: Six Congo Pygmies in Britain, 1905–1907" (156–87) and Z. S. Strother's "Display of the Body Hottentot" (1–61), each groundbreaking works.
24. Traveling north from Goma, Elisofon stopped at Escaliers de Venus waterfall at Mount Hoyo in the Virunga National Park to have a picture taken of him posing in front of the spray from the waterfall. It was not a whim.
25. The SIRIS photo caption, "Traditional hairstyle among Mangbetu women," is misleading.
26. It was the same politicized dress ritual that Nyim Kot a Mbweeky III [Kwete Mboke] of the Kuba performed, which Elisofon photographed a couple of weeks later at the king's formal (state) visit to Bungamba, a village between Mweke and Luebo in Kasai Occidental. Kwete Mboke shifted from wearing the elaborate state dress at the ceremonial photo sitting to the simple navy blue wool abacost, the Mobutu obligated attire, when he positioned himself at another photo session later in the day, a remodeling we never saw his predecessor, Mbop aMabiinc maKyeen [Bope Mobinji Kena], undergo, Elisofon photographing him in 1947 and 1951 then with Belgian colonists controlling the scene. EEPA EECL 2212, EEPA EENG 08592.
27. But *National Geographic* did not give up on either Zaire/Congo or Elisofon. During the four months of January–March 1972, he was given a new chance by the magazine to photograph in the country, which only meant that he returned to the well-known sites he had visited before on other occasions, reproducing more or less the same motifs and images. The photos selected by the editor for a chapter in the 1973 magazine were picked from the two certified trips but rigidly adjusted to go along with John P. Putman's dichotomous text called "Yesterday's Congo, Today's Zaire" (*National Geographic* 143.3 [1973]: 398–432). Stanley had been condensed into a footnote and Mobutu, as we will see, raised to stand up triumphantly as Zaire's unquestioned leader with the American president at his side.
28. His successor, Deane R. Hinton, on the other hand, was declared persona non grata after ten months' service (June 1975) to become U.S. ambassador to the European Union.
29. "USIA's Right-Wing Bias: Director Frank Shakespeare's Missionary Zeal Is Directed at Stopping Communism," *Boston Sunday Globe*, 9 January 1972. EEPA Y-4.7.
30. "The Outlook for the Congo," 22 July 1970, Foreign Relations, 1969–1976, vol. E-5,

Documents on Africa, 1969–1972, National Intelligence Estimate Number 65–70, U.S. Department of State Archive, http://2001-2009.state.gov/r/pa/ho/frus/nixon/e5/54753.htm.

31. Besides the letters that I have already annotated, of even more importance were the two (dated 30 August and 19 October 1970) that J. Verschuren, director of Institute de la Conservation de la Nature au Congo, wrote to him at the advent of his second and third 1970s trips. EEPA, W-1, 31.1, W-1, 39.1.
32. In a conversation with me in April 2010.
33. He took pictures of the same troops in 1967.
34. http://www.lexpress.fr/actualite/monde/afrique/le-roi-des-belges-roi-souverain-du-congo_1271318.html.
35. Here is a passage from their conversation: "President Nixon asked what forms the subversion takes and what form of opposition President Mobutu faces domestically? President Mobutu responded that he has no opposition in the Congo having squashed it when he came to power, but there are 6 to 8 thousand Congolese refugees in Tanzania all of whom are trained and equipped by the Chicoms. . . . [Nixon asked what] could be done to stop the Communist operations from Zambia and Tanzania. President Mobutu pointed out the ease with which Lake Tanganyika can be crossed at night and ammunition and supplies landed in the bush and the interior. . . . President Nixon thought that some of the riverine craft now used in Vietnam might be gotten to President Mobutu." Foreign Relations of the United States, 1969–1976, vol. E–5, pt 1, Documents on Sub-Saharan Africa, 1969–1972, document 235, http://history.state.gov/historicaldocuments/frus1969-76ve05p1/d235.
36. William T. Close, *Beyond the Storm: Treating the Powerless and the Powerful in MOBUTU'S Congo/Zaire* (Marbleton, WY: Meadowlark Springs Productions, 2007), 245. Mobutu gave him money to pay for his daughter's, actress Glenn Close's, wedding, which, he explains, he could not have afforded otherwise (247–48). These were Nixon's words of welcome to Mobutu in Washington: "We know that you will be meeting with our Government leaders and also later with business leaders in New York, who may be interested in making an investment in the Congo." U.S. Department of State Office of the Historian. Document 235. Memorandum of Conversation, Washington, 4 August 1970, http://www.presidency.ucsb.edu/ws/index.php?pid=2610.
37. White had written the much-discussed articles "Behind the Headlines in Viet Nam" (February 1967, 149–63) and "The Mekong: River of Terror and Hope" (December 1968, 754–55, 764–65).
38. In order to testify to the strict particularities of a typical Elisofon itinerary, here is the

one from January–March 1972, his last trip to the Congo (based on HRC 38.9). January 19: Arrival Kinshasa (from New York), 27: depart Kinshasa for Isiro, Dungu (city south of the Garamba National Park), 28: Garamba National Park, Gangala na Bodio, Mbuti people. February 1–3: Isiro, 3–5: Kisangani, 5: Kinshasa, 9: depart Kinshasa, 10: Kananga, 11: Mushenge village, Kuba, people, 14–15: Bulape, south of Mweka, Kuba people, 16: Kananga, 17: Mbuji-Mayi, mining company-diamonds, southwest of Kananga, 19: Kinshasa, 23: depart Kinshasa for Lubumbashi, Kolwezi (mining city), Lofoi Falls waterfall in Kundelungu National Park, Katanga Province), 27: Kinshasa, OAU village, Inga dam. March (accompanied by Elin and Jill Elisofon) 6: Goma at Lake Kivu, 7: Mount Nyiragongo, 8: Goma, Tutsi dancers, 9: Virunga National Park, Rwindi camp, Vitshumbi (at Lake Edward), 10: Beni, 11: Epulu, Ituri forest, Mbuti people, Ndaka people, 15: Kisangani, Zaire river boat, 17: Lisala, 19: Mbandaka (disembark), 20: near Mbandaka fishing village, 21: Kinshasa.

39. The photo album of the Congo was presented to Mobutu on the fifth anniversary day in October 1970.
40. Bulape is a city in Kubaland, between Mushenge and Mweke, the site from where many of Elisofon's photographic sessions in the area had started since 1947.
41. Here Putnam took a remarkable picture of Elisofon photographing an "Mbuti" child, a scene of vulnerability that breathes Elisofon's frustration with the pouring rain, his struggles in arranging the shooting, and the seeming composure of the small child (EEPA EENG 08487).
42. *Tribute to Africa: The Photography and the Collection of Eliot Elisofon* (Washington, D.C.: Museum of African Art, 1974), 9.
43. Elisofon's field-note reads: "Special fetish dance meant to frighten other people fighting them. These sticks are shoved thru one cheek but after dance no wound or scar can be seen, no explanation for this" (EEPA EENG 02513, EEPA EENG 02503).
44. These were pictures he took at a Protestant secondary school in Mbandaka (formerly Coquilhatville) on the Congo River, where he stopped on his return by boat to Kinshasa. His documentation of activities on the Colonel Ebeya centered on two major topics: women's hairdressing and the transportation of fish to the deck side.

### Chapter 8. The Politics of the *Black African Heritage* Series, 1970–1972

1. Bond, EEPA X-7, 1 (1); Davis, EEPA X-7, 2 (2); Angelou, EEPA F-2, 2 (3); Park, EEPA X-2, 2 (4). The numbers in the parentheses, preceded by *BAH*, will henceforth identify the particular film.
2. See Yale Richmond, *Practicing Public Diplomacy: A Cold War Odyssey* (New York:

Berghahn Books, 2008), 128–36.

3. See Tom Tuch interviewing Eugene Kopp, former deputy director of the USIA (7 March 1988), "The Association for Diplomatic Studies and Training Foreign Affairs Oral History Project Information Series." http://lcweb2.loc.gov/service/mss/mssmisc/mfdip/2005%20txt%20files/2004kop01.txt.
4. Both men were part of Nixon's political entourage at the détente policy-making meeting in Moscow in May 1972. Shakespeare did not shrink from communicating with his staffers his dislike of easing the tensions with the Soviet Union, clashing openly and provocatively with the State Department. He was at war; the USIA officials were his soldiers.
5. Shakespeare became executive vice president of Westinghouse in 1973.
6. After finishing the *BAH* footage, on 4 May 1971, he wrote a circular letter of accolade to Senator Edmund Muskie (Maine) and Senator Jacob J. Javits (New York), praising Frank Shakespeare and the USIA for the "willing and intelligent assistance I received from every one of their officers in Africa" (HRC 18.3).
7. Letter to John E. Garner, 15 October 1970; Garner's reply, letter 24 October 1970 (HRC 49.1).
8. Letter to John Shellenberger, 8 October 1970 (HRC 49.1-2).
9. Letter John H. Thompson to Shellenberger, 23 October 1970 (HRC 50.1).
10. Letter to P. A. O. Stanley Alpern, the American Embassy, Abidjan, Ivory Coast, 28 July 1970 (HRC 49.1, 50.4-5).
11. Letter from F. Wenston Fenhagen to Elisofon, 30 September 1970 (HRC 50.4, 51.5).
12. "Autorisation," Ministère de l'Information, République de la Côte d'Ivoire, le Cabinet, 27 février 1971; "Monsieur ELIOT ELISOFON propose d'effectuer un court métrage [short film] sur l'heritage Africain des noirs Américains." HRC 68.7-8, 69.1.
13. Letter to Frank Shakespeare, 27 July 1970 (HRC 49.8, 68.5).
14. Letter to Ekpo Eyo, 12 December 1970 (HRC 57.6), and another to Shellenberger,14 December 1970 (HRC 50.1-2) with the frustrated comment: "I am beginning to wonder if making these films is really worthwhile. I am so occupied with logistics and bureaucracy that I could give up."
15. Letter to Shellenberger, 10 May 1971 (HRC 50.1-2).
16. Elisofon, "Focus on Africa" [1] (HRC 44.1).
17. These are the prefatory historical data he wished to share with the viewers about the Congo: it is "one of the most magic names of Africa" where slavery became "important . . . when it was outlawed by the British, . . . there are some tribes which have remained unchanged since Henry Stanley opened up the basin and gave it to King Leopold of Belgium."

18. HRC 44.1. For another version, see EEPA X-8.2.
19. Letter to Shellenberger, 8 October 1970 (HRC 50.1-2).
20. Shakespeare telegrams, 15 October 1970 (HRC 49.1, 49.8).
21. The Macmillan book series would include the "three-river-story" (the Nile, the Congo, the Niger), two of which (the Nile and the Congo) he had already obtained enough to fill two dugouts each. One of the two other booklets was on an African "tribe" (the Yoruba); the second was on an "African nation" (Ghana). Letter to Elisofon from Macmillan (G. Gross and J. Elder), 24 November 1969; the contract with Elisofon was signed on 4 August 1970 and canceled on 21 December 1971. See correspondence HRC 56.8, 57.6.
22. From one of the many synopses of the *BAH* project Elisofon wrote for Westinghouse (HRC 48.12-13; see also 49.1 and 49.4).
23. I will add "71" to photos that he took during the second footage period (J2 and J3). Photos lacking a tag were taken during the first period (J1).
24. Pascal James Imperato, *A Wind in Africa: A Story of Modern Medicine in Mali* (St. Louis: Warren H. Green, 1976), 316.
25. See the *BAH* segment of the Bambara that includes the weaver dancing and playing his flute, pounding of millet (an Elisofon classic), a picture of the different types of antelopes (Tyi Wara and Sogoni Koun), and the masquerades. EEEP, 2:2–8.
26. Pierre Haffner, *Essai sur les fondements du cinéma africain* (Abidjan: Nouvelles editions africaines, 1978), 16–17.
27. Maya Bracher in a letter to her parents in Switzerland. Private communication with me.
28. In the first segment of the *BAH*, the "Congo Show," with Julian Bond as presenter [EEPA, X, 7–1 [4–5]). As also part of the Rwenzori visual-spiritual narrative, the "Congo" recites the historical gloss about Ptolemy as the "Mountain of the Moon" name-giver and teller of a half-truth, and now corrected by Elisofon: the rains divide on Ruwenzori, "one side starting the White Nile, the other going to the Congo River." This picks up the discussion earlier in this chapter about the meaning-making tropes related to the myths about this geography. As writer/photographer of both the Nile and the Congo, Elisofon is deeply implicated, so also the lizard that the filming team observes ascending the mountain, "its strange hand-like feet and independent revolving eyes also [lycopods, an early form of plant life] suggest the past." Africa belongs to the Old World.
29. After mountain climbing, they filmed in Ituri forest, in Virunga National Park, in the Lake Kivu area, and the Nyiragongo volcano; went for a brief visit to Ekulu and the Mbuti (called Pygmies in *BAH*, EEPA 1:6); filmed Enia fish traps at Moleka (Stanley Falls) (*BAH*, EEPA 1:7); and flew from Kisangani to the Mushenge area to film the (BA)Kuba people, Kot a Mbweeky III, and a whole museum of artifacts (*BAH*, EEPA 1:8–14).

30. The total sum for the SIRIS documents encapsulating the Dama masquerades in the Dogonland of his photography from 1959 and the four jaunts (J1, J2, J3, and J4) is 508. These also include his lengthy documentation of Dolo, the blacksmith and woodcarver, in Ogol du Haut village (J3) (EEPA EENG 02926).
31. "To the Dahomey, the mask is only one part of the masker, and by no means the most important one. It is not so much the masks as the accessories and attributes that determine the masker's identity" (EEPA staff note). To this could be added the Achebe wisdom that as much insight dwells with the partaker/participant of the dances and his or her positioning vis-à-vis the masquerader in motion.
32. His photos of the "women warriors," embodying "Amazons as a fighting force in Dahomey's [Bénin] foreign wars" (EEPA staff note), dancing for him, were of a different order. They were taken at the royal palace in Abomey, in the Fon people region (EEPA EENG 02204) (71).
33. In Chadawanka village, the camera turned on the Wodaabe male performers at the jeerewol celebration with equal relish for the spell of their bodies.
34. Secular photographic alternatives were that of the old town site at Elmina Castle, Elmina, Ghana, (71) and, more generally, the Tuareg. See SIRIS, Timbuctoo, Mali, 1970.
35. Here he took hundreds of pictures of Dolo, the carver and blacksmith, at work with his son Samuel producing a Kanaga mask, from the felling of the tree to the masquerader wearing Dolo's carved mask.
36. These pictures were accompanied by hundreds of aestheticizing close-up shots of the Wodaabe in Abouza and Chadawanka, young and old, women and men, at work, dancing, in a hallowed unity with their individual granaries (1970–1971). *BAH*, EEPA 2:8–11.
37. It is doubtful that cameraman King ever turned up in Bénin. At least he never materialized in the archival world.
38. The couple did small jobs for the French Cultural Center and the USIA, she as a photographer, he as a cameraman, and were both passionately engaged in the circle around Sembène Ousmane, the Senegalese filmmaker and writer. Georges Bracher was cameraman for Ben Diogaye Beye's *Les Princes Noirs de Saint-Germain-des Pres* (1975), and for Djibril Diop Mambéty's semifictional *Contras'city* (1968), and, likewise, for the semifictional *Touki Bouki* (*Le Voyage de l'hyène*) (1973). Maya did the still photographs for Sembène Ousmane's feature film *Mandabi* (*Le Mandat*), story by L. S. Senghor (1968), and the sound in Safi Faye's *Lettre Paysanne* (1975).
39. Matt Levine, "Touki Bouki," *Joyless Creatures* (blog), 7 March 2014 http://www.joylesscreatures.com/review-archive/touki-bouki.

40. See SIRIS, Elisofon archive, under Maya Bracher.
41. "Muriel Balash Notes" were enclosed in the letter (EEPA, x-3, 17).
42. The adverb "still" indicated that this was their second attempt at adjusting Elisofon's footage.
43. Elisofon was paid $200,000 for his *BAH* work, plus a share of the distribution profits for the four programs and their rights grants (HRC 46.11).
44. *BAH*, EEPA 2, 18–21.
45. Connie Perdreau, "To the Editor," *Ohio University Post* 63.19 (18 October 1972).
46. *BAH* or parts of the films were shown at a conference of African American parliamentarians in Lusaka (Zambia) on 17–18 January 1972 with President K. D. Kaunda as host. "Faces of Africa: Diversity and Progress; Repression and Struggle, Report of Special Study Missions to Africa," http://www.aluka.org/action/showMetadata?doi=10.5555/AL.SFF.DOCUMENT.uscg006.
47. What she watched was some or a mixture of the Westinghouse press release films collected from the films. Such were segments on Timbuktu and the Dogon masks; African iron working and the slave trade; musical instruments, the Bapende ceremony; and African dance. George E. Moynihan, the Westinghouse program manager, on the other hand, reporting from the same event (he too in a letter to Elisofon), was jubilant, also because the markets were competing for the product. He asked Elisofon to bring (buy) him another artwork from Africa for his "collection" (letter, 2 March, HRC). Elisofon was an African "art" courier for several friends of his.
48. The words are Warren Robbins' (HRC 45.12). See also Rick on Theater, "National Museum of African Art," *Rick on Theater* (blog), 19 January 2015, http://rickontheater.blogspot.se/2015/01/the-national-museum-of-african-art.html. Robbins and Elisofon were a tandem, both avid collectors of African art and lobbyists for their own causes. The difference was firsthand knowledge about Africa. Robbins visited the continent for the first time in 1973.
49. MAFA was expanded in 1971 with three adjacent outhouses and a modern wing, the first extension of the site since Robbins bought the Frederick Douglass property in 1964. The reopening was celebrated with an exhibition of 250 pieces of African sculptures and masks, among them artifacts from Gaston de Havenon's New York collection. "Washington's Museum of African Art," *Palm Beach Post-Times*, 22 May 1971.
50. The article "Albert National Park: Where Pygmies and Wild Elephants Play," *New York Times*, 27 February 1972, by Eliot Elisofon reads both as an advertisement for American tourism (enclosed is the address of a Kinshasa travel bureau for a seven-day trip) and a personal recital of Rwenzori heroism. What is objectionable is that the ten photos it

published were taken by Maya Bracher, not by Elisofon, and she was given no credit by the *New York Times*. "Quel honneur! mes photos publiées dans le New York Times! et le découvrir 43 ans plus tard!" was Bracher's courteous response (email to me, 23 March 2015).

51. The price of the three filmstrips was $54 and with records and audiocassettes $60. A teacher's guide was included at no cost.
52. Such as: "Through Wartime Africa with Knife and Fork," "Elisofon and the African Queen," "Climbing the 'Mountains of the Moon,'" and "People of Africa: the Baluba." To these, and many more, were added captivating summaries of his adventurous life among wild animals, "primitive Africans," beautiful Hollywood actresses, and prints of iconic Elisofon photographs (HRC 46.8–9; 51.8). The mythology of Elisofon is far-reaching, extending and swelling throughout the 1950s, 1960s, and into the 1970s, to be revitalized by the Smithsonian curators in 2014 for the fortieth jubilee of the EEPA, obfuscating a generation of intellectual insights, delaying and impeding scholarship from studying his photography and what a much-quoted Elisofon comment such as the following really carries with it: "I am really a visual man. . . . Although I write, lecture and do other things, my business is aesthetics and the study of people."
53. Bob Foster, "Screenings," *San Mateo Times*, 12 May 1972. Robbins had an identical comment about his museum project, repeating it on many occasions at this time.
54. She formulated this observation as a question, as she did regarding another microscale African institution, "the pyradimic establishment of responsibility," "the complex yet subtle political/social structure in an African tribe." Naturally, she insinuates, a skilled photographer can produce visual storylines to demonstrate cultural signatures of this kind. Angelou points to the full-fledged gender disproportions in Elisofon's photography.
55. In a letter to Elisofon in reference to his letter to the editor, Angelou wrote: "If I were to do an article on Israel, I could never approach the task with the same emotion as one whose relatives had suffered at Dachau and died in that madness" (letter to Elisofon, 25 May 1972, HRC 51.2).
56. These were "Paramount Collection Featuring Works Collected in Africa by Eliot Elisofon," Museum of African Art, 11 April–14 May 1972; Elisofon lecturing and showing *African Gift* at Colorado College Summer Program in Arts, Colorado Springs, 26 June 1972; lecture and showing of the *BAH* films, City College, New York, 11–13 October 1972; "African Art in Tribal Society" and "African Art for the Museum of Primitive Art Exhibition," Museum of Art, Rhode Island School of Design, 25 October 1972; "African Art of the Dogon: The Lester Wunderman Collection," Brooklyn Museum, 4 April–20 May 1973; "Wildlife Photography," "Africa's Gift," "The Future of Photography," University of

Wisconsin–Milwaukee, 5–7 March 1973 (the site of Elisofon's last public appearance and lectures).

57. Elisofon interviewed by Dave Skal, "Filmmaker Perplexed by Black Response," *Ohio University Post*, 63.19 (18 October 1972).
58. "The 28 women who carried water, the 14 boys who rowed the equipment, and the single policeman," Elisofon wrote in his field-notes from his days with the film team on the Ruiki River raft working on *The African Queen*, "did not like to work, being lazy by nature," noting that Lauren Bacall got her "baked beans, clam chowder, fresh tomatoes" directly by air from London (HRC 16.18, 21 September 1951). Katherine Hepburn had her "personal 'boy'—mine! Tahiti Bokumba" who provided her hot water every evening so she could wash her hair (picture by Elisofon, one of seventeen of his, in her diary). *The Making of* African Queen *or How I Went to Africa with Bogart, Bacall and Huston and Almost Lost My Mind* (New York: Alfred A. Knopf, 1987), 41, 48. "Life Goes on Location in Africa, *LIFE*, 17 September 1951, 173–79. See Jann Matlock, "Analysis," *The African Queen*, Colonial Film website, 2010, http://www.colonialfilm.org.uk/node/1067. "In this film, all the whites are taking land that does not belong to them."

## Chapter 9. Elisofon Collecting Artifacts and Elisofon Curated: Colonialist Power

1. See "Perfect Documents: Walker Evans and African Art, 1935," curated by Virginia-Lee Webb, archivist of the Photograph Collection in the Metropolitan Museum of Art, http://www.metmuseum.org/about-the-museum/press-room/exhibitions/2000/perfect-documents-walker-evans-and-african-art-1935. See also Virginia-Lee Webb, *Perfect Documents: Walker Evans and African Art, 1935* (New York: Metropolitan Museum of Art, 2000), 36.
2. Elisofon's watercolors and drawings are in the collections of the Museum of Modern Art, the Philadelphia Museum of Art, Colby College in Maine, the Pennsylvania Academy of Art, the Fogg Art Museum, and art museums in Dallas and Honolulu, as well as the Museum of Western Art in Tokyo.
3. Eliot Elisofon, "African Sculpture," *Atlantic Monthly*, 23 April 1959, 47.
4. Johannes Fabian, "Curios and Curiosity: Notes on Reading Torday and Frobenius," in *The Scramble for Art in Central Africa*, ed. Enid Schildkrout and Curtis A. Klein (Cambridge: Cambridge University Press), 100.
5. Emil Torday and T. A. Joyce, *Notes ethnographiques sur les peuples communément appelés Bakuba, ainsi que sur les peuplades apparentées les Bushong* (Brussels: Musée du Congo Belge, 1911). It was a formidable book containing 403 fieldwork photographs

and drawings, twenty color drawings, and fifty-three photographs of carved figures and objects.

6. Anne Maxwell, *Colonial Photography and Exhibitions* (London: Leicester University Press, 1999), 9.
7. As early as September 1952, two of Elisofon's artifacts were represented at the "African Exhibit" at the Museum of Modern Art.
8. Elisofon, "African Sculpture," 49.
9. Visiting the Bamana region (Mali) both in 1970 and 1971, he took pictures of antelope headdress manufacturing and mask performances.
10. Elisofon, "African Sculpture," 50.
11. Eliot Elisofon, "The Dance: What It Means to Me," *Dance Magazine* 33.8 (August 1957), tear sheets, HRC 38.17.
12. Constantine Petridis, "Luluwa Masks," *African Arts* 32.3 (1999): 43. Elisofon's photo is enclosed in the article. See 22923, C-4, 17.
13. Elisofon was seldom confronted by Africans by means other than the "look" signifying obliged acceptance, silence, passivity, anger, or unwillingness to cooperate. For colleagues or peers, the response to his aggressive self-importance shifted between benign moderation, tolerance, and grave irritation. For example, John Huston who had hired Elisofon as the color consultant for his second motion picture, *Moulin Rouge* (1952), made him a target of a series of practical jokes to assuage his "pompous egocentricity," with no lasting effect. Elisofon "even insisted on having a chair with his name on the back, so Huston had one made that said, '*Elisofon Go Home*.'" Lawrence Grobel, *The Hustons: The Life and Times of a Hollywood Dynasty* (New York: Skyhorse Publishing, 2014), 125–26.
14. Joan claimed that "no American woman has ever gone as high as I did" [the third stage] in a letter of 24 April 1951 to her parents. HRC 61.5–6.
15. Letter of 15 May 1951 from Joan Elisofon to her family, HRC 61.5–6. Apart from the grim climbing experiences, which Elisofon always called the "nine worst days of my life" (*LIFE*, 4 May 1953, 186), the couple had spent two to three days (9–10 April) at Camp Putnam (now Epulu), the "dude ranch" in the Ituri forest near Réserve de Faune à Okapis that the ethnologist Patrick Tracy Lowell Putnam had established in 1927 (collapsed in 1953), a combination of a guest house for traveling Westerners and a medical clinic for the Mbuti. "The place gave me creeps," Joan moaned. Putnam and his wife, Anne Eiser, were also collectors of masks. Elisofon took a bevy of photos of Joan and the "Pygmies" ("the ugliest people I have ever seen" [Joan]) and of Putnam's masks (not available in EEPA).
16. They were also fortunate at running into the Belgian cineast André Cauvin shooting a

wedding scene for his the semidocumentary film *Bongolo et la princesse noire* (1952). Joan observed "We watched them change the simple city [*sic*] into what resembled a baronial mansion. . . . This village which was once one of the most beautiful of African kings' palaces is rapidly disintegrating. The walls and houses are leaning and crumbling to bits and no or little repair work is going on" (Letter 3, HRC 61.5–6).

17. But not only Elisofon. Nine years later Terence Spencer, another *LIFE* photojournalist, visited Bope, now called King Lukenge, to find him and his entourage in misery and disintegration. Spencer used two of Elisofon's iconic 1947 photos, the portrait of the 165-pound "fetish King" and the picture of a bare-breasted dance scene, to contrast his own of the "morose monarch" who had been bereft by the new regime of his "family" and of the three remaining wives "sewing lonesomely" in a corner of the "harem." Terence Spencer, "Polygamy Passing: Congo King Loses 750 of His Wives," *LIFE* (12 December 1960): 79–82.
18. The following camera metaphor is one of Elisofon's most-quoted sayings: "Photography has enriched my life. It has enabled me to travel . . . to almost every corner of the globe, using my camera as a magic carpet to see and study the meaning and beauty of civilizations and environments besides my own." In his lecture "The Camera—My Magic Carpet," at "Symposium on Photo Journalism in the West," Asilomar, California, 26–29 September 1961. HRC 43.35.
19. Robert Taylor, *Boston Sunday Herald*, 26 October 1958. See also Constantine Petridis, "Bwadi Bwa Chikwanga: A Ram of the Bakwa Luntu," *African Art* 38.2 (2005): 50–63. Petridis comments on Elisofon's peculiar purchase of it and its obscure provenance.
20. Jan Vansina, *Being Colonized: The Kuba Experience in Rural Congo, 1880–1960* (Madison: University of Wisconsin Press, 2010), 302.
21. Marilyn R. Johnson in a letter to Elisofon, 15 October 1970, HRC 42.11.
22. Wenston Fenhagen in a letter to Elisofon, 19 February 1971, HRC 42.12.
23. Elisofon in a letter to Bayard King, 29 July 1970, HRC 42.11. King had sent five packages in all to Elisofon in February, which he did not open until he was back home in July. He received another mask sent by King exactly a year later (10 February 1971, HRC 42.12). Responding to him a couple of days later (13 February 1971, HRC 42.12), he had this information to share: "Simon Makonde was here [New York] with three excellent Mwaasaa/MBOY masks. I helped him sell one to Paul Tishman, another to Freida Rosenthal and I have the third, which was the newest, on a swap for two other pieces of mine which a collector wanted. The total price for the three was 4,500. Not too bad for Makonde. He has promised to get me the companion mask to the one with the bulging forehead called Mboom. He intends to hand it over to you. Also some old cowrie shells

and beads that Tishman wants to repair for his mask."

24. Leonard H. Goldenson in a letter to Elisofon, 23 June 1966, EEPA, V-2, 43.
25. George E. Moynihan in a letter to Elisofon, 2 March 1972, in which he also reported on the reception of *BAH* at the UN. The theater was "filled to capacity." "Ambassador Bush told me that he had seen the first episode on the Congo in Kinshasa last week. I assume that you had set it up and were probably at that screening" [he was not] (HRC 42.12).
26. Elisofon in a letter to Moynihan, 13 November 1972, HRC 42.12.
27. Sarah van Beurden, "Authentically Africa: African Arts and Postcolonial Cultural Position in Transnational Perspective," University of Pennsylvania, 2009, ProQuest 3381878, 358. As a complement to transnational art studies, she suggests (an analogy of my approach) consulting the Archives of the USIA. "African Art at the Museum of Primitive Art," Ohio State University, Columbus, 2011, http://www.rockarch.org/publications/resrep/vanbeurden.pdf.
28. Elisofon, "The Camera—My Magic Carpet."
29. "Growth and Change in a Photographer: Eliot Elisofon," lecture given at Wilson Hicks International Conference Communication Arts, Miami, 1966, in *Photographic Communication: Principles, Problems and Challenges of Photojournalism*, ed. R. Smith Schuneman (New York: Visual Communications Books, Hastings House, 1972), HRC 58.51.
30. Eliot Elisofon, Review of *Vanishing Africa* by Mirella Ricciardi, *African Arts* 5.2 (Winter 1972): 73–74.
31. Amy J. Staples, "Visualism and the Authentification of the Object: Reflections on the Eliot Elisofon Collection at the National Museum of African Art," *Collections: A Journal for Museum and Archives Professionals* 3.2 (2007): 185.
32. Another early exhibit of African artifacts was organized at the Museum for the Arts of Decoration, Cooper Union for the Advancement of Science and Art, March–June 1951. HRC 57.7.
33. They were among his twenty-two that he had photographed and printed in his *Sculpture* book.
34. "Around Chicago . . . or the institute," "This Week in Chicago for 9 February, 1952," HRC 62.8.
35. "This approach, rooted in twentieth-century Modernism, presented African art as a wholly formalist aesthetic experience," explains Kathleen Bickford Berzock. He "compelled the viewers to draw visual comparisons, but not to learn about art's deeper connection to African cultures." "The installation with a Kuba drinking horn from his own collection with his photo of the patterned scarifications of a Kuba woman's back

was such an example." Kathleen Bickford Berzock, "African Art at the Art Institute of Chicago," *African Arts* 32.4 (1999): 24, 25.

36. "Exhibition of African Negro Sculpture. View at Museum," Press Preview, 1 July 1952, the Museum of Modern Art, New York.
37. Elisofon in a letter to Brew, 12 February 1958. Brew replied that the price of around $7,000 was too high but that he was willing to negotiate with Klejman (who had accessed one and who also held some of Elisofon's objects for donation or selling) about an exchange with the museum. Eventually Peabody bought the Nima mask (25 February 1958). EEPA, N-3, 1–26 contains the 1958 correspondence between Brew and Elisofon about his nomination to be a Research Fellow of Primitive Art at Harvard as well as the discussion about the Peabody Nima mask acquisition, and Elisofon's role as mediator and curator for the Boston Museum of Fine Arts exhibition of Masterpieces of Primitive Art, 16 October–23 November 1958. For the exhibition, see HRC 57.28, 73.10.
38. Ten years later (1969) Peabody appointed him Honorary Associate in Primitive Art.
39. "Memorandum of conversation between Perry Rathbone, Eliot Elisofon and J. O. Brew, on 26 June 1959, with some additional comments," HRC 58.25, 57.28, 54.11.
40. T. H. Parker, "Art and Artifacts," *Hartford* (*Conn.*) *Courant*, 5 October 1958.
41. He gave a lecture on African sculptures as part of the conference Institute of Design, Chicago, February 1961; lectured at a "primitive exhibition," William Rockhill Nelson Gallery of Art, Atkins Museum of Fine Arts, Kansas City, January 1962; lectured on "African Venture" at City Art Museum of St. Louis, 5 June 1960; lectured on African art at an exhibition/sales (six hundred objects) by the Carlebach Galleries at Famous-Barr, Clayton, St. Louis, 1964. He had a heavy hand in the organization of the photographic exhibition on Africa that took place in the Museum of Science, Boston, in October 1961.
42. See the photo at SIRIS captioned "The first United States exhibition of a special collection of African contemporary stone sculptures from the Gallery of African Art, Johannesburg, displayed at the offices of South African Airways, New York, opening Sept 1972 / preface, Anatole Yaron."
43. Warren Robbins to Eliot Elisofon, 25 March 1963, HRC 44.2, 62.9. On 16 March 1970 he nominated him a curatorial associate (EEPA N-1, 3), and on 9 April 1970 he qualified this, asking him while traveling to keep an eye on artifacts for the museum that could be sent, he believed, via his diplomatic channels (EEPA N-1, 5). At this stage, if not earlier, Elisofon considered donating his collection to Warren's museum.
44. For release Sunday, 1 November 1969. "Masterpieces of Black African Art," Peabody Museum of Archeology and Ethnology, Harvard University, 13 October 1969. On 4 November, in conjunction with the exhibition, Elisofon gave a slide lecture that he called

"African Adventure," speaking, as he told Steve Williams, the Peabody director (letter 9 October), also about "his personal experiences in Africa" driving "an ex-army ambulance from Capetown to Cairo . . . [beginning in 1947] his well-known collection of African Sculpture, many pieces of which have been given to the Peabody Museum." HRC 54.4.

45. Rosalinde G. Wilcox, "Commercial Transactions and Cultural Interactions from the Delta to Douala and Beyond," *African Arts* 35.1 (Spring 2002): 42–55, 93–95.
46. His second *New York Times* article about the Museum of African Art, "Somebody's Doing Something Right," appeared a year later (13 June 1971). It was occasioned by the opening of the new wing of the museum. He concluded the article with a hopeful reflection on the museum's capacity to replace racial myths with "accurate information." It will contribute to understanding lies. HRC 74.18–19.
47. Roy Sieber's exhibition: https://www.moma.org/momaorg/shared/pdfs/docs/press_archives/4887/releases/MOMA_1972_0116_109.pdf?2010.
48. During the fall of 1972, he finished a film about the Tishman Akan collection and wrote an article about it, "Africa's Ancient Splendor Still Gleams in the Akan People's Golden Art," *Smithsonian Magazine* 3.10 (January 1973). HRC 43.8.
49. Elisofon in a letter to Warren Robbins, 17 October 1972 (HRC 52.9).
50. Of the 405 photographs of African artifacts that Elisofon had photographed for the book, 388 were taken of artifacts at galleries, museums, and private collections in the West; seventeen stemmed from African museums (Ife Museum, six; Jos Museum, four; K. C. Murray, four; Musée de la Vie Indigène, two; Rhodes-Livingstone Museum, one). Of the forty-five holders (museums, galleries, or private collectors) of the artifacts, twenty-three (thirteen) were American, sixteen (ten) European, one (one) Latin America, five (one) African (the figure in the parentheses indicates privately owned).
51. "Museum object photography" is Christraud M. Geary's term. See Christraud M. Geary, "The Incidental Photographer Roy Sieber and His African Images," *African Arts* 36.2 (2003): 77, where she also makes the comment about Fagg.
52. Gwilym Iwan "G.I." Jones, review of *The Sculpture of Africa* by Eliot Elisofon, *Journal of the International African Institute* 29.2 (1959): 198–99.
53. Deborah Stokes, "Documentary Observations: The African Photographs of William B. Fagg, 1949–1959," *African Arts* 36.4 (2003): 64.
54. William Fagg, *Nigerian Images: The Splendor of African Sculpture*, photographs by Herbert List (New York: Frederick A. Praeger, 1963), 16.
55. Raoul J. Granqvist, "Eliot Elisofon's Africa: Old, Updated, Worse," *Africa Is a Country* (blog), 13 February 2014, http://africasacountry.com/eliot-elisofons-africa-old-updated-worse/.

56. Elisofon to W. B. Fagg, 21 January 1964, HRC 53.21.
57. William Davenport, review of *The Tribal Artist in Tribal Society, Proceedings of Symposium Held at the Royal Anthropological Institute*, ed. Marian W. Smith, *American Anthropologist* 65.1 (1963): 146–48.
58. Eliot Elisofon, "How to Photograph Primitive Art," eight text pages, two-page list of illustrations, in HRC 54.6.
59. This is the EEPA data for Elisofon's picture: "Three masked performers, one wearing male horizontal Chi wara headdress, the two others wearing double-headed horizontal Chi wara headdresses, both referred to as n'gonzon-koun, Bamako (national district), Mali 1970 [slide]." EEPA EENG 01606. See also Pascal James Imperato, "Sogoni Koun," *African Arts* 14.2 (1981): 38–88.
60. It was filmed by Georges Bracher for *BAH.*
61. Elisofon's lecture at the Peabody-CAAS symposium, 4–7 May 1971, page 4 (HRC 59.6).
62. In his paper (not in the lecture?) he referred to other photographs of his own making that exposed the multiple view scenarios: in a chapter in the *LIFE*-Time series *Great Ages of Man: African Kingdoms* by Basil Davidson (1966) ("African Kingdoms," 156–57, 159, 164–65, 232, 248) and in his and Fagg's *Sculpture* book (plate 96).
63. Elisofon's lecture at the Peabody-CAAS symposium, 4–7 May 1971, page 4 (HRC 59.6).

## Conclusion

1. He started to work for *LIFE* as one of the first African photojournalists to be contracted by the magazine and moved back to Kenya in 1963 to document the weakening of the independence movements in the Congo, Rhodesia, and South Africa. He was killed by Biafrans in an ambush outside Owerri in the Nigerian Civil War on 2 October 1968. Joseph Haner, "Showcase: Finding Priya Ramrakha," *Lens* (blog), *New York Times*, 2 October 2009, http://lens.blogs.nytimes.com/2009/10/02/showcase-finding-priya-ramrakha/?_r=0.
2. HRC 4.20. "Elisofon's Text and Images of Concentration Camp in French Morocco," Gitterman Gallery, http://gittermangallery.com/exhibition/67/press_release/.
3. Steve Martinot, *The Machinery of Whiteness: Studies in the Structure of Racialization* (Philadelphia: Temple University Press, 2010).
4. See Fiona M. Dejardin, "The Photo League: Aesthetics, Politics, and the Cold War," University of Delaware, ProQuest Dissertations Publishing, 1993, 270–72, 312–13.
5. The Radical Camera: New York's Photo League, 1936–1951, the Contemporary Jewish Museum, Artdaily.org. http://artdaily.com/index.asp?int_sec=2&int_new=59844#.

Vh9TvnIsxMs.

6. Candide, "Only Human," [*New York*] *Evening Mirror*, 5 April 1939. C. E. Sloan wrote down the following comment in the guest book: "Here's hoping these pictures open the eyes and pocketbooks of the lucrative exploiters of the poor; and lift part of our 1/10 out of the mire of degradation and corruption into the enlightenment of wholesome living." http://newdeal.feri.org/pn/pn439.htm.
7. See Patricia Vettel Tom, "Naked Shots: The Masculinization of American Photography, 1945–1960," Ph.D. diss., Washington University, 1998.

# Bibliography

Achebe, Chinua. [1958] 1978. *Things Fall Apart.* London: Heinemann.

———. 1988. "An Image of Africa: Racism in Conrad's 'Heart of Darkness.'" *Massachusetts Review*, 18, 1977. Rpt. in Heart of Darkness: An Authoritative Text, Background and Sources Criticism, ed. Robert Kimbrough, 251–61. 3rd ed. London: W. W. Norton. Http://kirbyk.net/hod/image.of.africa.html.

———. 2012. *There Was a Country: A Personal History of Biafra.* New York: Penguin.

Agrell, Wilhelm. 2006. *Stockholm som spioncentral* [Stockholm as a Center for Espionage]. Lund: Historiska Media.

Aitken, Ian, ed. 2012. *The Concise Routledge Encyclopedia of the Documentary Film.* London: Taylor and Francis.

Akama, John S. 2004. "Neocolonialism, Dependency and External Control of Africa's Tourism Industry: A Case Study of Wild Life Safari Tourism in Kenya." In *Tourism and Postcolonialism: Contested Discourses, Identities and Representations*, ed. C. Michael Hall and Hazel Tucker, 140–52. London: Routledge.

Amkpa, Awam. 2014. "Africa: Colonial Photography and Outlaws of History." *Academia.* Https://www.academia.edu/4889353/Africa_Colonial_Photography_and_Outlaws_of_History.

Anderson, Martha G., and Lisa L. Aronson. 2011. "Jonathan A. Greene: An African Photographer Hiding in Plain Sight." *African Arts* 44.3 (Autumn): 38–49.

Anderson, Martha G., and Philip M. Peek. 2002. "Ways of the Rivers: Arts and Environment of the Niger Delta." *African Arts* 35.1 (Spring): 12–93.

Angelou, Maya. 1972. "'For Years, We Hated Ourselves.'" *New York Times*, 16 April, 14–15.

Archive-org-com. [1967] 2014. "Chronology of the Democratic Republic of Congo/Zaire (1960–1997)." Online Encyclopedia of Mass Violence. Http://archive-org.com/org/m/massviolence.org/2014-09-02_4514382_25/Chronology_of_the_Democratic_Republic_of_Congo_Zaire_1960_1997_Online_Encyclopedia_of_Mass_Violence/.

Ardrey, Robert. 1961. *African Genesis: A Personal Investigation into the Animal Origins and Nature of Man*. New York: Atheneum.

———. 1966a. "Man Is a Territorial Animal." *LIFE*, 2 September, 50–59.

———. 1966b. "The Basic Drive—for Territory." *LIFE*, 26 August, 40–59.

———. 1966c. *The Territorial Imperative: A Personal Inquiry into the Animal Origins of Property and Nations*. London: Collins.

Arendse, Herman. 1966. "Like Snoek en Patats, the Coons Belong to Cape Town." In "Chronicle of the Kaapse Klopse with some documents on the sources of their music." Compiled by Denis-Constant Martin, Fondation nationale des sciences politiques, Centre d'études et de recherches internationales, Paris, 2007.

Armengol-Carrera, Josep M. 2011. "Race-ing Hemingway: Revisions of Masculinity and/as Whiteness in Ernest Hemingway's *Green Hills of Africa* and *Under Kilimanjaro*." *Hemingway Review*, 31.1: 43–61.

Arndt, Richard T. 2005. *The First of Kings: American Cultural Diplomacy in the Twentieth Century*. Dulles, VA: Potomac Books.

Arnoldi, Mary Jo, Christraud M. Geary, and Kris L. Hardin, eds. 1996. *African Material Culture*. Bloomington: Indiana University Press.

Ashcroft, Bill, Gareth Griffiths, and Helen Tiffin. 2000. *Post-Colonial Studies: The Key Concepts*. 2nd ed. New York: Routledge.

Beach, D. N. 1970. "Afrikaner and Shona Settlement in the Enkeldoorn Area, 1890–1900." *Zambezia* 1.2 (October): 25–34.

Bechtolsheimer, Götz. 2012. "Breakfast with Mobutu: Congo, the United States and the Cold War, 1964–1981." PhD thesis, London School of Economics. Http://etheses.lse.ac.uk/403/1/Bechtolsheimer_Breakfast%20with%20Mobutu.pdf.

Behdad, Ali. 2006. "On Globalization, Again!" In *Postcolonial Studies and Beyond*, ed. Ania Loomba, Suvir Kaul, Matti Bunzl, Antoinette Burton, and Jed Esty, 62–79. Durham, NC: Duke University Press.

"Belgian Congo at War, The." Published by the Belgian Information Center, New York. Http://www.ibiblio.org/hyperwar/UN/Belgium/Congo/.

Beneduce, Roberto, Luca Jourdan, Timothy Raeymaekers, and KoenVlassenroot. 2006. "Violence with a Purpose: Exploring the Functions and Meaning of Violence in the Democratic Republic of Congo." *Intervention* 4.1: 32–46.

Bhabha, Homi K. 1994. *The Location of Culture*. New York: Routledge.

Bickford Berzock, Kathleen. 1999. "African Art at the Art Institute of Chicago." *African Arts* 32.4: 18–35, 93.

Biebuyck, Daniel P. 1973. *Lega Culture: Art, Initiation, and Moral Philosophy among a Central African People*. Berkeley: University of California Press.

Black, Cobey. 1955. "The Cosmopolitan Eye" [Who's News]. *Honolulu Star*, 11 May.

Bliss Jr., Edward. 1991. *Now the News: The Story of Broadcast Journalism*. New York: Columbia University Press.

Blixen, Karen. [1938] 2002. *Out of Africa*. London: Penguin Modern Classics.

Boateng, Osei. 2008. "Nigeria: Squalid End of Empire." *New African*, 20 November.

Bossche, Adrien Vandem. 1952. "Art Bakuba." *Brousse*, new series no. 1, 11–26.

Campbell, Alexander. 1953. "Africa, a Continent in Ferment: A Special Issue." *LIFE*, 4 May, 1–179.

———. 1954. *Heart of Africa*. New York: Alexander A. Knopf.

Canaday, John. 1970. "In Its Own Language, For a Welcome Change." *New York Times*, 12 July.

Cary, Joyce. [1936] 1951. [*The African Witch*. London: Michael Joseph.

———. [1939] 1952. *Mister Johnson*. London: Michael Joseph.

Cedrone, Lou. 1972. *Baltimore Evening Sun*, 15 March.

Churchill, Winston. 1908. *My African Journey with Illustrations from Photography by the Author and Lieutenant-Colonel Gordon Wilson, and Three Images*. London: Hodder and Stoughton.

Clarke, Michael Tavel. 2007. *These Days of Large Things: The Culture of Size in America, 1865–1930*. Ann Arbor: University of Michigan Press.

Cloete, Stuart. 1938. *The Turning Wheels*. Leipzig: Albatross.

Close, William T. 2007. *Beyond the Storm: Treating the Powerless and the Powerful in MOBUTU'S Congo/Zaire*. Marbleton, WY: Meadowlark Springs Productions.

Conrad, Joseph. [1902] 1994. *Heart of Darkness*. London: Penguin Books.

Cookman, Claude Hubert. 2009. *American Photojournalism: Motivations and Meanings*. Evanston, IL: Northwestern University Press.

Coombes, Annie E. 1994. *Reinventing Africa: Museums, Material Culture and Popular Imagination in Late Victorian and Edwardian England*. New Haven, CT: Yale University Press.

Cornelis, Sabine. 2008. "Culture coloniale, acteurs culturels et arts visuels au Congo

(1920–1950)." In *Aspects de la culture à l'époque colonial en Afrique centrale: Le corps—L'image—L'espece*, 166–67. Paris: Harmattan.

Coughlan, Robert. 1959a. "Black Africa Surges to Independence." Part 1. *LIFE*, 26 January.

———. 1959b. "Stormy Future for Africa: Eruption of Black Africa." Part 2. *LIFE*, 2 February.

———. 1961a. *Tropical Africa. LIFE* World Library. New York: Time.

———. 1961b. "Black Magic: Vital Force." *LIFE*, 21 April, 118–21.

Davenport, William. 1963. Review of *The Tribal Artist in Tribal Society, Proceedings of Symposium Held at the Royal Anthropological Institute*, ed. Maria W. Smith. *American Anthropologist* 65.1: 146–48.

Dejardin, Fiona M. 1993. "The Photo League: Aesthetics, Politics, and the Cold War." University of Delaware. ProQuest Dissertations Publishing.

Donald, James, and Ali Rattansi, eds. 1992. *'Race,' Culture and Difference*. London: Sage Publications.

Doss, Erika. 2001, ed. *Looking at* LIFE *Magazine*. Washington, D.C.: Smithsonian Institution Press.

Dudley, Sandra H. 2010. "Museum Materialities: Objects, Sense and Feeling." In *Museum Materialities: Objects, Engagement, Interpretations*, ed. Sandra H. Dudley, 1–17. New York: Routledge.

Duncan, David Douglas. 1953. "A French Administrator in Youkounkoun." *LIFE*, 4 May. 47–48.

Dunn, Kevin C. 2003. *Imagining the Congo: The International Relations of Identity*. New York: Macmillan.

Edozie, Rita Kiki. 2008. "Nigeria's 2007 Elections in Comparative Perspective: Democratic Capitalism and the Crisis of Democracy in Africa." In *Nigeria's Stumbling Democracy and Its Implications for Africa's Democratic Movement*, ed. Victor Oguejiofor Okafor, 141–64. Westport, CT: Praeger Security International.

Elicif [pseudonym for Eliot Elisofon]. 1944. [Report about a travel to Malmoe 23 September 1944]. *Sydsvenska Dagbladet*, 29 October.

Elisofon, Eliot. 1939. "Finland: Soviet Russia Crowds a Nation of Democrats." *LIFE*, 30 October, 69–76.

———. 1943. "Allies Overrun of North Africa." *LIFE*, 17 May, 20–21.

———.1944. "En amerikan ser på Norden. Fotografier från Sverige och Finland, akvareller och teckningar av Eliot Elisofon, *Life Magazine*" [An American's View of Scandinavia: Photographs from Sweden and Finland, Acquarelles and Paintings by Eliot Elisofon]. Booklet. Stockholm: Svenska turisttrafikförbundet.

———. 1945. "Sweden's Model Apartments: Stockholm Building Is Wonderful for Wives Who Work." *LIFE*, 12 March, 112–14.

———. 1947. "African Big Shot: A Fat Black Monarch of the Congo Rules His Tribe with a Heavy Hand." *LIFE*, 31 March, 129–32.

———. 1948. *Food Is a Four Letter Word*. New York: Lee Rinehart.

———. 1950. "The Nile: Its Course Unfolds Mighty Panorama of River People and Civilizations." *LIFE*, 20 November, 118–29.

———. 1952. "Mystic Art of Tribal Africa: Images of Early Negro Culture Influence Native Life of Today." *LIFE*, 8 September, 116–25.

———. 1955. "Voyages to Paradise: A Camera in South Seas Seeks Famous Scenes in Literature." *LIFE*, 24 January, 60–77.

———. 1957. "The Dance: What It Means to Me." *Dance Magazine* 31.8, tear sheets.

———. 1959. "African Sculpture." *Atlantic* (April): 46–60.

———. 1960. "The Hopeful Launching of Proud and Free Nigeria." *LIFE*, 26 September, 54–68.

———. 1961a. "A Writer's Land of Primitive, Eloquent Beauty: Storied World of Africa." *LIFE*, 13 October, 66–87.

———. 1961b. *Color Photography*. New York: Viking Press.

———. 1964. *The Nile*. New York: Viking Press.

———. 1966. "Growth and Change in a Photographer: Eliot Elisofon." Lecture given at Wilson Hicks International Conference Communication Arts, Miami. In *Photographic Communication: Principles, Problems and Challenges of Photojournalism*, ed. R. Smith Schuneman. New York: Visual Communications Books, Hastings House, 1972.

———. 1969. *Java Diary*. London: Macmillan.

———. 1972. Review of *Vanishing Africa* by Mirella Ricciardi. *African Arts* 5.2 (Winter): 73–74.

———. 1973a. "Africa's Ancient Splendor Still Gleams in the Akan People's Golden Art." *Smithsonian Magazine* 3.10:20–29.

———. 1973b. *Zaire: A Week in Joseph's World*. New York: Crowell-Collier Press.

Elisofon, Eliot, and William Fagg. 1958. *The Sculpture of Africa*. New York: Fredrick A. Praeger.

Elisofon, Eliot, and Marvin Newman. 1967. *African Animals*. New York: Ridge Press.

Elkins, Caroline. 2006. *Imperial Reckoning: The Untold Story of Britain's Gulag in Kenya*. New York: Henry Holt.

Enwezor, Okwui. 2006. *Snap Judgments: New Positions in Contemporary African Photography*. New York: International Center of Photography.

Enwezor, Okwui, and Octavio Zaya. 1996. "Colonial Imagery, Tropes of Disruption: History, Culture, Representation in the Works of African Photographers." In *In/sight: African Photographers, 1940 to the Present*, ed. Thomas Kreis, 17–47. Guggenheim Museum, 24 May–29 September 1996. New York: Guggenheim Museum Publications.

Erlmann, Veit. 1999. "'Spectatorial Lust': The African Choir in England, 1891–1893." In

*Africans on Stage: Studies in Ethnological Show Business*, ed. Bernth Lindfors, 126–33. Bloomington: Indiana University Press.

Fabian, Johannes. 1998. "Curios and Curiosity: Notes on Reading Torday and Frobenius." In *The Scramble for Art in Central Africa*, ed. Enid Schildkrout and Curtis A. Klein, 79–108. Cambridge: Cambridge University Press.

Fagg, William. 1963. *Nigerian Images: The Splendor of African Sculpture*. Photographs by Herbert List. New York: Frederick A. Praeger.

Fanon, Frantz. 1967. *The Wretched of the Earth*. Harmondsworth: Penguin Books.

Firchow, Peter Edgerly. 2000. *Envisioning Africa: Racism and Imperialism in Conrad's Heart of Darkness*. Lexington: University Press of Kentucky.

Flukinger, Roy. 2000. "'To Help the World to See': An Eliot Elisofon Retrospective." In a booklet of the same title by Harry Ransom Center, University of Texas at Austin.

*Foreign Relations of the United States, 1964–1968*. Vol. 23, Congo, 1960–1968, 714–15. Department of State, Washington, D.C.

Foster, Bob. 1972. "Screenings." *San Mateo Times*, 12 May.

Foucault, Michel. 1979. *Discipline and Punish: The Birth of the Prison*. Trans. Alan Sheridan. New York: Knopf Doubleday.

Frömming, Urte Undine. 2009. "Kilimanjaro's Melting Glaciers: On the Colonial and Postcolonial Perception and Appropriation of African Nature." *Ethnográfica* 13.2 (November): 295–316.

Gabriel, John. 1994. *Racism, Culture, Markets*. New York: Routledge.

Geary, Christraud M. 1993. "Two Days in Mushenge: Eliot Elisofon's Images of the Kuba (1947)." *African Arts* 26 2: 72–77.

———. 1995. "Photographic Practice in Africa and Its Implications for the Use of Historical Photographs as Contextual Evidence." *Fotografia e Storia dell'Africa*, 103–30. A cura di Alessandro Trulzi. Napoli: Istituto Universitatario Orientale.

———. 2002. *In and Out of Focus: Images from Central Africa, 1885–1960*. Washington, D.C.: Smithsonian National Museum of African Art.

———. 2003. "The Incidental Photographer Roy Sieber and His African Images." *African Arts* 36.2: 66–97.

———. 2004. "Through the Lenses of African Photographer: Depicting Foreigners and New Ways of Life, 1870–1950." In *Through African Eyes: The European in African Art 1500 to the Present*, ed. Nii O. Quarcoopome, 86–99. Detroit: Detroit Institute of Arts.

Gide, Andre. [1927] 1994. *Travels in the Congo*. Trans. Dorothy Bussy. Hopewell, NJ: Eco Press.

Gikandi, Simon. 1997. "Aesthetic Reflection and the Colonial Event: The Work of Art in the Age of Slavery." *Journal of the International Institute* 4.3 (Summer): 1–51.

Gilman, Sander L. 1992. "Black Bodies, White Bodies: Toward an Iconography of Female Sexuality in Late Nineteenth-Century Art, Medicine and Literature." In *'Race,' Culture and Difference*, ed. James Donald and Ali Rattansi, 171–97. London: Sage Publications.

Gilroy, Paul. 1992. "The End of Antiracism." In *'Race,' Culture and Difference*, ed. James Donald and Ali Rattansi, 49–61. London: Sage Publications.

Goldberg, David Theo, and Ato Quayson, eds. 2002. *Relocating Postcolonialism* Oxford: Blackwell.

Gorer, Geoffrey. 1935. *Africa Dances: A Book about West African Negroes*. London: Faber and Faber.

Granqvist, Raoul J. 2002. "Through a Swedish Looking-Glass: Photographing the Congolese Body." In *Palavers of African Literature: Essays in Honor of Bernth Lindfors*, ed. Toyin Falola and Barbara Harlow, 1:228–56. Trenton, NJ: Africa World Press.

——— 2003. "Romance and Racism: One Hundred Years with Joseph Conrad's *Heart of Darkness* in Sweden." In *Conrad at the Millennium: Modernism, Postmodernism, Postcolonialism*, ed. Gail Fincham and Attie de Lange, with Wieslaw Krajka, 467–97. New York: Columbia University Press.

———. 2012a. "Elisofons möte med Jean Sibelius: nationalism och jazz" [Elisofon Meeting Jean Sibelius: Nationalism and Jazz]. *Nya Argus* 105.4: 89–92.

———. 2012b. "Photojournalism's White Mythologies: Eliot Elisofon and *LIFE* in Africa, 1959–1961." *Research in African Literatures* 43.3: 84–105.

———. 2013a. "Fieldwork as Translation: Linnaeus' Apostle Anders Sparrman and the Hottentot Perspective." In *African Literatures and Beyond: A Florilegium*, ed. Bernth Lindfors and Geoffrey V. Davis, 149–76. New York: Rodopi.

———. 2013b. "The Story of How the Most Famous Portrait of Young Chinua Achebe Was Taken." *Africa Is a Country* (blog). 18 September 2013. Http://africasacountry.com/2013/09/eliot-elisofons-famous-portrait-of-chinua-achebe.

———. 2014. "Eliot Elisofon's Africa: Old, Updated, Worse." *Africa Is a Country* (blog). 13 February. Http://africasacountry.com/eliot-elisofons-africa-old-updated-worse/.

Gray, Stephen. 2013. "Soul-brother Eugène N. Marais: Some Notes towards a Re-edit of His Works." *Tydskrif vir Letterkunde* 50.2:63–80.

Green, Jeffrey. 1999. "A Revelation in Strange Humanity: Six Congo Pygmies in Britain, 1905–1907." In *Africans on Stage: Studies in Ethnological Show Business*, ed. Bernth Lindfors, 156–87. Bloomington: Indiana University Press.

Greenblatt, Stephen. 1991. *Marvelous Possessions: The Wonder of the New World*. Chicago: University of Chicago Press.

Grobel, Lawrence. 2014. *The Hustons: The Life and Times of a Hollywood Dynasty*. New York:

Skyhorse Publishing.

Grootaers, Jan-Lodewijk. 2002. "Lega: Ethics and Beauty in the Heart of Africa." KBC Bank Gallery Brussels, Belgium, 4 May–28 July.

Haffner, Pierre. 1978. *Essai sur les fondements du cinéma africain*. Abidjan: Nouvelles editions africaines.

Halmi, Robert. 1962. "I Go Visit a Chief's Son: An American Boy's Storybook Adventure in Deepest Africa." *LIFE*, 13 April, 74–87.

Hamovitch, Susan. 2013. "Drew, Robert (1924–)." In *Encyclopedia of Television 4 Vol. Set*, ed. Horace Newcomb, 761–63. New York: Fitzroy Dearborn Publishers, Routledge.

Haner, Joseph. 2009. "Showcase: Finding Priya Ramrakha." 2 October. *Lens* (blog), *New York Times*. Http://lens.blogs.nytimes.com/2009/10/02/showcase-finding-priya-ramrakha/?_r=0.

Harley, J. B. 1992. "Deconstructing the Map." In *Writing Worlds: Discourse, Text and Metaphor in the Representation of Landscape*, ed. Trevor J. Barnes and James S. Duncan, 231–47. New York: Routledge.

Hemingway, Ernest. [1935] 1963. *Green Hills of Africa*. New York: Scribner.

———. 1937. "The Short Happy Life of Francis Macomber." In *The Complete Short Stories of Ernest Hemingway*, 5–28. The Finca Vigia Edition. New York: Charles Scribner's Sons.

Hepburn, Katherine. 1987. *The Making of* The African Queen *or How I Went to Africa with Bogart, Bacall and Huston and Almost Lost My Mind*. New York: Alfred A. Knopf.

Hesse, Barnor. 2006. "Forgotten Like a Bad Dream: Atlantic Slavery and the Ethics of Postcolonial Memory." In *Relocating Postcolonialism*, ed. David Theo Goldberg and Ato Quayson, 143–73. Oxford: Blackwell.

Heyns, Jackie. 2007. "How to Cheat Fate—Be a Coon, Undercurrent Affairs." *Post*, 9 January 1966. In "Chronicle of the Kaapse Klopse with Some Documents on the Sources of Their Music." Compiled by Denis-Constant Martin, Fondation nationale des sciences politiques, Centre d'études et de recherches internationales, Paris.

Higham, Charles. 1983. *Trading with the Enemy: An Exposé of the Nazi-American Money Plot 1933–1949*. New York: Delacorte Press.

Holmström, Lauri. 2010. "Finland in American Intelligence 1941–1944." *Intelligence and National Security* 25.4: 479–99.

Hulme, Peter. 2006. "Beyond the Straits: Postcolonial Allegories of the Globe." In *Postcolonial Studies and Beyond*, ed. Ania Loomba, Suvir Kaul, Matti Bunzl, Antoinette Burton, and Jed Esty, 41–61. Durham, NC: Duke University Press.

Hyam, Ronald. 1992. *Empire and Sexuality: The British Experience*. Manchester: Manchester University Press.

Imperato, Pascal James. 1976. *A Wind in Africa: A Story of Modern Medicine in Mali*. St. Louis: Warren H. Green.

———. 1981. "Sogoni Koun." *African Arts* 14.2: 38–88.

Jacobson, Louis. 2013. "Reviewed: Eliot Elisofon at the National Museum of African Art." *ArtsDesk* (blog), *Washington City Paper*, 27 November. Http://www.washingtoncitypaper.com/blogs/artsdesk/visual-arts/2013/11/27/reviewed-eliot-elisofon-at-the-national-museum-of-african-art/.

Jay, Martin. 1994. *Downcast Eyes. The Denigration of Vision in Twentieth-Century French Thought*. Berkeley: University of California Press.

Johnson, Osa. [1940] 1997. *I Married Adventure: The Lives of Osa and Martin Johnson*. New York: Kodasha, America.

Jones, Gwilym Iwan ("G.I."). 1959. Review of *The Sculpture of Africa* by Eliot Elisofon. *Journal of the International African Institute* 29.2: 198–99.

"Känd USA-fotograf: 'Sverige vackrast'" [Famous U.S. Photographer: "Sweden is the Most Beautiful"]. 1948. *Stockholms-Tidningen*, 23 July.

Kaplan, Caren. 1996. *Questions of Travel: Postmodern Discourses of Displacement*. Durham, NC: Duke University Press.

Kaplan, E. Ann. 1997. *Looking for the Other: Feminism, Film and the Imperial Gaze*. London: Routledge.

Karlsson Blom, Lisa, and Mikela Lundahl. 2012. "Haunted Museums: Ethnography, Coloniality and Sore Points." *Glänta*, 18 December. Http://www.eurozine.com/pdf/2012-12-18-blom-en.pdf.

Kasfir, Sidney Littlefield. 2007. *African Art and Colonial Encounter: Inventing Global Commodity*. Bloomington: Indiana University Press.

———. 1992. "African Art and Authenticity: A Text with a Shadow." *African Arts* 25.2 (April): 40–53, 96–97.

Kipling, Rudyard. [1902] 1971. "The Elephant Child." In *Just So Stories: For Little Children*, 63–81. London: Macmillan.

Koivunen, Leila. 2006. *Visualizing the "Dark Continent": The Process of Illustrating Nineteenth-Century British Travel Accounts of Africa*. Turku: Department of General History, University of Turku.

Kozol, Wendy. 1994. LIFE*'s America: Family and Nation in Postwar Photojournalism*. Philadelphia: Temple University Press.

———. 2001. "Gazing at Race in the Pages of *LIFE*." In *Looking at* LIFE *Magazine*, ed. Erika Doss, 159–75. Washington, D.C.: Smithsonian Institution Press.

Kreis, Thomas. 1996. Preface in *In/sight: African Photographers, 1940 to the Present*.

Guggenheim Museum, 24 May–29 September 1996. New York: Guggenheim Museum Publications.

Landau, Paul, and Deborah Kaspin, eds. 2002. *Images and Empires: Visuality in Colonial and Postcolonial Africa*. Berkeley: University of California Press.

Langford, Martha, and John Langford. 2011. *A Cold War Tourist and His Camera*. Montreal: McGill-Queen's University Press.

Latz, John. 1966a. [The Mercenaries]. *Chicago Tribune*, October 4.

———. 1966b. [Mobutu]. *Chicago Tribune*, October 2.

Leed, Eric J. 1991. *The Mind of the Traveler: From Gilgamesh to Global Tourism*. New York: Basic Books.

Levine, Matt. 2014. "Touki Bouki." 7 March. *Joyless Creatures* (blog). Http://www.joylesscreatures.com/review-archive/touki-bouki.

Levine, Philippa. 2008. "Studies of Undress: Nakedness and the Colonial Imagination." *Victorian Studies* 50.2: 189–218.

———. 2013. "Naked Truths: Bodies, Knowledge, and the Erotics of Colonial Power." *Journal of British Studies* 52.1: 5–25.

Lidman, Sara. 1963. *Jag och min son* [I and My Son]. 1961. Rev. ed. Stockholm: Albert Bonniers Förlag.

Lindbergh, Anne Morrow. 1966. "A Safari Back to Innocence: Immersion in Life, Journey to East Africa.". *LIFE*, 21 October, 88–94, 97–98.

Lindsay, Vachel. 1926. "The Congo." In *Collected Poems*. Rev. and illustrated ed. New York: Macmillan Edition.

Lippard, Lucy R. 1997. *The Lure of the Local: Senses of Place in a Multicentered Society*. New York: New Press.

Lindfors, Bernth, ed. 1999. *Africans on Stage: Studies in Ethnological Show Business*. Bloomington: Indiana University Press.

Littell, Blaine. 1966. *South of the Moon: On Stanley's Trail through the Dark Continent*. London: Weidenfield and Nicolson.

Littell, Blaine, and Eric Robins. 1971. *Africa: Images and Realities*. New York: Ridge Press.

Loengard, John. 1998. LIFE *Photographers: What They Saw*. Boston: Little, Brown.

Loomba, Ania, Suvir Kaul, Matti Bunzl, Antoinette Burton, and Jed Esty, eds. 2006. *Postcolonial Studies and Beyond*. Durham, NC: Duke University Press.

Luig, Ute, and Achim von Opper, eds. 1997. *The Making of African Landscapes*. Stuttgart: Steiner.

Mark, Joan. 1998. *The King of the World in the Land of the Pygmies*. Lincoln: University of Nebraska Press.

Martinot, Steve. "The Coloniality of Power: Notes toward De-Colonization." Steve Martinot: Writings. https://www.ocf.berkeley.edu/~marto/coloniality.htm.

———. 2010. *The Machinery of Whiteness: Studies in the Structure of Racialization.* Philadelphia: Temple University Press.

Matlock, Jann. "Analysis." *African Queen*, Colonial Film website, 2010. Http://www.colonialfilm.org.uk/node/1067.

Maxwell, Anne. 1999. *Colonial Photography and Exhibitions.* London: Leicester University Press.

Mayer, Ruth. 2002. *Artificial Africas: Colonial Images in the Times of Globalization.* Hanover, NH: University Press of New England.

Mayys, Stan. 1967. "Dark Continent Also Long Continent." *North Adams Transcript*, 26 August.

McClintock, Anne. 1995. *Imperial Leather: Race, Gender, and Sexuality in the Colonial Contest.* New York: Routledge.

McDowell, Linda. 1999. *Gender, Identity and Place: Understanding Feminist Geographies.* Minneapolis: University of Minnesota Press.

McElhaney, Joe. 2009. *Albert Maysles (Contemporary Film Directors).* Chicago: University of Illinois Press.

Meyer, Hans. 1944. "Soldat med kamera" [A Soldier with a Camera]. *Folket i bild* (7 May): 3–5, 24–25.

Mignolo, Walter. 2000. *Local Histories/Global Designs: Coloniality, Subaltern Knowledges and Border Thinking.* Princeton, NJ: Princeton University Press.

Mirzoeff, Nicholas. 1999. *An Introduction to Visual Culture.* New York: Routledge:

Moorehead, Alan. [1957] 1959. *No Room in the Ark.* New York: Harper and Brothers.

Murray, Brian H. 2012. "'Stanley and His African Dwarfs': Exploring the Pygmy Imaginary." In "H. M. Stanley and the Literature of Exploration: Empire, Media, Modernity." Thesis, King's College, University of London. Https://kclpure.kcl.ac.uk/portal/files/13148415/Studentthesis-Brian_Murray_2012.pdf.

———. "Henry Morton Stanley and the Pygmies of 'Darkest Africa.'" *Public Domain Review.* Http://publicdomainreview.org/2012/11/29/henry-morton-stanley-and-the-Pygmies-of-darkest-africa/.

Ndlovu-Gatsheni, Sabelo J. 2013. *Coloniality of Power in Postcolonial Africa: Myths of Decolonization.* Dakar: Council for the Development of Social Science Research in Africa, Codesria.

Negro Art. "Genuine Congo Art Is Never Vulgar." In full text of "Belgian Congo at War." Published by the Belgian Information Center. Https://archive.org/stream/BelgianCongoAtWar/BSW2_djvu.txt.

Newman, Arnold. "Bope Mabinsha King of the Bakubas' Congo 1958." The Arnold Newman Website. Http://www.arnoldnewmanarchive.com/media-gallery/detail/58/294.

Ngugi, wa Thiong'o. 1981. *Writers in Politics: Essays*. London: Heinemann.

Nycop, Carl-Adam. 1944. "Svensk byråkrati" [Swedish Bureaucracy]. *SE* 25 (July): 24–31.

O'Connell, P. J. 2010. *Robert Drew and the Development of Cinema Vérité in America*. Carbondale: Southern Illinois University Press.

Parry, Benita. 2006. "Directions and Dead Ends in Postcolonial Studies." In *Relocating Postcolonialism*, ed. David Theo Goldberg and Ato Quayson, 66–81. Oxford: Blackwell.

Paton, Alan. [1948] 1974. *Cry, the Beloved Country: A Story of Comfort and Desolation*. Harmondsworth: Penguin Books.

Perdreau, Connie. 1972. "To the Editor." *Ohio University Post* 69.19 (18 October).

Petridis, Constantine. 1999. "Luluwa Masks." *African Arts* 32.3: 32–47, 91–94.

———. 2005. "Bwadi Bwa Chikwanga: A Ram of the Bakwa Luntu." *African Arts* 38.2: 50–63.

Polier, Rex. 1972. "'Black African Heritage' Takes Museum Approach." *Philadelphia Evening Bulletin*, 31 March.

Pratt, Mary Louise. 1992. *Imperial Eyes: Travel Writing and Transculturation*. London: Routledge.

Putman, John P., and Eliot Elisofon. 1973. "Yesterday's Congo, Today's Zaire." *National Geographic* 143.3: 398–432.

Py-Lieberman, Beth. 2013. "Meet the Real 'Most Interesting Man in the World,'" Smithsonian.com, 6 December. Http://www.smithsonianmag.com/smithsonian-institution/meet-the-real-most-interesting-man-in-the-world-180949043/?no-ist.

Quarcoopome, Nii O, ed. 2004. *Through African Eyes: The European in African Art 1500 to the Present*. Detroit: Detroit Institute of Arts.

"'The Radical Camera: New York's Photo League, 1936–1951' on view at the Contemporary Jewish Museum." *Artdaily.org*. Http://artdaily.com/index.asp?int_sec=2&int_new=59844#.Vh9TvnIsxMs.

Ravenhill, Philip L. 1996. "The Passive Object and the Tribal Paradigm. Colonial Museography in French West Africa." In *African Material Culture*, ed. Mary Jo Arnoldi, Christraud M. Geary, and Kris L. Hardin, 267–87. Bloomington: Indiana University Press.

Richmond, Yale. 2008. *Practicing Public Diplomacy: A Cold War Odyssey*. New York: Berghahn Books.

Rick on Theater. 2015. "National Museum of African Art." 19 January. *Rick on Theater* (blog). Http://rickontheater.blogspot.se/2015/01/the-national-museum-of-african-art.html.

Roosevelt, Theodore. 1910. *Africa Game Trails: An Account of the African Wanderings of an American Hunter-Naturalist*. London: John Murray, Albemarle Street.

Rosaldo, Renato. 1989a. "Imperialist Nostalgia." Special Issue: Memory and Counter-Memory. *Representations* no. 26 (Spring): 107–22.

———. 1989b. *Culture and Truth: The Remaking of Social Analysis*. Boston: Beacon Press.

Rose, Gillian. 1996. *Feminism and Geography: The Limits of Geographical Knowledge*. Cambridge: Polity Press.

Ruark, Robert. 1955. *Something of Value*. London: Hamish Hamilton.

Ryan, Simon. 1996. *The Cartographic Eye: How Explorers Saw Australia*. Cambridge: Cambridge University Press.

Said, Edward. 1983. *The World, the Text, and the Critic*. Cambridge, MA: Harvard University Press.

Saunders, Nicholas. 2009. "Ulysses' Gaze: The Panoptic Premise in Aerial Photography and Great War Archaeology." In *Images of Conflict: Military Aerial Photography and Archaeology*, ed. Birger Stichelbaut, Jean Bourgeois, Nicholas Saunders, and Piet Chielens, 27-40. Cambridge: Cambridge Scholars Publishing.

Schildkrout, Enid, and Curtis A. Keim. 1998. "Objects and Agendas: Re-collecting the Congo." In *The Scramble for Art in Central Africa*, ed. Enid Schildkrout and Curtis A. Klein, 1–36. Cambridge: Cambridge University Press.

Schrire, Carmel. 2002. *Tigers in Africa: Stalking the Past at the Cape of Good Hope*. Third Glynn Isaac Memorial Lecture, Cape Town 1999. Charlottesville: University Press of Virginia.

Scott, John. 1944a. "Finland: Death in an Empty Room." *Time*, 1 May.

———. 1944b. "Finland: Fateful Hour." *Time*, 3 July.

———. 1944c. "U.S. Miscellany." *Time*, 13 March.

Sekula, Allan. 1984. *Photography against the Grain: Essays and Photowork, 1973–1983*. Halifax: The Press of Nova Scotia College.

Shaw, Carolyn Martin. 1995. *Colonial Inscriptions: Race, Sex, and Class in Kenya*. Minneapolis: University of Minnesota Press.

Siollun, Max. 2009. *Oil, Politics and Violence: Nigeria's Military Coup Culture 1966–1976*. New York: Algora Publishing.

Skal, Dave. 1972. "Filmmaker Perplexed by Black Response." *Ohio University Post* 63.19 (18 October).

Smith, Jonathan. 1992. "The Slightly Different Thing That Is Said: Writing Aesthetic Experience." In *Writing Worlds: Discourse, Text and Metaphor in the Representation of Landscape*, ed. Trevor J. Barnes and James S. Duncan, 73–85. New York: Routledge.

Solinger, Rickie. 2001. "The Smutty Side of *LIFE*: Picturing Babes as Icons of Gender Difference in the Early 1950s." In *Looking at* LIFE *Magazine*, ed. Erika Doss, 201–19. Washington, D.C.: Smithsonian Institution Press.

Soyinka, Wole. 1976. *Myth, Literature and the African World*. Cambridge: Cambridge University Press.

———. 2007. *You Must Set Forth at Dawn: A Memoir*. New York: Random House.

Spencer, Terence. 1960. "Polygamy Passing: Congo King Loses 750 of His Wives." *LIFE*, 12 December, 79–82.

Spicer, Paul. 2010. *The Temptress: The Scandalous Life of Alice de Janze and the Mysterious Death of Lord Erroll*. New York: St. Martin's Press.

Spurr, David. 1993. *The Rhetoric of Empire: Colonial Discourse in Journalism, Travel Writing, and Imperial Administration*. Durham, NC: Duke University Press.

Stamberg, Susan. 2013. "Africa ReViewed: The Photographic Legacy of Eliot Elisofon." November 2013–August 2014, Smithsonian Institution, National Museum of African Art. Https://africa.si.edu/exhibits/africa-reviewed/index.html.

Stanley, Henry Morton. 1886. *The Congo and the Founding of the Free State: A Story of Work and Preparation*. Vol. 2. London: Marston, Searle and Rivington.

———. 1890. *In Darkest Africa: or, the Quest, Rescue, and Retreat of Emin, Governor of Equatoria*. Vol. 2. London: Sampson, Low, Marston.

Staples, Amy J. 2006. "Safari Adventure: Forgotten Cinematic Journeys in Africa." *Film History* 18:392–411.

———. 2007. "Visualism and the Authentication of the Object: Reflections on the Eliot Elisofon Collection at the National Museum of African Art." *Collections: A Journal for Museum and Archives Professionals* 3.2: 181–88.

Steiner, Daniel. "Do You Have Obsessive-Compulsive Photography Disorder (OCPD)?" *Illuminations Photoblog* (blog). Https://danielstainer.wordpress.com/2009/11/25/do-you-have-obsessive-compulsive-photography-disorder-ocpd/.

Stokes, Deborah. 2003. "Documentary Observations: The African Photographs of William B. Fagg, 1949–1959." *African Arts* 36.4: 58–71, 95–96.

Strother, Z. S. 1999. "Display of the Body Hottentot." In *Africans on Stage: Studies in Ethnological Show Business*, ed. Bernth Lindfors, 1–61. Bloomington: Indiana University Press.

Sturken, Marita, and Lisa Cartwright. 2003. *Practices of Looking: An Introduction to Visual Culture*. Oxford: Oxford University Press.

Tashman, George. 1972. [*BAH* review.] *The Independent*. 16 May.

Taylor, Robert. 1958a. "The Many Masks of Eliot Elisofon." *Boston Herald*, 7 November.

———. 1958b. Review of exhibition "Primitive Masterpieces on View." *Boston Sunday Herald*, 26 October.

Teicher, Jordan G. 2014. "Celebrating One Photographer's Rare 20th-Century Look Africa."

*Behold: The Photo Blog* (blog), *Slate*. 4 February. Http://www.slate.com/blogs/behold/2014/02/04/national_museum_of_african_art_presents_the_exhibition_africa_reviewed_the.html.

Tom, Patricia Vettel. 1998. "Naked Shots: The Masculinization of American Photography 1945–1960." Ph.D. diss., Washington University.

Torday, Emil, and T. A. Joyce. 1911. *Notes ethnographiques sur les peuples communement appelés Bakuba ainsi que sur les peuplades apparantées les Bushongo*. Brussels: Musée du Congo Belge.

Torday, Emil, T. A. Joyce, and T. A. Hardy. 1910. *Notes Ethnographiques sur le Peuples Communément Appelés Bakuba, Ainsi Que sur les Peuplades Apparentées—les Bushongo*. Brussels.

*Tribute to Africa: The Photography and the Collection of Eliot Elisofon*. 1974. Washington, D.C.: Museum of African Art.

Tweet, Terje. 2010. *The River Nile in the Post-Colonial Age: Conflict and Cooperation among the Nile Basin Countries*. London: I. B. Tauris.

van Beurden, Sarah. 2009. "Authentically African: African Arts and Postcolonial Cultural Position in Transnational Perspective." Diss., University of Pennsylvania. ProQuest 3381878.

———. 2011. "African Art at the Museum of Primitive Art." Ohio State University, Columbus. Http://www.rockarch.org/publications/resrep/vanbeurden.pdf.

van der Post, Laurens. 1952. *Venture to the Interior*. London: Hogarth Press.

Vansina, Jan. 2007. "La survie du royaume kuba à l'époque colonial et les arts." *Annales Æquatoria* 28: 5–29.

———. 2010. *Being Colonized: The Kuba Experience in Rural Congo, 1880–1960*. Madison: University of Wisconsin Press.

*Vecko-Tidningen Såningsmannen*. 1944. Interview with Eliot Elisofon. 38. 16 September, 6, 19–20.

Vokes, Richard, ed. 2012. *Photography in Africa: Ethnographic Perspectives*. New York: James Currey.

Webb, Virginia-Lee. 2000. *Perfect Documents: Walker Evans and African Art, 1935*. New York: Metropolitan Museum of Art.

Wilcox, Rosalinde G. 2002. "Commercial Transactions and Cultural Interactions from the Delta to Douala and Beyond." *African Arts* 35.1 (Spring): 42–55, 93–95.

Wittenberg, Hermann. 2004. "The Sublime, Imperialism and the African Landscape." PhD diss., University of the Western Cape. Http://etd.uwc.ac.za/xmlui/bitstream/handle/11394/1340/Wittenberg_DLIT_2004.pdf?sequence=1.

Wright, Roger. "Hitler, Bogart, and the Banker." *Chicago Guy's Blog* (blog). Http://chicagoguy14.wordpress.com/.

Wrong, Michela. 2000. *In the Footsteps of Mr. Kurtz: Living on the Brink of Disaster in Mobutu's Congo.* New York: Harper/Perennial.

Young, Robert. 1992. *White Mythologies: Writing History and the West.* New York: Routledge.

———. 1995. *Colonial Desire: Hybridity in Theory, Culture and Race.* New York: Routledge.

Zabus, Chantal. 1991. *African Palimpsest: Indigenization of Language in the West African Europhone Novel.* Amsterdam: Rodopi.

# Index

## F



## G



## H

## N

## Y



## Z